THE FIGHTING TENTH

*How would posterity and the youth
of Britain remember my men who had
died in such a desperate battle?
Unless they were told the story
they would have nothing to remember.*

Rear-Admiral G. W. G. Simpson, CB, CBE
Captain of The Tenth Submarine Flotilla,
Malta, GC, 1941–1943.

THE
FIGHTING
TENTH

THE TENTH SUBMARINE FLOTILLA
AND THE SIEGE OF MALTA

JOHN WINGATE
DSC

LEO COOPER
LONDON

Dedicated
to
Our Submariners

First published in Great Britain 1991 by
LEO COOPER
190 Shaftesbury Avenue, London WC2H 8JL
an imprint of Pen & Sword Books Ltd
47 Church Street, Barnsley, S. Yorks S70 2AS

Copyright © John Wingate 1991

A CIP catalogue record for this book is available from The British Library

ISBN: 0 85052 200 5

Printed and bound in Great Britain by
Mackays of Chatham PLC, Chatham, Kent

CONTENTS

No one was there to witness
The fate of 'boats' destroyed:
A sudden inrush of water,
A merciful, quick death — a void.

Their remains are still at the bottom
Encased in a tomb of steel;
No headstone to see and ponder:
They went as they fought — unreal.

When Remembrance Day comes along,
My thoughts are down in the deep,
Thinking of all Submariners:
Can you wonder why I weep?

We that are left ARE old,
But we did come home again.
Today, I often wonder,
Was it all in vain?

A Gunlayer of The Tenth:
Leading Seaman C. H. A. Balls, LR/2

Alexandria,
December, 1940.

'Your object is to cut the
enemy's sea communications
between EUROPE and TRIPOLI'

. . . The verbal order of the
Commander-in-Chief, Mediterranean,
Admiral Sir Andrew Cunningham, to
Commander (S), Malta, Commander G. W. G. Simpson.

Maps
Drawn by Captain Chester Read RN (Ret'd)

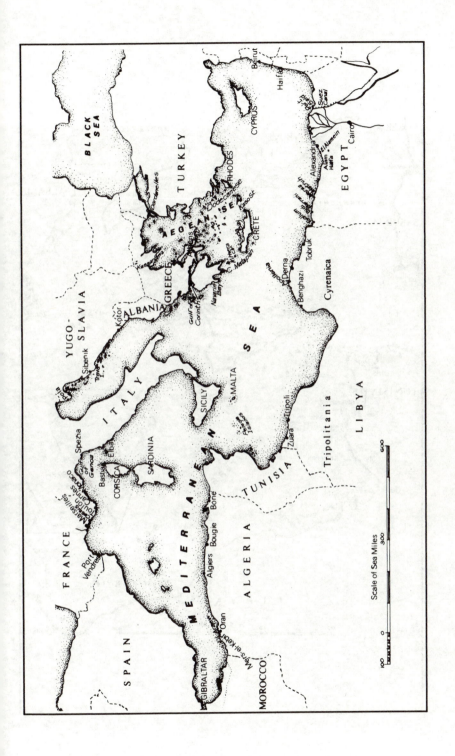

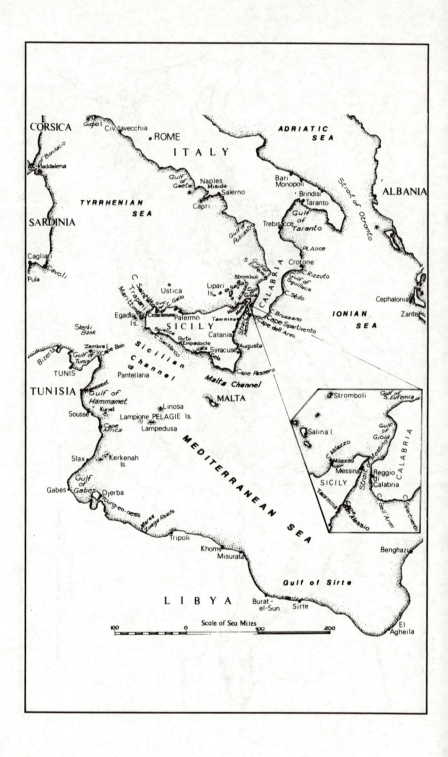

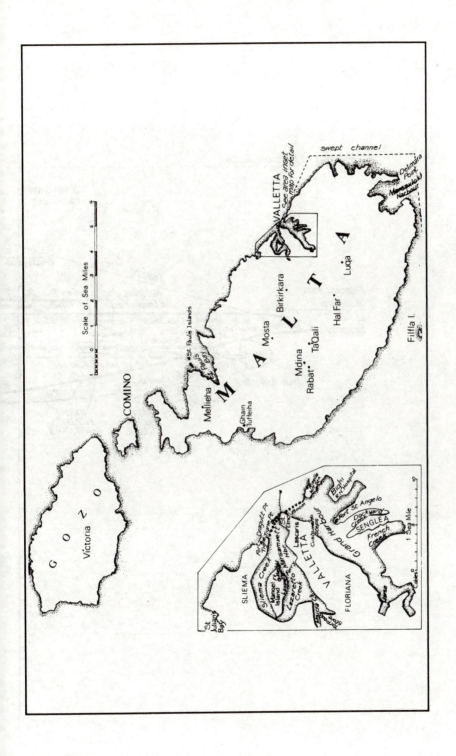

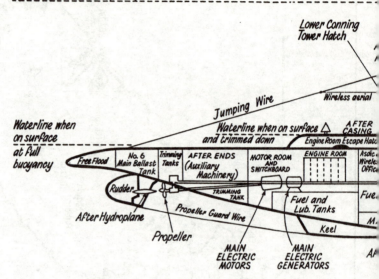

Waterline at periscope depth

Lower Conning
Tower Hatch

Jumping Wire

Wireless aerial

Waterline when
on surface

Waterline when on surface
and trimmed down

AFTER
CASING

Waterline when
on surface
at full
buoyancy

Free Flood

No. 6
Main Ballast
Tank

Trimming
Tanks

AFTER ENDS
(Auxiliary
Machinery)

MOTOR ROOM
AND
SWITCHBOARD

ENGINE ROOM

Engine Room Escape Hatch

Asdic
Wireless
Office

Rudder

TRIMMING
TANK

Fuel and
Lub. Tanks

Fue.

After Hydroplane

Propeller Guard Wire

Keel

M.

Propeller

MAIN
ELECTRIC
MOTORS

MAIN
ELECTRIC
GENERATORS

AF

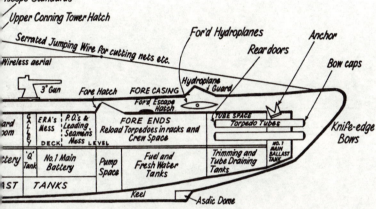

ope
- -

riscope Standards

Upper Conning Tower Hatch

Serrated Jumping Wire for cutting nets etc.

Wireless aerial

For'd Hydroplanes

Anchor

Rear doors

Bow caps

3" Gun   Fore Hatch   FORE CASING   Hydroplane Guard

Ford Escape Hatch

ard   GALLEY   ERA's Mess   P.O.'s & Leading Seamen's Mess   FORE ENDS   TUBE SPACE   Knife-edge Bows
om   Reload Torpedoes in racks and Crew Space   Torpedo Tubes
                            DECK   MESS LEVEL

tery   'Q' Tank   No.1 Main Battery   Pump Space   Fuel and Fresh Water Tanks   Trimming and Tube Draining Tanks   NO.1 MAIN BALLAST TANK

AST   TANKS   Keel   Asdic Dome

Periscope
ell

Length 196ft.   Beam 11ft.

Surface displacement.. 600 Tons   Max. surface speed.... 10 Knots
Dived displacement.... 800 Tons   Max. dived speed..... 7 Knots

FOREWORD

by
Captain George Phillips, DSO, GM, RN.,
Captain, The Tenth Submarine Flotilla, Malta, 1943-44.

It was a great honour to command the Tenth Submarine Flotilla during World War II, in succession to my friend, Captain G. W. G. Simpson, CBE, RN, and it delights me that a number of those who served in this remarkable unit have now got together to provide the material for this book. It is the story of a group of young men who fought the most concentrated submarine battle in history, from the beleaguered island of Malta.

They came from all Naval sources: Regular, Reserve and Volunteer Reserve, and from all walks of life. They suffered severe casualties and knew only too well the chill of the vacant chair; but they remained steadfast and cheerful and they won.

Submarine warfare is normally in the wide open spaces and targets may be hard to find, but for the Tenth Flotilla this was not so. With the German Army in North Africa, and Malta virtually on its supply routes to Italy, the targets and their offensive escorts were numerous. Within a short time of sailing for patrol, the submarines would be in action and experiencing the inevitable depth-charge counterattack. It was no fault of Malta that there was little to offer the crews in the way of food and relaxation on their return to harbour.

It would be appropriate to add a note about the Base Staff who dealt with the flotilla armaments and maintenance. Not for them the well-stocked spare parts store or a regular supply; rather, the exercise of great ingenuity in cannibalizing the incoming submarine for any part required by the next one to sail. I do not remember one submarine being delayed.

One thing which sticks firmly in my mind is that after the German surrender in North Africa, the Naval Liaison Officer on the Eighth Army Staff sent me an air note. It said that Rommel's Staff, in discussing their defeat, admitted that they were never able to plan ahead with any confidence, owing to the losses to their supplies caused by British forces in Malta.

INTRODUCTION

by
Admiral of the Fleet
The Lord Fieldhouse, GCB, GBE

As a post-war submariner I am honoured to have been invited to introduce the reader to the history of the Tenth Submarine Flotilla, operating from Malta and Maddalena between 1940 and 1944. It is a history of remarkable achievements attained by sheer hard work, dedicated attention to duty, remarkable personal bravery and high standards of professionalism - unfortunately at a tragic cost in human life. As such it will serve as inspiration to all our submariners present and future. It was not by accident that, when the Royal Navy was entrusted with the responsibility of deploying the national nuclear deterrent, the new Squadron formed by the Polaris submarines was entitled the 'Tenth'.

Rommel's Chief of Staff for the Afrika Korps, General Bayerlein, commented after the war: 'We should have taken Alexandria and reached the Suez Canal had it not been for the work of your submarines'. The attention of Hitler was drawn to the implications of the damage being inflicted on the shipping required to supply the army in North Africa and his reaction is recorded in the minutes of a meeting held in Berlin in March, 1943. 'It is therefore necessary at the present time to confront the Italians boldly with the alternative of making an all-out effort to get through supplies regardless of personnel considerations, or to lose Tunisia, and with that also Italy'.

As early as September, 1941, our own Commander-in-Chief, Mediterranean, Admiral Sir Andrew Cunningham, wrote to the Admiralty: 'Every submarine that could be spared was worth its weight in gold'. He was not an officer given to exaggerated expression; and even by that measure the 730-ton U-class submarines, which bore the brunt of the long battle, would not have been greatly overvalued.

Then, as nowadays, the quality of the support provided in harbour was vitally important for the Tenth. False pre-war economy had prevented the provision of secure base facilities at Malta with the result that the Engineers and Storekeepers worked under well-nigh intolerable conditions to prepare the submarines for patrol. That lesson, at least, has been learnt: the Faslane Base presents a very different picture today.

In conclusion I can do no better than repeat the unique Admiralty message following the sinking of HMS UPHOLDER on 14 April 1942: 'The ship and her company are gone but the example and inspiration remain'. We must learn the lessons from the history contained in this very readable book and act upon them.

AUTHOR'S PREFACE

"How would posterity and the youth of Britain remember my men who had died in such a desperate battle?" asked Rear-Admiral G. W. G. Simpson. "Unless they were told the story, they would have nothing to remember."

It was Anthony Daniell who proposed that the history of the Tenth Submarine Flotilla should be written, and it is fitting that out thanks should first go to him.

Contributions have come in from all quarters of the globe, from the submariners of the Royal Navy, the Commonwealth Navies and from our wartime Allies. They have responded unreservedly and to them we owe our deep appreciation. Inevitably, because of the constraints of space, it has not been possible to include all the material sent to me with such generosity. I offer my apologies to those who may have been disappointed. As an ex-submariner myself, the Tenth. with its *Us*, was the flotilla I knew best. When *Sor T*-class submarines were loaned to S 10 at Malta, their operations have been included in this history.

During the battle, a third of us did not return from patrol. By 1942/'43, replacement Commanding Officers were barely keeping pace with submarine losses. Churchill's words were no understatement: ". . . submarine COs are worth a million pounds each."

Such a serious situation affected submarine training. Not all officers and men could follow the tradition of being volunteers. The case of one lieutenant was not unique: joining submarines in June, 1942, he was appointed to his first submarine at Malta in September, 1942. In July, 1943, he was on his way home for his 'perisher': 13 months since he joined 'The Trade', as the Submarine Service used to be known.

During the years of Malta's Second Great Siege, the fortitude of the Fortress Island's people was inspired by the combined leadership of Lt-General Sir William Dobbie and the Bishop of Malta, Archbishop Mgr Dom Maurus Caruana, OSB: both great men, in the right place at the right time.

Britain's worst *uninterrupted* Luftwaffe blitzes upon her cities were measured in weeks. The inhabitants of Malta's tiny islands suffered more than *six thousand* air raids over *two years*. In Kesselring's last frenzied attacks from Sicily, the bombing continued day and night for *five months*. At one moment during this mass murder, *seven* RAF fighters, all the island possessed, grappled with 110 bombers, escorted by over 100 Messerschmitt fighters. Proportionately compared to Britain, the number killed and wounded among the Maltese population was 200% higher. No one knew how many homes and buildings were destroyed. We, the Servicemen, though we shared the ordeal of the Siege, were but temporary visitors.

Among the contributions which I have been privileged to include are those from the surviving Commanding Officers of the Tenth Flotilla. At the time, these captains were almost all lieutenants in their twenties:

P 34	Lieutenant P. R. H. Harrison.
Ultimatum	Lieutenant W. H. Kett, RNR.
Una	Lieutenant C. P. Norman.
Unbeaten	Lieutenant E. A. Woodward.
Unbending/P 37	Lieutenant E. T. Stanley.
Ultor/P 53	Lieutenant G. E. Hunt.
Unison/P 43	Lieutenant A. R. Daniell.
Unique	Lieutenant A. F. Collett
United/P 44	Lieutenant T. E. Barlow.
	Lieutenant J. C. Y. Roxburgh.
Unruffled/P 46	Lieutenant J. S. Stevens.
Unseen/P 51	Lieutenant M. L. C. Crawford.
Unshaken/P 54	Lieutenant J. Whitton.
Unsparing/P 55	Lieutenant A. D. Piper, RNR.
Upright	Lieutenant E. D. Norman
Upstart/P 65	Lieutenant P. C. Chapman.
Ursula	Lieutenant I. L. M. McGeoch.
	Lieutenant A. R. Hezlet.
Utmost	Lieutenant J. H. Eaden.
D. S. Dolfijn/P 47	Lt.-Commander H. van Oostrom Soede, R.Neth.N.
Safari/P 211	Commander Ben Bryant.

Sahib/P 212	*Lieutenant J. H. Bromage.*
Saracen/P 247	*Lieutenant M. G. R. Lumby.*
Splendid/P 228	*Lieutenant I. L. M. McGeoch.*

When considering the number of submarines who did not return from patrol, 'cause unknown, presumed mined', we should not forget that these small *U*s were very sensitive. In bad weather and in the varied densities of the Mediterranean summer seas, an error in drill, a minor defect or slackness on the part of one individual could develop with lethal swiftness into disaster. As Admiral Sir Max Horton, FO(S) from 1940 to 1942, told his men:

"There is no margin for mistakes in Submarines: you are either alive or dead."

It has been of especial satisfaction to record the exploits of our Allies, the Poles, the French and the Dutch. These resolute submariners renounced everything to join us. To operate efficiently and safely their *U*s which were re-named, our Allies had to make war using an alien language. Fighting under assumed names, many had no next-of-kin, their families having been exterminated or incarcerated.

The Poles, French and Dutchmen have all contributed their stories; sadly, there has been no response from our Greek friends who fought alongside us in the dangerous waters of the Aegean. Surmounting daunting political difficulties and fighting in older submarines, the Greeks nevertheless sorely discomfited the enemy, for the loss of four of their boats.

Without Anthony Daniell this history would never have been launched; *sans* Jack Michell, never finished. The Committee which Anthony formed made possible the publication of this book: Tubby Crawford, John Roxburgh, Jack Michell, Richard Compton-Hall, Frank MacVie, Johnnie Coote, Peter Piper, Gus Britton, George Taylor. And in Australia, George Hunt's help has been invaluable.

It is to them, and particularly to Captain John Coote (so tireless in his efforts), that we owe our gratitude.

I thank them all very much.

John Wingate

Prelude

1

On 10 June, 1940, the people of Malta heard with deep fore-boding the news that Italy had declared war on Britain and France. At 0630 the next morning they were woken by the wail of air raid sirens. The warnings had been sounded before, but this was no practice alarm: this was the real thing. Twenty minutes later, the first bombs were being unleashed over the RAF airfield at Hal Far. By the end of the day there had been seven more raids and the islanders were already mourning their dead.

The Acting Governor and Commander-in-Chief of Malta, Lieutenant-General Sir William Dobbie, proclaimed his faith in Divine Providence and in 'the cordial support and tried fidelity and determination of the people of Malta'. That fidelity to the Allied cause was to be more severely tested, in the months and years to come, than anyone could have foreseen.

For nearly a century and a half Malta had been home to Britain's Mediterranean Fleet, an invaluable base for repairs and maintenance; but in September, 1939, on the eruption of war in Europe, the fleet was moved. The Italian Air Force, with bases only sixty miles away in Sicily, was too formidable a threat.

The decision came as a particular blow to Admiral Sir Andrew Cunningham, Commander-in-Chief of the Mediterranean Fleet, which would now be based at the Egyptian port of Alexandria. He believed that Malta was crucial to British interests in the Mediterranean, but he had to accept the conclusions of the War Cabinet in London. The fleet had therefore moved out of the familiar haven of Grand Harbour and sailed for Alexandria, to leave behind a handful of motor torpedo boats and submarines.

The fleet's departure was a sad loss to the people of Malta whose fortunes had long depended on those of the British. At this stage of the war, in 1939, Italy was not involved; perhaps the maelstrom would pass the island by. It was a vain hope. As so often before in history, Malta would provide a focal point for opposing sides.

A rocky limestone outcrop in the Mediterranean Sea, Malta is smaller than the Isle of Wight. Even with the attendant isles of Gozo and Comino, the land area is little more than 120 square miles. But it is not Malta's size that has attracted attention throughout the ages, it is her geographical position, midway between Europe and Africa, Asia and the Atlantic, at the narrowest part of the sea.

First colonized about 6,000 years ago, Malta still displays the remnants of her remarkable early inhabitants, whose temples, tombs and artefacts continue to intrigue the archaeologists today. But this early civilization declined very suddenly, for reasons that remain unclear, and the island succumbed to less cultured invaders from the north. It seems to have been the Phoenicians who gave the island her name: 'Mlt', meaning shelter, no doubt derived from the fact that the superb natural harbours gave a welcome haven to the Phoenician ships as they plied the Mediterranean in pursuit of trade. The Phoenicians arrived in about 800 BC, and after them the Carthagians, whose most notable legacy is their Semitic language.

Following the Second Punic War, Malta was absorbed into the Roman Empire. Some 270 years later, in AD 60, a prisoner on his way for trial in Rome was shipwrecked off the coast. He was Paul the Apostle, who converted the islanders to Christianity and later appointed the 'chief man of the island, whose name was Publius' *(Acts of the Apostles* 28,7) as the first Bishop of Malta.

During the Dark Ages the island fell under Saracen domination, until in 1090 the arrival of Count Roger d'Hauteville restored Christianity and signalled the start of Norman rule from Sicily. The marauding Turks continued to threaten the islands, and in 1530 the Emperor Charles V offered Malta to the Knights of St John on condition that they held the island against the onslaught of Islam. Led by the splendid Grand Master, Jean Parisot de la Vallette, seventy-two years old, the Knights and loyal Maltese held out against Suleiman the Magnificent and his Saracen hordes for four terrible months, from May to September, 1565. It was the first Great Siege of Malta.

Gradually weakened by wealth and inertia, the one-time crusaders were eventually subverted by the revolutionary republicanism that was sweeping Europe two hundred years ago, and soon the Maltese found they had a new master — Napoleon. But in their better days the Knights had created not only stout fortifications in the city of Valletta, named in honour of their valiant Grand Master, but also a sturdy independence of mind in the Maltese islanders who now resisted the harsh demands of Napoleon's occupying troops. They forced the French to seek refuge inside the battlements of Valletta, and with the help of Nelson's fleet, which was returning after its victory of the Nile, laid siege to their own capital city. The French capitulated.

It was now, in the year 1800, that the British link with Malta was forged. The Maltese clamoured to join the British Empire, and their wish was fulfilled by the Treaty of Paris in 1814 when the islands of the Maltese archipelago were formally annexed to the British Crown. Throughout the nineteenth century, Malta provided the Royal Navy with a matchless base at the heart of the Mediterranean; in return the Maltese enjoyed a growing prosperity, particularly after the opening of the Suez Canal, when merchant ships sailing to and from the Far East now stopped off to refuel at Malta. Travellers were often surprised to find such affluence as well as such an agreeable welcome in Malta, though one traveller who was less favourably impressed was Byron; he paid the island a visit in 1811 and ended up in quarantine.

Such a curious connection, between one island preoccupied with all the privilege and responsibilities of Empire, and another much smaller island where the people belonged to the Roman Catholic faith and a totally different culture, might have seemed likely to collapse in mutual hostility; yet it lasted well into the twentieth century, fostered by the warm relations between islanders and men of the Royal Navy. In the 1930s, despite pressure from the judiciary, the Church and reactionary elements who favoured Italian as the official language, the islanders even opted for a combination of English and their own unique language of Maltese: a happy compromise that has stood them in good stead ever since.

To the Maltese people the outbreak of war between Britain and

Germany seemed a distant event. It was inconceivable to these islanders, so many of whom had relatives and friends in Sicily, only sixty miles away, that Italy might enter the war and that Malta herself might be threatened.

Hitler might regard him with scorn but Mussolini saw himself as Il Duce, a world leader to rank alongside the Führer. His own troops were already in Eritrea, Abyssinia and Libya; his intention was to dominate the whole of North Africa and the sea that he called 'mare nostrum'. In March, 1940, he ordered the Italian navy to its War Stations and to prepare an 'offensive at all points in the Mediterranean and outside'.

When German troops began storming into Holland and Belgium and threatening France, it finally became clear that Italy was on the point of joining her Axis partner. Belatedly, Britain set about reinforcing her forces in the Mediterranean; ten submarines from the China and East Indies stations were recalled in April, 1940. But, to defend the skies over Malta, the only aircraft which could be spared were four old Gloster Gladiator biplanes, and one of those was destroyed in the first day's encounter with the enemy. The island had been endowed with an early version of radar, but it served only to increase the islanders' frustration when they received advance warning of aerial intruders but were unable to send up any fighters to deter them. Although the three biplanes climbed into the air with dependable regularity, thereby winning the affectionate nicknames of 'Faith', 'Hope' and 'Charity', they were no match for the swift and well-armed attackers.

Thus, the Regia Aeronautica, the Italian Air Force, could come and bomb the island with virtual impunity. The intention was partly to destroy the dockyards and airfields, but also to demoralize the people of Malta. In this latter respect they failed. Like any small community (the islanders numbered only about 250,000 at this time) the Maltese closed ranks against the threat from outside. Seeking shelter in tunnels dug into the limestone rock, and in the ancient battlements raised by the Knights of St John, they prepared to withstand the second Great Siege of Malta. For the next few years scarcely a single day would pass without bombs screaming down from the sky.

While the Maltese sought safety underground, the British

Chiefs of Staff in London reviewed their policy for the Mediterranean. Vulnerable though it was to Mussolini's bombers, Malta's strategic importance was now enhanced — for, on 22 June, France had surrendered to Nazi Germany. It was now imperative to reinforce Malta's defences; the alternative was to move the fleet from Alexandria to Gibraltar, abandoning not just Egypt and Malta but the whole of the eastern Mediterranean. Churchill himself, the new Prime Minister, vetoed the move. Malta was to be held.

To fill the vacuum in the western Mediterranean, the Admiralty now created a squadron called Force H, which would be commanded by Vice-Admiral Sir James Somerville and based at Gibraltar. One of the first tasks of Force H, in August, 1940, was to protect a convoy of supply ships intended to help the besieged Maltese. Despite an operation earlier that month, in which twelve Hurricane aircraft had flown off the old carrier *Argus* to land safely in Malta, the island was fast running out of food, aircraft fuel, ammunition and other supplies.

In April, 1940, a week before Italy's formal declaration of war, the ships of the Mediterranean Fleet had already taken up War Stations. Among them were four of the large and ageing O, P and R-class submarines recalled from the east. They sailed for their designated war patrols on 10 June, with the two minelayers, *Grampus* and *Rorqual*. Within six days, two of the four, *Odin* and *Orpheus,* and the minelayers *Grampus,* had been lost. Over 170 officers and men had perished. Only two of the Rs and *Rorqual* survived.

Although Valletta's Grand Harbour had long been home to the Mediterranean Fleet, the submarines had so far been obliged to make do with a floating base, a depot ship moored in the dockyard. What the submarines needed were purpose-built pens, protected from the air and secure from surface attack; pens*, tunnelled into the sandstone rock, had been begun in 1934 but, by a political decision, had been abandoned because of the cost (the price of one T-class submarine). Now there was neither time nor manpower to spare to finish the job. This deficiency meant that

---

* On the jacket illustration appear three large cavities in the rock: the start of excavations for the submarine pens.

Malta's submarine base on Manoel Island was still not properly established at the end of 1940. This in no way reflected on the efforts being made by Lieutenant-Commander R. G. Giddings. Known to all as 'Pop', this retired Reserve Officer and representative of the wine merchants Saccone & Speed, led a ship's company of thirty-five Maltese sailors; he had been doing his level best to meet the demands of the visiting submarines after their passage from the east. But it was a hand-to-mouth existence, for equipment and personnel were virtually non-existent.

Giddings' methods did not always meet with the approval of his Maltese sailors, one of whom complained that 'he had told them that they deserved to be bombed and bloody well, too'. And, official complaint channels having evidently failed, the stone lintel above one stairway proclaimed plaintively: 'R. G. BASTID IS.' But, thanks to Giddings and his crew, the embryo submarine base eventually began to take shape.

The base itself occupied the buildings of a former lazaretto or leper hospital, which stood on the southern shore of Manoel Island in Marsamxett Harbour. This little island of fifty acres, which derived its name from the stone edifice of Fort Manoel on its eastern shore, was joined by a causeway at its western extremity to Sliema, a residential suburb of Valletta. Submarines could lie alongside the hospital's southern walls which rose sheer from the water's edge or at buoys laid in Lazaretto Creek, protected from seaborne attack by a defensive boom (nets slung from buoys) which stretched across the harbour mouth. Constructed like most of Malta's buildings with huge blocks of stone, the base could survive all but a direct hit; impervious to incendiary bombs, it soon acquired a battered facade from the bombing – but in the dark years ahead, the first sight of these Lazaretto walls was always exhilarating to submariners returning from patrol.

In June, 1940, the loss of the three submarines, *Odin*, *Orpheus* and *Grampus,* within so short a time was deeply felt at Lazaretto. The balance was redressed somewhat on 20 June when an Italian U-boat was sunk by *Parthian* (Lieutenant-Commander M. G. Rimington), based at Alexandria. This was the first British submarine success in the Mediterranean, and it did much to improve morale; but the sinking was one of the few notched up during the first six months of the war. In all, 398 officers and men did not return from patrol during these opening months of submarine warfare in the Mediterranean: peacetime trained, experienced, dependable crews, who could not be replaced. They paid a cruel price: their O-, P- and R-class submarines were not merely outdated, but too cumbersome and unwieldy to be effective in this theatre of war.

Admiral Cunningham was well aware that his submarines, despite the valour of their crews, were unsuitable and ill-equipped to meet the challenge. He also knew that they were having communication troubles: deficiencies in wireless reception, which had not come to light during peacetime exercises, meant that W/T signals from submarines in the Strait of Messina and the area south of Sicily were seriously delayed in reaching Malta. Cunningham was determined to attack the enemy's shipping routes between Italy and North Africa: Malta was the ideal base from which to launch such an offensive, as he impressed upon the Admiralty. First he needed submarines which were better suited to conditions in the central Mediterranean: smaller, more manoeuvrable submarines, particularly for the shallow, inshore waters where manoeuvrability was all-important. What he wanted were the Us, who were performing so well in the North Sea.

In London, the Admiralty agreed that Cunningham should have his Us — as soon as they were built and could be spared. In the meantime it was decided to send four of the powerful, modern T-class out to Malta.

In early September, 1940, Lieutenant-Commander R. G. Mills was summoned to the headquarters of Flag Officer, Submarines (FOS), at Northways, Swiss Cottage in north London. Here he met FOS, Vice-Admiral Sir Max Horton, who told him to take four Ts from the Third Flotilla in the River Clyde and sail for Malta. As Senior Submarine Officer there, he was to take control of the embryo submarine base until the arrival of Commander G. W. G. Simpson. For, on 7 September, Simpson had been appointed Commander (S) of what would become the Tenth Submarine Flotilla. He would not arrive in Malta until January '41, but as swiftly as possible Us would sail out to Malta to join the new flotilla.

By 20 September all four Ts were on patrol in the Mediterranean: *Truant* (Lieutenant-Commander H. A. V. Haggard) and *Triad* (Lieutenant-Commander G. S. Salt) in the Tyrrhenian Sea, with *Triton* (Lieutenant-Commander G. C. I. St B. S. Watkins) and *Tetrarch* (Mills himself) in the Gulf of Genoa. In due course, Ronnie Mills, experiencing the handiwork of Pop Giddings and his men, reported that the new base, despite continuous attention from the Regia Aeronautica, was functioning well. Mills was appointed Acting Commander (S) until Simpson's arrival. He was responsible to Captain (S) 1 in Alexandria, and at the end of the year was promoted to Commander.

Now the gloves were off. The *T*s were formidable boats, commanded by senior COs with harsh experience of Norwegian waters and the Atlantic, and soon they were drawing blood. By the end of the year they had sent 20,000 tons of Axis shipping to the bottom. But *Triad* and *Triton* had already paid the penalty: *Triad* presumed mined off the Calabrian coast, *Triton* in the southern Adriatic.

The Italian minefields were to prove a serious menace for our submariners. According to the Admiralty: 'Minelaying on a considerable scale was undertaken by the Italians during June, 1940.' In addition to minefields off all major Italian ports, the approaches to some North African ports were also mined, Tripoli, Benghazi and Tobruk in particular. As the official Admiralty records state:

> The Cape Bon — Sicily mine barrage was commenced on 8th June and reinforced on the 12th. Between 6th and 25th June 12,900 mines were laid, many of them before the outbreak of war, and some of them well outside the declared areas. The majority of the shallow anti-surface ship fields were backed up with deep anti-submarine fields.
>
> During the period July to December, 1940, 2,890 mines were laid, mainly to supplement the previous programme. Minelays to the eastward of Malta were undertaken in September, and Italian U-boats laid small fields off Haifa and Alexandria. Mines were also laid off Rhodes.

In the months and years to come further lays were carried out and old ones reinforced. By September, 1943, when the Italians surrendered, they had laid a total of 54,000 mines in the Mediterranean, and the Germans later augmented them.

It was a vicious welcome that was waiting for our *Us*, now heading one by one from the builders' yards and the cold grey waters of the North Sea for the warmer Mediterranean.

2

The *Unity*-class submarine was to prove uniquely suitable for war-time conditions in the Mediterranean, yet ironically it had been conceived with a very different purpose in mind. Uncomplicated in design and relatively simple to build, the *U*s were originally intended to be used as 'clockwork mice', for training surface ships in anti-submarine detection. It was the Admiralty's good fortune that they were already in production when war broke out.

Built at Barrow-in-Furness by Vickers Armstrong, whose then chairman, Sir Charles Craven, was himself a former submarine officer, the first three *U*s were launched in 1937 — *Undine, Unity* and *Ursula*. Captain George Phillips, DSO, GM, who would take command of the Tenth Flotilla in Malta in 1943, as a Lieutenant-Commander was appointed in command of *Ursula* for the first of the class trials. It was an interesting job for a junior officer, he remembers, as he was able to gain an insight into Admiralty thinking:

> The Staff requirement for the *U*s was as a replacement for the *H* class as a 'first command' submarine. When the building programme started, there was so much criticism that it looked possible that the design might be scrapped. Too small, too slow, too lightly armed: the interest was with the other new class, the *T*s.

But 'war noises were getting louder' and the Admiralty had no alternative but to press ahead with construction of these small submarines as originally planned.

> Technically, the big innovation was commercial, off-the-shelf generators. This was a great point at Malta because the flotilla

depended on cannibalizing for engine and all other spares. It also greatly helped the big expansion in building. Previously, main engines had been one-off, hand-made and good, but slow to produce.

These were the 400hp Paxman diesel generators, two of which were fitted in each of the *Us*, to provide the power to drive the two electric motors which then turn the propeller shafts.

In appearance the early *Us* were remarkable for their bulbous bows, which housed two external torpedo tubes; but these were later removed to improve trimming and partly to accelerate production. The principal advantage of this class was the speed with which the boat* could dive: the 'quick diving tank', or Q tank†, permitted a diving time of as little as sixteen seconds from surface to periscope depth. Set just forward of the submarine's centre of gravity, to give her a slight bow-down angle on diving, the Q tank held ten tons of seawater which displaced air. Q could be vented either inboard or outboard.

Apart from Q there were six Main Ballast tanks; two were external and free-flooding, flooded by opening main vents fitted in the top of the pressure hull; the other four were internal and set amidships. All were fitted with valves operated from the control room. The riveted steel hull, half an inch thick and designed to withstand the pressure at a depth of 250 feet, was subdivided into eight watertight compartments.

All the teething troubles had been dealt with by the time war broke out, but two inherent defects were to cause untold frustration to COs in the Mediterranean. One was the *U*'s extreme trimming sensitivity, even in a moderate sea, when at periscope depth. In the words of the distinguished submariner, Rear-Admiral Ben Bryant CB, DSO, DSC: 'A submarine is a very self-willed lady who must be humoured . . . If you were to keep her under perfect control, you had to anticipate and start correcting the wayward lady almost before she started to stray.'†† This was particularly true of the *U*, which could 'break surface' in bad weather or on firing a full salvo of torpedoes. Keeping the boat

* The submariner refers to his 'boat' rather than his 'ship'.
† See Glossary, p370.
†† Bryant: *One Man Band* (William Kimber, 1958).

perfectly trimmed, at all times and in all conditions, called for concentration and experience.

The diesel-electric propulsion system was a new departure and proved excellent under wartime conditions: no unwieldy clutches to operate to disconnect the main engines; and the battery charge could be 'floated' once the 'box was up' (batteries fully charged).

The second deficiency lay with these two generators which provided the electrical charge for the two main batteries; these two diesel generators initially gave considerable trouble when the Us first arrived in Malta. The diesels could be run only on the surface because they needed air: the Schnorkel breathing tube was not adopted by the Admiralty until after the war. It was therefore essential for the boat to come to the surface whenever the batteries had to be recharged. And, with a maximum surface speed of only ten knots, the Us were frequently unable to catch their faster prey.

Despite their shortcomings, the first three Us were hastily brought to war readiness: two torpedoes in the external bow tubes, four in the internal tubes; four reload torpedoes were stowed in the torpedo stowage compartment where the fifteen junior ratings lived and slept. To reload, their whole living quarters had to be removed. In order to speed construction of the next six boats in the class *(Utmost, Upright, Unique, Urge, Upholder* and *Unbeaten)* the external tubes were removed, leaving only *Ursula* with a salvo of six. Each was then armed with the ineffective 12-pounder gun: it was later replaced with the harder-hitting 3-inch gun.

By 4 December, 1940, when *Upright* nosed into Marsamxett Harbour, the first of her class to arrive in Malta, the Us had been tested and proved in the toughest of circumstances, fighting a determined enemy in the Norwegian campaign. Two had already been lost, *Undine* and *Unity*, but more were under construction in the shipyards of Vickers-Armstrong at Barrow-in-Furness, Vickers-High Walker at Newcastle and the Royal Dockyard, Chatham. Many of these new boats were destined for a gruelling commission in the Mediterranean, and some of them would never return to their home waters.

Already the Mediterranean conflict was developing in intensity.

Earlier, in July, 1940, Admiral Cunningham's ships had their first encounter with the Italians off Calabria, which resulted in the Italian battleship *Cesare* being hit and the rest of the enemy fleet retreating in haste. It was an encouraging start for the Mediterranean Fleet, strengthened the following month by reinforcements from the UK, including the new aircraft carrier *Illustrious*. Belatedly, at the height of Hitler's European 'blitzkrieg', London was trying to make good the lack of preparations in this theatre of war, and for the next few months both Cunningham's fleet and Somerville's Force H were kept busy escorting convoys of supply ships heading east from Gibraltar.

On 28 October Mussolini's troops invaded Greece. In response the British established a garrison on the island of Crete, with a rudimentary naval base at Suda Bay; despite the intermittent flow of reinforcements, war *matériel* and other supplies were becoming dangerously stretched. Nevertheless, on 11 November the British hit back: thanks to accurate reconnaissance by aircraft based in Malta, a surprise attack was launched on the enemy naval base at Taranto, where Swordfish bombers from *Illustrious* managed to sink three Italian battleships at their moorings. The dramatic success of this raid was noted with approval not only in London but in Tokyo; in December, 1941, without formal declaration of war, the Japanese would use identical tactics in their assault on the American fleet at Pearl Harbor.

On land, too, the Italians were retreating. In Egypt their early advances were now wiped out. General Wavell's Army of the Nile already had them on the run, pursuing them westwards to the Libyan region of Cyrenaica and beyond; soon the Italian-held port of Benghazi would be in British hands, and then, perhaps, even Tripoli . . .?

In Malta, despite the continued attentions of the Regia Aeronautica and the privations caused by the siege, the year was ending on an optimistic note. At last, it seemed, London had woken to the island's importance and was beginning to provide the military supplies needed for its defence. As well as the reconnaissance aircraft now based on the island, the air defences had been boosted by a score of Hurricanes. A flotilla of modern submarines was even now converging on Malta. On 20 December Admiral Cunningham himself arrived in his flagship *Warspite*.

Sailing into Grand Harbour for discussions about the supply situation with Governor Dobbie and the Vice-Admiral, Malta, Sir Wilbraham Ford, he was greeted with effusive warmth from fast-gathering crowds, for the islanders now knew they had not been forgotten. The rejoicing in Malta would have been considerably muted had anyone known that the Germans were even now arriving in the Mediterranean.

Hitler was not interested in the Mediterranean: frustrated in his ambition to invade Britain, he was nursing a new obsession with the Soviet Union, theoretically his ally. But his advisers persuaded him that British interests could best be damaged now by attacking in North Africa and the Mediterranean. Clearly the Italians could no longer be relied upon; German forces would have to intervene.

At a meeting with the Führer on 6 September, Admiral Raeder had warned that 'the Mediterranean question must be cleared up during the winter months [of 1940/41]'. Field-Marshal Kesselring insisted that the key to success lay in the invasion of Malta, and General Rommel concurred. But Hitler rejected their arguments; he considered invasion to be unnecessary when the Luftwaffe could finish off what the Regia Aeronautica had begun. He gave orders for Fliegerkorps X, triumphant after its success in the Norwegian campaign, to be moved south to bases in Sicily. 'The most important task is to attack the British Navy,' he proclaimed, 'particularly in [Alexandria and the Suez Canal] and in the straits between Sicily and the north coast of Africa.'

And so, throughout the second half of December and all January, 1941, Kesselring supervised the transfer of Fliegerkorps X: Junkers 87s and 88s, Heinkell IIIs medium bombers, Messerschmitt 110s, the twin-engined fighters, all dispersed across Sicilian airfields in preparation for the assault to come. German troops, too, were moving south, ready for shipping into North Africa where they intended to show the crumbling Italians how to fight.

This was the scenario awaiting the Us now on passage from Britain.

At least the long passage out from the UK allowed the crews time to get to know their boats before going on patrol in the unfamiliar conditions of the Mediterranean. 'There is no margin for mistakes in submarines,' Admiral Sir Max Horton used to tell his men; 'you are either alive or dead.' Any minor defect in the boat itself, any slip on the part of one of the crew, could develop with lethal swiftness into disaster; and the Mediterranean with its sudden changes of depth or salinity, could quickly destroy the trim of the sensitive Us. So the men worked doubly hard on their passage to the Mediterranean, learning about the boat, the routines, the skipper, themselves.

The submarine's equivalent to Action Stations in a surface ship is Diving Stations, a drill that prepares the crew not only for diving but for surfacing or for an attack. The captain or officer of the watch *(OOW)* calls 'Dive, dive, dive' down the voice-pipe and activates a klaxon to alert the crew. Within sixteen seconds the conning tower is under water, which leaves little time for the OOW to shut the upper hatch and join the lookouts descending the conning tower ladders into the control room.

Meanwhile, in the control room the duty watchkeeper (an engine room artificer (ERA) or the stoker petty officer) pulls levers on the diving panel to open the main vents on all six Main Ballast tanks, while the hydroplane operators turn their wheels to 'hard-a-dive', the coxswain on the crucial after-planes and the second coxswain on the fore-planes.

Between the two planesmen stands the first lieutenant, also known as Number One or Jimmy. He is watching the depth gauges and the bubble in the inclinometer, and waiting for the shout ("First clip on!") which indicates that the conning tower's upper lid has been shut. The boat is now watertight, and when the lower lid is clipped to shut off the conning tower from the main pressure hull, the first lieutenant knows it is safe to continue diving the boat. When the depth gauge shows twenty feet, the top of the periscope standards are below the surface, while the boat has a bow-down angle of perhaps as much as fifteen degrees. He blows Q tank empty. Depending on whether there is anyone 'up top' (an enemy surface ship or aircraft) he now uses the inboard or outboard vents to allow the air in Q to escape; using the outboard vent produces a large bubble of air which may betray the boat's presence to the enemy.

The submarine should now, theoretically, be in perfect trim at neutral buoyancy.

Before surfacing, the routine is reversed except that at night there is a preliminary degree of readiness. Twenty minutes before the boat starts to surface the order is given to 'Shift to night lighting'. The object of this routine, replacing white bulbs with red ones, is to help night vision: doctors having found that twenty minutes was the optimum time it took for a man's eyes to grow accustomed to darkness. When the first lieutenant has checked that the main vents are shut and that all preliminary drills have been carried out, he reports to the captain: 'Ready to surface, sir.'

The CO orders the higher submarine detector (the senior skilled asdic operator) to carry out an all-round listening sweep. As soon as the captain is satisfied there is nothing 'up top', he gives the order to surface. The first lieutenant blows One and Six main ballast tanks and the planesmen put hard-a-rise on their planes; if the captain wants 'to have a look' at periscope depth, the boat is planed up to twenty-eight feet, but if he wants to surface fast the main motors are speeded up and the submarine goes swooping upwards. Binoculars round his neck, the captain climbs the control room ladder. As Number One calls out the depth at forty feet, the captain opens the lower hatch. At fifteen feet he opens the upper lid and scrambles, half-drenched, out on to the bridge. His first action is to open the voice-pipe cock. Checking that the horizon is clear, he shouts down the voice pipe: 'Look-outs on the bridge. Start the generators.'

In the control room the helmsman has drained the voice pipe by holding a bucket beneath the bell-mouthed pipe, then opening the cock. In the engine room, high pressure air starts the two diesel generators which suck air down into the boat through the conning tower. At last the fug and stench of humanity is replaced by God's fresh air. While the generators rumble and roar, pumping amps into the batteries, the first lieutenant checks that the battery ventilation is running and orders: 'Carry on smoking.'

He now adjusts the boat's buoyancy according to the captain's orders to reduce the boat's silhouette to a minimum.

In fair weather he will leave her trimmed down as far as can safely be risked, without fear of diving again involuntarily. He floods Q tank in readiness for a sudden dive. When dived, he has to control the trim carefully, particularly in heavy weather. So sensitive is the *U* that the boat can break surface merely by one or two heavily built men moving aft from for'ard.

On the bridge, when the captain is certain that all is well, he orders: 'Patrol routine.' Normally, one-third of the crew is on duty, the officer of the watch and two lookouts being on the bridge. One of the first and most vital operations now is disposing of the malodorous rubbish which has accumulated to overflowing in the buckets lined up below in the control room. 'Permission to ditch gash, sir?' someone requests the OOW, on the bridge, who grants permission only if there is no potential risk; extra men in the conning tower might block an emergency dive. Permission given, some six ratings are required to man the ladders of the tower, so that the slopping buckets can be passed up to the bridge, hand over hand, until all their contents have been emptied over the side.

The *U* is not endowed with a cook, so one of the ratings, often the gunlayer, is co-opted as the boat's chef. The small galley with its electric stove exudes increasingly strange cooking smells as the chef does his best to feed his fellows. His is a thankless task, made more difficult by the food shortages that will soon begin to pinch. Even water is to be used with care; one of the limiting factors for the length of patrol is the capacity of the two fresh-water tanks, port and starboard.

Facilities generally, even aboard a modern boat such as the *U*, are not designed primarily for comfort. The only bunks are in the wardroom and senior ratings' mess, where the incumbents sleep 'hot bunks': the man coming off watch taking his turn in the bunk when the watchkeeper goes on duty. Otherwise the junior rates turn into hammocks swinging between torpedo racks or sleep on the deck in the torpedo stowage compartment. There are three lavatories ('heads', in naval terminology) per boat, and even they cannot be 'blown' until nightfall for fear of giving away the boat's position. And yet man is an adaptable animal: he learns to live with what he has, to find pleasure in the smallest things of life: a game of Uckers with his companions, perhaps enlivened with a tot of rum; or perhaps a cup of 'ki' ('pusser's cocoa'), then a blanket over his head.

As yet, facilities for the repair and maintenance of our submarines were at best patchy – and not just in the Mediterranean, as many of the crews could testify.

Jack Michell, then a young lieutenant in *Osiris*, remembers a catalogue of near-disasters following a refit in Chatham dockyard. When *Osiris* sailed for her static dive, Michell noticed that 'every nook and cranny in the control room was full of inflatable lifebelts', and on asking why he was told: 'They're there to be handy when the boat sinks.' Then, on convoy duty, enemy bombers forced *Osiris* to dive – except that she refused to dive; later it was discovered that the after-planes 'had been connected up arsey-facey in the dockyard'. During another patrol the boat was found to be leaving a telltale streak of oil on the surface; but the worst was yet to come:

> On a return trip from Alexandria, after a short patrol in the Adriatic in August 1941, one of *Osiris's* main motors failed. Halfway across the Med, the other main motor failed. She continued *on the surface* and then one diesel packed up. Just outside Alex harbour, the final diesel threw in its hand. She had to be towed in. When finally she got alongside the jetty, the battery blew up.

Such was the quality of submarine mechanical reliability in the early years of the war.

Osiris was twelve years old, whereas the *U*s were brand new; but it was 2,500 miles from home waters to the central Mediterranean, and there was abundant opportunity for mishaps on passage to Malta. Although *Upright* was the first of her class to arrive in Malta, she had overtaken one of her sister *U*s on the way out: *Utmost* found herself unavoidably delayed in Gibraltar.

The first commanding officer of *Utmost*, Lieutenant John H. Eaden (now Commander Eaden, DSC), kept a diary of her early days. In June, 1940, he visited her before she even left the Vickers shipyard at Barrow; in July and August he saw her through the early trials; in September he took her up to the Clyde for further trials. On Sunday, 16 September, her last day before heading south, *Utmost* was berthed alongside the submarine depot ship *Cyclops* in Rothesay Bay when a nearby merchant ship was hit by a German bomb. Twenty-one men were killed. Eaden later recorded in his diary the scenes of horror he found on boarding the ship with the CO of *Cyclops*:

> Saw three men amidships sitting on a raft. One man had something on his lap which he was crooning to. Went over to talk to them and discovered the man had a decapitated head on his lap — apparently belonging to his best friend. The men were completely shocked. Removed the head as gently as possible and dropped it overboard. Surprised how heavy it was.

The following day *Utmost* set sail for Portsmouth and, six weeks later, after a nine-day patrol off Le Havre, she finally sailed for Gibraltar. It was Monday, 28 October.

One man who almost missed the boat was Leading Telegraphist G. Gregory, a survivor of the *Unity* tragedy of 29 April, 1940, when she was rammed and sunk by a Norwegian merchant ship off the Tyne estuary, with the loss of four lives. Gregory had suffered ever since from ear trouble, and Lieutenant Eaden was, in Gregory's words, 'a bit shy about having me after reading the quack's report on my lugs'. But Gregory managed to coax his way on to *Utmost* — although he nearly came to regret it.

'Things went OK until we were nearing Gibraltar,' he writes. *Utmost* was proceeding at periscope depth when four surface ships were spotted, a cruiser and three destroyers. Having received no reports of British ships in the area, and supposing these to be Vichy French, the submarine prepared to attack. At the last moment the nearest ship was identified as the Royal Navy destroyer, *Encounter*.

> By this time the ships were almost upon us and the skipper realized we would certainly be picked up by their asdics and depth-charged. Fortunately there was a procedure for such an occasion: the submerged sub would fire a yellow smoke candle. On seeing this, the surface ship would stop engines and tell the sub to surface and identify herself. Failing to do this, the attacker would depth-charge her.
>
> Well, we fired the ·candle and saw it smoking away on the surface. After four minutes, the skipper fired the second candle. After waiting a short while, we surfaced.

We hadn't been up many seconds when 'Abandon ship! Shut watertight doors!' came from the bridge.

I thought to myself, What, again? and promptly scrambled up the conning tower ladder. When I got on the bridge I saw *Encounter* staggering around with her bows stove in and *Utmost* bow down in the water. It appears that when we surfaced *Encounter* thought we were a Jerry and decided to cut us in two. He came full speed at us and, just before he struck, he realized it was one of his chums and swung his wheel over to starboard, giving us a nasty dent on the starboard side of our fore-ends.

Gregory's skipper, Lieutenant Eaden, recorded the same incident in his diary for 6 November, 1940, adding that the 'cruiser' he had so nearly attacked was the battle-cruiser *Renown*. He concludes his account:

It was with a certain sardonic interest that I noticed that our starboard fore-plane had cut open *Encounter's* side, forward, for some thirty feet, just like an opener on a sardine can . . . Resumed our course for Gibraltar in company with *Encounter*. On arrival, we were first in the dock together for repairs. The Admiral is reported to have said: 'Put them in the same dock and let them sort it out between themselves.'

Although the initial confusion could be attributed to what Eaden calls 'the fog of war', the fact that the two yellow candles had been ignored was a puzzle — until he learned that the Admiralty had recently issued a warning to all ships that 'our S/M (submarine) recognition signal had been compromised and should be treated with suspicion'. Eaden adds dryly: 'Tough on our S/Ms!'

Utmost was still in Gibraltar when *Upright* arrived from the UK. In addition to repairs, she had to wait for a new commanding officer, Lieutenant-Commander R. D. Cayley; and then she was still further delayed, according to Lieutenant Anthony Daniell, the Number One of *Upright*, 'because her cat had gone adrift on her "run ashore" and the sailors would not go to sea without her'.

Upright (commanded by Lieutenant F. J. Brookes) thus became the first *U*-class submarine to enter the Mediterranean, leaving Gibraltar on 19 November. On the way to Malta she carried out her first patrol — 'a blank patrol north-west of Sicily', as Daniell writes — and finally arrived at her future base on 4 December, 1940.

Daniell, for one, was not a little dismayed by the lack of facilities at Lazaretto. 'There was *no* base, as such,' he remembers, not even a depot ship:

> On arrival at Manoel Island we found Lieutenant-Commander Giddings, who had long since retired, acting as Executive Officer of the Base; Chief Writer Lyon constituted the Secretariat; and 'Sunny' Warne was the Gunner (T). This was, at the time, the total staff to run a submarine base. Facilities were zero: the Lazaretto was completely bare, the same as when Byron stayed there.

But appearances were deceptive: although the base staff was still minimal, and machinery and engineering facilities were negligible, co-operation with the dockyard officers was excellent. At least the Regia Aeronautica was not interfering unduly with progress; the high-level bombing was not very accurate and the Italians had no idea that these old buildings would soon be home to the British submarines.

It was still a meagre existence, with shortages of every kind enforcing frugality in the harbours as on the land, but Pop Giddings was gradually turning the old leper hospital into a viable submarine base. And, like many in Malta at the end of December, 1940, he had high hopes that the siege would soon be lifted.

3

By the beginning of 1941, the War Cabinet was well aware of the new threat in the Mediterranean, a threat posed by the arrival of the Luftwaffe in Sicily. Moves were already afoot to counter this development and at the same time to relieve the besieged island of Malta. In addition to the *U*-class submarines now converging on the island, more RAF aircraft had been earmarked for delivery to the Maltese bases of Luqa, Hal Far and Ta' Qali. A vast and complex operation was being planned to convey military supplies and reinforcements, not only to Malta but to the Greek army, which was valiantly holding out against Mussolini's troops, and to our new base at Suda Bay in Crete.

Operation 'Excess', as it was codenamed, would involve the entire Mediterranean Fleet, including the Gibraltar-based Force H under Admiral Somerville. While Force H covered the eastward-bound convoy as far as the Narrows — the straits between Sicily and Cape Bon — Admiral Cunningham's main force of ships would sail westward from Alexandria to meet them, simultaneously covering the transfer of eight empty merchant ships that had been trapped in Malta. With the Alexandria fleet would sail the two cruisers, *Gloucester* and *Southampton,* carrying troops to the island, and *Essex* laden with 4,000 tons of ammunition.

Such a bold and dashing plan was characteristic of Admiral Cunningham, who had already stamped his mark upon the Italian fleet the previous November. By asserting his presence in the central Mediterranean he now hoped to avert the German menace. Yet, for all the firepower of his heavy ships, backed up by the air support of the carrier *Illustrious,* he knew they would face furious opposition from the enemy; apart from other considerations, surprise was not a weapon available to him. Even as the first ships left Alexandria on 5 January, and Gibraltar on the 6th, their movements were tracked by enemy reconnaissance aircraft.

The opening stages went well. The two cruisers from Alexandria reached Malta on 8 January and landed their precious cargo of troops, reinforcements for the hard-pressed defenders. Another newcomer to the island that day was a passenger in *Janus*, one of the shepherding destroyers; he was Commander George Simpson, and he was to take command of the *U*s now on passage for Malta — the first of the modern, small submarines that later in 1941 would be transformed into the Fighting Tenth.

Simpson's arrival coincided with a moment of high expectation in Malta. Not only did it seem that the siege had been lifted, with troops already disembarking and supplies even now on their way from the west, but the Italian army in North Africa was crumbling under pressure from General Wavell's Army of the Nile. British ascendancy in the Mediterranean had apparently been reestablished.

On 10 January, 1941, all illusions were shattered. The Royal Navy and the Luftwaffe met in their first head-on clash in this theatre of war, and, as in the North Sea and the English Channel, the skill and determination of the German pilots won the day.

The previous evening the eastbound convoy from Gibraltar had reached the Narrows; Somerville and Force H, having handed over control of the convoy to Cunningham's ships, had fulfilled their half of Operation 'Excess' and now were sailing back to base. In the early afternoon of the 10th, to the north-west of Malta, the carrier *Illustrious* (Captain Denis Boyd) came under attack. Before the carrier's Fulmar fighter planes could gain sufficient height, the first of the enemy dive bombers, Junkers 87s (Stukas), were plunging out of the sky. Diving almost vertically, they dropped their 1,000lb bombs on the carrier, pulled out at 500 feet and made their escape at flight-deck level.

Within minutes it was over. 'We could not but admire the skill and precision of it all,' Cunningham commented later. But the significance of the attack was not lost on him; the intervention of the seasoned veterans of the Luftwaffe, with their superior modern aircraft, meant that the Mediterranean Fleet had acquired a dangerous new adversary.

Six direct hits had grievously wounded the carrier and caused appalling casualties; the damage would have been worse but for the armoured deck. Her steering gear crippled by shrapnel, it was only by skilful manoeuvring on main engines that Captain Boyd was able to nurse the stricken ship back to Malta's Grand Harbour.

That evening the people of Malta watched *Illustrious* limping into harbour. Holding their breath, they awaited the inevitable *coup de grâce* for the shattered carrier.

Meanwhile the Stukas had turned their attention to the two cruisers, which, having disembarked their troops, had then caught up with Cunningham's main force. Both the *Gloucester* and her sister ship *Southampton* were hit, and the latter was sunk. The rest of the fleet escaped more or less intact and managed to complete their escort duties: the convoy reached its destination safely. Operation 'Excess' had achieved its aims, but at a heavy price.

As soon as the German pilots discovered where *Illustrious* was berthed (in French Creek, off Grand Harbour) they began a long and sustained campaign to annihilate her where she lay. Repeatedly they returned to batter her with bombs, not only the carrier, but the dockyard too, as well as the rest of the island. The Maltese people had become used to the constant high-level bombing of the Regia Aeronautica, but now the raids took on a new and terrible ferocity as the siege of Malta was intensified. No records remain for the number of raids during that awful January of 1941, but, to all who remember it, the real beginning of the 'blitz' was indelibly linked to the damaged carrier.

For the next thirteen days, despite the screaming Stukas and their bombs, the dockyard personnel worked feverishly to make the carrier seaworthy; they could not offer the full-scale repairs she needed for lack of resources, but they could patch her up well enough for a night-time dash to Alexandria and better facilities. That she was not sunk alongside was miraculous; that she was able to sail at sunset on 23 January was due to the bravery and endurance of the dockyard workers and *Illustrious's* unflinching ship's company.

One of the attacks on the carrier was witnessed by Lieutenant Dudley Norman, who had taken over *Upright* after her first patrol. He happened to be in Barracca Gardens with a grandstand view of Grand Harbour when the attack began. 'It was a fantastic sight,' he remembers, 'with some of the aircraft finishing their attack so low that they had to pull up to clear the breakwater.'

> I was deafened not only by the *crump!* of bomb explosions and the noise of every available weapon, but also the *'Zzzzphut'* of falling shrapnel all around me. I suppose the whole attack lasted less than fifteen minutes, after which an eerie silence descended for a few moments. Then came the 'All Clear'. I got a *dghaisa* [one of the colourful Maltese 'taxi' gondola-type boats] across the harbour and picked my way through the rubble towards *Upright*, catching on the way a piece of paper which blew into my face. It was a demand note for stores signed by me a few weeks earlier! *Upright* was, happily, unharmed. Our signal-man-cum-anti-aircraft gunner claimed to have hit one of the Stukas with a bullet from his Lewis gun. I'm afraid that he was never credited with a kill!

Another eyewitness was Victor Coppini. 'I thought it was the end of the world,' he recalls. 'I sometimes wonder how we in Valletta came out alive from that inferno of exploding ack-ack shells and aerial bombs.' For the anti-aircraft batteries responded in kind, using a new technique called the 'box barrage' which according to Mr Coppini was 'a defensive procedure conceived by Major Fenech, a Maltese Army officer':

> In simple terms it was a plan by which ack-ack guns protecting a target area, like Valletta's Grand Harbour, would fire in a fixed direction, simultaneously and constantly, thus creating a box of flying shrapnel which would down any plane that dared enter into it. It must also have had a deterrent effect on the would-be bombers. The guns were controlled from GOR (Gun Operation Room) sited somewhere deep down in the bowels of the earth . . . This 'box barrage' was later used at El Alamein: set areas were earmarked for concentrated and devastating bombardment by artillery. Not even scorpions had a chance to survive! When the 'box barrage' was over, the Eighth Army advanced.

But the triumph of El Alamein was still a long way off: nearly two grim years would have passed before that battle marked a turning point in Allied fortunes in North Africa.

The German raiders, thwarted in their efforts to destroy *Illustrious,* were seemingly attempting to sink what Winston Churchill would call 'that unsinkable aircraft carrier' – the island itself. Though the carrier remained the principal target, Kesselring's orders to his pilots were to terrorize the Maltese population and to reduce their island to rubble. The Afrika Korps, under General Rommel, was about to arrive in North Africa; and this air assault was intended to reduce the risk of counterattack by British forces based in Malta.

The fifteen RAF Hurricanes, outnumbered and outclassed, their airfields barely usable, fought until overwhelmed. Ammunition and spare parts were running out. From now on every submarine on passage from Britain to Malta was crammed with extra stores. Except for the brief visits of surface warships from the middle of April until October '41 and until Malta could be adequately defended from the air, the island's sole offensive potential now consisted of the smallest submarines in the Mediterranean fleet, the Us.

Throughout this onslaught, work was continuing on the Lazaretto submarine base. As the submarines arrived they had to spend a few days storing and refuelling, and the crews required a short rest before sailing on patrol, so the need was urgent. Under the guidance of Commander Simpson and his engineer officer, Sam MacGregor – who had arrived on 10 January, with the western half of Operation 'Excess' – the base on Manoel Island was at last taking shape.

One priority was bomb-proof shelters for some of the base facilities, such as engineering workshops and the sick bay. Burrowing into the rock behind the old hospital buildings, the frantic tunnelling work began. Soon everyone was lending a hand, Maltese labourers and submariners alike. At present other quarters were within the Lazaretto itself, where the names of those once quarantined here were scratched into the wall at the western end, including that of Byron whose sour verdict on Malta was:

Adieu, thou damnedest quarantine
That gave me fever and the spleen . . .

26

This western end was to be turned into barracks, with officers' cabins on the first floor and a large hall serving as wardroom and mess. Later on a small chapel would be tunnelled out of the rock close by, where the Chaplain could celebrate Holy Communion on Sundays.

Along the southern side of Lazaretto, looking across Marsamxett Harbour to Valletta, there ran an imposing arched arcade supporting a first-floor gallery. Extending the full length of the block, this long open corridor would become a haven for off-duty COs, whose cabins, like Simpson's quarters and office, opened off the gallery.

Moorings for the submarines were laid in an arc around Lazaretto, head and stern buoys being spaced at varying distances to take the different classes of boats. The privileged 'wardroom berth', on the southern frontage where the water was deep enough to accommodate a boat alongside, was usually occupied by a submarine about to go on patrol, particularly in bad weather, as there were no unstable pontoons to negotiate when provisioning the boat and preparing for sea.

Bomb-proof shelters for the boats themselves were simply not feasible. 'Pens would have made a terrific difference,' writes Anthony Daniell, the Number One of *Upright;* but time was short and there was just too much to do. Already men were working flat out, and this on reduced rations as food shortages on the island began to bite. As further protection, Simpson issued strict orders that the White Ensign should *not* be flown at Lazaretto and that all men in uniform *must* take cover as soon as the alert was sounded; by these means, even the low-flying Stukas and Ju 88s were for months kept unaware of the exact location of the base.

While work continued at Lazaretto, Sam MacGregor spent long days over in Grand Harbour, scouring the docks for machinery, tools and stores, begging and 'borrowing' whatever he needed for the workshops now being dug out of the rock. Sam would soon become a central figure in the lives of the submarine COs; either he or his right-hand man, the Commissioned Engineer Officer, Mr L. A. Creed (known as 'Creedy') would always be waiting on the pontoon when a boat secured after a patrol. According to Anthony Daniell, Sam's standard question on boarding the boat was: 'Has the chain come off?' No defect, however complicated, ever seemed to worry him or the laconic Creedy.

The only other officer on the base when Simpson arrived was someone he already knew: 'Sunny' Warne, the Commissioned Gunner (T). In 1925 both men had been in the submarine *L7* when she became stuck on the bottom of the China Sea; perhaps the incident had taught Mr Warne to make light of the inconveniences of siege conditions, for the constant smile that earned him the nickname could not otherwise be reconciled with the difficulties of his job. In his torpedo workshop in 'Torpedo Creek', as ill-equipped as Sam MacGregor's, he would have to care for a perplexing array of different torpedoes – Mark IVs, VIs, VIIIs and the CCR pistol as well. Under Lieutenant 'Wiggy' Bennett, the Torpedo Officer, Sunny Warne was the man upon whose shoulders would rest responsibility for the future flotilla's armament.

Overall command remained with the new Commander (S), Commander George Simpson, the first commanding officer of HMS *Talbot*, as the base was known officially.

George W. G. Simpson was a man apart. As Commander (S) 10, later as Captain (S) 10, he was an exceptional leader of men. Despite a caustic exterior, he is remembered by the author particularly for his kindness, and he left an indelible image on the minds of all his COs.

Short of stature and stocky of build, Simpson was known to all as 'Shrimp'. Now approaching the age of forty, he was much older than most of his COs, who tended to be in their middle to late twenties, and this disparity in age served to emphasize the loneliness of his position. It was also a source of niggling annoyance to him, as his men realized: 'I knew, as did everyone in the flotilla, that Shrimp would far rather go to sea himself than have to send us,' writes Anthony Daniell, who had sailed with Simpson before the war, when the latter was skipper of *Porpoise*. The same opinion is echoed by Mr Wingrave Tench, OBE, a Civil Administrator in Malta who became Simpson's trusted friend: 'Most of all, Shrimp regretted his age. At thirty-nine, he was too old to be out on patrol, where he longed to be, sharing the risks and opportunities with his friends.'

The COs were indeed his friends, and the growing strain upon Commander Simpson as they failed to return from patrol was a burden Tench was unable to share. 'Gravy' Tench and his wife Greta opened their home, Pembroke House in St Julian's Bay, to Simpson and his COs, and they knew best of all how much he suffered. Yet Gravy Tench retains a vivid impression of Simpson's 'irresistible sense of humour' and the mischief that sometimes twinkled in his piercing blue eyes:

> In spite of the crushing burden he was carrying, he always exuded confidence and optimism. It was his humour, enthusiasm and a mind full of ideas to improve his men's lot which endeared him to his submariners and Maltese sailors alike.

Lieutenant Dudley Norman, CO of *Upright,* who remembers Simpson as 'a brilliant leader', also recalls the sense of humour that characterized the man:

> At a time when wines and spirits were still obtainable, it was possible to exceed one's wine bill. One day, Shrimp sent for Lieutenants Cayley, Norman and Wanklyn. In a very serious voice, he informed us of the amount by which each one of us had exceeded his allowance. Then, with a twinkle in his eye, he added: 'I cannot allow this situation to continue, unless my wine bill is greater than yours. Gentlemen, we will proceed to the wardroom immediately to put that matter right . . .'

Whereupon, Norman concludes, 'We did'.

When Simpson arrived on 8 January there were no submarines in harbour. *Upright,* with Lieutenant E. D. (Dudley) Norman now in command, was on her second patrol since arriving in Malta; the first one had been an uneventful visit to the shallow waters of the Kerkenah Bank off Tunisia, from 14 to 24 December. With another submarine based in Malta, the Free French *Narval,* she had been sent to patrol off the Libyan coast, to intercept any enemy troops attempting to escape from the advancing Army of the Nile.

Narval was an ancient submarine of the *Requin* class, built in 1923 and modernized in 1937. Commanded by Commandant François Drogou, *Narval* was the only French submarine in the Mediterranean to continue the struggle with us in 1940.

Ignoring orders, Drogou sailed from Sousse in Tunisia on 24 June, 1940. Whilst on passage to Malta where *Narval* arrived on the 26th, Drogou made his historic signal to all his compatriots: *'Trahison sur toute la ligne, je fais route vers un port Anglais.'* His was the first French ship to respond to General de Gaulle's *appel* on 18 June, 1940.

Overcoming appalling manning and training difficulties, *Narval* carried out three patrols off Libya from Malta. She sailed on 29 December, 1940, for the Derna area, but was overdue on 14 January, 1941. She was rammed by the Italian torpedo boat, *Clio*, who suffered damage herself. There were no survivors, but *Clio* picked up several of *Narval's* named lifebelts. A tragic end to a company who had proved their loyalty and tried so hard.

And so, on 14 January, 1941, it was Simpson's sad duty to make his first 'missing' signal to his Commander-in-Chief: 'Regret to report *Narval* now three days overdue and must be considered lost.'

The next *U* to arrive in Malta, *Unique* (Lieutenant A. F. Collett), sailed for her first patrol on 16 January and six days later was the first of her class to carry out an attack: she fired one torpedo at a ship off the Kerkenah Bank. It missed; but the *U*s had thrown down the gauntlet.

Now the *U*s were coming thick and fast. *Upholder* (Lieutenant-Commander M. D. Wanklyn) arrived on 14 January, followed by *Utmost* (Lieutenant-Commander R. D. Cayley), *Ursula* (Lieutenant A. J. Mackenzie), and then, on 17 January, *Usk* (Lieutenant-Commander P. R. Ward). *Usk* was in a bad way, after a long and traumatic passage from the west coast of Scotland; she limped into Marsamxett Harbour on five cylinders of one diesel generator, the remaining main bearings having run. The trouble was traced to carborundum dust in the reserve lubricating oil tank: deliberate sabotage. Nor was this the only case of sabotage among *U*s, a crime which Commander Simpson laid at the door of British traitors: at this stage of the war, five months before Germany attacked Communist Russia, Stalin was

Hitler's ally and consequently Britain's enemy. *Usk* went straight into the dockyard for repairs. Unhappily, under the strain of coaxing his sabotaged submarine all the way from Scotland, her captain's health had cracked, and following *Usk's* first attack, on a convoy off Tripoli on 9 February, she was sailed under the command of the Spare CO, Lieutenant G. P. Darling.

Upholder had arrived in Malta without one of her original crew. On passage from Britain to Gibraltar, she had met very bad weather, as a result of which a heavy bulkhead door swung loose from its retaining catch and smashed on Chief ERA Baker's hand, almost severing the tips of three fingers. Lieutenant-Commander Wanklyn, having first given Baker a pain-killing injection, sorted out the mangled fingers with infinite patience; then strapped them up and dressed them for the next four days, until the boat arrived at Gibraltar when Baker could be transferred to the Military Hospital. It was entirely thanks to Wanklyn's care that, apart from a slight malformation on one finger, Baker regained the full use of his hand.

Upholder had sailed from Gibraltar in company with *Triumph*, and on their way to Malta the two submarines had been used to provide cover for the western half of Operation 'Excess'. On 8-9 January, while in their billets south of Sardinia, they were ordered to raise their wireless masts above the surface while dived: the object was to improve the quality of transmission and reception of sighting reports from RAF aircraft. The COs did as ordered, although the huge plume of white water that was raised by each boat's mast would vastly increase the risk of detection by enemy aircraft. Fortunately they were not seen, but Captain S. M. Raw, commanding the First Submarine Flotilla at Alexandria, was so fiercely critical of this suicidal procedure that the Admiralty was obliged to issue a Fleet Order against the practice in future.

As the *U*s arrived in Malta, they took over the patrol areas which had formerly been the responsibility of the *R*- and *T*-class boats, particularly the shallow coastal waters off North Africa where the smaller *U*s were less restricted in their manoeuvres. But their COs quickly found that the Mediterranean lived up to its reputation. The fluctuating salinity levels, the unpredictable currents, the abrupt changes in weather, all combined to keep even the most experienced men on their toes. Moreover, the pellucid blue of the sea meant that submarines were visible even seventy feet below the surface; in an effort to camouflage them, all boats had to be painted a vivid blue by their crews on arrival at Gibraltar.

The hard-working *Upright,* after another blank patrol, returned to base on 19 January for ten days' rest and recuperation. Despite the bombs and hectic activity, Dudley Norman's recollections of life in Lazaretto at that time are not all grim. 'Life on the base at the beginning of 1941 was fairly comfortable,' he writes. 'Food was good and in fair supply; the sailors had their rum and the officers their gin. This was not to last,' he adds. However, he goes on to recount the story of how Lazaretto came to acquire its own farm. Two of the submarine COs, Dick Cayley and Tony Collett, went for a walk in the countryside where

> they came across an elderly Maltese who was sitting on a wall playing operatic excerpts on a violin.
> 'Harmonica Dick', an expert on the mouth organ, joined him on the wall and a lively concert ensued. After a time the Maltese farmer took them back to his farm, where they sampled the local wine . . . When Dick and Tony left, he insisted on giving them a little piglet. They carried it back to the base, brought it into the wardroom and gave it a saucer of beer. I protested that the animal was improperly dressed, in fact totally naked. Tony Collett went out and returned with a bow tie which he put round the piglet's neck. Thus was honour satisfied. Later the piglet was taken out to a disused, enclosed area which had a certain amount of grass, and invited to make itself at home.

The piglet gave Commander Simpson an idea.

The submarine *Triumph,* which had arrived on 14 January with *Upholder,* was on her way to Alexandria with an unusual passenger on board: Commander James Fife of the US Navy, an official observer (this was nearly a year before the United States entered the war). While *Triumph* underwent routine maintenance in Grand Harbour, Commanders Fife and Simpson had quickly become friends, and one day Simpson invited Fife to visit a country market to buy the first 'gilts in pig'. Simpson had decided that a pig farm would not only guard against rainy days ahead but would also help his men's morale, so now he and the American were attending a country sale of Middle Whites. After some careful thought he purchased two pregnant sows.

Back at the base, Simpson posted a notice to inform the ship's company that 'your pigs' were being safely installed in their prepared pens, cared for by Pop Giddings and a team of pig keepers. The two sows caused unanimous enthusiasm, though Sam MacGregor was heard to remark: 'I see both pigs are twelve-cylinder jobs. What happens if the sows give birth to fourteen pistons?'

Simpson later had misgivings about the pigs when he learnt that, under Maltese law, pig meat was not legally fit for human consumption, unless the animal had been killed in the official slaughterhouse. According to Dudley Norman:

> Shrimp, concerned that some of the pigs might be killed by the blast of a near-miss, invited the Maltese Minister of 'Ag & Fish' to come to the base and discuss the problem. His solution was to invite Shrimp to send any pig which had suffered such an unhappy fate to the slaughterhouse where they would be killed again.

This problem resolved, the 'piggery' went from strength to strength and 'soon expanded with chickens'.

James Fife never forgot the friendships he made in Malta during a sojourn that corresponded with the Luftwaffe's furious raids on *Illustrious*. Later, when in the Pacific he became Admiral Commanding Submarines of the US Navy's 7th Fleet, he would command our Far East submarines, and they could not have been better looked after.

By the end of January, 1941, the mood in Malta was one of greater realism. With the siege tightening on the island, basic foodstuffs like tea and sugar were in short supply; conscription was about to be introduced for the first time since 1792; life was constantly disrupted by bombs and enforced spells in the air raid shelters. And yet the Maltese people remained defiant, even as they began to wonder if the Germans were planning to invade.

As it happened, Hitler was not planning to invade. On the contrary, he was so worried by British advances in North Africa that he was moving half his Fliegerkorps X to Tripoli, as well as General Erwin Rommel and his panzers, to lend support to the crumbling Italian troops. Although the incessant raids on Malta would continue throughout February and March, they would not have quite the same intensity.

The islanders' defiance was matched only by that of the Fleet. Fortified temporarily by the extra supplies delivered by 'Excess' and by each new submarine arriving from Gibraltar, the Navy and the dockside workers were determined to carry on despite the bombs. And then, at sunset on 23 January *Illustrious* sailed out of Grand Harbour on her way to Alexandria, the gallant carrier a symbol of defiance. With the new *Us* now patrolling the central Mediterranean, hopes were high that German plans in this theatre of war, whatever they were, could be frustrated.

The Pioneers

4

JANUARY/FEBRUARY, 1941

FOLLOWING the assault on Operation 'Excess', Admiral Cunningham had warned the Admiralty in London that future convoys through the Mediterranean could not be possible until they had air support. Fuel, ammunition and other military provisions were desperately needed in Malta, in addition to food supplies and certain other basic commodities like soap and matches. But until Cunningham had the wherewithal to tackle his well-armed and skilful adversary, he was not going to risk his ships on convoy duties. The grim truth, as he saw it, was that Malta was now on her own; she would 'have to fight it out with Sicily'.

Ironically the Fliegerkorps in Sicily was now seriously depleted, as Hitler ordered Kesselring's pilots to prop up the Italians in North Africa. But Hitler, keeping one eye on Greece, had also ordered the installation of air bases in Rhodes and the Dodecanese. The Luftwaffe would henceforth be a major threat to the Mediterranean Fleet based in Alexandria. Moreover, the Germans were now within easy reach of the Suez Canal; if they could close the canal they would destroy the lifeline not only to the Navy but also to the British Army; though convoys could no longer use the Mediterranean, they were still arriving via the Red Sea, by sailing all the way round the Cape and up the East African coast.

Already, on 30 January, enemy aircraft from Benghazi had mined the Suez Canal. Despite the frantic efforts of our minesweepers, this inevitably caused delays to reinforcements arriving via the Cape, which included the new aircraft carrier, *Formidable*. And at this stage the need for reinforcements was particularly crucial, as General Wavell, sweeping ever westwards with his Army of the Nile, was in danger of overstretching his supply line. On 22 January the triumphant British troops took Tobruk; on 6 February they captured Benghazi. They would have pressed on even further west to Tripoli if events on the opposite side of the Mediterranean had not cheated them of this final goal.

On 1 March Bulgaria declared war on the Allies and was soon swarming with German troops. Spurred by this new development, the British planners set up Operation 'Lustre' to transfer and transport Wavell's troops and munitions to Greece. Thus, even as Rommel and Kesselring were arriving in North Africa to bolster the Italians, our own victorious army was being removed from the scene. With the rest of the Mediterranean Fleet involved in the enormous operation to ferry 45,000 troops from Egypt to Greece, and all available aircraft providing the necessary cover, virtually the sole obstruction in the flow of supplies to Rommel's army in this spring of 1941 was the handful of submarines at Malta.

In London it was the intention of Admiral Sir Max Horton, Flag Officer, Submarines, to base ten U-class submarines at Malta. In fact, replacement barely kept pace with losses and never more than eight were able to operate at one time. As the Us arrived they relieved the older boats, who now sailed to join the First Flotilla and its depot ship *Medway* at Alexandria. The nucleus of another flotilla, the Eighth, had been formed at Gibraltar, the flotilla consisting of the new S-class boats: in March, 1941, 'Mother' *Maidstone* would arrive as their depot ship. The Eighth's task involved both defensive convoy work in the Atlantic and patrolling in the western Mediterranean, while the Us were intended to lead the offensive in the central Mediterranean. But, incredible as it now seems, our submariners were still fighting with one hand tied behind their backs: 'Sink at sight' applied only to ships within thirty miles of the Italian and Libyan coasts.

By February, 1941, Simpson had acquired some vital support at Lazaretto: both a deputy Commander(S) 10 and a Staff Officer, Operations (SOO). Lieutenant-Commander H. A. L. Marsham, Simpson's deputy, had been Commanding Officer of *Rover*, recently operating out of Malta; his experience and knowledge of these waters would be invaluable. The SOO or 'Staffie' was Lieutenant-Commander Bob Tanner; forced to leave submarines when his eyesight deteriorated, Tanner's dry sense of humour and unflappable qualities were an appreciable asset in times of stress. With this competent and devoted team around him, Simpson was now able to delegate much of the day-to-day planning while he concentrated on the main objectives.

The priority, of course, was to harry the enemy along the coasts of Italy and North Africa; but as the Us arrived after their long passage from the UK, they inevitably required some attention. Sam MacGregor was still licking his workshops into shape and was obliged to send the boats round to Grand Harbour for any repairs and routine maintenance, where the dockyard officers and their 'maties' worked miracles with depleted supplies. In the meantime the crews managed to snatch a brief run ashore, and Simpson was able to explain his plans to the Commanding Officers.

These first Commanding Officers, pioneers of the future Tenth Flotilla, were men of exceptional calibre who would set a high standard for those who followed. As Simpson well knew, it is the men who make a submarine, and the Commanding Officer who moulds the men. The captain bears unique responsibilities to his crew, because only he can look through the periscope during an attack; only he can make the decision to seize an opportunity or let it slip, the decision that may mean life or death.

In his book *Periscope View,* Simpson has described these pioneer Commanding Officers in glowing terms and identified some of the qualities that made them so successful as leaders: their 'ability, prescience and intelligence', their tenacity, loyalty and bravery. But the single most important quality that Simpson looked for in his Commanding Officers was the ability to make instant decisions, for this is what reaps reward in submarine warfare. As for success in attack, Simpson judged that it depended at least partly on what he called 'the knack':

I have heard it said in submarine circles that to be a good submarine attacker it is necessary to be a good mathematician. My experience does not corroborate this, although a quick calculating brain must be of value. Wanklyn was a case in point; although he was an excellent mathematician he could not hit his targets for three months. Then suddenly he got the knack . . .

Lieutenant-Commander David Wanklyn, Commanding Officer of *Upholder,* usually known as 'Wanks', had been Simpson's first lieutenant in *Porpoise,* just before the war, so they already knew each other well. A tall man, over six feet, Wanklyn had all the qualities that Simpson required of his Commanding Officers. Although it was months before he demonstrated his ability to hit a target, he would more than make up for his disappointing start.

In fact, none of the Us had much success during their first few weeks in the Mediterranean. In retrospect, the reasons are manifold. The thirty-mile restriction was not lifted until 22 February, as we shall see. The Us were commanded by men who lacked experience of Mediterranean conditions. The faulty engines meant that the boats needed long hours of repair and modification in the dockyards. And, most frustrating of all, there was an acute shortage of torpedoes. Under such difficult conditions it is surprising that any of the Us had any luck at all.

Still intent on catching the enemy off the North African coast, Simpson continued to send the Us to the Kerkenah Bank northwest of Tripoli. *Upholder* (Lieutenant-Commander Wanklyn) sailed on 24 January, followed a few days later by *Ursula* (Lieutenant-Commander Mackenzie), *Utmost* (Lieutenant-Commander Cayley) and *Usk* (Lieutenant-Commander Ward), and then on the 29th by *Upright* (Lieutenant Norman), by now on her third patrol.

Upholder sighted her first target at 0130 on 26 January, a supply ship being escorted by a destroyer. *Upholder* surfaced and attacked with two torpedoes. While evading the destroyer, another supply ship was sighted and two more torpedoes were fired, but all four missed. Two days later, another two supply ships were sighted. After the experience of the earlier attack, Wanklyn closed in to 900 yards before firing two torpedoes, one of which hit an 8,000-ton ship believed to be the German *Duisburg*. But the ship was still afloat some hours later.

On the afternoon of 30 January Wanklyn's asdic operator reported hydrophone effect (HE) to the west, and not long afterwards a convoy and its escorts were sighted through the periscope. The boat manoeuvred into position and the remaining two torpedoes were fired at a 5,000-ton ship; one hit was claimed but never confirmed. A heavy and noisy depth-charge attack followed, but Wanklyn, listening to the reports from his asdic operator, quietly manoeuvred *Upholder* clear. As all torpedoes had been expended, course was set for Malta where the submarine arrived on 1 February, in the middle of yet another air raid.

Upholder's opening patrol had demonstrated two important facts. First, the *U*s lacked surface speed; if Wanklyn had two more knots (the *S*s had 13 knots, the *T*s 15) he could have been in position to attack all three ships during the night of 27 January. Second, in low night visibility, and even with the noise of the generators charging the batteries, the asdic operator often gave earlier warning of the approaching enemy than could the bridge look-outs. On his return to base Wanklyn made his report to Simpson and in future Shrimp would warn his Commanding Officers: firstly to think ahead, to make up for the lack of speed; and secondly to trust their asdic.

Ursula, on 8 February, made two attacks and missed with both; following the second, she was nearly rammed. But she had evidently stirred up the opposition, because when *Utmost* attacked another convoy on the evening of the 9th, the ships promptly adopted a frantic zigzagging course which allowed them to escape. Three days later *Utmost* fired the last of her torpedoes at one of a three-ship convoy; her target stopped, stern down, but did not sink. Unable to deliver the *coup de grâce, Utmost* retired to Malta.

On the same day, 9 February, *Usk* was in the shallow mined waters off Tripoli when she sighted a convoy and made an attack. She missed; but three hours later a 3,000-ton supply ship in the same convoy was sunk by *Truant* (Lieutenant-Commander H. A. V. Haggard). During the subsequent counter-attack, *Truant* suffered battery damage; instead of proceeding to Alexandria, she returned to Malta for repairs, where she arrived safely on 12 February.

Unique (Lieutenant Collett) missed with his two torpedo

attacks off the Tunisian coast, and two further sightings could not be followed up for lack of identification, though the ships concerned were suspected to be Vichy ships coast-crawling.

Then, during mid-February, *Upright* sailed for yet another patrol inside the Kerkenah Bank, where 'it was thought that perhaps the bay and port of Sfax might be being used as a convoy assembly anchorage,' writes Lieutenant Dudley Norman, whose memories of the patrol are particularly vivid. His fellow officers included 'Tiger' Daniell as first lieutenant, 'Vasco' Walmsley, Lieutenant RNR, as navigator, 'and "Shaver" Swanston, Lieutenant, completed as fine a team as you could hope for'. But, even before leaving Malta, *Upright* had to negotiate a new threat: acoustic mines, which the Italians were now dropping in the harbour approaches:

> In an attempt to set these off before passing over them, we were advised to fire machine-gun bullets into the water about a hundred yards ahead of the submarine. I think that we were the first to prove the success of the ploy; after passing through the spray of the explosion, we received a quick signal from base: *'Good shot.'*
> On our second night out, we sighted an unescorted tanker, proceeding southwards. Two torpedoes fired at 2,000 yards resulted in an enormous explosion and set her on fire from stem to stern. Most members of my crew had a chance to look at her through the periscope before what was left of the tanker sank.

The crew were 'in fine fettle', Norman reports, and no doubt their good humour was increased by this success. His own response was clear: 'If you were lucky you found some worthwhile targets; if not, you spent the time gazing at acres and acres of "Sweet Fanny" .' But such tedium was not to be his lot on this patrol. On 21 February *Upright* entered the port of Sfax, dodging erratic fishing boats while looking for the suspected enemy vessels. But none were sighted, and 'as we were then scraping along the bottom at periscope depth,' Norman writes, 'it seemed prudent to reverse course and retire to the open sea.'

Following orders, Norman now took *Upright* eastwards to patrol the route between Sicily and Tripoli. On the night of 25

February the boat was surfaced as usual when David Swanston, the officer of the watch, sounded the night alarm. Norman had been down below examining the charts and he needed a few moments to accustom his eyes to the dark but 'Shaver' Swanston had everything under control. The target was 'a cruiser or a very large destroyer, escorted by two destroyers, one on each bow.' Norman checked her course and speed, then fired four torpedoes:

We dived as soon as the last torpedo had gone, and turned to get away from their tracks. As I got below, the periscope was going up. I got it on the right bearing in time to see the first torpedo hit, in the light of which I considered that the target was probably a cruiser. A number of depth-charges were dropped, but none close enough to do any damage. We crept quietly away. Dawn showed that the two destroyers were evidently engaged in picking up survivors, and we left them to it. With only two torpedoes left, we decided to return to base to replenish.

Norman was right; she was the 5,000-ton Italian cruiser, *Armando Diaz*. For this first major success, *Upright's* crew were duly rewarded, as Anthony Daniell, her first lieutenant, recalls:

The standard procedure was to dish out 'gongs' for the sinking of enemy fighting units, so automatically the Skipper got the DSO; as Number One I got the DSC; Cox'n the DSM, Chief ERA the DSM, then one or two others of the crew also were recognized. One was very conscious that one was wearing these decorations for the *whole* crew who were all in it together, down to the humblest.

Norman notes that one of those who very properly received a decoration after the sinking of the cruiser was 'Able Seaman Smith (if that was his real name)':

It was he who made the first sighting and kept the target in sight throughout the twelve minutes of the attack. He should not have been there: he had not yet reached the age at which volunteers were accepted for submarines, a fact that was not mentioned in his citation!

As a footnote to this story, Norman adds that *Upright* had been carrying a couple of passengers, two soldiers 'who were due to carry out a landing operation on a later patrol. I asked one of them how he enjoyed being depth-charged and got the reply, "Champion!".'

The two soldiers on *Upright* were with a party of sixty, members of the army's No. 1 Special Commando Battalion, who had arrived in Malta in January with the *Illustrious* convoy. Led by three officers under Captain Taylor of the Liverpool Scottish, their task was to carry out various clandestine operations, dreamed up in London by MI6 and the army planners, to harry the Hun and the Wop. These forays would involve the submarines, for the commandos had to be ferried to and from their destinations.

At Simpson's invitation, the kilted Captain Taylor had decided to install his unit on Manoel Island, and so the men had taken up residence in the barracks alongside Lazaretto. With their plastic explosives, grenades, tommy guns, daggers, cheese wire and all the rest of their lethal paraphernalia, they were a formidable lot, and itching for action. Already well trained in cloak-and-dagger techniques, they were now training in conjunction with the submarines, rehearsing how to launch and man their Folbots (two-man collapsible canvas canoes).

Simpson and his SOO, Bob Tanner, spent much of February working on plans with Captain Taylor for special operations to take place later in the year; but already Simpson was beginning to doubt the wisdom of involving his *Us* on such missions. One incident some weeks later merely confirmed his doubts, and underlined his determination to keep a close eye on all future operations involving his *Us*. As Commander (S) he was asked to release *Utmost* for a top-secret mission on 1 March. Lieutenant-Commander Dick Cayley, the Commanding Officer of *Utmost*, was one of only five individuals who knew the details of the operation, the others being three army officers and one woman. Simpson told Cayley that *Utmost* could go if Cayley considered there was no exceptional risk. It was the first and last time that Simpson allowed one of his submarines to operate without his knowledge: 'a very stupid act on my part,' he confessed later.

Though Cayley was awarded the DSO for this exploit, the operation remains a mystery to this day. The only clues emanate from *Utmost's* log of 1 March, 1941:

0200. Stop Shebka El Cazel, 8 fathoms.
0300. Boat landed and brought off British Officer (Second Lieutenant Fairclough).

'Shebka' is the Arabic word for salt-marsh, salt-lake or salt-lagoon, but the author has been unable to identify the landing site, nor trace 'Second Lieutenant Fairclough'. The entire episode remains obscure.

But Simpson was too busy to spend all his time discussing the details of cloak-and-dagger missions scheduled for some later date. In February and March he was preoccupied with his *U*s and their progress, as well being responsible for other submarines working from Malta during this period. Apart from the two surviving *T*s, *Truant* (Lieutenant-Commander Haggard) and *Tetrarch* (Commander Ronnie Mills), recently joined by *Triumph* (Commander W. J. W. Woods), there were one minelayer *Rorqual* (Lieutenant-Commander R. H. Dewhurst), *Regent* (Lieutenant-Commander H. C. Browne) and Hubert Marsham's *Rover*. Finally there was *Parthian* (Commander M. G. Rimington) who had achieved the first British submarine success in the Mediterranean. The hard-won knowledge and experience of their Commanding Officers and crews could thus be profitably shared with the *U*s.

Truant had a close shave during February, although her crew did not know it at the time. *Upholder* was just a few hours from Malta on her second patrol, soon after dark on 12 February, when the look-out sighted a small object to the south. Wanklyn identified it as a submarine and hopes ran high through the boat at the prospect of an attack. As there were no reports of any Allied submarines in the area, it seemed reasonable to suppose that the submarine was Italian. But, distant though it was, Wanklyn identified the submarine as one of our *T*s. Just to be sure, he ordered the challenge signal to be made. There was no response. He repeated the signal three times, but no reply was received. Nevertheless, Wanklyn was so sure of his identification that he withheld fire and it transpired that the submarine was *Truant,* returning early from patrol with her wireless out of action. Thanks to Wanklyn's mastery of his job, a potential tragedy had been averted.

It was during this same patrol that *Upholder's* captain realized how visible the submarine must be from the air, particularly during calm weather when the Mediterranean water is clear and glassy smooth; and even more particularly when an aircraft's attention had been drawn to the area by the disturbance caused by a raised periscope. The forward casing of the submarine, Wanklyn noticed, some twenty-five feet below the surface, could clearly be seen through the periscope. But there was no solution to the problem other than painting the submarine blue in an attempt to camouflage it. Fortunately, only a slight breeze was needed to disturb the surface and restore the submarine to invisibility.

On 22 February British restrictions on their submarines were lifted; from now on, 'Sink on sight' would apply to all ships found within an area roughly rectangular in shape, including Sardinia and Sicily, Cape Bon and Benghazi. Apart from a strip in the Adriatic to safeguard Yugoslavia, and the three-mile limit still allowed to the Vichy French in Tunisian waters, virtually the whole of the central Mediterranean was now a legitimate hunting ground. But this welcome move, allowing our Us far greater initiative than before, was made in response to an ominous announcement from the Italians: they had established much enlarged minefields, particularly in the Narrows.

And there was worse to come. Despite the victorious offensive by Wavell's Army of the Nile, our troops were now being diverted from North Africa to Greece just as the Germans were arriving; in mid-February Rommel had taken over command of the Afrika Corps. And in Sicily, Kesselring had reinforced the Luftwaffe with Me 109s, piloted by men who had learnt their lessons in the Battle of Britain. During the next few months Fliegerkorps X, with this strong fighter cover, would step up the raids on Malta: in February 107 raids; in March 1,050. And still the slaughter continued.

5

MARCH/APRIL, 1941

'Treat your COs as Derby winners,' was Admiral Sir Max Horton's advice and Simpson never forgot it. He knew it was asking for trouble to concentrate all his COs in one spot, especially when bombs were falling; the entire flotilla could be neutralized by one unlucky hit. As Dudley Norman recalls, the raiders were already getting too close for comfort:

> On one occasion, the bombs were close enough to shatter a large part of the glass in the windows. I had just returned from a rather exhausting patrol and was evidently so tired that I slept right through the raid and knew nothing about it until I awoke to find, not only the floor of my cabin but also my bed, covered in glass.

Consequently Simpson now issued orders that his COs should if possible find billets off the base: Dudley Norman, for example, found 'a bed in the air raid shelter built in the cellar of a house in Sliema'. As 'Gravy' Tench recalls, Simpson 'did all he could to take his submariners' minds from the war', encouraging the runs ashore 'when a boat's whole company would for a brief evening forget together the earnestness of their trade'. Ever mindful of the safety and well-being of his men, he would continue to think up ways of reducing the stresses on them.

Despite the constant disruption of raids, and despite the lack of calories which was already affecting the health of the toiling men, everyone was working to the limit. Even ashore the submarine crews were kept busy, helping on the base itself or touching up the blue paint on their boats; and the dockyard officers and 'maties' were continuing to do a superb job of maintenance. Meanwhile, inexperienced junior officers were practising skills they had barely had time to acquire at home, often taking command of the U while in the safety of harbour, especially during the routine manoeuvres known as 'trot fobs': moving between moorings in Lazaretto Creek, visiting the Torpedo Depot in Msida Creek, or refuelling at the oil barge in the centre of Marsamxett Harbour.

These trot fobs were a source of regular merriment for more experienced officers watching from the vantage point of Lazaretto gallery, such as the occasion when a Third Hand, an RNVR officer who had been a farmer in days not long past, was conning his U towards the wardroom berth. Cheered on by a large 'goofing' party, the submarine was sweeping at too obtuse an angle and much too fast towards the solid frontage of Lazaretto. The onlookers held their breath. The gap of water between boat and building was rapidly diminishing. Then, as the boat's momentum finally began to ease, everyone burst out laughing, for across the water came the ringing West Country tones of the officer carrying out the trot fob: 'Whoa-a-a, starboard! Tchk-tchk!, port!'

But such moments of laughter were rare during these black days for Malta. The indiscriminate bombing, combined with food shortages, was wearing everyone down. Although stubbornly determined to resist this second Great Siege of Malta, the islanders could not expect further supplies to arrive until Operation 'Lustre' was over, for the Mediterranean Fleet was busy ferrying British reinforcements to Greece.

Air reconnaissance in early March had reported a surprising number of merchant vessels off the Tunisian coast and at least ten warships, which hinted at some large operation: the Us would have to investigate. *Ursula* (Lieutenant Mackenzie) had been patrolling off Lampedusa (largest of the three Italian Pelagie islands, midway between Malta and Tunisia) when she was diverted to probe the enemy's convoy routes off Cape Bon. *Utmost* (Lieutenant-Commander Cayley) was despatched on 6 March, to relieve *Unique* (Lieutenant Collett) whose time on patrol had already been extended; *Utmost* herself had enjoyed only one day in harbour since completing her last patrol.

In the Gulf of Hammamet, on 9 March, *Utmost* sighted a two-ship convoy; she attacked and torpedoed the trooper, *Cap Vita*, 5,683 tons. On the 10th, the last day of her patrol off the Kerkenah Bank, *Unique* torpedoed and sank the *Fenicia*, 2,584 tons. At last the *U*s were finding 'the knack'.

Utmost's patrol had to be cut short, as the moon was waxing and the bright moonlight combined with increased anti-submarine activity represented an unacceptable risk; she returned to base for a brief respite. Since 4 February she had been at sea for thirty out of thirty-eight days, a dangerous precedent. *Ursula* had less success; but by observing enemy tracks and by judicious use of her mine detector unit, she brought back much useful information about enemy minefields off Cape Bon. On 19 March *Utmost* sailed from Lazaretto again, making for the Kerkenah Bank. At first her patrol was uneventful; but then, on the 31st, a six-ship, heavily escorted convoy bore down from the north. At close range, *Utmost* torpedoed another of Rommel's troopships, the German *Herakles* of 1,927 tons. With the escort busy picking up survivors, Cayley was then able to give some of his crew an opportunity to see what was going on 'up top'. One of the company, Mr J. Murdoch of Leeds, recalls:

> It was an unusual attack because there was no retaliation from the escorts. When the Skipper took a look through the periscope, the sea was littered with bodies, which explained the reason for no depth charges. Lieutenant-Commander Cayley then permitted those of the crew on watch in the control room to take a look at our handiwork: it took me years to get over the sight of that stricken ship and the men struggling in the sea.

Utmost returned to Malta at the end of her stint on April Fool's Day.

Truant (Lieutenant-Commander Haggard), still operating from Malta, was patrolling in the Gulf of Sirte. Hugh Haggard had sighted an enemy supply ship entering a small port called Burat-el-Sun and on the night of 19 March he planned a quick foray into the harbour to attack her. At 2000 he passed the buoy marking the harbour entrance: 'It was now very dark and the buildings ashore could only be seen when they were lit up by lorry headlights,' he records. At 400 yards, he fired. But, to his intense chagrin, the torpedoes ran harmlessly beneath the target 'as the ship had discharged cargo during the day and was now in ballast'. To clear the harbour *Truant* had to pass within a few yards of the ship and, as she did so, someone appeared from below, leaned over the guard rail 'and had a good deal to say'. With a cry of '*Il Duce!*' from *Truant,* she then proceeded out of harbour on main engines.

Upholder had a similarly frustrating time in March. Leaving harbour on the 10th to carry out a patrol off Tripoli, Wanklyn sighted a northbound convoy, but they were only small ships, mostly in ballast, and, conscious of the shortage of torpedoes, he withheld his fire. The rest of the patrol was disappointing; nor was there any incident to enliven the reconnaissance patrol she made during the second half of the month.

In the eastern Mediterranean, Operation 'Lustre' had gone well. Not only had Cunningham's fleet successfully transported most of Wavell's army to the Piraeus, not a single British soldier was lost, despite frequent attacks by German aircraft from their new bases in Rhodes and the islands of the Dodecanese. The fleet had itself been reinforced by *Formidable,* the armoured aircraft carrier intended to replace *Illustrious.* She had squeezed through the Suez Canal to enter Alexandria on 10 March, and with her she brought good news from East Africa: Mussolini's Abyssinian empire was collapsing. Although it was two months before the last remnants of the Italian force were swept out of the area, Britain now had control of the Red Sea.

As for Malta, *Formidable*'s arrival in the Mediterranean meant that once again the fleet could defend itself from air attack; at last Cunningham would be able to send a convoy to relieve the island. Nine days later a small convoy of four store ships set off from Alexandria, arriving safely in Malta on 23 March. But the following day two of the four ships were sunk in harbour, with half their cargo still unloaded.

This most galling loss was compounded a few days later by sad news from Suda Bay. *York,* the only 8-inch gun cruiser in the Mediterranean Fleet, had been struck; she was torpedoed on the 26th by an Italian one-man torpedo boat, and, having lost all power, she sank on the rocks. Not only that, but *Rover,* Hubert Marsham's previous command, who was sent to help her, was bombed and damaged beyond repair. The Italians, deriving support from their Axis allies, had demonstrated that they were not finished yet. Cunningham resolved to teach them a lesson.

On 27 March he received RAF reports that the Italian fleet was some 300 miles west of Crete and steaming south-east towards Alexandria. Although the enemy had numerical superiority, Cunningham decided that he would lure them into a confrontation: the bait would be four cruisers under Vice-Admiral H. D. Pridham-Wippell. On the 28th the enemy took the bait and Cunningham closed in. By midnight that night, off Cape Matapan, he had destroyed three Italian cruisers and two large destroyers; although the enemy's new battleship *Vittorio Veneto* managed to escape, she too had been damaged, torpedoed by Swordfish of the Fleet Air Arm. Despite later drastic reverses to our Mediterranean Fleet, Admiral Iachino, the Italian Commander-in-Chief, never again managed to seize the initiative from his British adversary.

The victory at Matapan was the last good news for some time. Within the week Rommel's Afrika Korps would have recaptured Benghazi, virtually abandoned now by Wavell's army. For all the efforts of our submarines, most of Rommel's troopships and supply ships had managed to reach Libya, and had quickly established bases on the eastern coast of the Gulf of Sirte. And when the Germans invaded Greece and Yugoslavia on 6 April, the threat not only to Malta but to British interests in the whole of the Mediterranean was plain.

Rommel's sudden advance took everyone by surprise, even his own superiors, and threw the British into confusion. Clearly Rommel must be stopped, but how? It was eventually decided to make a stand at Tobruk. Meanwhile, Rommel's supply line must be cut, and in particular Tripoli must be attacked, for this was his main port of entry. As the submarines could not be expected to achieve this on their own, Cunningham informed the Admiralty on 8 April that he was sending four destroyers to Malta in order to step up the pressure on the German convoys.

The Admiralty retorted that this was not enough and ordered Cunningham to sink his own battleship *Barham* as a blockship in the port of Tripoli. Although this plan bore the hallmark of the Prime Minister himself, Cunningham refused even to countenance such a deliberate blow to the morale of his own men. Fortunately, he would be saved from outright defiance by the success of the four destroyers.

Throughout April Simpson was dispatching his *Us* primarily to the Tunisian coast, where enemy convoys hugged the shoreline all the way from Cape Bon to Tripoli. The *Us* were to attack at every opportunity, by day and by night, along every mile of the route. The other submarines still operating from Malta were to do likewise, as well as mining the enemy ports and taking part in other less straightforward activities.

During the second half of April, for example, *Regent* (Lieutenant-Commander H. C. Browne) paid a successful visit to the Yugoslavian port of Kotor, in order to rescue the British Minister and his mission; for this operation Lieutenant-Commander Browne was awarded the DSO. *Triumph,* too, was on clandestine work in April. After an operation involving paratroops under Major Pritchard of the Welch Fusiliers, and Lieutenant Deane-Drummond, the object of which was to attack a Sicilian aqueduct and thus interrupt the enemy's water supply, the soldiers were to be picked up by submarine. Simpson detailed *Triumph* to go but her position was compromised and she had to be recalled. As it turned out, the paratroops had all been captured on their way to meet the submarine.

Simpson felt that the other services invariably underrated the threat to his boats. In his mind, a submarine compromised was a submarine and her company lost. If she was obliged to linger on the surface she was in continual danger of being spotted, and once spotted she was too easy a target. Despite his doubts, in April he also had to send *Utmost* on two cloak-and-dagger operations; but now he was determined to keep his hand on the tiller. The first such mission, to land secret agents in Sousse Bay, was successfully completed on 19 April, although Dick Cayley complained afterwards that when a convoy of four ships passed within five cable-lengths of him, 'Owing to her position and the nature of her occupation, *Utmost* was unable to do anything about it.' The second operation began when army intelligence asked Simpson if he could help them rescue one of their officers from Tunisia. Having talked the matter over with Cayley, Simpson made careful arrangements which were then transmitted to the army officer concerned. He was to 'borrow' a rowing boat on the evening of 28 April and row two miles out into the bay south of Hammamet as if to go fishing; if all was safe he should tie his shirt to an oar and hold it up; if not he should display a pair of trousers instead. The operation was a complete success.

At the beginning of the month, both *Unique* and *Upright* had disappointing patrols, and *Upholder*'s fourth patrol, starting on 3 April, was no more successful than her earlier ones. On the 10th Wanklyn twice sighted convoys off Cape Bon but both attacks went wrong; his first target was at extreme range and during his second attack the torpedo tracks were seen, leading to a prolonged counter-attack. That night a single ship was also attacked, but the torpedo was a 'wanderer': some mechanical fault caused it to deviate from the set course and, in order to avoid it, Wanklyn had to take *Upholder* deep.

By now *Upholder* had fired both salvoes; but instead of returning to Malta, Wanklyn decided to reconnoitre, to watch enemy movements in the area and report them to base, for he had been forewarned of the planned assault by Cunningham's four destroyers. His prescience was rewarded on 12 April when five big ships with an escort of three destroyers and three aircraft were sighted to the northward. *Upholder* duly surfaced to pass her W/T enemy report, but was sighted by one of the enemy aircraft and forced to dive. Thirty minutes later she repeated the procedure until receiving an acknowledgement from Malta. Then, that midnight, on passage back to Malta, *Upholder* overheard an aircraft's W/T report of an oncoming convoy; Wanklyn promptly diverted to intercept it. Proceeding at full speed, he managed to catch up with the enemy convoy and, while passing another report to base, he fired starshell into the night sky. The convoy immediately reversed course and returned whence it had come.

Cunningham's destroyers – *Jervis, Janus, Mohawk* and *Nubian* – had arrived in Malta on 10 April, with Captain P. J. Mack in *Jervis* as Captain D. After a few short hours in harbour, they were out on the prowl, waiting for just such a report as Wanklyn made on the 12th. They failed to make contact with the convoy which *Upholder* had intercepted, but on the night of the 16th they sighted another: five merchant ships and an escort of three destroyers off Sfax. In a brilliant night action, Captain Mack annihilated the entire convoy, for the loss of *Mohawk*.

This bold strike against Rommel's supply line resolved the impasse between Cunningham and London. The Admiralty planners now ordered Cunningham to bombard the port of Tripoli, which had been his intention from the first. With the Luftwaffe concentrating on our forces in Crete and the Piraeus, he judged that his ships would meet little resistance. On 18 April the Mediterranean Fleet sailed from Alexandria and at dawn on the 21st arrived at the assembly point off Tripoli, marked by the submarine *Truant* (Lieutenant-Commander Haggard). According to Cunningham's memoirs, Hughie Haggard later told him what a thrilling moment this was, watching the huge shapes of the warships looming up out of the dark, in a silence that was broken only by 'the rippling sound of our bow waves, the wheeze of air pumps, and the muffled twitter of a boatswain's pipe'.

Despite the shortage of aircraft in Malta (in the words of one sailor, explaining why he always wore an inflated Mae West lifebelt: 'It's the only effing air support I'll ever get!') every available Wellington and Swordfish had already begun the bombardment of Tripoli thereby helping to cover the fleet's approach. At 0500 Cunningham's ships opened up. Within an hour the enemy was reeling from the damage of his big guns; the whole port seemed to be ablaze. Two days later the fleet was safely back in Alexandria.

The tremendous success of this operation was underlined by another, subsidiary operation, smaller but just as important in the eyes of those in Malta. Under cover of the main force's movements, Cunningham had passed a fast merchant ship, *Breconshire*, from Alexandria to the beleaguered island. Another vital cargo of supplies had arrived.

When *Upholder* returned to Malta on 14 April at the end of her fourth patrol, she had fired another eight torpedoes without result. Doubts were surfacing about Wanklyn's competence. Even Simpson, who had such a high opinion of Wanklyn's capabilities, was beginning to wonder whether he could afford to retain a commanding officer who used up valuable torpedoes to no effect. As Simpson later wrote in his book *Periscope View:*

> Wanklyn made such a poor start in February, March and early April, 1941 (by which time he had expended about twenty torpedoes without result) that I feared he might never make the grade.

The shortage of torpedoes was now so acute, particularly after the numbers used in the Battle of Matapan, that the Torpedo Depot was adapting ancient Mark IV torpedoes to issue to the *U*s, and this vintage stock was not exactly reliable.

And yet, despite the failures of the past three months, the morale of Wanklyn's ship's company was high. It was a measure of the man's character that even when other *U*s were scoring successes, the ship's company of *Upholder* continued to demonstrate their complete confidence in him. He, for his part, remained outwardly calm and cheerful, though, as he set off for his fifth patrol on 21 April, he must have suffered twinges of doubt.

Three days later, off the Tunisian coast, Wanklyn broke the spell — he fired a torpedo at the *Antonietta Laura*, 5,428 tons, and sank her. The following day *Upholder* was ordered to close the Kerkenah Bank, where an enemy destroyer and supply ship had run aground and been abandoned. These shallow waters were a potential death-trap for a submarine; it would not be possible to dive should enemy ships or aircraft appear. But in order to save torpedoes, Wanklyn took *Upholder* alongside the supply ship, the *Arta*. A boarding party searched the ship, which had obviously been carrying a number of troops and was still loaded with transport and munitions; then, having laid their demolition charges on both the *Arta* and the destroyer, they returned to *Upholder* with the inevitable souvenirs — German tin hats and the like. Thankfully, *Upholder* then set course for deeper waters while the demolition charges did their work.

Wanklyn's new-found knack did not desert him when, just before the end of this patrol, *Upholder* sighted a convoy of five ships with four escorting destroyers. It was very rough weather, making depth-keeping and periscope observation difficult, but Wanklyn fired a salvo of four torpedoes. He scored a hit with three: two sank the German ship *Leverkusen*, 7,386 tons, and a third stopped the *Arcturus*, 2,597 tons. The destroyers launched a counter-attack while the rest of the convoy slipped away, but they soon gave up and left, allowing Wanklyn a chance to finish off the damaged ship with his last torpedo. Triumphantly flying the Jolly Roger flag indicating that she had finally scored, *Upholder* returned to Malta on 3 May.

By the end of April, therefore, Simpson had good reason for satisfaction with his *Us*' progress. In addition, two of the other submarines based in Malta had left their mark on the enemy: *Truant* (Lieutenant-Commander Haggard), before acting as a beacon for the fleet at Tripoli, had sunk the 279-ton schooner *Vanna*, which, though small, had been carrying vital fuel for Rommel's tanks; and in the same area, *Tetrarch* (Commander Mills) had sunk the tanker *Persiano*.

Malta had received considerable naval reinforcements during April: a cruiser, a new minelayer and six destroyers, as well as more Hurricanes, flown off from *Ark Royal* on the 3rd and again towards the end of the month. The submarines were no longer on their own in their fight to stop enemy supplies reaching Tripoli.

Sadly, the *Us* had suffered their first casualty. After constant engine trouble caused by the sabotaged oil tank, *Usk* left for patrol on 19 April with Lieutenant Godfrey Darling in command. Her destination was Cape Bon, but on the 25th she reported that she was withdrawing because of 'intense anti-submarine activity in the area'. She was never heard from again. It is thought that she was mined, probably off Cape Bon on the 26th. It was less than a year since *Usk* had been launched.

And the news from elsewhere in the Mediterranean was not good. In North Africa Rommel seemed invincible. By 12 April he had surrounded Tobruk and, leaving the port invested, swept on eastwards with his Afrika Korps; thus the remaining elements of Wavell's army in Tobruk found themselves dependent on convoys of supplies from Alexandria. In Greece the Germans were storming south; the British army faced an impossible task, so far from its own base across the sea, and the decision was made to withdraw to Crete and Alexandria.

Once again the fleet was mobilized to ferry our troops across the Mediterranean's eastern basin. Operation 'Demon' began on 24 April; on the 27th, as the last of our ships sailed from the Piraeus, the Germans entered Athens. The Luftwaffe had clear control of the skies, with bases established in all the main Greek islands; now it seemed that Britain's lonely base in Crete was their target.

6

MAY, 1941

It was at this disastrous moment of the war that the next four Us nosed through the mine-swept channel and into Marsamxett Harbour. First came *Undaunted* (Lieutenant J. L. Livesay), followed on 3 May by *Union* (Lieutenant R. M. Galloway), *Unbeaten* (Lieutenant E. A. Woodward) and *Urge* (Lieutenant E. P. Tomkinson).

Urge had already made her mark on the enemy. According to Lieutenant Ian McGeoch, who was to be the new Spare Commanding Officer in Malta and who was taking passage in *Urge,* they were in the Atlantic west of the Bay of Biscay on 18 April when they encountered a large tanker steering eastward. Poring over 'Talbot-Booth', the *Manual of Merchant Ship Identification,* which was, as McGeoch says, 'our only means of recognizing merchant ships', Lieutenant Tomkinson − known to all as 'Tommo' − decided to attack:

> Torpedoes were fired from a good position, with fairly confident target data, and we all kept perfectly quiet, counting the seconds against our private estimates of what the running time of the torpedoes might be − the range was not more than 2,000 yards, as I recall.
>
> After about a minute and a half, we all heard a faint 'tonk'.
>
> 'Damn!' said Tommo. 'The bloody thing hasn't gone off. Stand by, Three and Four tubes. Keep thirty feet. We'll get the bastard yet!'
>
> With the fruit machine* set up and Three and Four tubes reported 'ready', Tommo slowed the motors and came back to periscope depth. As the periscope, at full height and set to the

---

* A calculating machine into which all relevant attack data is fed, and from which the necessary information is extracted to carry out a torpedo attack.

new DA*, broke surface, Tommo, eyes glued to it, suddenly yelled, 'It's OK, boys; I can see the water going down her funnel!'

Urge had sunk the *Franco Martelli*, 10,535 tons, an 'Italian blockade-running tanker' returning from Brazil.

Teddy Woodward was much impressed by the submarine activity in Malta. There was *Upholder* and David Wanklyn returning to base 'because he wanted to get some more torpedoes'; Hughie Haggard and *Truant* sailing off with 'not even one day's shore leave between patrols'; *Triumph* ordered to enter Benghazi to 'engage the shipping there by gunfire'; 'Hairy' Brown in *Regent* recently returned from 'his spectacular entry into Kotor'. As Woodward writes, the boats 'were certainly being kept busy'. Within days, he and *Unbeaten* would be just as busy, leaving harbour to join the rest of the Us on patrol.

The tragic news about *Usk* had caused not only sorrow among the ships' companies of her sister Us, but anger as well; they set off on their next patrols determined to avenge her loss.

During the second week of May, *Undaunted* sailed for the busy waters of Tripoli. It was her first patrol from Malta; it was also to be her last. From Italian records, it seems that she was attacked by torpedo boats escorting a convoy that was heading back to Sicily, for they reported dropping depth-charges and seeing a large oil slick afterwards, but it is also possible that she may have run into one of the extensive new minefields. Now the Us had two of their number to avenge

The drama of *Unbeaten's* first patrol, in an area not far from *Undaunted,* along the coast toward's Benghazi, is best conveyed in the words of her captain, Lieutenant Teddy Woodward:

> Our first attack was on Wednesday, 14 May, our third day out. A convoy of five small ships was heading eastwards, coast-crawling only about a mile off the coast. I was handicapped by a small tunny vessel which we had to pass only about 600 yards away. My speed was restricted, as I did not want him to see

*Director Angle: the amount of 'aim-off' required to allow for the course and speed of the target.

my periscope wash. I was only able to get within 4,500 yards of the rear but largest vessel. In spite of the long range and the necessity of not wasting torpedoes, which had to be brought all the way out from England and were scarce in Malta, I decided the importance of the target, although small, merited the risk of three torpedoes, which were fired. An explosion was heard a little over three minutes after firing and, when I and my navigator had a look through the periscope some time later, we could see only four ships. One of them, a trawler, had turned towards us and, in case she was armed with depth-charges, we got the hell out of it by going deep and turning away. Luckily, the Italians did not have very good anti-submarine detectors at that time.

The next day we were off Khoms when we saw a small (800 ton) three-masted schooner making for the harbour. As she was apparently not fully laden, I decided not to use valuable torpedoes but to try a gun attack in the harbour at dusk.

At 1830 we closed to within 1,500 yards of Khoms anchorage. The target appeared to be a normal merchant schooner with no 'Q'-boat signs* and there were no visible gun batteries ashore. At about 2030 we went in, bumping gently along the bottom until we got as close as possible with twenty-five feet on the diving gauge. We surfaced at 2049, only 1,000 yards from the target and closed, opening fire at 2054 at a range of 700 yards. We continued to close to 400 yards, by which time we had fired twenty-one rounds of high explosive shells.

Had I surfaced a little earlier, or used starshell, the results might have been more satisfactory, but I felt that any additional illumination would greatly facilitate any shore batteries for we were very close inshore and only about 500 yards from the breakwater. As it was, the target was plainly visible to us, but *Unbeaten* must have been extremely difficult to see from the shore.

Each flash of our gun temporarily blinded the gun control officer, Sub-Lieutenant J. C. Varley, and the gunlayer, which made spotting difficult and the rate of fire slow. It was impossible to see for several seconds after each round, with the result that even direct hits could not be seen. But they could be heard,

---

* 'Q'-boats were anti-submarine ships disguised to resemble innocent-looking merchant vessels: originally a British ruse developed in the Great War by Commander Gordon Campbell, VC.

and we got quite a number, though some of them ricocheted to explode in the town beyond. We did manage to get her though, for as we proceeded to clear the harbour on a course of 040°, both the gunnery officer and the signalman said they saw her settling by the stern and that a small boat had been lowered and was pulling away from her.

Years later, after the war, Woodward happened to meet someone from Khoms who had been on the receiving end of his attack: in spite of which, he recalls, 'We had a friendly drink together.'

As Woodward continues, there was 'never a dull moment' on *Unbeaten's* first patrol from Malta. The following day, 16 May, 'two large transports and an escorting destroyer' were sighted, heading westward along the coast. Woodward was manoeuvring into a good attack position when *Unbeaten* 'struck bottom' (at thirty-five feet, though only yards away the depth was sixty feet) and was forced upwards. With the destroyer only 600 yards away at the time, and convinced that she must have seen him, Woodward took urgent avoiding action. As he noted later that same afternoon, after sighting another destroyer, 'We had been told not to waste valuable torpedoes on destroyers unless they were very special or proving to be a real danger to us. I let her go.'

Two days later *Unbeaten* was back in action. It was just after midday on 19 May when a 6,000-ton 'passenger-type merchant vessel' was sighted, escorted by a *Baleno*-class destroyer. Woodward continues:

At 1241 we fired three torpedoes at the merchant ship. Although we were in about fourteen fathoms of water and the submarine was on a level keel when we fired the first torpedo, it exploded on the bottom eight seconds after being fired; the torpedo lifted *Unbeaten* up to fifteen feet on the gauge. The second torpedo was fired with the bubble 1° aft, which is 1° bow-down. At this stage we took a very large angle bow-down and, although I tried, I was too late to stop the third torpedo from being fired. It went straight to the bottom and exploded and *Unbeaten's* stern came well out of the water. A muffled explosion was heard two and a half minutes after firing the second torpedo, so we assume we got a hit and, as no further hydrophone effect was heard from her propellers, we believe she sank [sinking not confirmed].

The first pattern of four depth-charges was dropped on us only three minutes after we had fired our first torpedo. We struck the bottom at seventy-six feet but, shortly afterwards, slid down to 140 feet with our quick-diving tank, 'Q', flooded. We didn't dare blow or run any pumps, as we knew he would be able to hear us. He dropped between twenty and thirty depth-charges during the next forty-five minutes, the last pattern of two charges being dropped at 1330. I can only assume he had run out of depth-charges, because he then lay stopped some way off on our starboard quarter.

I was anxious to get off the bottom and clear the area; so, three-quarters of an hour later, at 1415 we started the telemotor pump, but immediately the destroyer got under way at 200 revolutions, easing to 160 revolutions and then stopping a good deal closer to us. In spite of the possibility that he might be joined by reinforcements, I decided to lie doggo until after dark, when he would no longer have the advantages of shore fixes . . .

During the next four hours, the destroyer did use his propellers intermittently, presumably to maintain his position, but at 1815 there was quite a lot of activity and we wondered if he had been joined by another vessel, so I decided not to make a move until midnight.

At midnight we started pumps and blew very slightly to lift the submarine off the bottom. There was no hydrophone effect and, when we got to the surface, nothing in sight. With a sigh of relief, we cleared the area. We got our recall signal later and were back in Malta after a quite unforgettable first patrol on Wednesday, 21 May.

Back safe in Malta, Woodward made a full report to Simpson about this eventful first patrol, including a detailed list of the minor damage wrought by the exploding depth-charges: a few lights put out, loose articles flung around, 'a considerable number of leaks but no fractures' in the air lines, and so on. 'Surprisingly little damage was done,' he concludes, considering the 'heat' the boat had received. But he remarks particularly on the 'exceptional' morale of the whole ship's company during the long anxious hours of 19 May: 'We were able to have a meal and a large proportion of the ship's company turned in and slept. There was a good deal of joking and laughter in spite of the fact that most of us, at times, were frightened.'

Thanks to improved intelligence, including that supplied by reconnaissance aircraft now based in Malta, our submarines were concentrated more accurately during May. While the larger boats of the First Flotilla covered the Gulf of Sirte eastwards to their own base in Alexandria, the *Us* were focusing on the enemy's Sicily – Tripoli supply route, particularly the eastern seaboard of Tunisia.

It was in this area that *Urge* now struck lucky. Lieutenant 'Tommo' Tomkinson had been on patrol for five blank days when the Italian habit of dropping depth-charges irregularly ahead of their convoys alerted him to an approaching target. Two twin-funnelled cruisers with their screening destroyers passed out of range, but seven minutes later the convoy itself hove into sight: four big ships screened by five destroyers. Tomkinson attacked and the first two torpedoes hit what he later judged to be an oiler. The third one missed. But, according to his patrol report for 20 May, 1941*:

The fourth torpedo hit the transport, estimated range 500 yards, and made a terrific explosion. It sounded like a biscuit tin being scrunched up.

The fore-ends crew were thrown flat and had a few minutes of complete darkness. The stoker, alone in the auxiliary machinery space, a Hostilities Only rating and by profession a steeplejack's mate, was thrown right across the compartment and shaken up badly.

Drastic avoiding action was taken after firing the last torpedo, as the rear destroyer on the screen was very close.

After turning and slowing right down, the boat was very heavy due to flooding to get deep, and she went slowly down to 278 feet, with an angle of 10° bow up. Owing to depth-charging, it was not considered safe to speed up at all before reaching this depth. Except for a few leaky rivets, there was never any sign of stress or strain anywhere.

* Kindly provided by Mr. Francis Dickinson, grandson of Lieutenant Tomkinson.

Depth-charging stopped abruptly after eleven minutes, none of the ten charges fired being very close.

It is thought that the welcome cessation of those bangs was due to the troops in the transport partaking in the swimming gala. The transport was heard buckling up after the hit.

Urge had sunk *Zeffro,* 5,165 tons, and damaged *Perseo,* 4,800 tons. She had also exceeded the designed diving limits of the *U*s by twenty-eight feet.

On the next day *Urge* took a long-range shot at the passing cruisers but the attack was unsuccessful, and *Urge* returned to base on 24 May.

On that same day, the 24th, *Upright* was sailing for the Calabrian coast, for what her CO, Lieutenant Dudley Norman, later remembered as a particularly memorable patrol. On board were half-a-dozen soldiers led by Lieutenant Dudley Schofield, Royal Fusiliers. Their task was to blow up a railway line which ran along the Calabrian coast, close to the beach; reconnaissance teams had reported that the line was particularly vulnerable at the southern end of the bay, where it crossed a bridge over a small valley – 'an ideal pit into which to topple a train', as Norman writes:

> This was one of the first of many such operations and the equipment was, to say the least of it, primitive. Someone had designed a flat-bottomed, slab-sided, steel punt, large enough to carry the soldiers and a large quantity of ammunition and explosives. This was secured on to the [submarine's] fore-casing with large metal straps. It had two large circular holes in the bottom which allowed free access of water when the submarine dived. Two suitably sized screw-threaded plates were provided which could be inserted into these holes when the punt was required to float.
>
> The punt was far too heavy to be manhandled and was launched by the simple means of partly submerging the submarine until the boat floated off. We considered launching it fully manned but decided that the evolution was too dangerous, as the soldiers, loaded as they were with arms and explosives, would almost certainly have sunk if they were tipped into the water. Several practice launches proved that the best and quietest way to launch was for my crew to carry out the operation

and for the soldiers to man it with the crew holding it steady. The punt was propelled by four oars with a spare oar for steering.

Training and rehearsals completed, we set out for the Calabrian coast of Italy . . . The launch was successful, but the passage to the beach took longer than expected because one of the soldiers lost his oar. A hostile dog which barked caused some minor alarm, but the locals paid no attention.

The landing party had just about completed laying their explosives and were preparing to put in the detonators when a train was heard approaching. They took cover and completed the job after it had passed.

Meanwhile, *Upright* was waiting. Anthony Daniell, Norman's First Lieutenant, takes up the story:

We were feeling very naked in *Upright,* sitting on the surface just off the enemy shore, while daylight was increasing rapidly. When dawn was breaking, the seaward look-out said suddenly: 'There they are!'

Sure enough, there were Dudley Schofield and his men paddling like blazes away from the shore. They had paddled right past us in the dark and would have soon disappeared over the horizon!

'Some hours later, there was a very satisfactory explosion,' Norman writes. The raid had proved successful, but hard lessons had been learnt. 'The next landing operation was, I believe, carried out in folding canoes purchased from Gamage's store.'

The operation did have its lighter moments, however, particularly when they were rehearsing with what Daniell calls the 'tin bath contraption'. Everyone involved was issued with inflatable life-belts which had to be worn 'well up underneath your armpits', Daniell writes, otherwise 'you tended to float upside down'. There was always much good-natured rivalry and banter between commandos and submariners, but Daniell claims that the 'Pongos' (the naval term for British soldiery) were warned about this. However:

One of these Pongos had his life-belt somewhere around his

waist and he fell in. When we next caught sight of him, all we could see were his regulation boots sticking out of the water. Luckily the second Cox'n (who was the only one who wasn't doubled up with laughter) managed to get him upright.

Upholder's sixth patrol began on 15 May off the east coast of Sicily to intercept southbound traffic from the Strait of Messina. The patrol had an inauspicious start, as one of her loaded torpedoes developed a leak soon after she sailed and had to be exchanged for a reload; this involved a major upheaval in the crew space, but after much juggling the reload was inserted in the tube. Three days later a more serious defect occurred involving the asdic set, which robbed Wanklyn not only of the means of detecting the enemy but also of a valuable aid if he were forced to take avoiding action during a counter-attack. As indeed he was, just a few days later.

On 22 May an escorted convoy was sighted, including a 4,000-ton fuel tanker, a priority target worth three torpedoes. One hit was claimed. The next day another escorted convoy was encountered and another three torpedoes fired, this time hitting a tanker of 5,000 tons, *Capitaine Damiani*.* The latter attack produced a fierce response from the escorts and *Upholder* suffered some minor damage. On the following day, just after sunset, yet another convoy was sighted. Despite a heavy swell which made periscope observation difficult, and the fact that he had only two torpedoes remaining, Wanklyn made another attack. This was to earn him the award of the Victoria Cross, the first VC awarded to a submariner in the Second World War.

The attack is best described in the words of the citation:

> On the evening of 24 May, 1941, while on patrol off the coast of Sicily, Lieutenant-Commander Wanklyn, in command of His Majesty's Submarine *Upholder,* sighted a southbound enemy troop convoy, strongly escorted by destroyers.
>
> The failing light was such that observation by periscope could not be relied on, but a surface attack would have been easily seen. *Upholder's* listening gear was out of action.

* Vichy French ship, *Damiani* was being used by the enemy. Hit right aft, she managed to reach Messina under tow. The earlier hit was not confirmed.

In spite of these handicaps, Lieutenant-Commander Wanklyn decided to press home his attack at short range. He quickly steered his craft into a favourable position and closed in so as to make sure of his target. By this time the whereabouts of the escorting destroyers could not be made out. Lieutenant-Commander Wanklyn, while fully aware of the risk of being rammed by one of the escort, continued to press on towards the enemy troopships. As he was about to fire, one of the enemy destroyers appeared out of the darkness at high speed and he only just avoided being rammed. As soon as he was clear, he brought his periscope sights on and fired torpedoes, which sank a large troopship. The enemy destroyers at once made a strong counter-attack and during the next twenty minutes dropped thirty-seven depth charges near *Upholder*.

The failure of his listening device made it much harder for him to get away, but with the greatest courage, coolness and skill he brought *Upholder* clear of the enemy and safe back to harbour.

The troopship that Wanklyn had sunk was the 18,000-ton *Conte Rosso*. Of the 3,000 Italian troops on board, only 1,432 were saved, even though she was close to the coast.

The *Conte Rosso* was cruising at an estimated speed of twenty knots when Wanklyn sighted her: twice his own maximum surface speed. It had needed all his sharp wits and quick reactions to deal with such a target and her fast-moving escort. He had indeed found 'the knack'. Although the award was not gazetted, as we shall see, until the end of the year, the satisfaction of this major success — particularly after the months of failure — was shared by the whole ship's company. As the Commander-in-Chief himself recorded:

> HMS *Upholder*, under Lieutenant-Commander M. D. Wanklyn's command, is inflicting heavy losses on the enemy. Great credit is due to all on board.

Ursula's CO, 'Black' Mackenzie, had been stood down for a rest, and for one patrol in May she sailed under the command of Lieutenant I. L. M. McGeoch, the new Spare CO who had arrived with *Urge*. McGeoch was assailed by doubts. It was just six months since he had completed his 'perisher', the Commanding Officers' Qualifying Course. His first command, *H 43*, had been 'unfit to dive below periscope depth', and his second, *H 34*, had been 'solely on passage from Sheerness to Tobermory'; consequently, he had not had a chance to practice his new skills. 'I felt bound to say to "Shrimp" Simpson that . . . I had no confidence in attacking the enemy,' he writes. And so a plan was devised: 'I would sail in *Ursula* half an hour before Dick Cayley in *Utmost,* so that I could do a dummy attack on him as he left the harbour.' In fact, the practice attack never happened. 'Darkness fell and I had to press on without making contact. Just as well, as he would probably have torpedoed me!' But now McGeoch was out on patrol, and on his own:

> Bob Tanner had told me to patrol off Tripoli first, then off Zuara which was to the westward. After several hours on the surface in daylight, repairing a defective muffler valve, and feeling very exposed (luckily it was misty), I dived off Zuara.
> Next morning at twilight the Zuara lighthouse went on and I took up a position from which I expected to be able to see vessels approaching from the north, silhouetted against the dawn. And so it turned out. A supply ship with two escorts appeared, heading directly for Zuara harbour entrance. Unfortunately, just as I was ready to fire, on a nice track, the supply ship altered course about 90 degrees to port, evidently to make along the coast for Tripoli. So I fired two torpedoes, rather hopelessly, on a 170 degree (or thereabouts) track. 'to keep up the offensive'. Futile waste of fish. No more targets appeared, and when I got back to Malta, Shrimp was not madly enthusiastic about my performance!

However, as Spare CO, McGeoch was to be on frequent call during the months ahead, while other COs stood down for a few days' rest. In between patrols he helped Bob Tanner, the SOO, although he was 'somewhat inhibited by the security aspect'. Working at Lascaris, the military headquarters safe underground in Valletta, where Commander (S) had an office and where all the planning was done, McGeoch was privy to much restricted information, and, as he himself admitted, it was not beyond the bounds of possibility that he 'might one day fall into enemy hands, or make a compromising signal unknowingly'.

It was fortunate that he could not read the crystal ball, but he did fall ill, later in 1941, and had to return to the UK.

7

JUNE, 1941

At the beginning of May the Admiralty had to send a fast convoy of merchant ships through the Mediterranean, against the advice of the Mediterranean Fleet's Commander-in-Chief who feared that without air cover the convoy was doomed. But Operation 'Tiger' had successfully reached Alexandria with its load of tanks and supplies for General Wavell, and on the way had delivered some much-needed stores to Malta. Some ten days later the *Ark Royal* and *Furious* had flown off a total of forty-eight Hurricanes for Malta, all but one of which arrived safely, to form the island's first Hurricane squadron at Hal Far.

Encouraged by the success of these two operations, the War Cabinet now drew falsely optimistic conclusions. Perhaps, it seemed to them, the service Commanders-in-Chief were exaggerating the threat in the Mediterranean. Nothing could have been further from the truth.

The bombing of Malta had continued with unabated ferocity into early May, but by the middle of the month it had eased somewhat. Unknown to the suffering Maltese, the Luftwaffe was being redeployed in readiness for Operation 'Barbarossa', the German attack on Russia, which was due to start on 22 June. Kesselring had therefore withdrawn Fliegerkorps X from Sicily, which left the Regia Aeronautica to continue alone. The Luftwaffe was now firmly established in the eastern Mediterranean.

On 20 May the Germans launched a paratroop attack on Crete, a few miles west from Suda Bay, and the British decided to evacuate the island. Every available ship was summoned and every available aircraft, most from airbases in North Africa, over 400 miles away. On the 21st the destroyer *Juno* was sunk by German bombers. The next day several more of Cunningham's force were bombed, including his flagship *Warspite,* and the heavy cruiser so familiar in Malta, *Gloucester,* was sunk. And so it went on, until the end of the month. Day after day, the British fleet ran the gauntlet of German bombers in order to ferry troops and equipment back to Alexandria. Finally, on the 31st, the last 4,000 men were embarked. Although they reached safety, yet another British cruiser had been sunk. By the end of the Battle for Crete, as it became known, the Mediterranean Fleet had been decimated. The British army had completed its evacuation of Crete, but at appalling cost to the navy.

As a result of the fleet's losses, Malta was even less likely now to receive convoys of the supplies she needed so desperately. Apart from food, the island needed torpedoes, aviation fuel, ammunition — the wherewithal to strike at the enemy. For the offensive against Rommel's supply-line was now entirely dependent on the submarines and the few remaining aircraft.

The Germans had lost one whole paratroop division in the Battle for Crete, but in North Africa Rommel was still making progress. The Afrika Korps, poised on the Egyptian frontier, now had Benghazi as its main supply port. This meant that the convoys from Italy and Sicily were able to follow a more direct route across the deep open waters of the central Mediterranean; clearly our submarines would concentrate on the areas where shipping was heaviest, the Strait of Messina and off Benghazi; but anti-submarine forces would also focus on these points. It was time to reconsider the dispositions of our submarines.

The Admiralty having released the Ss with the Eighth Flotilla in Gibraltar from their convoy escort work in the Atlantic, Cunningham was now able to send them into the Tyrrhenian Sea. Here these superbly handy and hard-hitting boats were to harry enemy shipping, especially in the Naples convoy assembly point, in the bottleneck to the north of the Strait of Messina, and around the island of Sardinia. The Ts, from the First Flotilla in Alexandria, would now take over the pursuit of enemy supply ships converging on Benghazi. The Us, meanwhile, with their limited range and lesser draught, were to continue in their old haunts, but with the addition of the coasts of Sicily and the toe of Italy.

Unable now to fight his convoys through to Malta, Cunningham ordered that all submarines proceeding to Malta in future, both from Alexandria and from Gibraltar, should be loaded with stores. The minelayers and older, larger boats were removed from patrol duty and devoted temporarily to store-carrying. Their supply trips would become Malta's lifeline — 'magic carpet' runs, as they were known.

The first 'magic carpet' run was made by *Rorqual* (Lieutenant L. W. Napier). At the end of March, under her previous CO, Lieutenant-Commander R. H. Dewhurst, she had the satisfaction of torpedoing an Italian U-boat. She left Alexandria with two tons of medical stores, sixty-two tons of 100-octane aviation spirit for the RAF's Hurricanes, forty-five tons of kerosene cooking fuel, twenty-four passengers and 147 bags of mail, all of which arrived safely on 12 June. Having discharged her cargo, *Rorqual* then loaded up again: seventeen passengers, 146 cases of 4-inch gun ammunition for the First Flotilla, 130 bags of mail and ten tons of mixed stores which may have included a case or two of gin. She sailed from Malta on 16 June and reached Alexandria on 21 June, unloaded at once, and then reloaded again: sixty-four tons of aircraft petrol, forty-seven tons of kerosene, seven tons of stores, and twenty-one Army and RAF passengers. She unloaded at Malta, then reshipped her mine-casing doors which had been removed while she became a store-carrier. She was relieved by *Osiris* from Gibraltar.

Meanwhile another submarine in Alexandria was taking on stores for Malta: *Cachalot* (Lieutenant-Commander H. R. B. Newton). On 12 June, as she left Alexandria harbour, she did her trim dive to enable the CO to check her handling, an essential preliminary to sailing with an unusual cargo, and as she did so she became covered in oil scum that had been lying on the surface. For the whole of her passage to Malta, where she arrived on the 19th, an oil slick trailed astern of her. She was lucky.

Osiris (Lieutenant-Commander T. T. Euman) left Gibraltar crammed with stores on 25 June and arrived at Malta having sunk two caiques on passage. After unloading and reloading, she continued to Alexandria, where she discharged and reloaded, then sailed again for Malta. It was a constant and monotonous round of chores, but vital for the islanders' survival.

1. Captain G.W.G. Simpson, the first Captain of the Tenth Submarine Flotilla, Malta.

2. Captain J.S. Bethell welcomes *Ursula* back to Blyth in December, 1939. Her captain, Lt-Cdr G.C. Phillips, wearing his heavy-weather *'Ursula'* suit, was later to succeed Captain Simpson as S(10) at Malta.

3. The Commanding Officers and staff of the Tenth Submarine Flotilla when Admiral Sir Max Horton, FOSM, visited Lazaretto in October, 1941.

4. *Porpoise*, 'Shrimp' Simpson's last submarine command. The minelayers and Os, Ps, and Rs were all used as store-carriers to Malta during the siege.

5. The Submarine Base, Malta: behind the *T*-class submarine in the foreground are three Us. Astern of them lies the old monitor *Medusa*, who was to become HMS *Talbot*. She was used as an oil barge for the flotilla.

6. The ratings' messdeck in the Base.

7. The battery shed at Lazaretto. *Unbroken*'s battery had to be shovelled out of the boat at Malta, after she was severely depth-charged off Lampedusa.

8. A 'search' periscope being serviced in the periscope workshop. Note the smaller tube of an attack periscope at extreme right.

9. Officers relaxing on the balcony, Lazaretto. CO's and Captain(S) 10's cabins are on the right.

10. Lt–Cdr 'Pop' Giddings, first lieutenant at HMS *Talbot*, shepherds the sole survivors of the piggery : Mary and Annie. There were 70 pigs at one time during the siege, but lack of 'gash' reduced the number to two.

11. The control room of *Utmost* showing the captain, Lt–Cdr R.D. Cayley, at the periscope. On the right is the first lieutenant, Lt Oxborrow, supervising the trim; later, when CO of *Unshaken*, he was lost overboard. Lt Boyd, who is working the Fruit Machine, was to become CO of *Untiring*. Lt Archdale is on his left.

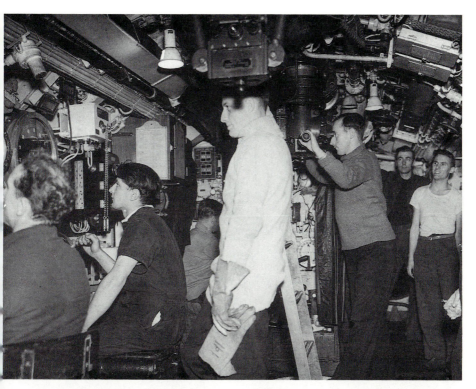

12. Lt J.S. Wraith at the periscope on *Upright's* return to the UK. Under the command of Lt F.J. Brooks, she was the first *U*-class submarine to carry out a patrol in the Mediterranean. Her first lieutenant, Lt J.F. Michell, between the two planesmen, is supervising the trim.

13. *Ursula* sailing for patrol. In action from the start of the war, she served from North Cape to Benghazi.

14. Back home at last! *Upright's* Jolly Roger is proudly displayed by her crew : red bars denote warships sunk; white bars, supply vessels.

Some weeks later, having just completed a run from Alexandria, *Osiris* was in Malta when her CO fell ill; his place was taken by Lieutenant C. P. Norman. Pat Norman, who had arrived in Malta with *Thrasher* to become another Spare CO for Simpson's *Us*, was aghast at the size of the job. Apart from fifty tons of destroyer ammunition which he was expected to deliver to Alexandria, and petrol in the ballast tanks, amid 'assorted stores' on board *Osiris* was 'the stem-piece of a *J*-class destroyer strapped to the casing'. Warily, before leaving Malta he 'insisted on a static trim dive between a couple of buoys', and was grateful ever afterwards that he had: 'I hit the bottom of the harbour with startling rapidity and a great thump. I still hesitate to imagine what would have happened if I'd done the trim at sea.'

> So off we went, with old *Osiris* noisily banging and rattling, towards Alexandria; she was also leaking petrol from the vents of the two partially petrol-filled ballast tanks and this left a lovely slick. To my horror, when only out from Malta twenty-four hours, I was detailed to approach Apollonia in Tripolitania to carry out a bombardment of an airfield. This we did and luckily with practically no retribution from the Italians.

In due course *Osiris* arrived safely at Alexandria where 'thankfully I was relieved of my command', writes Norman, who adds that he flew back to Malta in a Sunderland: one of his co-passengers was Churchill's then envoy in the Middle East, Oliver Lyttelton.

At the beginning of June *Upright*'s CO, Lieutenant Dudley Norman, became seriously ill and had to be sent back to England. Malta's hospitals, though excellent, were hard-pressed at this time of shortages, and it was felt that naval personnel should not add to the strain unless necessary. The general health of those who worked at the submarine base and of the ships' companies was looked after first by Surgeon Lieutenant Mills, and then by Surgeon Captain Cheeseman, who cycled to the base daily from his home in St Julian's Bay; later, a German bomb demolished the house, killing both Cheeseman and his wife.

Sometimes there was urgent need for hospital treatment, after an air raid or perhaps an accident in the dockyard, when naval facilities simply could not cope. On one occasion, while embarking torpedoes in *Upholder,* two men were overcome by carbon-monoxide fumes from a leaking torpedo. Petty Officer Carter tried valiantly to stop the leak but collapsed in the tube space; then, when Lieutenant Read, the torpedo officer, went to his assistance, he too was overcome. The two men had to be given artificial respiration and later admitted to hospital suffering from severe carbon-monoxide poisoning.

On board the boats themselves, the coxswain was 'doctor', aided and abetted by the captain and first lieutenant, though not all were as adept at fine surgery as Lieutenant-Commander Wanklyn. The coxswain usually underwent a course in First Aid and relied heavily on the Admiralty *Manual of Medicine* to help him in his ministrations. Each boat had its own medical chest, including standard items such as morphine, hypodermic syringes, surgical needles and thread; but the most widely prescribed and efficacious cure for all ills was undoubtedly the 'Admiralty Number Nine' pill, a powerful laxative.

Conditions in the submarines became increasingly uncomfortable during the summer months, when longer hours of daylight meant shorter hours of natural ventilation on the surface. The engine room, particularly, was a 'hard work section', remembers Polish-born Mr Antoni Banach:

> At dawn we would submerge, and after the first four hours the air inside the submarine would gradually deteriorate and become noticeably stale. After about ten to twelve hours the temperature would be about 80° Fahrenheit (27° Celsius), and breathing became more difficult. At the time I was twenty-two years old and found it uncomfortable, but the older men found it more difficult. By the time eighteen hours had passed since submerging, some of the crew were having a hard time. I was young, a non-smoker, and knew what to expect from previous experience. The last few hours before surfacing were the worst for the older crew and the inexperienced, who would by now be gasping and struggling for every breath and perspiring heavily.

And as Mr Banach points out, 'there were no baths or showers available'; hardly surprising, then, that the crews suffered periodically from scabies, for which 'the remedy would be quite painful – sitting in a basin of carbolic solution'.

At one stage, under the new management of Lieutenant J. S. Wraith, *Upright* took a medical officer on patrol, to let him see at first hand what conditions were like. As his report later stated, 'The health of this ship's company has not been of a very satisfactory standard', and he wanted to find out why. His report went on:

> Seamen's and stokers' messes in the torpedo stowage compartment are also the only available stowage for the majority of the three weeks' provisions carried for patrol. This compartment suffers from excessive sweating and is permanently damp. The Corticene* of the deck is completely sodden and requires constant renewal. Hammocks cannot be kept dry and bunks cannot be provided. Under these conditions it is considered that twelve days at sea is the maximum compatible with any degree of efficiency . . . Bad weather has a noticeably depressing effect on the ship's company, as sleep becomes impossible and even the old hands are seasick.

Now the medical officer understood why everyone was suffering from so many minor ailments, but there was not much he could do to help. Nourishing food was the men's main defence against illness, but this was becoming increasingly difficult to provide.

As time went by, these minor ailments combined to cause serious problems for Commander Simpson and his COs. Simpson did his best to ensure that there was normally a rest period of about ten days between patrols, when the submarine would be serviced and re-stored and the crews could take a break. He began to arrange rest camps in remote parts of the island, where the ship's companies could find relaxation away from the constant smell of engine oil and machinery, but everyone had to make their own recreation.

Drinking, naturally, was one popular way to pass the time ashore, and some of the crews invariably made a beeline for their favourite watering-hole as soon as they were released from duty – 'The Olde Dun Cow' and similar establishments in Sliema and

* Heavy-duty deck covering made of cork.

the other suburbs of Valletta. But drink, too, became increasingly scarce in the months and years to come.

In any case, for the officers at least there was invariably too much to do, as Pat Norman, the Spare CO, remembers. When he himself was not captaining a boat, he was helping Bob Tanner, the SOO, or lending a hand to Hubert Marsham and Pop Giddings at Lazaretto:

> During this period all officers and men, in their spare time, were digging away in the limestone rock underneath Lazaretto buildings. We made great progress with the help of Pop Giddings's ship's company; we ended up with about 200 yards of tunnelling and adequate space for workshops.

Norman also contributed to the success of the pig farm − 'at its peak we had 300 porkers' − and ran necessary errands whenever required. But it is, of course, the good times that he remembers of that summer of 1941: taking the pony and trap into Valletta to collect the shopping, or a rare afternoon off with a companion and a couple of girls in a whaler.

In mid-June General Wavell launched a counter-offensive in Libya, his main objective being to relieve the pressure on Tobruk, still under siege from Rommel's troops. Because the Luftwaffe was well established now in North Africa, merchant ships were unable to reach the port, where the garrison thus remained dependent on Cunningham's warships. But within three days Rommel had halted the British advance; our soldiers were driven back to their starting point, having lost most of their tanks. Tobruk was still encircled by the enemy, and the siege would last for another six months.

Already depleted by the losses of the Battle for Crete, the Mediterranean Fleet was sorely pressed by the need to continue these life-saving trips into Tobruk. Rommel's supply line, on the other hand, was going from strength to strength. It was not until the second half of June that the *U*s began to get their eye in.

In June, 1941, Simpson was operating seven *U*s. Four were sent to the now familiar hunting ground between the Kerkenah Bank and Lampedusa: *Urge, Unique, Upright* and *Union*. Only

Union (Lieutenant Galloway) had any success, on the 22nd she attacked and sank the *Pietro Querini* (1,004 tons). The other three *U*s went north to the Messina billet, where two of them fared little better.

To allow Wanklyn a rest, *Upholder* was temporarily under the command of another Spare CO, Lieutenant A. R. Hezlet. This was his first operational patrol, and it proved to be completely uneventful. The only vessel that was sighted was a hospital ship. *Unbeaten* sighted a much more hopeful target on the 16th, a 20,000-ton liner south-west of Sicily; but she was on a continuous weave, zigzagging wildly and escorted by numerous aircraft. Teddy Woodward fired an over-optimistic salvo which missed.

Utmost had a more interesting patrol. She was bound for the Gulf of Santa Eufemia, where the railway line from Naples to Reggio di Calabria ran alongside the sea, and on board she had a team of commandos led by Dudley Schofield, this time with two of the canvas Folbots instead of the unsatisfactory steel punts. But on the way to her destination, *Utmost* passed through the enemy's mine barrage between Cape Bon and Sicily, the very area in which *Usk* had disappeared. Dick Cayley later wrote in his patrol report:

> Coming up to periscope depth for a periodic all-round look, I found we were passing a domed object: it seemed like the top of a mine just buoyant and with no horns showing. I put the stick [periscope] up another three feet and took an all-round look. To my horror I counted about twenty within a hundred yards of me. Wondering what was my best way out of this danger from every quarter, the mine I was looking at grew a horn, opened an eye and winked. They were Mediterranean terrapins.

Successfully negotiating both terrapins and mines, *Utmost* rounded the coast of Sicily, passed the dull red, glowing volcanic cone of Stromboli Island on the night of the 23rd, and arrived at the appointed position on the 24th. The team of commandos departed in their Folbots, laid their explosives and waited: nothing happened. Schofield's fuses had failed. He returned to the scene and tried again – success!

While the enemy rushed to clear the track, *Utmost* dived for a brief foray into the northern end of the Strait of Messina where on 26 June she torpedoed and sank the *Enrico Costa,* 4,080 tons. Then, on the 28th, Schofield and his men tried another raid on the railway line, but this time the submarine was detected from the beach, so the landing had to be cancelled. *Utmost* returned to base on 3 July, complaining bitterly about the difficulty of clearing a W/T signal to Malta from that billet.

Urge, having returned from her earlier patrol, was then sent north with another train-wrecking party, this time led by Captain Taylor. During the night of 27/28 June he and his commandos were landed near the Sicilian town of Taormina to blow up the northbound express as it emerged from a tunnel near Cape San Alessio. They laid their charges and returned safely to *Urge* in their Folbots, then watched as the train approached along the coast. It disappeared into the southern end of the tunnel. A minute later there was a vivid flash: the mission had been successful. For three nights afterwards, patrolling submarines reported seeing oxy-acetylene cutters and flares being wielded as the wreckage was removed and the line repaired.

On the 29th *Urge* sighted two cruisers, escorted by four destroyers, and, despite the long range of 4,000 yards, Tomkinson attacked. He missed, but three days later, while returning to base, he sighted an armed merchant cruiser escorting a supply ship, and fired the last of his torpedoes. Although he heard one hit, Tomkinson was bitterly disappointed to see both ships continue northwards. Only later did intelligence confirm that he had in fact hit the ex-Norwegian *Brarena* (6,696 tons) and that she finally sank.

With Wanklyn back in command, *Upholder* too was in the Messina billet when, on 3 July, she sank the *Laura Cosulich,* 5,867 tons. The rest of this patrol, her tenth, was quiet and she returned to Malta on 8 July.

At last Commander Simpson could feel that his boats were beginning to make their mark. At the beginning of June there had been an encouraging signal from Admiral Cunningham:

> I wish to express my appreciation of the successes which have been achieved in the last few weeks by you and your command

in attacks against the Tripoli convoys. In these times of adversity, this work is more than ever important to the Empire's effort. Well done and carry on.

By the end of the month the Commander-in-Chief, Mediterranean, had sent another heartening message to be displayed on the notice boards at Lazaretto:

The strain of the continuous and arduous duties you are being asked to carry out is fully appreciated, but your fine actions clearly indicate that their necessity is very apparent to you and I am certain that you will carry on with the same ready efficiency.

Also at the end of June there came yet another appreciative signal, this one from Admiralty:

The steady ascending scale of success achieved by submarines in the Mediterranean indicates a very high standard of accuracy and resolution. If this scale of attack can be maintained or increased, it is probable that enemy operations will be hampered owing to lack of shipping. Congratulations to submarine crews and to all Naval Attachés whose efforts contribute to such successful results.

The Mediterranean submariners felt a quiet satisfaction that their efforts were being recognized, and were further cheered to hear that Cunningham had asked the Admiralty to send him all the submarines that could be spared. But the best reward of all was the news, which arrived on the last day of June, 1941, that their leader, Commander George Simpson, had been promoted to Captain.

8

JULY, 1941

In July a major operation began which would provide the beleaguered island of Malta with essential supplies and further reinforcements for her own defence. Code-named Operation 'Substance', the convoy of six storeships and a troopship was to be escorted from Gibraltar by the whole of Force H, with the addition of one battleship, *Nelson,* and three cruisers. Admiral Cunningham would initiate a diversion at the other end of the Mediterranean in order to distract the enemy, and Malta's submarines would play their part by keeping the Italian fleet busy. But the convoy would not sail from the UK until 11 July, and it would be another ten days before it reached Gibraltar. Until then the submarines would concentrate on the enemy's supply line that was still pumping life into the Afrika Korps.

The month began with patrols off the Tunisian shoreline. On 8 July *Unbeaten* (Lieutenant Woodward) sailed for Lampedusa in the Pelagie islands, but, sighting nothing, moved south to Marsa Zuaga roads, a shallow anchorage west of Tripoli. Here, on the 15th, she sank a big schooner, but the rest of her patrol was quiet and she returned to base without incident. In contrast, her spell back in harbour was somewhat eventful.

'As everyone knows,' says Teddy Woodward, 'many of us in submarines were superstitious in those days.' So when a sailor spotted a rat scuttling off the submarine at her mooring, the word quickly went round: 'Rats leaving the sinking ship.' *Unbeaten's* coxswain, Harding, warned his CO about what was happening; and, picturing half his ship's company suddenly going sick ('or, God forbid, jumping ship!') Woodward anxiously went to confer with Captain(S)10. Simpson simply advised him to speak to them. 'So I did. It wasn't easy,' remembers Woodward, who proceeded to tell his men that the rats were leaving because poison had been put down, emphasizing, 'What a hell of a patrol we would have if the pests stayed on board and then died: we would be cooped up with their ghastly smell for hours on end,' and adding a few yarns of his father's sailing ship days. And, Woodward concludes,

> It seemed to work, for they were all on board when we left for our next patrol, a few days later. True, we got quite a belting after one of our attacks, but I wish I could confirm the story of the rats coming back on board again when we got back to Lazaretto!

By now another *U*-class submarine had arrived, *P 33* (Lieutenant-Commander R. D. Whiteway-Wilkinson), and her first patrol from Malta, beginning on 11 July, took her west towards the Gulf of Hammamet. Here her duty was to carry out a reconnaissance, in preparation for another cloak-and-dagger mission a few days later when *Union* was to pick up spies from a fishing boat. But this first patrol was a good deal more dramatic than intended.

On the afternoon of 15 July, *P 33* was off the heavily fortified Italian island of Pantellaria, when she sighted 'a small but important enemy convoy', in the words of her fourth hand and torpedo officer, Lieutenant Jackie Fox, which consisted of 'two merchant ships, heavily escorted by maritime aircraft and six destroyers'. Fox later recorded his admiration of the CO's 'brilliantly executed submerged attack':

> Taking his submarine undetected through the destroyer screen, he fired four torpedoes from a range of 1,500 yards at his target . . . *[Barbarigo,* 5,293 tons]: she was hit by at least one torpedo and sank.
>
> To avoid the counter-attack, the Captain went deep and ordered 'Silent Routine'. But for an hour and a half, the destroyers carried out a series of persistent and accurate depth-charge attacks on *P 33:* some fifty explosions, very close, were counted in the submarine.
>
> The boat's Main Ballast pump, one main electric propulsion

motor, main lighting, the steering and the hydroplanes were put out of action by this battering. As *P 33* spiralled downwards out of control to a depth of 350 feet (deeper than any *U*-class submarine had so far been), the pressure hull creaked, rivets sprang, and the stern glands and hull valves leaked alarmingly. But a Main Ballast trim was skilfully caught before it was too late.

When the enemy were probably running short of depth charges (perhaps they thought the submarine was a 'goner'), the destroyers withdrew from the scene. Five hours later, after making good the worst of the damage caused by the counter-attack, *P 33* surfaced. Badly mauled, she limped back to Malta where she was docked for extensive repairs: not the least of the damage was a distorted pressure hull.

Some of the crew had become casualties too, including Fox who suffered a ruptured eardrum and had to take sick leave, as a result of which he missed *P 33*'s next patrol.

Union (Lieutenant Robert Galloway), for whom *P 33* had been due to carry out a reconnaissance, sailed from Malta on 14 July. She never returned. It is now known from Italian sources that on 20 July, south-west of Pantellaria, she attacked a small convoy of ships heading north — two salvage vessels and a supply ship, escorted by a torpedo boat and a seaplane. The sea was moderately calm and the CO of the torpedo boat, *Circe,* recorded that an oily slick on the surface betrayed the submarine's presence:

> The origin of the slick being only 1,000 metres off the convoy's track, *Circe* ordered the ships to turn away to the south-east, while the torpedo boat increased speed to twenty knots for a depth-charge attack. Turning to port under full rudder, she dropped six charges over the source of the slick, the settings being for 50, 75 and 100 metres.
>
> At 1131, 200 metres from *Circe,* a gigantic bubble of air from the submerged submarine erupted on the surface. Three more 100kg depth charges were dropped at short intervals; the escorting Z5O1 aircraft then dropped its A/S bombs. The contact's position was 36°26'N, 11°50'E.

So ended *Union's* short life, and her attacker would later become a thorn in the side of another *U*-class submarine.

Throughout July the 'magic carpet' runs continued, with the store-carrying submarines doing their utmost to keep Malta supplied. Every new submarine arriving in the Mediterranean would stop off at Gibraltar to load stores of one kind or another for the besieged island. *Talisman* (Lieutenant-Commander M. Willmott), on passage to Alexandria, called in at Malta with 5,500 gallons of 100% octane aviation spirit for the RAF in her tanks, while other submarines brought equally welcome though humbler supplies such as ordinary household kerosene.

Off the Libyan coast on 30 July, *Cachalot* (Lieutenant-Commander Hugo Newton) was in the middle of yet another run when she sighted an escorted enemy tanker making for Benghazi, and launched a surface attack. The tanker escaped behind a smoke screen. Hugo Newton now found himself under attack from the destroyer escort, the *Generale Achille Papa*. Hampered by patchy mist, and half-blinded by the flashes of his own gun (flashless ammunition did not reach Malta until September, 1942), Newton suddenly realized to his horror that the destroyer was about to ram him. She was only 800 yards away and her sharp stem was steering straight for the submarine.

Newton, turning hard-a'starboard, ordered his gun crew back through the gun-tower into the boat, but the control room reported a jam; the hatch could not be shut, so Newton could not dive. By the time the jam was cleared, *Papa* was only 300 yards away. Newton knew it was hopeless to start diving now and gave the order to abandon ship, hoping that at least a handful of men would be able to scramble out.

Papa rammed the submarine, but with a less than catastrophic blow. Despite damage to his external ballast tank, and the extra weight of all his stores and twenty-five passengers, Newton attempted to escape. But *Papa's* captain evidently lost patience: fire from the destroyer's high-angle guns started raking *Cachalot's* bridge and hull. Newton now had no option but to scuttle his boat.

All ninety-one people on board the submarine abandoned ship, and all but one — the Maltese steward — were picked up by *Papa*, whose captain showed his humanity by making repeated efforts to find the missing man. As *Cachalot* sank beneath the waves, bows down into 200 fathoms, Newton and his crew faced two long years in a prisoner-of-war camp. They were liberated in 1943.

By the end of July, 1941, the supply runs by store-carrying submarines such as *Cachalot* had been supplemented by Operation 'Substance'. The convoy passed through the Strait of Gibraltar on 21 July, escorted by Admiral Somerville's augmented Force H. Already the *Us* from Malta were in position, their number increased by the arrival of *P 32* (Lieutenant D. A. B. Abdy) on 17 July.

It was Simpson's intention to use all his submarines to deter the Italian battleships from leaving their bases in Palermo, Messina and Taranto. While the new boat, *P 32,* was to patrol off Sardinia, he sent *Utmost* to patrol north of the Strait of Messina, *Upright* and *Unique* to the south of the strait, *Urge* to Palermo on the northern coast of Sicily and *Upholder* to the west off Cape San Vito. With other submarines from Alexandria forming a line across the Gulf of Taranto, by 22 July all of Admiral Iachino's main bases were ringed. Further deterred by a stream of dummy W/T signals being emitted by two First Flotilla boats, *Perseus* and *Regent,* which persuaded him that the main British fleet was at sea in the eastern Mediterranean, his ships never emerged from their lairs.

On 24 July the 'Substance' convoy arrived safely at Malta, E-boats from Pantelleria had torpedoed one of the store ships but she managed to continue. The whole operation had been a resounding success and for a few weeks more Malta's survival was guaranteed.

By now the submarines had, at Simpson's instigation, adopted a new method of negotiating the mine barrage laid in the Sicilian Channel. The relatively shallow waters (the average sounding was 50 fathoms) were sown with a profusion of mines. Simpson explained to his team that in future all submarines were to use the same route through the channel; this would require accurate navigation which in turn demanded shore fixes through the periscope. The track therefore had to be within sight of the southern shoreline of Sicily. Consequently, a submarine had to time her night passage from Malta to arrive at dawn, ten miles off a headland called Cape San Marco, close to the small town of Sciacca.

There, having obtained an accurate fix, she would go deep to 150 feet, then steer blind on a course of 300° for fifty-five miles. Speed was to be adjusted so that the submarine need surface only after twilight, with the island of Marittimo ten miles to the north-east. The return journey would be exactly reversed.

Having summoned his COs and disclosed his plan to them, Simpson stressed that their navigation skills would be tested to the full. Then he asked for a volunteer to blaze the trail to Marittimo. Dick Cayley spoke up at once, and that night *Utmost* sailed. Two days later, a signal arrived from *Utmost* somewhere off Marittimo: '*Utmost* to S.10. Next please'.

Utmost's next operation after 'Substance' was to carry out another train-wrecking raid with the commandos in the Gulf of Santa Eufemia. The Folbot party paddled ashore on the night of 27 July, but their first effort was foiled by locals indulging in a moonlight swimming spree. Later that night they tried again, and succeeded in destroying a train and the track's overhead electric cable. On the next afternoon, while still in the gulf, *Utmost* sank the 1,466-ton *Federico;* her successes were becoming almost routine. Cayley then received orders to guard Palermo, in order to keep the Italians in port while our new light cruiser *Hermione,* which had rammed and sunk the Italian submarine *Tembien* off Tunis, dashed through to Malta for repairs.

Unique also landed a successful train-wrecking party near Messina at the end of July, but the greatest achievement of all was when *Upholder* made two hits during one attack on the 28th. Earlier, on the day the convoy reached Malta, *Upholder* had torpedoed and damaged an enemy supply ship, then diverted to Marittimo. This westernmost island of the Egadi group, off the western tip of Sicily, would become the Piccadilly Circus of submarines in search of prey, and *Upholder* was the first to pounce.

The day began in dense fog, but by the evening visibility had cleared sufficiently for Wanklyn to sight, at long range, two big ships steaming at speed towards him – the cruisers *Raimondo Montecuccoli* and *Giuseppe Garibaldi,* escorted by the destroyer *Bersagliere* and by aircraft. Wanklyn had only two torpedoes left and Lieutenant M. L. C. Crawford, *Upholder's* first lieutenant, recalls, 'Wanklyn once again demonstrated his quick thinking, as the whole attack took only a few minutes from sighting to firing the torpedoes.' Both torpedoes hit the *Garibaldi,* causing serious damage which took months to repair.

Upright, now commanded by Lieutenant Johnny Wraith, maintained her patrol in the Messina billet after 'Substance' and made what Lieutenant Anthony Daniell describes as 'the only attack in World War Two on a floating dock'. Daniell, as first lieutenant in *Upright,* was making his last patrol before returning home for the Commanding Officers' Qualifying Course, more usually known as the 'perisher'. This is his account of the attack:

> The dock was heavily escorted and was being towed by tugs along the Calabrian coast towards Messina. I think two torpedoes hit. The A/S conditions were very bad and, while being heavily counter-attacked, *Upright* dropped down out of control, with an 8° bow-down angle, to 340 feet. She survived these attacks but developed several leaks.
>
> Our elation at what we thought to be a sinking turned to disappointment later on, when we learnt that the dock, though damaged, reached harbour safely.

But as Daniell admits himself, 'A floating dock is divided into several compartments' and it would require more than usual skill to sink such a target.

Thirty-six hours after the safe arrival of the 'Substance' convoy, late on 25 July Captain Simpson was summoned to Lascaris, where the Combined Services' headquarters lay hidden in tunnels beneath Valletta. Simpson knew, as few others did, that Malta had a secret weapon − radar, or RDF (Radio Direction Finding) as it was known in those days − and the radar screen was showing a puzzling 'blip'. Until this echo could be identified, none of his submarines could sail from Lazaretto.

Still very new, Malta's radar was so 'Top Secret', according to Mr Victor Coppini of Valletta, that even those who worked on it referred to it by a code word. The installation consisted of 'a rotating hut, under camouflage . . . enclosed in a rambling circle of barbed-wire entanglements', with guards disguised as farmers patrolling the area 'with orders to shoot at sight any trespassers'. Mr Coppini's informant, a nineteen-year-old staff sergeant at the time and former university student, told him that he and his fellow operators 'worked right above two tons of TNT. Their hut revolved over enough explosives to blow it to smithereens at the first sign of invasion.'

What the radar screen had shown finally became clear on the morning of the 26th. The dawn silence was shattered by staccato gunfire, coming from Fort St Elmo at the tip of the Valletta peninsula. The Italians were making a daring attempt to penetrate Malta's harbours. The radar echo had been their midget submarines arriving off Malta with their mother ship *Diana,* accompanied by fast motor boats towing other boats packed with explosives.

The midget submarines were trying to pierce the defensive nets hanging from booms across the harbour mouths, thus creating gaps for the Motor Anti-Submarine (MAS) craft to dash through. But, one by one, the Maltese gunners picked them off. The explosive boats were blown out of the water, bringing down one span of the viaduct at the entrance to Grand Harbour. Hurricane fighters finished off the remaining boats, although *Diana* managed to reach Sicily safely. Eighteen survivors were taken prisoner, and the wreckage of the explosive boats was put on display, their bullet-ridden hulls a graphic reminder to everyone of the reality of the invasion threat.

The immediate objective of this Italian raid had been twofold: to sink the 'Substance' supply ships in Grand Harbour and to destroy our submarines in Marsamxett Harbour. By now the Regia Aeronautica had realized that Malta's submarines had their own base, and the Italians were itching for revenge on the men who were not only sinking their ships but landing the swift and lethal commando parties. The commandos, at little cost, were engaging at least 2,500 Italian soldiers in guarding their coastal railway lines, viaducts and tunnels, soldiers who could have been fighting our Desert Rats in North Africa. Although one of our submarines, bent on train-wrecking, missed an enemy convoy and earned Simpson a reprimand from Cunningham − 'Convoys are your main target' − the combined work of the submariners and commandos was rapidly accelerating the Italians' discomfiture.

Captain Simpson did not flinch from special operations. He

suspected that some officers in the other services did not fully understand the risks a submarine was facing when she went to fetch and carry special agents; one man in an aircraft could do some of the errands much more quickly and safely. He and the commandos based at Lazaretto understood each other's needs very well by now. But all too often these cloak-and-dagger forays put his boats at risk for dubious returns, and he was never happy about them.

At one stage, back in April, there had been a plan to kill Field-Marshal Kesselring, now in charge of Goering's Luftwaffe in Sicily:

> From: Commander-in-Chief.
> To: Submarines, Malta.
> Kesselring has established his HQ at the Miramar Hotel, Taormina. Eliminate him.

By chance, Taormina was where Wanklyn had spent his honeymoon and so *Upholder* was chosen to land the commando party. Captain Taylor's commandos launched enthusiastically into training, the best cricketers among them practising the hurling of dummy grenades; but, four days before the operation was due to take place, the Governor of Malta, General Sir William Dobbie, sent for Simpson and asked what was going on. When Simpson explained, as he writes in *Periscope View,* that this was 'a typical example of a combined operation', making the best of 'our meagre resources', Sir William expressed displeasure: 'You know Simpson, I abhor butchery.' Simpson says in his book:

> As I walked down that broad sweeping marble staircase, suits of armour with metalled gloves grasping embossed shields flanked my progress. I walked over to the nearest and tapping his cuirass I said, 'The days of chivalry are over, chum. You might tell the boss.' Then I felt ashamed that I should have sunk so low. I must attribute my fall to progress.

As it happens, the operation was postponed for reasons quite unconnected with anyone's squeamishness, and a fortnight later a further signal reached Simpson saying that Kesselring had left Taormina.

9

There is an intriguing contrast, at this crucial stage of the war, between the strategic thinking of Britain and Germany. Britain, with her overseas Empire, instinctively thought in terms of sea power; Hitler, the continental, thought more of his armies.

The War Cabinet in London knew that whoever controlled the Mediterranean would be able to reinforce his armies in North Africa and that Malta was the key to the Mediterranean. The German liaison staff in Italy understood this; Rommel did, too – but Hitler did not. Despite the efforts of his generals and his advisers, Hitler failed to grasp the importance of Malta to the North African campaign.

And yet, so far, the war in the Mediterranean was going much the enemy's way. Admiral Iachino was by no means a spent force and the Mediterranean Fleet was constantly menaced from the air. On land the Afrika Korps was consolidating its gains, thanks to supplies still streaming into the Libyan ports from across the sea. Our only hope, until Malta's aircraft could be built up, lay in our submarines, and not only for offensive purposes.

The store-carrying submarines continued to break the blockade on Malta by sailing from both ends of the Mediterranean with passengers, stores, mail, tanks of petrol and spares for the precious aircraft, among much else. *Rorqual, Osiris, Otus,* even *Thunderbolt* (formerly *Thetis,* who had sunk during trials in Liverpool Bay in 1939 and now had been salvaged) however old and bent, were much appreciated in Malta, and the devotion to duty of their ships' companies was beyond compare.

Captain Simpson was acutely aware of the strain under which his submarines and his men were working. The Mediterranean itself could be a threat, with its swift currents and shallow waters; the days of summer calm when the glassy surface betrayed a shape beneath (despite being painted 'Mediterranean blue', the submarine was obvious down to a depth of fifty feet or more) and even the faintest ripples pointed to an advancing periscope. Our charts were often out of date and inaccurate: it was not uncommon to find a boat running onto a sandbank in six fathoms where the chart showed a depth of twenty-five. The enemy was also developing more efficient anti-submarine measures, and increasing the number and density of his minefields.

The best Simpson could do was to ensure that his men made full use of their runs ashore, escaping to the bars as long as the drink lasted, or to the rest camps for a complete change; he encouraged them to relax in whatever way best suited them. In *Periscope View* he notes some of the pastimes that his early COs enjoyed, such as reading and needlework – Dick Cayley, 'Harmonica Dick', was not only an accomplished musician but an expert at gross-point tapestry; but when he writes of Teddy Woodward, CO of *Unbeaten,* it is possible to detect a note of awe. Commenting that 'Woodward was a young officer of exceptional physical stamina' and, incidentally, 'probably the best middle distance swimmer in the navy', Simpson writes:

> Teddy Woodward found that it suited him best to play the game of war in reverse. The pace he set himself during rest periods in Malta would have put most men in hospital. He would arrive at Lazaretto from the rigours of holidaying in Malta's 'watering resorts', which seemed never closed to Woodward, looking pale and in need of complete rest. He would climb to the conning tower and say, 'Let go everything. Slow ahead port,' and would escape from the dangers of a social 'sea lion' amongst the mermaids of Malta's coastline into the refuge of a wartime submarine patrol.
>
> Once clear of harbour his grand First Lieutenant (A. D. Piper, RNR) would take over and direct *Unbeaten* to her patrol position. By the time the submarine arrived Teddy was not thinking about the dangers ahead, but fresh as a daisy he could reflect with satisfaction on the dangers so recently surmounted whilst on leave.

It says much for the steadiness of Shrimp's men that, as he reported at the end of his time in Malta, not one man ever shirked a patrol deliberately. There were isolated cases of stress-related mental disturbance; it would be astounding if there were not. In *Upholder,* during the depth-charging that followed her attack on *Conte Rosso,* one man had to be forcibly restrained from trying to escape through the lower conning tower hatch. While *Urge* was being hunted, a hardened leading stoker, with years of submarine experience, temporarily went off his head and strode up and down the control room reciting the Lord's Prayer out loud. But the vast majority took their cue from their Captain (S) and turned their inner doubts and fears into a positive drive to defeat the enemy.

In this August of 1941 they would need all the self mastery at their command to survive the unremitting pressure. But some would not survive.

Simpson knew that if the enemy's anti-submarine forces could be dispersed, their efficiency would suffer. Accordingly he disposed his submarines as widely as possible, though always with the primary aim of catching the enemy's convoys as they sailed south from the Italian mainland.

Having received word from Intelligence that a fast convoy of four troop-carrying liners was heading for the Gulf of Hammamet, on 19 August Simpson sent *Urge* and *Unbeaten* to intercept them south of Pantellaria. Somehow the convoy managed to sail unscathed between them. *Unbeaten* fired a salvo at 6,500 yards, but a combination of human error, malfunctioning torpedoes and bad weather resulted in failure. *Urge,* after losing trim in the rough seas, was spotted by an escorting aircraft which put a destroyer on her tail, and she was then pursued for over an hour.

Also on the 19th, *Utmost* sailed for a special mission in the Gulf of Taranto, this time operating in company with *Triumph.* Both boats were laden with commandos and Folbots, which were safely launched on the night of the 26th. Some hours later, an important railway bridge was blown at Trebisacce on the gulf coast.

Two days later *Utmost* sighted a brace of *Cavour*-class battleships complete with destroyer screen and escorting aircraft. They were at extreme range, and *Utmost* was spotted by an aircraft. Because she could not attack herself, she immediately tried to report the enemy's movements to base, but it took almost twelve hours to raise Malta by W/T, by which time the report was less than useful. It was the same old communications problem that had plagued so many COs in the central Mediterranean. Lieutenant-Commander A. C. C. Miers, CO of *Torbay,* reported at one stage that even on the surface it took him two hours to transmit a W/T report from off Benghazi, and as he said, 'The long time taken to clear signals greatly increases the danger of making them.' As a result, steps were now taken to change both wavelengths and procedures.

In mid-August *Upholder* had sailed for her twelfth patrol: she was to take part in a commando raid on the north coast of Sicily near Palermo, and on board was a party of commandos with canoes. On the way to her destination Wanklyn first sank a trawler (*Enotria,* 852 tons) with two torpedoes. Then, a few days later on 22 August, a convoy of three supply ships escorted by three destroyers was attacked with four torpedoes; two hits accounted for a naval tanker (*Lussin,* 4,500 tons). And on the 24th the remaining two torpedoes were fired at a naval force of one battleship, two cruisers and six destroyers. It was thought at the time that one cruiser had been hit, but this was never confirmed. Even so, by the time *Upholder* reached the north coast of Sicily, on 25 August, she had already wreaked considerable havoc on the enemy.

That night the soldiers paddled ashore in their canoes to blow up the railway line to Palermo. Waiting offshore in the darkness, those in the submarine heard shots coming from the area where the men had landed, followed by a considerable disturbance; clearly the alarm had been raised. Time passed. In the submarine, anxiety turned to despair. The men must have been captured. The boat would have to leave without them. But suddenly the blue flicker of a torch was seen: the men were signalling that they were on their way back. It transpired that the soldiers had managed to hide their Folbots but, by the time they had thrown off their pursuers, the railway line was a long way away and it was time to turn back. Wanklyn thankfully withdrew from the coast and set course for Malta, arriving on 27 August.

Urge made a second patrol in August, off the island of Marit-timo, where she intercepted a southbound convoy. Tomkinson's attack began badly when one of his torpedoes jammed in the tube and he was forced to surface; he had the effrontery to continue the attack and managed to hit the fully-laden tanker *Aquitania,* 4,971 tons, but she did not sink. Moving north, *Urge* next inter-cepted a convoy of three heavily escorted troopships; she tor-pedoed and damaged the liner *Duilio* (23,600 tons) but failed to stop the other two, *Neptunia* and *Oceania,* so she passed an enemy report to Malta. Simpson promptly sent out *Upholder,* who had returned from patrol only two days earlier with *Ursula* who had been on a blank patrol in the Messina billet. *Ursula* sighted the ships on the 30th but they were beyond her range; at first light on the 31st *Upholder* fired four torpedoes, but again the range was extreme and both ships escaped.

Although *Triumph* had also damaged the heavy cruiser *Bolzano* on the 26th, this unsuccessful month was also to prove a tragic one for the submarines operating from Malta.

Simpson had sent *Unique* and the two new boys, *P 33* (Lieutenant R. D. Whiteway-Wilkinson) and *P 32* (Lieutenant D. A. B. Abdy), to the shallow waters off Tunisia and Tripolitania. At the moment this tended to be the quietest billet, where the new-comers could gain experience of Mediterranean conditions, although it was in the Gulf of Hammamet that *P 33* had suffered such a fierce attack in mid-July.

P 33 sailed from Malta on 6 August to a position seventeen miles west-north-west of Tripoli lighthouse. On the 12th *P 32* followed, to a position twelve miles north-north-east of Tripoli. On the 16th, with Lieutenant A. R. Hezlet standing in for Tony Collett, *Unique* sailed for a position between the other two *Us*. She arrived on the morning of the 18th and signalled them of her presence by sub-sonic transmission (SST: in effect, sending Morse code via asdic). Only *P 32* replied to the underwater call.

Shortly after noon *P 32* heard the singular, regular explosions of depth-charges: clearly an Italian convoy was approaching, this being a favourite anti-submarine measure of theirs. What was worrying David Abdy was that the explosions went on for two hours and that they seemed to originate from where the other two boats were. To reassure himself, Abdy went deep and ordered his asdic operator to contact *P 33* on SST. There was no reply, but the asdic operator reported that he could hear HE (hydrophone effect: the sound of ships' propellers). Abdy ordered Diving Stations and came to periscope depth. A convoy was entering the swept channel through a known minefield that protected Tripoli harbour.

Abdy decided to go deep, increase speed and pass underneath the minefield; he would then return to periscope depth ahead of the convoy in the swept channel. He ordered 'Group up' (batteries in parallel, for increased speed) and took the boat down to sixty feet. Ten minutes later he ordered 'Group down' (batteries in series) and the boat started planing upwards to twenty-eight feet.

Suddenly there was a shattering explosion from the port side, for'ard. All lighting failed. The for'ard control room bulkhead slammed and jammed shut. The boat took on a heavy list to port. Despite all emergency action, including blowing Main Ballast, she careered out of control to the seabed, hitting bottom at 210 feet. Everyone was hurled to the deck by the impact, which also smashed the bottle of hydrochloric acid to be used should it ever become necessary to destroy the Confidential Books. Lethal vapours wafted across the control room.

The coxswain, Acting Petty Officer Kirk, donned a DSEA set (Davis Submerged Escape Apparatus) and breathing through his mask attended to the spilt acid. Others were already wrestling with the bulkhead door to release their trapped messmates from the for'ard side. It was too late. The whole fore-part of the submarine was flooded and the eight men for'ard the bulkhead door were dead.

The twenty-four survivors maintained a disciplined calm while they fought to raise their mortally wounded boat. In vain. Miraculously, no seawater had yet reached No 1 battery compartment; otherwise chlorine gas would already be seeping through to kill them. That jammed door was containing the water, but for how long was anybody's guess. The captain gave the order to abandon ship.

Abdy mustered all hands in the control room and explained that when they reached the surface they should stick together; he could not be sure whether there were any ships in the vicinity to pick them up. The enemy convoy might not have noticed the explosion that had wounded *P 32* or might have attributed it to a faulty mine; no depth charges had followed, so no one could have seen the oil and debris that must now be gushing to the surface from the damaged submarine.

The DSEA sets were distributed and checked, and the escape drill recited. First the compartment would be flooded until air pressure within the compartment equalled water pressure outside. The 'twill trunk' would be rigged, a collapsible tube beneath the escape hatch; each man in turn, wearing his breathing apparatus, would enter the trunk, climb the ladder and then clamber out through the hatch.

All hands then moved aft to the engine room, where the escape hatch was sited at the for'ard end of the compartment. A count was made: twenty-four men, all squeezed into this cramped space, each wearing his bulky escape apparatus. It was clear that as the compartment flooded up, there would be precious little air (and that under considerable pressure) for the last men to breathe while waiting their turn in the hatch. Abdy decided to reduce the overcrowding by asking for volunteers to join him in the control room, where they could make an escape through the conning tower.

In the engine room the men had the added protection of another bulkhead door, in case the for'ard door burst or the chlorine gas started to escape. In the control room that protection was not available. But the coxswain, Acting PO Kirk, and the outside ERA, W. H. Martin, both volunteered to join the captain. Satisfied that two fewer men in the engine room meant more air for the rest, Abdy checked that the first lieutenant knew the drill; Lieutenant R. L. S. Morris assured him he did. So the captain and his two volunteers left the engine room and closed the for'ard engine room door while Morris and the others began the escape procedure.

Now Abdy opened the valve to start flooding the control room. It was at this moment that Kirk realized that there was a hole in the breathing bag of his DSEA set, the result of broken glass during his earlier efforts to clear up the spilt acid, and that he had used up all his oxygen. But, without saying a word to his companions for fear it might jeopardize their chances, he tried an old trick he had learnt during his training years ago in the tank at HMS *Dolphin*. He shut his exhaust valve and mouthcock, then, while there was still air in the compartment, he breathed in through his nose and exhaled into the bag, again and again, hoping that the inflated bag would take him to the surface; he might try holding his breath on the way up for as long as he could.

The water level rose in the control room. When the pressure was almost equalized, the three men mounted the control room ladder: Martin, then Kirk, then Abdy. They entered the conning tower. Martin mounted the upper ladder, and while he struggled to open the upper hatch Kirk gulped a last few lungfulls of air. The upper lid opened suddenly. As the sea poured in, Martin let go and escaped without difficulty. Kirk, holding his breath, followed suit. All too soon his breath gave out and he started swallowing mouthfuls of the Mediterranean, but the inflated breathing bag took him upwards. Suddenly he was floundering about on the surface, gasping for air, supported by the DSEA bag.

Seconds later Kirk saw the captain appearing on the surface nearby and then saw Martin. Abdy's ascent had been trouble-free, but something was wrong with Martin. Kirk swam over to him. He must have ascended too fast, for he was dead. His body drifted off in the tidal stream.

Abdy and Kirk kept together while they waited for the engine room party to reach the surface. No one appeared. They alone had survived.

It was now late afternoon. They could see the top of Tripoli's white lighthouse and judged land to be only five miles distant. With heavy hearts they began to swim. After a time they saw an Italian seaplane approaching. They waved and waved, but the aircraft flew off towards the coast and vanished.

The pilot of the seaplane, a Z501 from 145A Squadron, had sighted the two survivors from *P 32*. The aircraft was escorting the convoy which the submarine had been intending to attack, and had seen the explosion. The pilot's official report states:

> The observer sighted a column of water some twenty metres high, and 1,000 metres from the aircraft. The plane closed the

position, then circled for twenty minutes to discover the cause of the explosion: a small stream of air bubbles continued to well on the surface.

The amphibian then landed at Tripoli where the Naval Commander was informed of what had happened.

After refuelling, the aircraft took off for Pisida. But, having left Tripoli, the pilot decided to deviate his course to the scene of the explosion. Once again he approached the position, but now he sighted two survivors who were waving their hands, and *two corpses* in the water [author's italics].

Because the sea state did not allow a safe landing on the spot, the aircraft's observer signalled Naval Command to send out a . . . boat to pick up the survivors. Thus were the commanding officer and petty officer rescued from their submarine.

Soon afterwards, Lieutenant Abdy and Petty Officer Kirk were picked up by the Italians and taken to Tripoli hospital, and the following day they were interrogated. When Kirk discovered that the Italians thought he and his captain were survivors from the submarine that the convoy escorts had been attacking the previous morning, he did not disabuse them; he guessed that they had been attacking *P 33*. No one has ever discovered what had happened to the engine room party, but the Italian report states that Martin's was not the only body on the surface: one man at least had managed to escape from the engine room.

Abdy and Kirk soon found themselves interned in the PoW camp at Tarhuna, where they met survivors from *Cachalot* who had been sunk on 30 July. Later they were shipped back to PoW camps in Italy in the liner *Neptunia,* one of the two troopships that *Upholder* and *Ursula* were stalking at the end of August.

Lieutenant-Commander Abdy, who was promoted before being repatriated in an exchange of prisoners, considered that the mine which sank his submarine might have been an RAF ground mine laid in the swept channel. He was convinced that he had gone deep long enough and far enough to have cleared the minefield, and that when he had started planing upwards he had indeed been in the swept channel. He and Kirk were the only two men to survive from the thirteen *U*s to be lost in the Mediterranean.

It was never ascertained what had become of *P 33,* but the presumption must be that she was caught by the enemy's depth charges, or else she struck a mine. In Malta, all that was known was the fact of her disappearance; like that of *P 32*, her loss was attributed to the enemy's mines. When Lieutenant Hezlet in *Unique* arrived back at Lazaretto, he confirmed that his signal to *P 32* had been acknowledged but that *P 33* had not replied.

Unique herself had had a close shave. Her captain reports that on 20 August she sighted a convoy of troopships making for Tripoli, escorted by six large destroyers, a torpedo boat, two motor torpedo boats and three small sea-planes. 'As usual,' writes Hezlet, the convoy 'broadcast its approach by dropping single depth charges at intervals.' He decided to attack.

> I fired a full bow salvo of four torpedoes at 600 yards at the leading ship of the port column, which was the *Esperia*. We very nearly broke surface; apparently *Unique's* usual captain (Tony Collett) normally took charge of the depth-keeping when firing torpedoes, whereas in most boats this was done by the first lieutenant. We went straight down to sixty feet and increased to full speed to clear the torpedo tracks. Shortly afterwards a destroyer passed right overhead, but dropped no depth-charges: she presumably did not know we were there . . .
>
> During this time we heard what we thought to be three torpedoes hitting and breaking-up noises while *Esperia* sank. Some depth-charges were dropped in counter-attacks, but none were close.
>
> The torpedoes we used were destroyer-type Mark IV, which were all that were available in Malta at the time. We withdrew to the northward, still at sixty feet and in Silent Routine. When sure that all was clear we came to periscope depth: nothing was in sight, so we went deep again to reload the torpedo tubes, which took about an hour and a half.
>
> We then returned to periscope depth and patrolled to the northwards. The water was clear but there were white horses; nevertheless, we patrolled using the 'porpoising' routine, in which the submarine was normally at sixty feet but came up to periscope depth every five minutes to have a look.
>
> We continued thus for some hours, when the OOW (a sub-lieutenant RNVR) reported a small flying boat in the vicinity. Fortunately, I went at once to have a look and was just in time to see the flying boat banking steeply to attack. We went deep

at once and the first bomb exploded as we passed fifty feet. The second bomb, shortly afterwards, was very close indeed, putting out lights, etc.

We stayed deep until after dark and then surfaced. There was a strong smell of fuel and in the moonlight I could see we were leaving a substantial oil track: obviously the bomb had damaged a fuel tank. I therefore sent a radio signal to Malta saying I was returning to base.

When we were docked at Malta, several rivets were found to be loose in an internal [i.e. inside the pressure hull] fuel tank. I also learnt that both the other submarines [P 32 and P33] had been lost and that we were the only survivor of the patrol line. I returned to the spare crew and was later awarded the DSC for this patrol.

So ended August, 1941, a sombre month for Malta's flotilla of Us. Not only were two submarines lost, but only fourteen hits had been made out of twenty-three attacks (and only eight of the hits later proved to have been successful). The aged torpedoes were certainly an element in this lack of success; but a more fundamental truth is that the COs and crews, overworked as they were, had begun to show signs of severe strain.

At this time of low ebb, nine months after the arrival of *Upright,* Malta's *U*-class submarines were at last formally transformed into the Tenth Submarine Flotilla.

Phase II

Birth Of A Flotilla

September, 1941 – April, 1942

10

SEPTEMBER, 1941

The first Tenth Submarine Flotilla had been created at the beginning of the First World War, in December, 1914. Based on HMS *Forth* at Immingham, on the Humber, the flotilla comprised five of the petrol-engined *C*-class submarines and was commanded by Rear-Admiral G. A. Ballard. Later the flotilla's base was moved to HMS *Lucia* on the River Tees, under the command of Captain Martin Nasmith, VC, by which time there were twelve boats of four different classes. After the war, on 3 March, 1919, the Tenth was disbanded and merged with the Seventh Flotilla. Phoenix-like it later rose again, in March, 1940, when it consisted of twelve French boats working out of Harwich until the fall of France.

And now, on 1 September, 1941, a new Tenth Submarine Flotilla had been born. Based at Malta, it would comprise all the *U*-class submarines in the Mediterranean, with periodic additions from other classes of boat. Although Captain (S) 10 (captain of the Tenth Submarine Flotilla) was still answerable to Alexandria, the *U*s now had their own flotilla. Officially now, they also had their own 'depot ship', *Medusa,* the old monitor being used as an oil barge; she was renamed HMS *Talbot,* under the command of Captain George Simpson.

But the changes were little more than formalities. The flotilla had, in effect, been in existence since Simpson and the *U*s arrived in Malta. The pioneers had blazed a trail which now remained unchanged. The Malta submarines still had the same objectives: to harry the enemy all the way from Italy to North Africa; to mine all Rommel's embarkation and discharge ports; to launch commando raids and other special operations to keep the enemy hopping.

Simpson himself made few changes, declining to alter arrangements that had evolved over the past nine months. By custom the White Ensign should now be flying from the battered cross-trees of HMS *Talbot*'s mast, but Simpson would have none of this; it would confirm what the enemy, so far, only suspected: that this was the base from which the submarines sallied forth to attack Rommel's supply lines. Similarly, again by custom, Simpson as a captain was supposed to enter the wardroom mess only by invitation of the Mess President, at this time Lieutenant-Commander Hubert Marsham; but Simpson had continued to mix freely with his wardroom officers after his promotion to captain and he would continue to do so now. He found it useful to know their individual strengths and weaknesses; besides, they were all friends, and the wardroom officers would have been dismayed if he had suddenly distanced himself.

As Captain (S) 10, his plans for September began with a rest period for most of his *U*s; a major operation was being arranged for later in the month and the submarines would then be kept very busy. The operation, codenamed 'Halberd', was another large convoy of supplies and troops to be sailed from Gibraltar: nine ships in all, escorted by no less than two battleships, the carrier *Ark Royal,* five cruisers and eighteen destroyers.

The number of *U*s in the Tenth Flotilla had now risen to eight: the newcomer was *P 34* (Lieutenant P. R. H. Harrison). After the long passage from England, she was in need of the usual maintenance and her crew joined those of the other *U*s in Lazaretto, who were relaxing before the start of Operation 'Halberd'. The only excursion made in early September was *Unique*'s uneventful patrol off Capri. Because of the imminent convoy from Gibraltar, the 'magic carpet' runs were also diminished. *Osiris* and *Otus* made only one trip each from Alexandria with a reduced number of passengers and stores.

The submariners at Malta would have been considerably cheered if they had known how worried the Germans were. On 9 September the head of the German naval staff in Rome, Vice-Admiral Weichold, reported to Berlin:

Now, as formerly, the most dangerous British weapon in the Mediterranean is the submarine, especially those operating from Malta.

In the period covered [11 July – 31 August 1941] there were 36 submarine attacks in the Mediterranean, of which 19 were successful. In spite of improved harbour defences, submarines lurking in or just outside the harbours have sunk or damaged eight ships.

A very severe supply crisis must occur relatively soon. This is because Italian freight space which is sunk cannot be adequately replaced, and also because air transport can never be a complete substitute for sea transport.

A few days later the German naval supremo in Berlin, Admiral Raeder, replied to Weichold that he 'entirely agreed' with these conclusions. Because of the 'increasing deterioration in the sea transport situation and the very grave position in North Africa resulting therefrom', Raeder went on:

The Naval Staff considers it necessary to arrange immediately for the quickest possible transfer of anti-submarine vessels and motor minesweepers to the Mediterranean and the return of German air forces to Sicily. The escort of German and Italian transports to North Africa is a most vital task which must take priority over everything else in the Mediterranean . . . The main objective must be to reinforce our North African position.

And on 13 September Hitler's Headquarters Staff reported to the Führer:

Enemy submarines definitely have the upper hand. German and Italian naval and air forces for patrol and escort duties and for planned anti-submarine measures are inadequate both in numbers and equipment . . . There are constant shipping losses. The numbers of British submarines must be expected to increase and thus the situation will become even more critical.

And the picture for the Germans was not made any rosier by the diminishing oil stocks in Italy. The German invasion of Russia was barely three months old and was using oil at an alarming rate. Supplies from the Romanian wells had dried up. The Italians were already rationed: the Italian fleet alone needed 100,000 tons of fuel a month, though anti–submarine forces had priority.

With his attention still on Russia, Hitler now began to see the oil wells of the Middle East as the answer to his army's needs. Rommel, in Libya (where oil had not yet been discovered), would soon find that greater emphasis was laid on his continuing success. Swiftly the convoys from Italy were stepped up.

Intelligence was reaching Malta that a convoy of fast troopships was about to sail from Taranto. The three liners *Oceania, Neptunia* and *Vulcania* were raising steam in port, already laden with soldiers to join Rommel's Afrika Korps.

At 1430 hours on the afternoon of 17 September Captain Simpson consulted Bob Tanner, his SOO, to plan an immediate response. If the Tenth's submarines could sail within ninety minutes, they might be able to intercept the convoy; it was a slim chance, for the *U*s had a surface speed of barely ten knots, compared to the eighteen knots of the Italian ships, but it was an opportunity worth seizing.

Simpson knew from past experience that the troop convoys tended to follow a direct route across the Mediterranean by keeping well to the east of Malta and setting course for Khoms, fifty-five miles east of Tripoli. He decided to spread his submarines across the convoy's most likely approach to Khoms. Summoning all COs whose submarines were both seaworthy and armed (Wanklyn, Woodward, Wraith, Tomkinson and Hezlet) Simpson explained his plan. The submarines must sail within the hour. He realized they were exhausted and if any of them still felt tired or below top form this was the moment to say so.

Tomkinson asked to be counted out. He voiced doubts over the intelligence reports, which he believed needed more careful evaluation before action was taken. He honestly disliked spontaneous decisions.

Recording this incident in *Periscope View,* Simpson makes it plain that he did not hold Tomkinson's objections against him. On the contrary:

I knew very well that Tomkinson and his *Urge* would be the

first to volunteer if he were feeling rested and relaxed; obviously he was tired and on edge and had the guts to say so. It was just this relationship between myself as a member of the wardroom and a brother officer which was so invaluable to me in assessing the possible . . . The CO's needed to be studied and their idiosyncrasies respected.

By midnight on 17 September the submarines were in their billets: *Upholder* (Wanklyn), *Unbeaten* (Woodward) and *Upright* (Wraith) some sixty miles and 045° off Khoms, with *Ursula* (Hezlet) taking long-stop behind them and closer to shore.

At 0307 on the 18th *Unbeaten* sighted the convoy approaching. Woodward tried in vain to contact Wanklyn by SST, then took twenty-four minutes to clear a W/T report through to *Upright;* finally, after thirty-three minutes, he managed to reach *Upholder* by W/T. By this time *Unbeaten* was behind the convoy and she followed astern of the troopships to pick off any that were damaged.

Within ten minutes of receiving Woodward's report *Upholder* had herself sighted the convoy: 'three large two funnel liners escorted by five or six destroyers' remembers Lieutenant M. L. C. Crawford, Wanklyn's first lieutenant, who afterwards recorded his memories of the patrol. *Upholder*, already surfaced, immediately started her attack:

The gyro compass was out of action and there was a moderate sea running which made it difficult to steer a steady course. By skilful manoeuvring Wanklyn was able to fire his torpedoes as two of these ships overlapped, making a continuous target. The yawing of the submarine caused him to vary the normal sequence of firing. The first torpedo was fired at the bow of the leading ship, but the second torpedo was fired at the stern of the rear ship. The third and fourth torpedoes were spread across the centre of this large target as the submarine swung back. The range at the time was about 5,000 yards. *Upholder* then dived and, after what seemed like hours, at least two and possibly three torpedoes were heard to explode.

As no counter-attack developed, presumably because the escorting ships were busy recovering survivors, Wanklyn surfaced forty-five minutes later to survey the situation. As only one liner was lying stopped with destroyers fussing around her, one was presumed to have sunk. The third had been heard steaming away to the westward and it was hoped that she would be attacked by the other submarines on the patrol line.

It was now a question of finishing off the crippled ship, and so the submarine was dived to reload torpedoes and as daylight broke *Upholder* was closing the liner from up-sun to deliver the *coup de grâce*. Three of the destroyers were circling the ship and, just as Wanklyn was about to fire, one of them forced him to go deep. At this stage *Upholder* was so close to the target that the only solution was to dive under the ship and open out on the other side, turn and fire. This was successfully done and two torpedoes sent her to the bottom. Woodward *(Unbeaten),* who was closing from the other side, was amazed to see his target disappear just as he was going to fire. The two liners were the *Neptunia* and *Oceania* of 19,500 tons each.

The third boat, *Upright,* forging south to gain an attacking position, ran too far and the remaining liner, *Vulcania,* steamed past her to the northward. A *Navigatori* destroyer passed within range, but again Johnny Wraith was baulked: the torpedoes already loaded into his tubes ready for firing were the old Mark IVs, pre-set at a depth-setting of twenty-four feet for the troopships, and once in the tube the setting could not be altered.

According to *Ursula*'s CO, Lieutenant Hezlet, *Vulcania* 'was substantially faster than the other two (twenty-three knots instead of eighteen), so she surprised *Ursula* early'. Not yet realizing that the troopship's speed had been miscalculated, Hezlet's long-range salvo missed astern. It was, as Hezlet said, 'A pity, because the whole convoy would have been destroyed'.

Nevertheless, this joint action, which later became known in the Tenth as 'the Battle of Bottoms Up', had been a splendid success for Simpson and the COs involved. Simpson was characteristically generous in paying tribute to his COs, notably Wanklyn who had sunk two ships without the aid of instruments.

An inevitable consequence of the sinking of the two troop-transports was that many lives were lost: in his book Simpson put the number at 5,000. Many more, according to Wanklyn, were saved by the escorts; if it had not been for the pre-set Mark IV torpedoes, the escorts themselves might have been sunk. 'I thought about this quite a lot,' wrote Simpson later; 'I knew that to be merciful was something we were in no position to afford.' He was not naturally a ruthless man, but neither did he fudge the issue. Following another occasion when one of his submarines sank a cruiser, but then withdrew while escorting destroyers rescued the survivors, Simpson wrote:

> I thought this quite wrong . . . To me, it seemed that fully viable ships of war must be sunk under any conditions, and the troops on board them who were shortly to confront our own army must be drowned, because casualties largely decided the war militarily, so this was our duty.

War was a 'a foul business', but the sooner the enemy was destroyed the sooner the nightmare would be ended.

On the same day that the submarine pack closed in on the convoy, 17 September, 1941, Admiral Cunningham signalled to the Admiralty: 'Every submarine that can be spared is worth its weight in gold.'

Operation 'Halberd' began on 24 September, when the convoy of supplies left Gibraltar with its escort of a much augmented Force H. By now the submarines from Malta had been in position for two days, patrolling the Italian and Sicilian coastlines to keep watch on the enemy's movements. *Utmost* had been on passage for a special operation when she received word that the surviving liner from the enemy troop convoy, *Vulcania*, after landing her troops in Tripoli, was heading back to Italy. Although *Utmost* sighted the liner, *Vulcania* was at extreme range and Cayley had to watch her sailing safely off to Naples. His frustration was compounded when the two demolition sorties made by his commando party ended in failure.

The 'Halberd' convoy made good progress until the 27th when enemy aircraft found it and began to attack. Despite valiant attempts by fighters flown off from the *Ark Royal* the battleship *Nelson* was hit which reduced her speed. One transport, too, was hit and later sank, though not until her troops had safely been transferred to another ship. By now the convoy had reached the

Narrows and there was not much further to go. Aircraft from Malta arrived to give added air cover, and early on the 28th the triumphant convoy entered Grand Harbour to enthusiastic cheers from crowds of onlookers.

The submarines returned to base on 2 October, only *Upright* having had any opportunities to attack. She was in the billet north of the Strait of Messina on 27 September, when she heard a 'series of grunts and tappings' according to Jack Michell, her fourth hand and torpedo officer:

> These were followed by the prompt appearance of a *Generale*-class, three-funnelled torpedo boat. She started circling us, obviously trying to pinpoint our position. She steamed past our bows the first time and Johnny [Wraith] started the attack. We got One and Two tubes ready. Without altering course, at Slow Group Down [i.e. low speed] he fired two torpedoes as the torpedo boat came past for the second time. One torpedo hit. She sank. QED.

By the sinking of this torpedo boat, *Albatros, Upright* had avenged the loss of *Phoenix,* the submarine sunk by *Albatros* on 17 July, 1940.

Once again, army Intelligence had approached Captain (S) 10 to ask for a submarine for a specific operation. Last April *Utmost* had landed a Tunisian spy near Castellammares in western Sicily; now he had found his way to the west coast of Calabria and he needed money, fresh orders and new codes. This persuasive army Intelligence Officer, a major, persisted with his request. At first Simpson refused; why could not an RAF Hurricane do the job? But many were the reasons put forward until, reluctantly, Simpson gave in. He summoned Lieutenant Tomkinson and warned him of the danger of treachery, advising him to take particular care. The vital bag was to be handed over to the spy by Sub-Lieutenant B. N. T. Lloyd, one of the spare crew in Lazaretto, who would paddle ashore in a Folbot, guided by a blue light shone by the spy from a protected cove. The rendezvous was arranged for 0200 on the morning of 30 September; if that failed, the submarine would make a second attempt on the following night at the same time.

On the appointed night *Urge* entered the Gulf of Gioia and surfaced cautiously a mile offshore. Shortly before 0200 her asdic picked up fast-running HE − the propeller noises of an E-boat. An Italian MAS craft swept into the bay, stopped, listened for thirty minutes, then started up and headed out again at speed.

Tomkinson was convinced that the E-boat had been expecting to find a submarine in the bay. But he was not sure about the agent. Had the man they were trying to help betrayed them? The Intelligence Officer had been so certain the man was genuine. Tomkinson decided to send the sub-lieutenant ashore on the next night to find out.

In the early hours of 1 October, as arranged, Sub-Lieutenant Lloyd duly clambered into his Folbot and paddled off in the dark ness, watched through binoculars by Tomkinson. The canoe had barely entered the cove when a hail of bullets erupted from the shore. Lloyd was mown down before Tomkinson's eyes. Grimly, he gave orders to retire to seaward. *Urge* continued with her patrol, including an ineffective bombardment of the railway lines, before returning to Malta on 6 October.

It was later established that the Italians had captured incriminating material, and that the Tunisian spy was a double agent.

Simpson notes in his book that he got 'a well-earned reprimand from Admiral Horton' for selecting young Sub-Lieutenant Lloyd for this mission. Horton told Simpson, 'You have commando troops provided for this type of work, so use them.'

It was a distressing end to the first month in the life of the Tenth Submarine Flotilla.

11

OCTOBER/NOVEMBER, 1941

October, 1941, opened with the arrival of two new *U*-class submarines in Malta: *Sokol* (Lieutenant-Commander Boris Karnicki) and *P 31* (Lieutenant J. B. Kershaw) which thus brought the Tenth Flotilla's strength up to ten.

Sokol (the Polish word for 'Falcon') had been commissioned in January, 1941, as *Urchin,* but was then handed over to the Poles. Lieutenant George Taylor, RNVR, joined her in Malta as liaison officer. She would work alongside the British submarines, sharing their patrols, their duties and responsibilities, answerable to Captain(S)10 and in every respect like his other *U*s except that her captain and her crew were Polish. Hence the need for a British liaison officer.

Boris Karnicki had been first lieutenant in the submarine *Wilk* when she escaped from Poland after the German invasion. He later became her CO and carried out several patrols in the North Sea, during one of which he rammed a German U-boat. Taylor reports:

> The U-boat sank, but *Wilk* was so badly twisted that she was condemned to become a training boat. *Wilk's* ship's company then manned *Sokol* for her first commission. Boris Karnicki was appointed to command her and . . . Lieutenant-Commander Boleslaw Romanowski was his first lieutenant.

Sokol's first liaison officer was Lieutenant B. J. B. Andrew, then 'Geordie' Hunt, to be succeeded later by 'Pablo',★ and later still

---

★ The author has been unable to trace the identity of this officer.

by Lieutenant Godfrey Place before George Taylor joined her.

Place recalls that *Sokol's* CO had smoothed over the minor political problem 'that Poland had never declared war on Italy, or vice versa', to his own satisfaction, at least:

> 'When we had passed Gibraltar,' he reported later to Captain(S), 'we were submerged one morning and all was quiet. I summoned my ship's company into the control room. Then I announced very distinctly: "I, Boris Karnicki, commanding ORP *Sokol*, declare war on you, Benito Mussolini." So everything is in order.'
>
> 'I'm sure,' replied Captain(S) 10, 'that your government will take over details like the declaration of war.'
>
> 'They've not done so yet, sir,' Boris answered. 'Both countries being Roman Catholic, we have always been friends with Italy. So I have avoided any rudeness.'

The Polish crew had not all been submariners originally; as Place points out, some had come from surface ships, while others 'had been brought up in France and been in the Polish brigade in the French army, finally escaping to England on the fall of France in 1940.' Place also makes the point that

> Boris was determined that his boat should be considered just like any other British boat and that no one in Malta, Alexandria or London should consider a soft option for him.

And so *Sokol* was duly sent on patrol on 9 October, only nine days after arriving in Malta. It turned out to be a blank sortie, off the east coast of Tunisia, but on the 23rd she would set off on a second and much more eventful patrol.

At the beginning of October *Urge* and *Utmost* were both in the area of the Pelagie islands, *Urge* was patrolling off Lampione when she sighted the *Maria Pompei* (1,407 tons). Tomkinson fired a torpedo, which missed, but, on seeing the torpedo's track, the ship's crew abandoned their vessel and transferred to an escorting schooner. Tomkinson then sank his prey with another torpedo. On the evening of the same day he found another, larger victim: *Marigola* (5,996 tons). One torpedo sent her to the bottom,

·though, as she was in the shallows, she remained partly above water.

Utmost, under the command of Lieutenant J. D. Martin who was giving Dick Cayley a rest, was unaware of *Urge's* efforts and persisted in trying to sink *Marigola* by gunfire. That night she opened fire at a range of 400 yards. The fifty rounds of SAP (semi-armour-piercing) shells and high explosive were visible to the horizon. But the *Marigola,* blazing fiercely, remained obstinately where she had settled.

On the 17th *Ursula,* still with Arthur Hezlet standing in for 'Black' Mackenzie, sailed for a demolition raid in Calabria, but was diverted on passage to a billet off Lampedusa. A convoy from Naples had been reported sneaking round the west coast of Sicily and was making a dash southwards towards Tripoli. *Ursula's* new orders were to intercept this convoy. As Hezlet records,

> We ran at full speed all night and sighted the convoy after daylight. We were a very long way off and ran in at full speed submerged. Eventually we fired at long range, obtaining a hit on one ship; unfortunately she was only damaged and was towed into Tripoli.

That ship was the *Beppe* (4,859 tons). She was later repaired, but, a year later, was sunk by *Unbending* (Lieutenant E. T. Stanley — see page 222). Hezlet continues:

> Five days later, on 22 October, we tried to destroy a railway bridge on the coast of Italy, north of Cape Spartivento at Cape Bruzzano. We surfaced half a mile from the shore and opened fire with our 2-pdr gun. We hit the bridge a number of times, but each shell only removed a small quantity of the brickwork. We had cut through about a third of the thickness when an armoured car and a number of soldiers arrived. We shifted target to the armoured car, but one of the soldiers firing his rifle at long range began to get a bit close. At that point an aircraft arrived, so we had to dive and withdraw.

This patrol was *Ursula's* last before leaving for home, where she was due for a refit. With her, 'as first lieutenant to "Baldy" Hezlet', went Lieutenant Ian McGeoch, who had been seriously ill in

Im Tarfa hospital with an ulcer and then double pneumonia. He volunteered to return home because he felt that he had to 'go back to square one and get some more attacking practice in', he wrote later. After another spell in hospital he 're-qualified, informally, with the help of "Boggie" Bone who was running the perisher'. Thereafter he would return to the Mediterranean, in 1943, as CO of *P 228 (Splendid)*.

Another submarine sailing home for a refit at the end of October was *Rorqual* (Lieutenant Lennox Napier). A mine-laying submarine, she had completed sixteen very successful months of operational patrol in the Mediterranean; her mines had sunk six supply ships, a total of 16,455 tons. She had also sunk two torpedo boats and the Italian U-boat *Capponi* and in addition she had made two 'magic carpet' runs most of the time on short rations herself. Her crew certainly deserved a spell at home. During the summer of 1940, she spent 93 days out of 125 on patrol. Her place as mine-layer was taken by the newly arrived *Porpoise* (Lieutenant-Commander E. F. Pizey), who reached Malta with a precious cargo of high-octane petrol for the RAF's Hurricanes. *Porpoise* was the first submarine with purpose-built tanks to carry fuel supplies; a vast improvement on the four-gallon tins which, stowed in the casing, were often crushed when a submarine dived, so that the fuel leaked out and began to produce a tell-tale slick on the surface.

On 23 October, *Sokol* sailed from Malta on her second patrol, to the northern billet in and around the Gulf of Naples. This area was often busy with supply ships assembling in convoys before sailing southward, and, for protection, the Italians had laid dense minefields. The Italian mine defences were constantly being augmented by the Germans, particularly around the Sicilian coast. It may have been one of their mines that gave *Upright* a scare on the same day that *Sokol* left Lazarertto. Johnny Wraith was attempting to close the shore off Cape San Vito when 'two heavy bumps' were felt, followed by 'a loud scraping noise down the ship's side'. Although nothing was seen through the periscope, *Upright* altered course to the northward and continued with renewed caution.

By contrast, the first real threat that *Sokol* faced was shortage of rations.

According to Godfrey Place, *Sokol's* 'first success was a sizeable escorted cargo vessel, the *Citta di Palermo* (5,413 tons), followed by a couple of hours' counter-attack, noisily nowhere near.' The rest of the patrol was quiet, and the boat was about to return to base when word was received that a convoy might be heading her way; she was therefore ordered to extend her patrol. There was one problem, however; the Poles had nearly finished their rations. As Place explains, when the submarines left base they 'normally took three weeks' provisions with a further three weeks' emergency provisions'. This was more than enough for most patrols, which were often cut short when the boat returned to Malta to reload. But *Sokol's* ship's company had instituted an eight-meals-a-day routine.

In some submarines, particularly when patrols were expected to last longer than ten days, the daily routine was turned upside down: 'night-time' for the crew was during the hours of daylight, when the boat was submerged, while their 'day' lasted as long as darkness. They would thus expect breakfast at dusk, with other meals following accordingly. As Godfrey Place puts it: 'Not so the Poles. They had the best of both worlds, with eight meals a day.'

Sokol did not encounter the promised convoy and by the time she was on her way back to base the emergency rations were running very low. Then one night she sighted 'an unescorted merchant ship':

> It was deemed worth no more than two torpedoes, which produced the classic miss: too wide a spread — one in front and one behind. The ship's crew evidently saw the tracks and took to the boats, leaving the ship stopped. *Sokol* had only one torpedo left . . . but, despite a carefully aimed shot, this had a gyro failure: the track could be watched curving gently to starboard until out of sight in the darkness.
>
> So the ship was sunk by gunfire. She was in ballast and everyone was surprised to find how many shells were needed to sink an empty ship; it took all *Sokol's* ammunition outfit.
>
> South of Sicily, shortly before dawn on the way home, *Sokol* saw an Italian U-boat at 2,000 yards on the surface. 'We could do no more than just watch her go by,' Karnicki remarked. 'If I had even a loaf of bread, I'd chuck it at her.'

By this time, Place writes, 'The wardroom had been dicing for the largest piece of biscuit and there was no tinned meat left of any sort.' *Sokol,* having started her score card, continued her patrols with daring and success. When she returned to base there was a surprise awaiting the Poles.

> Proudly flying her Jolly Roger, with two new white bars stitched on to it, *Sokol* had entered harbour at 11.30 on 3 November. As she swung to starboard to come alongside the Wardroom Berth, Commander Boris Karnicki and his Polish company glanced upwards at the welcoming party grouped along the balcony. Standing next to Captain Simpson was a high-ranking officer whom they did not at first recognize, returning their salute.
>
> General Sikorski, their Polish Prime Minister and Commander-in-Chief, had flown in that morning unannounced to visit his compatriots.
>
> On the next day, at a quiet ceremony in the base attended only by the Polish submariners, General Sikorski removed his *Virtuti Militari* medal and pinned it on Boris Karnicki's chest. It was a moving moment.

The Polish CO was 'a much respected and popular officer in the wardroom at Lazaretto', Place writes, and 'the company of his junior officers was also greatly enjoyed'. But very few of the ratings spoke enough English to be able to mix with the other crews and, although none of them showed signs of self-pity, their lot was particularly difficult:

> The loneliness of a sailor fighting in a foreign war with no possible contact with his home was poignantly apparent in the signalled report of one killed in an air raid on Malta. The dull, standard format became tragically meaningful: 'No known next of kin.'

General Sikorski was not the only surprise visitor in Malta that month. Admiral Sir Max Horton, Flag Officer Submarines, was on a round of visits to all his submariners in the Mediterranean; he had already seen the Eighth Flotilla in Gibraltar and after Malta he would call on the First Flotilla at Alexandria.

Simpson, forewarned of the two-day visit, had arranged for as many as possible of his boats to be in harbour so that FOS could meet their crews; only *Unique* and the new boy, *P 31,* were away on patrol. As well as the other eight *U*'s, FOS also saw *Trusty* (Lieutenant-Commander W. D. A. King), *Thrasher* (Lieutenant H. S. Mackenzie),* *Perseus* (Lieutenant-Commander E. C. F. Nicolay) and, shortly before she left for home, *Rorqual* (Lieutenant Napier). Inspecting the Lazaretto base of the new Tenth Flotilla, he declared himself impressed by the half-finished excavations; he talked with all the submarine COs and listened to their grievances (such as the repeated gyro failures on torpedoes). He promised to do what he could to remedy the faults and spread confidence among the submariners that, when back in London, he would take immediate action. Then, addressing the assembled companies in the base, FOS delivered a personal message of appreciation and encouragement from the Prime Minister. He added his own thanks, which, coming from a man of his renown and submarine experience, lifted the hearts of all.

Sir Max also discussed quietly with Captain Simpson what could be done to ease the strain on the crews. As a result of these discussions, arrangements were made to limit a man's service to one year away from home, though this must depend on the rate of submarine construction. It was an important psychological move: a man now had a definite date to look forward to and knew that his time away would not extend into the vague future. Known as a loner, Sir Max spurned naval tradition by inviting publicity for our submarines, subject to security. Six weeks after his departure, Commander Anthony Kimmins arrived in Malta and went on patrol with *Upholder;* the result was a memorable series of broadcasts for the BBC. Furthermore, remembering his own experiences during the Great War, Sir Max insisted that awards of decoration for gallantry must be immediate: with losses running high, posthumous awards afforded precious little satisfaction.

Some disquieting news reached Malta at about the time of Sir Max's visit. Six German U-boats were now operating in the

---

* As Vice-Admiral Sir Hugh Mackenzie, KCB, DSO*, DSC, he became the architect of the Royal Navy's nuclear-powered submarine fleet: HMS *Dreadnought*, the first British 'nuke' to be built, was commissioned in 1963.

Mediterranean, after, one night, forcing the British-controlled Strait of Gibraltar. This did not bode well for future supply convoys to Malta, or for Cunningham's fleet.

One reason for the U-boats' arrival was that the Germans were increasingly concerned about their losses in the Mediterranean. In this one month alone, October, 1941, Axis tonnage sunk (18,800 tons) exceeded that which was delivered (18,400 tons). But the main reason for the U-boats' presence, which the British did not yet know, was that Berlin was planning a major offensive in the Mediterranean during November. Many more U-boats were already on their way; by the end of the year a total of twenty-eight would have been dispatched to these waters. Three were quickly sunk and another three were damaged and had to return to their Atlantic bases. As the German chiefs of staff soon realized, their submariners strongly disliked operating in the Mediterranean conditions; they felt caught in a trap.

Coincidentally, too, the British were planning a naval offensive in November. A small squadron called Force K had arrived at Malta on Trafalgar Day, 21 October, comprising the light cruisers *Aurora* (Captain W. G. Agnew) and *Penelope* (Captain A. D. Nicholl) and two destroyers, *Lance* and *Lively*, from Force H at Gibraltar. In the words of Lieutenant Donald McEwen, the navigating officer of *Aurora*, who 'saw all of that ship's battles from the bridge (and drafted all the reports afterwards!)', Force K was intended 'as a striking force to interfere with Axis shipping between Italy and North Africa', and her first strike was not long in coming.

Not only was there a naval offensive in the wings, but a major land offensive too. The Eighth Army, under its Commander-in-Chief, General Auchinleck, was planning to relieve Tobruk and push the Afrika Korps back westwards. Codenamed 'Crusader', this operation was due to start on 18 November, led by General Alan Cunningham, brother of 'ABC', as the Admiral was known to his navy.

But first Force K would go into action, backed up by the Malta submarines. 'Because of the overwhelming air superiority of the Axis, Force K could only operate safely at night, and would sortie at dusk,' writes Lieutenant Donald McEwen in *Aurora*, 'with the intention of returning to be under the air umbrella of Malta by first light.' The first skirmish took place on the night of 8 November, following reports of a large convoy sailing south from Cape Spartivento.

Simpson had disposed six of his submarines in two fixed patrol lines, one across the coastal corridor between Benghazi and Tripoli, the other astride the enemy's usual route south from Calabria. Well before the appointed time, the Us were in position: *Unique, Ursula* and *Unbeaten* in the coastal corridor; *Urge, Upholder* and the new boy, Lieutenant Harrison in *P 34*, in mid-Mediterranean. *Upholder* was the only submarine to see any profit for her labours.

Early on the morning of the 8th *Upholder* was on passage to her billet when an Italian U-boat was sighted; Wanklyn decided to make a dived attack and fired four torpedoes. He thought that he had obtained a hit, but Italian records show that the *Perla*-class submarine managed to return to base. That night *Upholder* surfaced to watch Force K in action. Captain Agnew and his ships had intercepted the convoy at 0040, during the Middle Watch, and according to 'Tubby' Crawford, *Upholder*'s first lieutenant, 'They laid on a magnificent firework display.'

McEwen in *Aurora* writes of the night action:

> The devastation caused was fantastic, despite the presence of two Italian heavy cruisers and an escort of about six destroyers. All nine of the merchant ships were left sinking and blazing wrecks, and two destroyers sunk.
>
> As we left the scene of the action at about 0140, we sighted from the bridge of *Aurora* a small light winking from the water, close to our track. This was the submarine *Upholder*, commanded by Lieutenant-Commander Wanklyn, who had witnessed the whole of our battle.

Upholder was flashing her Aldis lamp in order to help Force K home in on two of the surviving destroyers which were too fast for the submarine. The following morning Wanklyn moved in on the remnants of the feast and 'picked off' another destroyer, the 1,449-ton *Libeccio*, with a single well-aimed torpedo, remembers Crawford. And still Wanklyn had not finished:

Later that forenoon, a force of two *Trento*-cruisers and four destroyers were sighted. They had probably been sent to see what they could salvage from the previous night's scrap. Wanklyn managed to get in a long-range attack with his three remaining torpedoes but the centre torpedo ran wild. The other two torpedoes just missed ahead and astern of the cruiser, but one torpedo damaged one of the escorting destroyers.

Upholder now being out of torpedoes, she returned to base on 11 November, after a patrol of only four days and a score of one destroyer sunk, another destroyer damaged and a U-boat possibly sunk.

Force K returned to Malta during the early afternoon of the 9th, having dealt the enemy a severe blow: a whole convoy had been wiped out, and a large one at that. On the following day Rommel complained bitterly that out of the 60,000 troops he had been promised, only 8,093 had arrived.

Morale in Malta was high. Not only had the island acquired her own aggressive force of surface ships, but her air defences were rapidly being reinforced. In mid-October Admiral Somerville's *Ark Royal* had flown in more Blenheim bombers, and now, on 10 November, he sent the carrier to deliver more: thirty seven Hurricanes and seven Blenheims, all of which touched down safely on Maltese soil.

But the great carrier never returned to Gibraltar. On 13 November, 1941, she was attacked by a German U-boat, received one torpedo amidships and sank the following day.

The loss of *Ark Royal* was catastrophic. Cunningham no longer had an aircraft carrier at his disposal. *Illustrious* and *Formidable* were both in the United States, undergoing major repairs (this was the happy result of an agreement signed between London and Washington back in April), and the brand new *Indomitable* had gone aground off Jamaica while working up for her commission in the Mediterranean.

Nor was this the only blow in November: the month had begun with the tragic loss of *Tetrarch* (Lieutenant-Commander G. G. Greenway). She had been returning home for a refit and was due to call in at Gibraltar on 2 November, but never arrived; she is presumed to have struck a mine in the Sicilian Channel.

Her captain, George Greenway, had been in com mand for only three months, having taken over from Lieutenant-Commander R. M. Peacock who himself had taken over from Ronnie Mills in January.

At dawn on 18 November the long-awaited Eighth Army offensive began, taking Rommel completely by surprise. With inferior tanks and guns, the British troops made determined progress against a much stronger adversary. But suddenly, on 24 November, Rommel struck back and General Cunningham's offensive ground to a halt.

On the same day, the 24th, Force K sallied forth from Malta to tackle another important convoy, which was taking fuel from Greece to Benghazi, and sank two ships. This second success, so soon after the first, was rewarded by reinforcements in the form of Force B, under Rear-Admiral H. B. Rawlings, comprising five light cruisers: *Ajax, Neptune, Naiad, Euryalus* and *Galatea*.

One day later Admiral Cunningham suffered a serious blow when his battleship *Barham* was sunk by a U-boat. 861 officers and men perished, many of the survivors suffering shocking injuries while sliding down the capsized hull. *Barham* had not been in dock for over six months and her barnacles were of horrific size.

Admiral Cunningham's aims, during the land offensive, were twofold: to support the army by taking troops, ammunition and other supplies into Tobruk, where it was hoped that the besieged garrison would soon be relieved; and to divert the enemy's sea and air forces, while continuing to prevent the flow of his supplies. This latter task was now divided between Malta's submarines and surface ships. Their success to date was reflected in the reduced number of convoys that the enemy was attempting to sail, and in the proportion that was sunk: out of 37,000 tons sailed in November, 26,000 tons were sunk and another 2,600 tons damaged. But, because there were fewer convoys, there were fewer targets for Malta's Tenth Submarine Flotilla.

On 21 November *Utmost* was patrolling the Strait of Messina when Cayley received word that a northbound convoy might be coming his way. Having noted an increase in anti-submarine activity, and with his batteries fully charged, Cayley decided not to start up his generators when on the surface that night. Instead, *Utmost* surfaced in silence and lingered in the dark on her main electric motors, listening hard on asdics. Her wait was rewarded at 2300 when HE was detected. As he closed on the bearing, Cayley sighted three cruisers and three destroyers. He fired a salvo and his first torpedo struck home with a flash that lit up the night. He had hit the *Duca d'Abruzzi* (7,874 tons). Although she limped into Taranto, the cruiser had been severely damaged and would take months to repair. *Utmost*, having retired before the heat started, continued with her patrol but returned to base on the 27th without further sightings.

A few days earlier, *Sokol* had been patrolling off the Greek island of Zante, at the entrance to the Gulf of Corinth, when she received reports that a small escorted convoy of ships had taken refuge in Navarin Bay. According to Godfrey Place, *Sokol* was ordered to enter the bay and launch an attack: there were no nets or booms, she was told. Boris Karnicki made a cautious investigation and decided the attack might be possible. He summoned the crew and told them that he had seen no sign of the buoys that would be supporting nets or booms:

> He was very good at keeping everyone informed, speaking in Polish and French and, for the benefit of the liaison officer, English as well. He had barely finished speaking when wires could be heard grating on the hull. The mine-warning lamps flashed red and two or three small explosions made a tinkly noise.

Sokol had, after all, run into anti-submarine nets. Her after-planes had been damaged and the stern was rising, so Karnicki ordered all spare hands to go aft while he attempted to recover trim. A moment later the boat broke surface, and then, going full astern with a huge bow-down angle, began a steep descent. Karnicki ordered all spare hands to go for'ard. As Place comments, 'Planesmen don't get much practice while going astern at speed and man movement does not lead to fine accuracy in trimming.' *Sokol*'s rearward progress was marked by huge ungainly dips and jumps, with her depth varying wildly 'between 50 and 150 feet' before Karnicki managed to regain trim. As Place adds,

It was cheeky, perhaps, to return later and to fire the torpedoes set shallow to pass over the net. The range was extreme and, although explosions were heard, the result could not be seen. Following this incident, despite a flooded periscope, *Sokol* stayed on patrol and carried out three further attacks, but the hits she claimed were not confirmed.

At the end of the month, two *U*s were joined by *Thrasher* (Lieutenant H. S. 'Rufus' Mackenzie) from Alexandria to form a patrol line across the enemy's convoy route to Benghazi. *Upholder*, south of the Calabrian coast, sighted a small convoy on the 27th, but her attack was not successful. On the 29th *P 31* attacked three southbound cruisers, who on their return northwards came under renewed attack, this time from *Upholder*. Both attacks were unsuccessful. The *U*s then returned to base, their place taken by *P 34*. She patrolled off Calabria until 6 December, damaging an unescorted supply ship. *Thrasher* returned to Alexandria on 7 December, having had an uneventful patrol.

And so November ended with mixed results on both land and sea. Although the Eighth Army had forced Rommel on to the defensive, Tobruk was not yet relieved. The Mediterranean Fleet would have to continue its work running supplies from Alexandria, while the submarines and surface ships in Malta concentrated on the enemy's convoys. But Hitler was worried: he had at last begun to recognize the threat that the island forces posed to his ambitions in the Mediterranean. Stung by our offensives, he had transferred Kesselring's Fliegerkorps back to Sicily from the ice-bound Russian front: the relentless bombing of Malta began again, more than doubling from November (seventy-six raids) to December (169 raids). The smell of invasion was in the air.

12

Although there were many in Rome and Berlin who now considered that the threat of Malta could be suppressed only by invasion, Hitler paid no heed. In his view, the Luftwaffe would remove the island's offensive potential by reducing Malta to rubble. On 5 December he ordered Kesselring's Fliegerkorps to annihilate the fortress isle. But his advisers were already beginning to make tentative plans for a combined assault by seaborne and airborne troops (codenamed 'Hercules') to take place in the spring of 1942. Once the Fliegerkorps had done its work, 'Hercules' could proceed.

In Malta the expectation of invasion continued and precautions were stepped up. Security up till now had been somewhat fallible, as Dudley Norman remembers. One night he and Hubert Marsham were passing St. George's Barracks en route to the Sliema Club when they were challenged by a Maltese sentry:

> 'Halt, who goes there?'
> We replied 'Friend,' and waited for the invitation to proceed.
> After some delay we asked if we could come forward.
> 'No speak English,' the sentry replied.
> We retired quietly and went to the club by a different route.

The island's coastal patrols were increased and security tightened, especially in the vicinity of naval and military installations.

But the ordinary people of Malta were too preoccupied with their own survival to worry about enemy troops jumping out of the sky. In addition to deepening food shortages, fuel shortages, which had been acutely felt during this unusually cold winter, and rationing of all kinds providing a challenge to their ingenuity, they now had to survive the renewed onslaught of the German bombers.

The news from Pearl Harbor that Japanese torpedo-bombers had attacked the American fleet, without provocation, on 7 December, was as yet irrelevant to those in the Mediterranean, even though it meant that the United States now entered the war; much more immediate was the news that those two great ships, *Prince of Wales* and *Repulse,* had been sunk by the Japanese off Malaya on the 10th. Fortunately the effect on morale was relieved somewhat by successes nearer home.

On the first day of the month, Force K had made its third effective strike by sinking, first, an ammunition and supply ship and then, later the same morning, a tanker carrying both oil and troops. The tanker's destroyer escort fought valiantly but was blown out of the water before the tanker went up in flames. Further good news came from Tobruk, relieved at last, on 8 December.

Meanwhile, Malta's submarine flotilla was earning its nickname of 'The Fighting Tenth'. At the beginning of December four of the Us had been dispatched to the southern approaches to the Strait of Messina, but found little to interest them there. After a few days three of them moved on, leaving only *Unique,* backed up on 10 December by *Urge.* 'Tommo' Tomkinson, captain of *Urge,* had written home to his mother on 28 November: 'We've had a quieter time of late, but much the same amount of seagoing'. Almost enviously he mentioned 'this Libyan business' and added, 'I shall be hopping mad if they [the army] don't polish them off after all we've had to put up with.' A month later he would be writing a much more cheerful letter to his mother.

The three Us that had left *Unique* behind, *Upright, Utmost* and *Unbeaten,* had moved to a patrol line outside Taranto, the major Italian naval base. On 12 December they received orders to close in on the harbour. That evening *Unbeaten* surfaced and edged towards the harbour entrance. In the dark the lookout suddenly reported a strange red light flashing on and off irregularly. Very cautiously Teddy Woodward took *Unbeaten* towards the light, all tubes at the ready. Then, as the bridge team peered upwards, they saw the dull red glow lighting up the face of an Italian sentry: he was dragging at his cigarette while pacing the end of the breakwater. *Unbeaten* withdrew, but suffered considerable annoyance from intensive anti-submarine reaction by the enemy.

Later that evening *Utmost* attacked the leading half of a convoy; she claimed a hit on a 5,000-ton ship, and although no sinking was confirmed, she did have a witness to the hit — *Upright*, whose third hand and navigator, Jack Michell, later reported hearing 'the unmistakable "clang" of a torpedo hit to the south'. *Upright* herself now sighted the convoy just after midnight. 'Johnny Wraith was on the bridge and told us it was a convoy of two large transports steering north with destroyer escort,' Michell writes. At 0207 on the morning of the 13th, Wraith fired four torpedoes, then dived *Upright* and took the usual avoiding action:

> After the correct running time, we heard three 'clangs' from the hits on the leading troopship; and then, after a longer interval, a fourth 'clang' on the second troopship. We heard the breaking-up noises of the first ship ... and the second ship sank three minutes later. They proved to be the *Fabio Filzi* and *Carlo del Greco*, both new ships of 6,835 tons on their maiden voyage.
>
> We were depth-charged for eight hours at varying intensities, tailing away after seven hours. Johnny Wraith opened a tin of asparagus in celebration. We stayed dived all next day and when we surfaced at 1900 we were panting like tired dogs.
>
> I was asleep in the wardroom that same night when, at about 2100, the klaxons sounded. I rushed to the control room and Johnny Wraith tumbled down the ladder and said: 'Destroyer coming at us, 30 knots. Shut off for depth-charging.'
>
> What we did not know was that a stoker had pumped out the engine room bilges without telling anyone. Therefore we were light aft and with main vents open and both planes hard-a-dive and motors half ahead group up, we careered along with our stern on the surface and a bow-down angle of about 20°. The periscope standards must have been making a fine bow wave. Johnny said to 'Shaver' Swanston: 'Number One, get her down for God's sake...'
>
> Shaver was flooding X, O and M when the noise of an express train came thundering over our fore-casing with a swishing of propellers at high speed. There was a series of clicks, the sound of depth-charge detonators springing home. The Coxswain said to Johnny: 'Full pattern, sir.' All eyes in the

control room were looking upwards as about twenty depth charges, probably set to ten metres, exploded with an enormous detonation under us and around us. The boat was flung about like a leaf. The lights went out and the emergency lights came on, cork showered down on us, glass and crockery broke, the two shallow depth-gauges went off the board and their front glasses shattered, leaks were reported by the fore hatch and engine room muffler valves.

We then sank like a stone, due to the aeration of the sea from the depth-charge explosions . . . We blew No 1 and No 6 Main Ballast as we passed 100 feet and finally stopped at just above 300 feet. We started rising, with an audible sigh of relief from all aboard. We caught a trim at sixty feet, just as the destroyer passed directly above us again, and a second full pattern of depth charges came down on us. There was another almighty explosion ... and a noise like a pistol shot from aft, from a main motor fuse blowing.

The total damage was: shallow gauges 'kaput'; wireless telegraphy completely smashed; asdics smashed; batteries broken; and the side-plating of the pressure hull was corrugated.

Thank God, the destroyer thought that we had been sunk and sailed back to Taranto signalling to that effect. Shrimp Simpson signalled us three times and as we could not reply we were considered lost. We stayed in Taranto Bay for the remaining three days until the end of our patrol as we did not want to return unheralded with no W/T. When we did return, Shrimp and all Lazaretto were very surprised to see us, as they were about to report us to the Flag Officer Submarines at Northways as lost.

Later it was realized that the enemy had used D/F (Direction Finding) to pinpoint *Upright's* position – a sinister development in anti-submarine measures which the Germans were now teaching the Italians.

Jack Michell finishes his story by noting that Simpson naturally asked Wraith how the attack had gone: '"They simply committed suicide, sir," Johnny replied. "Just ran into my torpedoes."'

It was 0840 on 14 December, 1941. The wind was north-west force 3 with a few white horses. Through *Urge's* periscope, Tomkinson sighted the enemy battle fleet – a squadron of two battleships with twelve destroyers and torpedo boats.

The magnificent battleships were the pride of the Italian fleet — modern, fast and well-armed. *Littorio* (in the van) and *Vittorio Veneto* were thirteen miles from Cape dell'Armi and were heading north through the Strait of Messina. Zigzagging at twenty knots, they were surrounded by a close screen of escorting ships, with two aircraft patrolling overhead. *Littorio* was just altering course when *Urge's* torpedo struck the *Vittorio Veneto*.

The CO of *Clio*, one of the accompanying torpedo boats, explained later that neither the submarine's periscope nor her torpedo tracks had been sighted because the tracks were exactly 'up-sun' and the slight sea disguised the 'feather' of the periscope. By the time *Clio* and the aircraft had started the hunt, *Urge* was safely clear.

Tomkinson's hit put the 35,000-ton battleship out of action for the next few months. This triumph was recognized with several awards to *Urge's* officers and men; and to Tommo himself, who already had a DSO and Bar. He was honoured with what he himself described as 'a most unusual thing' — two years' seniority. Simpson must have recommended him a second bar to his DSO, which would have given him three DSOs, but evidently Tomkinson was pleased with this alternative for he wrote to his mother on 27 December that it was 'a pretty compliment'.

Urge's success cast a lonely ray of light amidst the gloom that afflicted Lazaretto towards the year's end. Another submarine had been lost; *Perseus* (Lieutenant-Commander E. C. Nicolay), who although based at Alexandria was well-known in Malta. Remarkably, there was one survivor, Leading Stoker John Capes, from whom the story of her fate later became known. Late on 6 December, off the Greek island of Zante, she hit a mine and sank to the seabed with most of her ship's company already dead; only six men survived the initial explosion, and of them only Capes managed to escape. He then swam nearly ten miles to land and was found by some Greeks who looked after him until he finally managed to return to Egypt in May, 1943.

Perseus was reported overdue on 12 December. On the 13th four of Admiral Cunningham's destroyers carried out a brilliant night action off Cape Bon. They torpedoed and sank two Italian cruisers that were laden with petrol for Rommel's tanks. A few days later Rear-Admiral P. L. Vian led a squadron of three cruisers and twelve destroyers into action in what later became known as the First Battle of Sirte.

Admiral Vian's primary aim was to escort the converted merchantman *Breconshire* to Malta with desperately needed oil and petrol supplies. Despite enemy air attacks, the ship arrived intact on the 18th. That afternoon the squadron ran into an enemy convoy, escorted by two Italian battleships, in the Gulf of Sirte. Despite their superior potential, the Italians rapidly disengaged. But British jubilation was short-lived.

On the following day, 19 December, pursuing another enemy convoy, Captain Rory O'Conor dashed out of Grand Harbour in *Neptune* with two other cruisers, *Aurora* and *Penelope*. With the four escorting destroyers, Force K ploughed into a minefield north of Tripoli. There was only one survivor from *Neptune*. *Aurora* and *Penelope* were both badly damaged and *Kandahar*, one of the destroyers, was sunk.

The tragedy marked the end of Force K. But this disastrous day was not yet over. At anchor in Alexandria, two of our battleships and several other ships were badly damaged in a brilliant attack by three 'human torpedoes' delivered by an Italian U-boat. *Valiant* sat on the bottom; *Queen Elizabeth*, Cunningham's flagship, was holed and flooded.

By the end of the year, as Cunningham admitted, the Mediterranean Fleet was at its lowest ebb. He identified, as the greatest single threat to the Allied cause, German supremacy in the air. With no aircraft carrier to provide the cover his ships needed, he told London that the fleet would have to abandon the central basin of the Mediterranean; and without the fleet to guard its flank and to ferry supplies, the Eighth Army advance could not continue.

On 24 December the army retook Benghazi. Thereafter the advance failed, its momentum exhausted. 'ABC' was right.

Unknown to David Wanklyn, his Victoria Cross was gazetted on 16 December. He was out on patrol with *Upholder* at the time, and when he returned to base on the 23rd no one said a word. While he was asleep that night, his shirt was removed from beside his bunk and Simpson arranged for the VC ribbon to be sewn on before it was replaced. Next morning Wanklyn woke up and dressed without noticing anything. As Jack Michell remembers:

> Nobody let on. It was only at lunch time, when Wanks was combing his hair, that he noticed the ribbon. He came into the mess asking who had the bad taste to play a practical joke like that on him. It was only then that Shrimp confirmed that Wanklyn had been awarded the Victoria Cross. A suitable celebration ensued, for his was the first VC to be given to a submariner in the Second World War.

A few days later, Wanklyn's great friend, Tomkinson, was told that he was being awarded two years' seniority. Simpson writes in his book:

> Tomkinson, whose skill was comparable and whose successes were not much less, said to me: 'I'm glad Wanks had got the VC. He's earned it. It suits him and it makes him so happy; but, sir, if you want to know what medal would make me most happy, it's one they haven't struck yet: the End of War medal.'

But Tomkinson was satisfied with the 'pretty compliment' he had been paid, and wrote a lively Christmas letter home to his mother:

> The little boat is working very well and all the sailors are in great heart. We gave them all a bottle of beer on Christmas Day and had a few minutes talking with them. They are so good and have to work very hard — but keep the boat looking like a new pin all the time. Thank goodness the army is at last doing its stuff in Libya . . . It's really quite cold out here and we have a wood fire in our cabin in the evenings — it makes things much more cheerful. There's no coal to be had here, so we have to go scrounging round for old boxes which we break up. We feed like fighting cocks all the time — in fact far better than we ever did at home. The only nuisance is from the sky — there are far too many bombs falling and barrages going up to be comfortable. I spend a lot of the day in a deep rock shelter, which I reckon to be the safest place to be found.
> I'd give a lot to be able to get home to see Myrtle and Bridget

[his wife and baby daughter], but we have to go on and smash
the foe out here, which I'm sure we shall do in due course.

Jack Michell, as duty officer for Christmas night, was alone in the
wardroom when Simpson walked in and offered him a drink: 'He
then told me he would take over my duty officer job and he
ordered me to go ashore and enjoy myself. I thanked him and did
so!'

Thus it was that Shrimp Simpson managed to gather in all his
ten Us for Christmas at their Lazaretto 'home'. This band of
brothers, whose like would never be seen again, celebrated for a
brief instant the birthday of Him for whom, at the root of things,
they were in truth fighting with their lives and with such ferocity. Of those original captains, only two would enjoy another
Christmas.

13

JANUARY, 1942

The new year of 1942 held out no great hope for the people of Malta despite Admiral Cunningham's brave assertion at the end of 1941. Reacting to suggestions that the intensified German bombing raids were an obvious preliminary to invasion, he had said: 'It is our intention to frustrate this with every ship we possess, air cover or none, come what might.' But, as Kesselring's pilots increased their onslaught, the islanders prepared for the worst; they tightened their belts and read the new leaflet issued by the Governor's office: *What to do in an Invasion.*

Early in January Vice-Admiral Sir Wilbraham Ford, for five years the popular Vice-Admiral, Malta, left the island, his place being taken by Vice-Admiral Sir Ralph Leatham. Just before his departure, the outgoing VAM wrote to his Commander-in-Chief:

> I've given up counting the number of air raids we are getting. At the time of writing, 4 p.m., we have had exactly seven bombing raids since 9 a.m., quite apart from over a month of all-night efforts. The enemy is definitely trying to neutralize Malta's effort, and, I hate to say, is gradually doing so.

Apart from causing terrible losses to the island's aircraft, he wrote, the raid interrupted work in the docks and hence slowed up vital maintenance of ships and submarines; if only his suggestion concerning 'underground shelters' had been pursued 'they would have been finished by now'. And because the enemy was now laying mines all round the island, 'poor *Abingdon'*, the only minesweeper, being machine-gunned in the hours of daylight, was 'trying to sweep during the dark hours'. It was a frustrating job, being VAM; as Sir Wilbraham put it, 'damnable to be quite useless'.

A similar frustration was felt by many of the submarine COs who shared these murderous times, for the crucial rest periods during which the boats were serviced were constantly interrupted and vital preparations severely curtailed. It became ever more dangerous merely to take the boat around the harbour, as Lieutenant C. P. ('Pat') Norman recalls. Simpson asked him to take *Upholder* out 'for a day's exercise' as spare CO while Wanklyn had a break. All went well until he returned, surfacing off Tigne Point just outside Marsamxett Harbour.

> We surfaced and almost immediately my signalman reported aircraft low over Valletta and coming towards us. 'Only Hurricanes,' we gaily said. But not a bit of it; they were Me 109s and we were well and truly shot up with cannon and machine gun.
>
> In the act of shutting the conning tower hatch, I was hit by machine-gun fire and a cannon shell exploded in the bridge casing just behind my head. I knew nothing further. Apparently I dropped like a stone to the control room. The signalman (bless his heart) forced his way up and shut the hatch just as the water started coming in. Number One (Lieutenant M. L. C. Crawford) took over immediately and did a U-turn submerged in the swept channel, just at the entrance between Tigne Point and Valletta. Very wisely he set out to sea again.
>
> Joe Martin* had also been out that day exercising in *Urge*. He was about two miles away and also dived. We sent a message by underwater telephone to him which merely said: 'Air attack. Stay dived. Captain shit.'
>
> This, I am glad to say, was followed shortly by another signal: 'For shit, read *shot.*'

Norman was rushed to Mtafa hospital where he stayed for three weeks and where, as he says, 'a most extraordinary thing happened':

> The German pilot who had shot me up was shortly after shot down himself. He was picked up and, being wounded, was put

* Lieutenant J. D. Martin, another spare CO.

in the next bed to me in Mtafa. We got on quite well; sometimes he won at Uckers and sometimes I did.

Norman further records that 'Wanks was on the whole very
decent to me on returning his lovely *Upholder* full of holes.'

The submarines in dockyard hands felt particularly vulnerable.
Upright's first lieutenant, Anthony Daniell, recalls:

> Our anti-aircraft armament was two 1914 Lewis guns. We got
> them up on the bridge and potted away at the dive bombers, the
> Ju 87s and 88s, as they came out of their dives; we had no hope
> of hitting anything or doing much damage but it did give us a
> bit of a lift. One thing we noticed was that the German dive-
> bombers were so accurate that we, not being their target in this
> instance, were in little danger of being hit.

A more serious incident occurred on 6 January, when *P 31* was
in for her periodical docking; a bomb landed alongside her in No.
1 Dock. Miraculously, only three of her crew were injured but
the boat suffered serious damage to her pressure hull and it took
three weeks to complete the repairs.

Thus, with no Force K and with the few remaining RAF aircraft grossly outnumbered by the Luftwaffe, Malta's fortunes
now depended very much on the submarines.

Upholder's first patrol of the new year began on the last day of the
old one. On the night of 3 January she was off Cape Gallo, north
of Palermo, when Wanklyn sighted two westbound ships.
Because of a bright moon he was forced to make a dived attack;
he fired three torpedoes, which all missed. Some hours later another ship was sighted, the destroyer *Sirio,* and again Wanklyn
dived for his attack. This time he had torpedo trouble, which left
him with only three 'fish'. He fired two. One plunged 500
fathoms to the seabed, exploding beneath the submarine and she
was lucky not to be damaged. The other torpedo struck *Sirio*
amidships, but the destroyer struggled on.

Upholder surfaced so that Wanklyn could continue the attack
with the 12-pounder gun, but the Italians returned fire with two
Breda automatic guns, their accuracy eventually forcing *Upholder*

to submerge. With only one torpedo remaining, Wanklyn withdrew.

Just before dawn the following morning Wanklyn was summoned to the bridge by his OOW: *Upholder* was being attacked apparently from the dark shoreline. Suddenly a gun flash lit up the dim silhouette of a U-boat. Emerging from the gloom, she was steering straight for *Upholder*. A shell whistled overhead and Wanklyn dived. He guessed that the U-boat was making for Palermo, and, confident that she would now turn away, he decided to dive for a counter-attack. During those twenty seconds of diving, Wanklyn began swinging *Upholder* to an approximate firing course, while she took up periscope depth. On his first look he sighted the U-boat at about 1,800 yards, swinging beam-on and steering west. Without instruments, Wanklyn fired his last torpedo which hit the U-boat amidships. She sank immediately. In broad daylight, *Upholder* surfaced and picked up four survivors from the *Ammiraglio Saint Bon,* an Italian U-boat. They provided much useful intelligence.

Unique had been sent north to the Gulf of Taranto, once again to form a line across the bay in company with *P 34* and *Thrasher* from Alexandria. *Unique* (Lieutenant Collett) arrived at her billet on 1 January, but all was quiet for some days. Then, on the 5th, HE was heard, followed by twenty distant depth-charges; the heavy units were returning to base. Soon afterwards Tony Collett sighted the fighting tops of the big ships coming straight towards him: a battleship, a cruiser, with five destroyers in 'V' formation, and an overhead escort of two seaplanes. *Unique* was in what Simpson later described as 'the precise position which any submarine officer must pray for and which, in less than one-in-a-thousand sorties, he was likely to experience'.

> This is the great occasion when the chances are 50:1 in the submarine's favour, provided the CO uses as little speed and periscope as possible − and very little of either are necessary. He must then dismiss the escorting destroyers from his mind. He must concentrate his attack upon the battleship, knowing that, if his attack is a real success, his escape is also virtually assured, since the destroyers will be busy life-saving.

15. Left: Lt A.R. Daniell when first lieutenant of *Upright*.

16. Right: CERA Anthony Townsend : *P31* (Lt J.B. Kershaw) dived involuntarily off Tripoli. At 80 feet, her first lieutenant, Lt J.P.H. Oakley, threw the switches to full astern, grouped up. CERA Townsend blew Main Ballast tanks when the sea deluged into the control room. The Captain was knocked unconscious; the Fourth Hand was swept over the side but climbed back on board; the Third Hand was drowned.

17. Lt Maydon at the search periscope of *Umbra*: he has just come down from the bridge. Note machine-guns, rifles and bayonets in the racks.

18. During the rest period, the submarine is overhauled and prepared for the next patrol : carrying out maintenance in the Engine Room.

19. Loading a torpedo, possibly in *Unbroken*. The 3″ gun is trained outboard to allow enough space for working. The torpedo officer, in shorts, is checking that the rollers on the lifting band will fit into place on the loading frame below the torpedo.

20. Lt–Cdr M.D. Wanklyn with the crew of *Upholder*, most of whom perished when this famous submarine was lost off Tripoli on 14 April, 1942. *Upholder*'s first lieutenant, Lt M.L.C. Crawford, is on his Captain's left.

21. The torpedo boat *General Achille Papa* manoeuvring in Tripoli harbour, 2 August, 1941, four days after sinking *Cachalot*.

22. *Oceania*, 19,405 tons, sunk in a night attack by *Upholder* off Tripoli, 18 September, 1941. Troops for the Afrika Korps can be seen scrambling down the lifelines.

23. *Pegaso*, 855 tons, torpedo boat, probably sank *Upholder* at 1600 on 14 April, 1942, north of Tripoli.

24. *Upholder* (left) and *Urge*, alongside each other at Lazaretto. Note the modification carried out to the bows of *Urge*.

25. Lt-Cdr E.A. Woodward, Captain of *Unbeaten*, Captain 'Tug' Wilson, centre and Lt D. 'Bobby' Lambert, later CO of *Surf*.

26. Right: 'Tommo' (later Lt Cdr) E.P. Tomkinson, Captain of *Urge*.

27. Below: The Italian submarine *Ammiraglio Saint Bon*, 1,461 tons, *Upholder*'s second Italian U-boat victim.

28. Dust and spray from exploding bombs shroud *U*-class submarines berthed off Lazaretto, Manoel Island: viewed from the Valletta side of Marsamxett Harbour.

29. Augusta, summer, 1942. A minelayer embarks her moored mines.

30. The bow of a *U*-class submarine, secured to a buoy off Lazaretto, is silhouetted against the nightly air-raid barrage.

31. *Sokol*: March, 1942. "*Many Happy Returns!*" Boris Karnicki, Lt–Cdr, DSO, VM, KW, Commanding Officer of *Sokol*, salutes Captain (S) 10.

32. The Maltese people played an essential part in keeping the Royal Navy operational: Officers' Steward Paul Camilleri proudly represented the Maltese when he became a member of *Sokol*'s crew.

33. CPO G. Selby, DSM★, BEM, the luckiest man in the Submarine Service. He left *Upholder* just before her last patrol; survived the sinkings of *P 39* and *Olympus*; left *Sickle* before she was sunk; left *Truculent* and *Affray* before these two boats were lost after the war.

34. HMS *Medway*, depot ship to the First Flotilla, Alexandria. Sunk by *U.372* on 30 June, 1942. She is seen here before the war, with her flotilla of Os (and one unidentified) alongside.

35. Right: The Submarine Service's most decorated rating, CPO 'Alfie' Mallett, who was awarded three Distinguished Service Medals and a Mention in Despatches whilst serving in submarines during the war. He was in *Ursula*, *Tigris* and *Tuna* in home waters; in *P 33* and *Una* in the Mediterranean; and in *Terrapin* in the Far East.

36. Depth–charged by the Italian torpedo-boat *Circe*, *Tempest* is forced to the surface. *Circe* destroyed three, possibly four, of our submarines: *Grampus*, *Union* (possibly), *Tempest* and *P.38*. (Photograph taken from *Circe's* upperdeck, 12 February, 1942.)

But, worried by the closeness of the destroyer screen and the overhead aircraft, Collett chose to attack on a broad track. He took *Unique* deep, running westward and turning on to a 120° track, and waited for the screen to pass.

On coming up to periscope depth the boat lost trim and Collett was forced to go deep again as a destroyer passed overhead. By the time he next had a periscope sighting, the battleship had altered course. *Unique* fired a full salvo of four torpedoes, but without result. It was, as Cunningham himself commented, 'most regrettable that such an opportunity . . . should have been missed' and no one was more furious than Collett himself.

While *Unique* returned to base, her place in the patrol line across the Gulf of Taranto was taken by two boats, *Sokol* and *Unbeaten*. But, after three blank days, on 9 January *Unbeaten* was ordered to shift billet south to Cape Spartivento. On the morning of the 12th, wind Force 5, she heard HE to the north-eastward. Two minutes later a U-boat appeared, steaming through the murk. Woodward fired a full salvo at a range of 1,300 yards. Two torpedoes hit, and the U-boat sank. Although he was close in to the coast, Teddy Woodward then surfaced and found the only survivor, a German, who revealed that the target had been *U.374*.

At Lazaretto the German seaman required some coaxing before he would reveal any more. Aided by Chief Petty Officer Domisch, *Sokol*'s German-speaking coxswain, Simpson interviewed the man. The German jeered at British incompetence. While boasting that *U.374* had evaded all our anti-submarine measures in the Strait of Gibraltar, he let slip that she had been at a depth of 260 metres (850 feet). He had provided important information: not only was it three times the depth that a British U could safely dive, but it was also much deeper than British depth-charge pistols could reach: their maximum setting was 500 feet.

Simpson immediately reported this vital intelligence to the appropriate authorities, but it was *over a year* before our anti-submarine forces were equipped with deep pistols for their depth-charges.

The German prisoner also revealed that *U.374* had been on

the surface by day because her captain, an experienced CO, considered the weather too rough for submarine attack.

Following her attack on the U-boat, *Unbeaten* made two torpedo hits on a tanker, causing serious damage. She returned to Malta on 19 January. Like *Upholder* before her, who returning to base on the 8th, had been harassed by a Junkers 88, *Unbeaten* was attacked as she surfaced off the harbour entrance. A roving Me 109 suddenly appeared. The fighter showered *Unbeaten's* conning tower with cannon shells and bullets, but she was already diving, and no one was hit.

From this day onwards, Captain (S) ordered that all submarines returning from patrol should stay submerged until within one mile of St Elmo lighthouse, at the tip of the Valletta peninsula, and then should surface only if the red flag was *not* flying at the Castille; further, that the CO should not man his bridge until the submarine was inside the breakwater.

In mid-January it became clear that another submarine had been lost: *Triumph* (Lieutenant J. S. Huddart) was overdue on the 9th. She had successfully landed a rescue party in Greece to collect some escapers. She was due to pick them up again a few days later but nothing more was heard from her. It is presumed that she was mined.

At the same time, another three *U*s had arrived, and a fourth was on her way; by the end of the month the Tenth Flotilla consisted of twelve submarines (excluding *Ursula* who was on her way back to the UK for a refit). First to arrive was *Una* (Lieutenant D. S. R. Martin), entering Marsamxett Harbour on 4 January, after an eventful passage from home. Firstly, she had come under torpedo attack, being forced to dive in the Bay of Biscay; but the incident was encouraging, remembers her first lieutenant, Rocky Hill, because it gave the crew 'confidence in our boat and in our captain'. Then, arriving at Gibraltar, the electrical engine controls on the upper bridge suddenly failed and *Una* 'left a V-shaped souvenir of our visit in the dock gate'; fortunately, the boat was not damaged. Lastly, when *Una* was 'on the final run to Malta', somewhere off the Sicilian coast the unmistakable sound was heard of 'another submarine venting its ballast tanks as it dived'. Afterwards the other submarine was discovered to have been all of fifteen miles away. As Rocky Hill reports, 'The incident made us all realize how far sound can carry on a quiet night'.

On 5 January, the day after *Una* arrived, she was joined by *P 35* (Lieutenant S. L. Maydon); on the 15th they were followed by *P 36* (Lieutenant H. N. Edmonds, DSC), and on the 27th by *P 38* (Lieutenant R. J. Hemingway).

P 36, having embarked two secret service agents in Gibraltar, landed them near Cannes, in the south of France, on 9 January. One was Captain Peter Churchill, who was delivering money to the French resistance movement in Marseilles. According to *P 36*'s telegraphist,* destined for spare crew duties, she arrived in the middle of an air raid.

Two of the new boys sailed for their first patrol to the usual billet off the coast of Tunisia. *Una* had a dull introduction to life with the Tenth but *P 35* was very soon in action. She was ordered to investigate a reported infringement of the rules by Vichy ships at Sousse, and on the way Lynch Maydon sighted at 0311, 17 January, what he took to be a U-boat. Nine minutes later he had fired three torpedoes, one of which blew the target to bits. According to Petty Officer Telegraphist Fred Buckingham, *P 35*'s PO Tel., Maydon then took his boat 'back to the scene of the crime' and found one man sitting on a raft. He was Italian but knew some English and Buckingham soon found that 'Joe', as they nicknamed him, had been 'on a salvage vessel engaged in trying to raise the submarine *P 32*'. Buckingham goes on:

Joe was a stoker and was actually engaged in shovelling coal into the furnace when our torpedo had struck. The next thing he remembered was coming to the surface and banging his head on something which turned out to be the raft. He climbed aboard to find that he was the only survivor. All those engaged in salvage work on the upper deck had disappeared. If Joe had been a disbeliever before, he must surely believe in miracles now. Mussolini was apparently to blame for this and all Italy's troubles, and the sooner he was defeated the better.

Joe did his best to thank us for picking him up. He worked

*This telegraphist kept a daily and fascinating log of his life in the Tenth.

like a Trojan, helping to reload the tubes with spare torpedoes, working in the galley, and generally making himself useful. One day he was helping the wardroom steward. The steward disappeared and then the wardroom bell sounded. Joe entered the wardroom and said: 'What you want? More tea?' No prizes for guessing where he picked up that bit of excellent English . . .

He wasn't too happy later on when we fired our other four torpedoes at an escorted convoy, and loads of depth-charges were dropped around us. Neither was I, for that matter.

The salvage vessel which Maydon had sunk was the 301-ton *Rampino*; though small, she had been invaluable to the enemy who were dependent on salvage for replacing losses. 'Joe' provided grist to our intelligence services with his enthusiastic explanation of enemy techniques in disembarking stores at Tripoli, despite RAF minelaying and bombing. The convoy that *P 35* attacked, and was later attacked by, turned out to have been Vichy ships, well within their permitted waters. Fortunately Maydon's torpedoes had missed.

The only other hit by one of the Tenth Flotilla's boats was made by Lieutenant Harrison in *P 34*. She was patrolling the southern approaches to the Strait of Messina, on 25 January, when a large southbound ship was sighted, escorted by one destroyer. Harrison fired a full salvo, and, despite one gyro failure, hit the fully laden target, the *Dalmatia* (3,320 tons), which later sank. The destroyer mounted an ineffective counter-attack, but when two flying boats arrived Harrison decided to withdraw.

The tide was running very much in the enemy's favour. During the first week of January, despite the efforts of our submarines, two sizeable convoys had reached Tripoli. Rommel was thus able to launch a strong counter-offensive and on 21 January he attacked. The Eighth Army was taken completely by surprise. By 7 February the Allied troops were withdrawing from Cyrenaica, pursued eastwards by Rommel and his Panzer corps, aided by the Luftwaffe flying in from Crete.

On 12 February, far away in France, the two German battle-cruisers, *Scharnhorst* and *Gneisenau* slipped out of Brest, evaded the British and dashed up-Channel to their home ports. The success of this operation so pleased Hitler that he was in amenable mood when Admiral Raeder saw him the next day. Raeder explained, once again, the tremendous advantage to be gained by a Mediterranean victory. Patiently he emphasized how this would lead to disintegration of the British Empire and would allow the Herrenvolk to link up with their Japanese allies across India. At the same time, the Middle East oil wells would fall under German control.

Hitler was impressed as Raeder explained his strategy. Rommel was now making progress in Libya; the Luftwaffe had total supremacy in the eastern Mediterranean; the British fleet had been decimated. The only real stumbling block was the island of Malta. Hitler told Raeder to get 'The Great Plan' under way. With feverish enthusiasm, the German staffs revived Operation 'Hercules', while Kesselring and the Axis navies were ordered to tighten their grip on Malta.

Because of his recapture of the Cyrenaican ports, Rommel's convoys of supply ships from Italy could now be dispersed, some to one port, some to another. In future they would be much more difficult targets for our submarines to intercept.

14

FEBRUARY 1942

The bombing was seriously hampering life at Lazaretto. By now Simpson had issued strict orders that *everyone* must take immediate shelter when the alarm was raised: COs, officers, ratings, base staff, visitors. Much of Sliema had been reduced to rubble, and the COs with billets ashore had returned to take up quarters in the base itself; like everyone else, they repaired to the shelters whenever a raid began. The deep tunnels so laboriously dug out of the rock assured everyone's safety, but the frequent raids enforcing long spells in the shelters (up to five hours at a time was not uncommon) were a constant source of annoyance.

On 13 February, 1942, there was another red alert: the enemy was dropping parachute mines. Two of these fiendish devices landed on the Lazaretto buildings, while eight more fell elsewhere on Manoel Island. In the laconic words of our telegraphist's unofficial log:

> *13 February:* Big air raid. Direct hits scored on Base, Sick Bay, Cinema, Laundry and Mess Decks demolished, two killed, five injured. Practically all my kit lost.

Three days later the entry reads:

> *16 February:* To sea at 1930 . . . It is a relief to be at sea after the continuous air raids.

The casualties were from the visiting Greek submarine *Glaukos,* whose CO was holding a conference with his officers; apparently disregarding the alert, they had carried on their discussions in direct contravention of Captain (S)'s orders.

The base had been half-demolished and the sight that greeted those emerging from the shelters was ghastly. The work load was now redoubled, as everyone struggled to recover whatever possible from the ruins and clear up the mess. They were dark days and would become darker. But one lighter moment came with the discovery that Sam MacGregor's precious bagpipes had miraculously survived.

From now on, all officers and men would mess together in the rock shelters. Everyone slept in relays in the long lines of two-tiered bunks, under or upon trestle tables. Simpson's day cabin had lost its roof, and he found alternative accommodation in a huge disused oil tank half-buried in the rock, where here too some of the officers slept. The foul stench of oil pervaded clothing, bedding, everything, but a chest of drawers was installed and duckboards rigged across the remaining oily slush. With her table and typewriter, Simpson's secretary, the unflappable Miss Gomer, added a certain elegance to the scene.

Fortunately the damage did not extend to the hot water boiler or the galley, and an approximation to the usual routine was soon established. The soldiers' barracks adjoining Lazaretto suffered even worse damage and three men died as the parachute mines did their dreadful work. It seemed that the enemy was now turning the full force of his attention on the island site of the submarine base.

Pat Norman took *Upholder* to sea on the first day of February to give Wanklyn a rest. On the fourth he sighted an eastbound Italian destroyer off Cape San Vito and he fired three torpedoes. Their tracks must have been seen because the enemy immediately counter-attacked, fortunately without success. Three days later, on the 7th, Norman sighted an eastbound convoy in the same area and fired another three torpedoes. This time he succeeded in sinking the *Salpi* (2,710 tons) and damaging the *Duino* (1,334 tons); the latter went on to hit a mine and finally sank.

Upright, too, was under temporary command in early February while her usual CO, Johnny Wraith rested; his stand-in was Lieutenant J. W. D. Coombe. With *Una* (Lieutenant D. S. R.

Martin) and the newly arrived *Tempest* (Lieutenant-Commander W. A. K. N. Cavaye), *Upright* sailed to form a patrol line across the Gulf of Taranto; this 'Iron Ring', as this tactic became known, was intended to catch any enemy warships entering or leaving Taranto. The primary objective on this occasion was to prevent the enemy interfering with a vital convoy of supplies leaving Alexandria.

On the morning of 12 February the three submarines were in position, ten miles apart, across the gulf. Their sailing orders contained this Admiralty signal:

> The Italian tanker *Lucania* (8,100 tons) will sail from Taranto 11 February on passage to the Atlantic. She will not be zigzagging, will not be escorted and will be marked on both sides amidships with the Italian flag. *Lucania* has been promised safe passage by the British Government and is not to be molested.

The tanker had been guaranteed immunity from attack because she was delivering fuel to a repatriation ship returning with civilians from Mombasa. This was not *Lucania's* first such errand: our submarines and the RAF had previously received similar orders to let her pass, though they complained of her inadequate and dirty markings.

At 1010 on the 12th, *Upright* sighted the tanker, correctly identified her and let her pass. About two hours later, *Una's* captain, D. S. R. Martin, sighted smoke to the northward, with a monoplane overhead which he took to be an escort for the as yet unidentified approaching ship. He fired three torpedoes from a range of 2,000 yards. Captain (S) 10's subsequent report states: 'One hit, and the ship sank after some hours. Periscope observation a few minutes after the hit showed that the vessel was in fact the *Lucania,* with correct though very indistinct markings.'

It later transpired that Martin was ill. On return to Malta, he was found to be suffering from double pneumonia and had to spend two weeks in hospital. But his Number One, Lieutenant L. F. L. ('Rocky') Hill, RNR, who affirms that ' "D. S. R." was a good CO', believes that Martin might not have seen the Admiralty signal before sighting the Italian ship. 'It *is* possible,' he insists, 'because I (the first lieutenant and second-in-command) had not seen it before the attack.'

Before sailing from Lazaretto, *Una's* third hand, Sub-Lieutenant R. L. Jay, had presented the signal log to Martin in the usual way. Martin declined to read it, saying that he had already studied the latest signals in the Staff Office in the base, before coming on board, a procedure which was not uncommon.

Signalman H. Thomas remembers that Martin allowed his control room team to look through the periscope. Thomas saw a large white circle on the ship's side, for'ard; her bows were canted in the air, the remainder of her hull now sliding beneath the water. Thomas writes: 'The general feeling in *Una* was that we had been involved in an "accident of war".' The 'Skipper' was, in his words, 'an honourable and highly professional submarine commander'.

While Martin then retired to his bunk, Hill took *Una* back to Lazaretto.

Even as Martin lay in his hospital bed, the repercussions of his mistake were echoing around Whitehall. Two weeks later he was sent back to the UK on a priority RAF flight, to explain in person to Anthony Eden, the Foreign Secretary, why he had sunk the wretched tanker. After his convalescence, Lieutenant Martin was appointed CO of *Tuna,* in whom, in April, 1943, he won the DSO by sinking *U 644*.

There was one immediate consequence of this tragic incident. Hearing *Lucania's* SOS on the afternoon of 12 February, the Italians despatched both air and sea assistance to the stricken ship with further orders to find the submarine responsible. That night, in deteriorating weather, the Italian torpedo boat *Circe* detected the echo of a submarine and went to action stations. Early on the morning of the 13th the Italians started dropping depth-charges, and according to the report of *Circe's* CO he soon saw 'two blue spouts of air bubbles', followed by an oil slick. His report continues:

> I am now convinced by the air bubbles that the submarine has been severely damaged and will therefore soon be forced to surface. I signal to Taranto that I have only one pattern of depth charges remaining. At 0917 I start my final attack. Running in

at 0942 on a course of 090° at 1,000 metres, I sight two enormous air bubbles. Three minutes later, the submarine surfaces on my port quarters.

The boat was, in fact, *Tempest* (Lieutenant-Commander Cavaye), whose CO and crew were now destined for prisoner-of-war camps.

Meanwhile, the all-important convoy of supplies from Egypt had been attacked from the air. Despite a cruiser escort under Rear-Admiral Vian, the merchant ships were either sunk or forced to turn back to Alexandria. Malta would continue to rely almost solely on those supplies brought by submarine, such as those carried by the valiant *Porpoise* who made two storing runs during March. This, surely, was the moment for the enemy to invade.

Returning on 17 February to Malta from patrol, *Unique* was making a blind approach to the island, ('she was not yet radar-fitted', explains her navigating officer, Lieutenant Jackie Fox) when she ran ashore. As Fox continues:

> There she was, high and dry. Dawn was beginning to break. In the shocked silence, the click of a rifle bolt was heard on shore, close to the submarine.
>
> 'Halt! Who goes there?' challenged a perplexed army sentry and guardian of the coast.
>
> 'British submarine *Unique* ashore here!' was the captain's reply in a calm English voice.
>
> Apparently satisfied with this explanation of the unusual, the sentry resumed his patrol without further ado. He disappeared into the semi-darkness.

The captain, Tony Collett, was not enjoying his predicament. German marauders often visited Malta's coastline, Me 109s and Ju 88s shooting up anything they saw. *Unique* would be a sitting duck. A W/T signal failed to raise any response, presumably because the boat was blanketed by the shoreline. Clearly someone would have to go ashore. Collett himself takes up the story:

> My third hand, Lieutenant Dick Silver, leapt off the fo'c'sle end

and on to the rocks. He then climbed through the barbed wire, by which time the sentry had returned. Dick Silver was dressed in a voluminous dirty submarine sweater. He was unwashed, unshaven and wearing an old pair of grey flannel trousers, and, in this state, the sentry guided him back to the Army Officer's Mess. After Dick had finally phoned Shrimp Simpson and been given hot tea, the army apologetically told him that they had no transport on this particular day, so Silver decided to run to Dockyard Creek, cross Grand Harbour by *dghaisa* to Valetta, run again over the top, through Floriana and down to Sliema Creek, where he hailed another *dghaisa* to land him directly at our Lazaretto base: a distance of some four and a half miles.

The army was infuriated (this was at the height of invasion fever) because not once was Dick Silver challenged, not even at the main dockyard gates in Dockyard Creek. Then someone let the cat out of the bag. It wasn't long before a huge headline appeared in the *Malta Times:*

MALTA INVADED!

Fox writes that *Unique* was soon towed off the rocks, having suffered 'surprisingly light' damage, but, as Tom Lancaster reports, 'Shrimp was being pressurized into court-martialling *Unique's* officers':

> But Shrimp pointed out in no uncertain terms that such a course of action was the last thing that he was concerned about; he was extremely thankful to have the boat and her crew safely back, regardless of circumstances.

After a spell in dockyard hands, *Unique* was soon ready to return home for her refit at Chatham. But, as we shall see, the long-awaited day would be further postponed.

In mid-February the Tenth Submarine Flotilla was joined by another new *U, P 39* (Lieutenant N. Marriott). Her first patrol was with *P 34, P 38* and *Una,* all of them forming a line to stop a southbound enemy convoy, with a strong destroyer escort. To the chagrin of the *Us,* the one attack by *P 34* was unsuccessful and the convoy reached Tripoli in safety: three 6,000-ton liners laden with supplies for the Afrika Korps, another bitter disappointment for the hard-pressed Tenth.

On 8 February 1942, *Sokol* was patrolling in the Gulf of Gabes when she sighted and chased the Italian schooner *Guiseppina* (392 tons). The Italian crew having abandoned ship, Boris Karnicki sent a boarding party across to destroy the vessel. They returned with a picture of Il Duce, an Italian helmet and *Guiseppina's* cat. Suggestions from Lieutenant Taylor, the liaison officer, that the schooner be towed back to Malta were treated with scorn by Karnicki who wanted to continue his patrol. It had been uneventful, save for thick fields of seaweed which proved a nuisance off Djerba Island, west of Tripoli, and *Sokol* returned to base with her booty on 20 February.

To the east of *Sokol* was *P 31*, back on patrol again after being bombed in the dockyard. She attacked an enemy ship but in vain, and saw nothing else worth pursuing. Then, at dawn on 12 February, the third hand, Lieutenant M. H. Gardner, and Sub-Lieutenant Roger Bucknall were on the bridge with 'Shirty' Kershaw, the CO, when an elderly, recalled leading stoker misunderstood orders and suddenly caused the boat to dive 'at a horrible angle.' Gardner and Bucknall were both washed overboard, and Kershaw was knocked unconscious. He dropped down into the control room with a 'wall of water', remembers John Oakley, the first lieutenant. Scrambling into the tower Oakley found that the upper hatch had somehow shut itself, but 'we were then at eighty feet'. With the submarine back under control, Oakley found Bucknall still on the bridge: 'I asked him if he minded staying up there while I cleared up below, little realizing that he had climbed back on board.' Of Gardner there was no sign. Two days later *P 31* returned to Malta.

Our spare crew telegraphist had been drafted to *P 39*, who, with eight other submarines, including *Una* and *P 34*, were spread across the line of advance of an important convoy: three troopships of 6,000 tons each. The *Us* lay in wait north of Ras-el-Hamra, east of Tripoli, where the enemy made his landfall after crossing the Mediterranean.

On 23 February the convoy passed between *Una* and *P 34*, the latter being heavily counter-attacked after an unsuccessful attack. *P 39* survived 127 depth-charges and was recalled on the 25th.

27 February. Arrived Malta. Machine-gunned by two MEs when entering boom. Arrived alongside Lazaretto. Bombs dropped on wardroom and 0.5 inch gun position. Two officers killed. Dived in creek at 2000. We are now working Patrol Routine in reverse: diving during dark hours, on surface in day-time.

Sitting in a submarine 'on the bottom of the creek with awful noises up top and unable to do anything about it': this was the ultimate in frustration for Lieutenant Oakley, the Number One of *P 31*. Yet there was no respite to be found anywhere in Malta these days, even in the rest camps. Oakley recalls one particular break he took at Ghain Tuffieha, the rest camp in the north-west of the island, when Lynch Maydon (CO of *P 35*) started shooting with a rifle at German fighters:

Swift retaliation came in the form of a cannon attack. I was woken up by shells coming into my room and was lucky to survive. Others did not.

All seaworthy submarines were doing their best this month, but success was hard to find. *Urge* was detailed for another special operation, this time in Castellammare Bay on the north-west coast of Sicily, but again Tomkinson found reason to be suspicious when an E-boat slowly circled the bay, and, recalling what had happened before when he ignored his instincts, he abandoned the landing and returned to Malta.

On 15 February, patrolling the southern approaches to the Strait of Messina, *P 36* (Lieutenant H. N. Edmonds, DSC) made a fruitless attack on two cruisers at a range of three miles, and for her pains was subjected to a vicious counterattack; but she did manage to hit the modern destroyer *Carabiniere,* one of the escort ships.

Another success during February was achieved by *P 38* (Lieutenant R. J. Hemingway), who had sailed for her first patrol off Lampedusa on 8 February. On the 19th she attacked and sank the 4,200-ton *Ariosto,* and was then diverted to intercept a west-bound enemy convoy crossing the Gulf of Sirte. Part of the powerful escort for this convoy was the Italian torpedo boat

Circe, who only ten days earlier had sunk *Tempest. Circe* was about to strike again.

According to the report of *Circe's* CO, she was thirty-two miles north of Misurata on the 23rd, when he got a good sonar contact. His counter-attack was quickly supported by three *Navigatori*-class destroyers.

> As I pass over the position indicated by the sonar and the tell-tale bubbles, I let go a depth-charge pattern set to 75 metres. I increase to full speed to avoid damage to *Circe.*
>
> As I am clearing the area the pattern explodes. Soon afterwards the submarine is blown to the surface on my port quarter, stern down and bow pointing towards the convoy.
>
> No one leaves the submarine. I alter to starboard to close, but meanwhile *Antoniotto Usodimare* has opened fire with her main armament and machine guns. Some of her rounds are 'over', so I am forced to alter course abruptly.
>
> In the middle of my turn, I watch the air escort machine-gunning the submarine and, as she begins to dive again, a second aircraft drops bombs . . . Suddenly the submarine breaks surface on Red 150°. Her bows rear into the air; she is leaping and diving; a few minutes later she is at a 40° bow-down angle, with her propellers turning in the air and her after hydroplanes at hard-a-rise. She had made her last effort to reach the surface.

Interrupted by two other destroyers, *Circe's* CO had to abandon his search for the submarine for a few minutes, but later returned to find nothing on the surface but 'large air bubbles and gobs of oil':

> The oil slick is widening and, as I cross it, I see small bits of wood, a canvas bag and human remains. I lower the seaboat and recover three pieces of wood: one is a grating which still has linoleum glued to it; the other two are parts of a locker door . . . Two black flags and three Union jacks are in the canvas bag.

This most humane of men concludes his report with a precise note of *P 38's* last resting place, and adds that before leaving the spot 'I call my crew to attention, at Action Stations. I and my crew then salute the ship's company of the stricken submarine.'

It was up to *Upholder* to score the last hit for the Tenth during February. With Wanklyn back in command after his rest, she sailed on the 23rd: coincidentally, this would be her twenty-third patrol. With *P 35, P 36* and *Unbeaten* (under Lieutenant J. D. (Joe) Martin, standing in for Woodward who was ill) she was hoping to intercept a Tripoli-bound convoy, but bad weather forced a change of plans. *Upholder* now started patrolling between Djerba Island and longitude 13°E. At 1843 on the 27th she sighted a supply ship escorted by only one destroyer, steaming westwards along the coast. At 1905 Wanklyn sank the ship with three torpedoes. After dropping eight depth charges, the destroyer began picking up survivors from the stricken ship.

This brought the Tenth Flotilla's total to five supply ships sunk for February, an improvement on January, despite all the extra difficulties. At the end of the month, the German raiders returned and again Manoel Island came under attack. By now the Royal Malta Artillery had ringed Lazaretto with four Bofors batteries, but even their valiant efforts could not deter the determined and daring German pilots. Still the onslaught continued.

15

MARCH, 1942

The month's innings began with a hit by *Unbeaten* on a Vichy tanker working for the Germans. Joe Martin, still in command while Woodward was off sick, fired three torpedoes at *PLM 20* (5,147 tons) and sank her on 1 March. On passage back to Malta she sighted the wreckage of an Italian fighter, but it was the German bombers that wreaked most havoc.

Upright was due to leave Malta on 2 March, to sail back home for her refit. Jack Michell, her third hand, records what happened:

> On sailing day, I was on the bridge, testing main vents with the blower on. I then saw a Heinkel bomber flying quite low up the creek. I just had time to order 'Stop the blower, shut Kingstons, shut off for depth-charging' before he dropped a 1,000kg bomb about thirty feet to starboard of us.
>
> *Upright* keeled over to starboard about 70° and then slowly righted herself. A ton of evil-smelling water then dropped onto the bridge. After I had picked myself up, I heard a voice calling up the voice pipe.
>
> 'Control room bridge?'
>
> 'Bridge control room,' I replied.
>
> 'Excuse me, sir, are we sinking?' I recognized the cox'n's voice. I peered over the side. 'No,' I replied. 'Why are you asking?'
>
> 'The lights are out,' the cox'n said, 'and we can smell chlorine.'

Upright had almost all her battery cells smashed; the gyro compass was completely broken and the W/T was damaged. She had to be towed round to the dockyard for repairs; it would be nearly three weeks before she was able to sail for home. The disgust of her ship's company can only be imagined; but one of them was able to vent his fury on the raiders a few days later. Jack Michell again:

> One forenoon, while alongside in the dockyard, I was on the bridge talking to two ABs, Sprattling and Woolley, when a Maryland bomber-reconnaissance plane flew over very low, pursued by two Messerschmitt Me 109Fs.
>
> 'Can I have a go, sir?' Sprattling asked.
>
> I agreed and Woolley slammed a pan on the old Lewis gun. Sprattling emptied the drum in the general direction of the Me 109s. Down came a wheel and the fighter plunged straight into the drink in Grand Harbour. Unhappily, so did the Maryland.
>
> We were accused of shooting down both aircraft, but we modestly claimed only the Me 109F.

Finally, on the 19th, *Upright* sailed for home.

Another *U* was about to return to Britain when an unfortunate incident forced a postponement: *Unique*. Patched up after her misadventure on the rocky shore, she had only just been declared seaworthy when a deranged sailor who wanted to stay in Malta with his girlfriend broke into her pistol locker and then emptied a revolver into the control room complex. The submarine was thus compelled to return to the repair yards yet again.

Simpson dealt with the man in forthright fashion. He would now be sent back under arrest to the UK, to be dealt with by the naval authorities in Devonport. He would sail not with *Unique* but in *Clyde*, a minelaying submarine converted to store-running, but now on her way back home. Simpson sent for *Clyde*'s CO, Lieutenant R. S. Brookes, and her coxswain and chief stoker. He ordered them to take the man back for court-martial on the charge of sabotaging one of His Majesty's Submarines in time of war. If the offender gave them any trouble whatsoever, Lieutenant Brookes was to surface, shoot the man on the fore-casing, then dive again. Did everyone understand his orders? Solemnly, they all agreed that they understood. And with that Simpson gave the man into their care. *Clyde* sailed the next day.

There were some who criticized Simpson for such ruthlessness, but two years later Simpson was delighted to hear that the offender had become a leading seaman in one of the frigates fighting the battle of the Atlantic, and that he was a thoroughly dependable man.

Unique finally sailed for the UK on 7 March, having completed eighteen patrols and sunk five ships totalling 14,720 tons.

Another example of Simpson's unorthodox methods is recalled by Dudley Norman. One of the COs reported to Simpson that a key rating had failed to return from overnight leave, though on this occasion, Norman writes, 'It was not the ladies but the drink that was the cause of the trouble'. The man finally appeared, 'singing, shouting and swearing that he was not going to go out on any effing patrol for any effing officer, etcetera, etcetera'. Simpson ordered everyone to muster on the jetty, including the drunk. Then, in front of everyone, he asked, 'Are you going to join your submarine?' Defiantly the drunk retorted:

> 'I'm not joining any effing sub'.
> Shrimp ordered that a heaving line should be produced and tied round the rating.
> 'Throw him in the water,' he ordered. Seconds later he added:
>
> 'Pull him out'.
> The man was hauled out and brought dripping before S 10.
> 'Are you going to . . .?' Shrimp began.   'I'm not . . .'
> 'Throw him in'.
> The rating was thrown in and hauled out four times before the Captain.
> 'Are you . . .?' Shrimp began.
> 'Of course, sir. Thank you, sir'.

And that, according to Norman, was the end of the matter.

Jack Michell, sailing for home in *Upright* this March, was to have an extraordinary experience in London. At the end of the previous November he had been at Lazaretto when an air raid began. It was a 'Double Red' alert, meaning that the raiders were definitely heading for Malta's harbours. Running for the shelters, he and 'Rastus' Platt, *Upright*'s fourth hand, passed another cabin where two officers were playing chess. One was Brian Band, Crawford's replacement as first lieutenant in *Upholder*.

> 'It's a "Double Red",' we shouted to them. 'Come on down to the shelters.'
>
> 'I'm considering my next move,' Brian called out. 'We'll follow you.'

But Michell returned to find Brian Band dead: 'Not a mark or wound on him, but killed by blast.' The dead officer was buried and that, thought Michell, was 'the last of the sad incident'.

But in this spring of 1942, during Michell's leave, he visited the Café Royal in London and found himself in conversation with an army officer on a bar stool beside him.

> One thing led to another: I was in submarines; he had had a son killed in submarines. The officer proved to be Brian Band's father. The Admiralty had never told him how Brian had died, so he and his wife had always been worried that their son had suffered a painful or lingering death. Brian's father said that now that he knew that his son had died instantly, his wife and he would be much relieved. The army officer concluded: 'I've been brought to the Café Royal on the only day when I've been in London: I've been placed alongside you at the same time, at the same bar. Our meeting can have happened only by the hand of God.'

On 6 March Manoel Island took a further battering from the Luftwaffe. Once again all electricity and telephone lines were cut. The boats themselves were being attacked. The log of our spare crew telegraphist, still with *P 39,* describes one raid on that day:

> *6 March.* Three bombs dropped alongside, one sinking the oil lighter that was tied up alongside. I was sitting in the wardroom of *P 39.* One 'bang' sounded as if the S/M had been hit for'ard. It must have been the bomb hitting the lighter. There was a shower of broken glass as all the wardroom and control room fittings were torn from the bulkhead by blast. A list to starboard had developed and water was pouring down the conning tower hatch. Thinking that the boat was sinking, we climbed to the

bridge. Arriving on the bridge, we could see nothing. It was like a thick, thick fog in London. The oiler was on fire and gradually sinking. The S/M was gradually reverting to an even keel. Except for loose fittings and a strong smell of battery gases, nothing seemed the matter.

P 39 had been very seriously damaged and had to be towed into dock: 172 of her vital battery cells were cracked; warheads were wrenched from her torpedoes; machinery bedplates were fractured. The fuelling lighter sank shortly afterwards, covering the entire harbour in shale oil.

From now on, Simpson ordered, all submarines would have to spend the hours of daylight on the bottom of Marsamxett Harbour, and only surface at night to prepare for the next patrol. Only one boat at a time would remain alongside Lazaretto, so that all maintenance staff could concentrate on her. Submarines in the dockyard would be evacuated; only a skeleton fire party was permitted to remain on board.

The stress on his COs was worrying Simpson. He knew that even in harbour they were becoming exhausted. He therefore issued further orders that all boats were to dive 'on the watch', meaning that just one-third of the crew was on board, under the command of the first lieutenant or third hand. The boats would be secured by their bows to a mooring buoy; they would submerge by day and surface after dark. Meanwhile the COs were all to find whatever relaxation they could at one or other of the rest camps, and the crews, when not on watch, would have to find entertainment closer to the base.

One former source of entertainment was in Sliema, across the causeway from Manoel Island, where there were numerous bars all haunted by 'ladies of the town', according to Dudley Norman, Wraith's predecessor in *Upright*:

> Unfortunately, the incidence of VD began to climb accordingly, which affected the numbers available for patrol. Shrimp wrote a letter to the Chief of Police, headed 'Confusion of Enterprise', pointing out that, whereas he was trying to keep his sailors fit for operational duty, some 'ladies' were ensuring that they were not. Could he therefore do something about it?

Sadly for the sailors, the Chief of Police then launched a crackdown on the women and the sick bay at Lazaretto gradually became less busy.

But there was little for the sailors to do, as *P 35*'s Petty Officer Telegraphist, Fred Buckingham, remembers. 'It was almost impossible to get a meal ashore and there was very little beer to be had,' he writes.

> Life was far from pleasant. After fourteen days on patrol, where we saw no daylight, we spent the day on the bottom of a creek when on duty and most of the time in the shelter when not on duty.
>
> Very often we took a chance and had a run ashore. Half the crew were in The Olde Dun Cow one day when the Ju 88s came over and bombed the creeks . . . José, the landlord, dived for the shelter at the first bleep of the siren, leaving us to help ourselves. Strange as it may seem, we paid for what we took.

Buckingham was on watch in *P 35* on the morning of 8 March. The crew had worked all night, reloading torpedoes and filling the fresh-water tanks. Their work completed, most of the crew then took to their bunks for the day, either in the base or at Ghain Tuffieha, the rest camp in the north of the island. At dawn the submarine would dive, according to Simpson's orders, in the harbour. On board as Duty Officer were Lieutenant K. H. (Ken) Martin, brother of J. D. (Joe) Martin, with the Chief ERA and Fred Buckingham.

'We had been bombed daily and were dog tired,' writes Ken Martin, explaining rather than excusing a serious omission which now led to the boat being very heavy forward. He was not worried by the boat's descent to the seabed, but Buckingham reports that *P 35* 'hit the bottom with a hard thump':

> Seconds later, Leading Stoker Richardson dashed from the tube space and called to me: 'Water's pissing in for'ard'. I nipped smartly in and had a look. That was enough. I withdrew and we shut the watertight door. I ran to the control room and reported to the Officer of the Watch, Martin.

Martin and the Chief ERA immediately blew all the Main Ballast tanks at full pressure. Martin recalls:

> At first the response was encouraging, but just before surfacing the boat took a rapidly increasing bow–down angle; the bows were on the bottom and the stern showing above the surface. There was no point in keeping this alarming and uncomfortable angle; every moveable object had shifted with a frightening noise, so we opened the Main Ballast vents again and allowed *P 35* to settle on the bottom once more.

After checking the boat and helping to shut two ventilation trunkings against the inrush of water ('to the detriment of my wedding present, a Rolex Oyster, which never subsequently recovered') Martin settled down with the Chief ERA to consider what to do. The torpedo tube space was filled with water which somehow had to be removed.

> We got out the ship's drawings which showed that the cubic capacity of the tube space was thirty-six tons: an enormous weight, either to be removed or compensated for. There were emergency compartment 'blows' fitted for just such an event, and so this was our first recourse . . . But again the submarine practically stood on her head and we had to open main vents to let her return to the bottom.
>
> Meanwhile, on the terrace outside the wardroom on Manoel Island, my brother John was sitting drinking a post-breakfast cup of coffee with his great friend Pat Norman [Lieutenant C. P. Norman] while they awaited the first air raid of the day. My brother was Spare Crew Commanding Officer, while Pat Norman was commanding *Una*. Looking across the creek, Pat Norman saw the whole tail-end of *P 35* rise out of the water and then disappear again. He had time to say, 'What the hell is that young brother of yours doing, Joe?' before a smoke candle billowed out yellow smoke on the surface. I had decided that it was time those 'up top' were alerted to the problem. The two onlookers called for the flotilla *dghaisa* and set off for the rescue.

Deciding that the first objective was to pump out the fresh water tanks, while everything heavy was moved from forward to aft, in order to reduce weight forward, Martin was now dependent on the Chief ERA adapting a valve connection, while his own thoughts turned to communication with 'them up top'.

> I had read of French letters being used as waterproof containers and the gimmick appealed to me; so I wrote an account of the circumstances, tied a knot in the French letter and blew it to the surface through the underwater signal projector, accompanied by a smoke candle. An hour later a second was sent up; but alas, used French letters were not an uncommon sight in the creek, despite Malta being a bastion of the Roman Catholic faith. So the searchers in the *dghaisa*, now joined by other boats, saw nothing unusual in them and delicately ignored them. "Why didn't I write on the smoke candles?" I was later reasonably asked.
>
> *Upholder* was for some reason on the surface alongside the base and her famous commanding officer, Lieutenant-Commander Wanklyn, VC, was personally operating the asdic in an endeavour to contact *P 35*. We could hear the SST (known as the 'underwater telephone') vaguely through our hull, but we could not respond as our asdic gear was in the tube space, flooded and inoperable.
>
> Suddenly the engine room telegraph jangled: 'Full Ahead' then back to 'Stop'. It gave us an eerie shock for a moment until we realized that a diver had been sent down; and he was operating the mechanical telegraph from its inter-connected bridge position. We rang a reassuring reply.

At long last, early that afternoon, after the Chief ERA's talents had been taxed to the full, the boat returned to the surface, 'still down by the bow but safely afloat'. While Jimmy Launders, the first lieutenant, now took *P 35* in charge and delivered her back to her night moorings in Lazaretto Creek, the younger Martin found himself immediately summoned to face an investigation committee 'including my strict and not-at-all amused commanding officer, Lieutenant S. L. C. "Lynch" Maydon, whose first, and perhaps natural assumption was that I had made some gross error!

Martin's indignation was proved to be justified when a large triangular hole was found in the pressure hull, probably caused by a discarded anchor, upon which *P 35* had in her overweight condition rather clumsily sat.

Though no one was hurt and Martin was exonerated, the incident gave him serious pause for thought: aged just twenty-two at the time, he realized that the outcome might have been very different. 'We all knew,' he writes, 'that although escape by using the Davis Submerged Escape Apparatus was possible under ideal conditions, it had never been 100% successful and was susceptible to human error.'

After the *Lucania* incident, Pat Norman took command of *Una*. Her next patrol, beginning on 7 March, was 'off the port of Tripoli where we were to intercept small craft running arms into Africa,' writes Rocky Hill, the first lieutenant:

> This was a quiet patrol and our only target was a small Italian coaster running into Tripoli with arms. This was too small for a torpedo, so we surfaced and sank her by gunfire, after the crew of five had taken to their lifeboat and pulled for the African shore which was only ten miles away.
>
> Our next target was a salvage vessel heading for Tripoli, escorted by two armed trawlers. This was successfully sunk with one torpedo, the target just disintegrating. Expecting a counter-attack from the escorts, we went deep; but nothing happened and we heard the enemy propeller noises returning to the north from whence they had come. We returned to periscope depth and cruised through the debris when, to our amazement, we saw a man clinging to some of the wreckage . . . we picked up this survivor.
>
> At this time, small submarines did not have a qualified cook and it was the practice to appoint one of the seamen for this duty. Our particular choice was far from good: he tried to boil 7lb of dehydrated spinach in a large saucepan, with the result that the spinach overflowed into the bilges and all over the small galley. The boat smelt of bad spinach for days afterwards. Even our prisoner did not appreciate our cook's efforts, so the Italian volunteered to take over as chef. This we allowed, not knowing what to do with him; he proved to be an excellent cook and we had never lived so well since we left home .
>
> On return to Malta he offered to stay with us as cook for the duration of the war, but to our regret he was marched off as a prisoner of war. One other attack was carried out during this patrol, on an escorted convoy of three small cargo boats heading

for Tripoli and escorted by armed trawlers. It was not successful, due to counter-attack, and our POW was most upset: not
because of the counter-attack, but because we had missed.

Una returned safely to Malta on 21 March. Her patrol area had
been shared by *P 31*, *P 35* and *Sokol*, of which both *P 31* and
Sokol had a little luck.

P 31 (Lieutenant J. B. Kershaw) was off the island of Lampione
on 5 March in glassy calm conditions when she was forced to go
deep by aircraft obviously carrying out a sweep ahead of an
oncoming convoy. Returning to periscope depth, Kershaw
sighted a southbound ship, with two destroyers escorting her,
zigzagging at speed and 'coming towards'. Kershaw, noting that
the target was probably on a steady course of her 'zig', went to
forty feet and fired a salvo by asdic. All torpedoes hit at a range
of 800 yards.

Six minutes later the submarine was counter-attacked. After
nine depth charges had exploded uncomfortably close, Kershaw
decided to bottom *P 31* gently in the 180 feet shown on the chart.
Taking her down 'dead slow', she actually touched bottom with
240 feet on the gauges. While *P 31* lay bottomed at this extreme
depth, the two destroyers, apparently in contact overhead,
dropped another thirty charges extremely close to the submarine.
It was some hours before the harassed *P 31* was able to return to
the surface. On resuming periscope depth, Kershaw saw nothing
but an empty sea. The hunters had moved off and the *Marin
Sanudo* (5,081 tons) had sunk to the bottom.

Sokol was temporarily under the command of Boris Karnicki's
first lieutenant, George Koziolkowski, for this patrol. Off Lampedusa she sank a tug and gunned a schooner. Meanwhile, her
usual CO was attending a conference with Captain (S) 10 and all
those of his COs who were in harbour.

Simpson's worries had been increasing with the number of
enemy fighters concentrating on the submarine base. The shortage of ammunition in Malta compelled the four Bofors gun batteries on Manoel Island to engage only the German bombers; the
fighters were therefore swooping at will over Lazaretto and
Marsamxett Harbour. How low they flew was recorded by
Shrimp. One officer came running into the shelter yelling: 'The

Luftwaffe are down to their "pansies" now. A pilot waved to me as he flew past: the bastard had painted finger nails!'.

Even with the submarines sheltering on the seabed, it was all too possible that a bomber would get through the Bofors barrage and unleash its terrible cargo over the harbour. The fighters were repeatedly shooting up any submarine in the dockyard or found on the surface. The Tenth Flotilla could not afford to lose any more boats. So Simpson came to the conclusion that, for a limited period, it would be necessary to keep the boats almost constantly at sea. In order to achieve this, the incoming boat would enter harbour at dusk, refuel and re-arm overnight, while a fresh crew took over during the middle watch, ready to sail again before dawn the following morning.

These were alien and desperate measures. But the urgency of the situation persuaded most of the COs reluctantly to accept them. Only Tomkinson refused. Quietly he followed Simpson back to his cabin and explained that he could not share *Urge* and his men with anyone else. He was capable of continuing indefinitely at sea, returning only to re-arm and refuel. He told Simpson that he saw no reason to part from his beloved *Urge* 'just because some enemy airmen are piddling around overhead. My *Urge* is one hundred per cent efficient and my duty is to command her and to beat this devilish outfit, ' he asserted. And then, in a final impassioned outburst, he declared that if Simpson insisted on the scheme then he, Tomkinson, would resign his command. Simpson took Tommo's reaction to heart; the time was not yet right for resorting to double crews. The scheme was left in abeyance. Judging that Tomkinson was under considerable strain, he dispatched *Urge* next on a relatively quiet 'cloak-and-dagger' patrol with Captain Wilson, RA.

Admiral Cunningham had been planning a further convoy to be sailed through to Malta with the support of all three services. The convoy would comprise four ships — the old warrior *Breconshire*, with *Clan Campbell*, *Pampas* and *Talabot*. Escorting this vital convoy would be the 15th Cruiser Squadron, under the command of Rear-Admiral Vian in *Cleopatra*. It was due to leave Alexandria on 20 March, while the army and the RAF staged diversions elsewhere to keep the enemy busy.

Well before the 20th Simpson's submarines were taking up patrol positions in order to intercept any enemy fleet movements, most importantly around Sicily and off Taranto.

On the 14th *P 34* (Lieutenant P. R. H. Harrison) was off the south Calabrian coast when she sighted the conning tower of a northbound Italian U-boat. Harrison identified her as *Millo* (1,461 tons), one of the larger submarines which the Italians used to ferry stores to Africa. It seemed strange that the enemy boat was on the surface in broad daylight and proceeding at only about six knots, but at the time Harrison was concentrating on his attack in ideal conditions. When two of his four torpedoes struck *Millo* forward and amidships, Harrison writes, 'she sank almost immediately'.

> After the attack, *P 34* surfaced and closed the position and those on board *Millo* who managed to escape — there had been many on her bridge when hit — were rescued from the sea: fourteen survivors were picked up. Rescue operations were in full view of the shore and took some time as *P 34* had to be manoeuvred alongside each survivor in the water; whilst this was going on we believed that ineffectual fire from the beach was directed against the submarine, and she was no doubt reported. In due course, the expected flying boat arrived over the area but not, again fortunately, until after rescue operations had been completed and the submarine submerged. In view of the numbers of survivors on board a small submarine, *P 34* returned to Malta and landed them the next day. She then resumed her patrol.

According to one of the Italian officers, *Millo* had been on the surface because the captain wanted to smoke.

Two days later, and a few miles south of *P 34*, *Unbeaten* attacked a troop transport. Now with Teddy Woodward back in command, fit again after his illness, *Unbeaten* was close under the cliff of Cape Spartivento on the 16th when he torpedoed and damaged the *Pisani* (6,339 tons). The counter-attack from three destroyers was ineffectual, but at one stage when the submarine came up to periscope depth she was very nearly rammed. After withdrawing westwards, *Unbeaten* was close to Cape dell' Armi just before dawn the next morning when HE was heard and Woodward glimpsed another U-boat on the surface (*Guglielmotti*,

896 tons). He went deep, turned *Unbeaten* at full speed to a 100° track, then returned to periscope depth, ready to fire. But the target had vanished. Suddenly it reappeared, but well past the D.A. Swinging *Unbeaten*, Woodward fired a full salvo. One hit was heard, followed by the sounds of a submarine breaking up under water. *Unbeaten* surfaced to try and pick up a group of twelve men in the water, but an approaching aircraft and several E-boats forced Woodward to dive and he left them to pick up the survivors. The enemy then dropped twenty-four depth charges, but without damage to *Unbeaten*.

Upholder was on her twenty-fourth patrol. According to Captain M. L. C. Crawford, DSC★, Wanklyn's original first lieutenant (at this time Crawford was in Britain taking his 'perisher'), 'Wanklyn had always been asking for a patrol in the Adriatic and on 14 March he sailed for this area'.

> He closed Brindisi and, observing that traffic did not appear to be following swept channels, he felt it was safe to go really close in to the coast. He was justified in this decision by sighting a *Perla*-class U-boat but this passed out of range. Later another U-boat was seen and, although four small fishing vessels in the area complicated the attack, he managed to get off four torpedoes, two of which sank the submarine *Tricheco*.
>
> A chance to use the gun came when a small trawler and three small fishing vessels were sighted close inshore. Wanklyn surfaced very close by the trawler and ordered the crew to leave before sinking her with a very small expenditure of ammunition. The Italians equipped many such vessels with A/S equipment and small guns and they could be a menace to submarines.
>
> *Upholder* was then ordered to shift patrol to an area off Taranto to watch for movement of the Italian fleet, and so course was set to pass through the Otranto Strait. On 23 March, in very rough weather and in poor visibility, the asdic operator reported the noise of enemy propellers and Wanklyn was just able to make out the top of a battleship. It was almost impossible to control the depth of the submarine at periscope depth, but an attack was made, firing four torpedoes but with no success.
>
> Having fired all her torpedoes, *Upholder* returned to Malta,

arriving on 26 March, and all the crew had a few days' break in
a rest camp.

On the pitch–dark night of 19 March *P 36* (Lieutenant H. N.
Edmonds) was off Taranto when the enemy fleet made its move.
At 0050 *P 36* heard the HE of heavy ships approaching from the
north. At 0125 Edmonds dived to avoid a destroyer screen. Minutes later the boat returned to the surface. Nothing was visible,
but Edmonds immediately started transmitting his 'enemy
report': the enemy battlefleet might be a threat to the all-important convoy and its escort of the 15th Cruiser Squadron.

Thanks to Edmonds's signal, the convoy's escort was able to
dispose itself between the battleship and our four merchant ships.
The confrontation finally occurred on 22 March in the Gulf of
Sirte, and an unequal battle it was, with the Italian battleship *Littorio*, three fast and powerful cruisers and heavy destroyer screen
facing our four light cruisers. In a bold and brilliant action which
later became known as The Second Battle of Sirte, Rear-Admiral
Vian held off the enemy warships while the convoy slipped
round towards Malta.

Pursued by enemy aircraft, first *Breconshire* was hit, though she
managed to limp through to Malta; then *Clan Campbell* was bombed and sunk twenty miles from safety. *Pampas* and *Talabot*, the
other two ships, arrived in Grand Harbour, but, while their
supplies were still being unloaded, both were bombed and sunk
alongside. Only 5,000 of the 26,000 tons of the convoy's supplies
were safely unloaded.

The month was ending in near despair. Lethargy and exhaustion due to semi-starvation were producing the first signs of a
terrible apathy. It was only a stubborn will to survive that kept
most people going – an obstinacy aided by the store-running
submarines, *Porpoise*, *Olympus* and *Pandora*.

Malta could not hold out much longer.

16

MARCH/APRIL, 1942

Whether or not Malta could survive the ferocious bombing, the question was by now being asked whether the Tenth Submarine Flotilla could afford to stay there. Conditions were so severe that it was only by superhuman efforts the submarines were kept functioning. Although crews were usually able to reach the shelters, the boats were at constant risk. In the dockyard they were totally vulnerable and there was nothing anyone could do to protect them. Camouflage netting was of little value when the enemy was using saturation tactics like these.

P 39, after the damage caused to her batteries by the near miss off Lazaretto, was still undergoing repairs in the dockyard on 26 March, just across the creek from *Sokol* who had also suffered some damage in harbour. At 1800 that evening a bomb fell between the two submarines. *Sokol* was unaffected, but *P 39* was split in twain. She was towed off and beached by the stern, her stores and gear being removed to Lazaretto. One less submarine for the Fighting Tenth. Captain Simpson's worst fears were coming true.

Urge, having had generator trouble off Pantellaria, returned to Malta on the 23rd. For once, the raiders did not interfere with repairs and she sailed again on the same day. The following day, a Tuesday, Tomkinson wrote home to his mother:

> I've been sleeping for nearly thirty-six hours with only a short break for meals and one or two calls, so am completely recover-ed from the very severe blitzing the filthy Hun has been giving us — you probably read about it in the papers . . . My boys are all very well and the boat seems to just keep on going, thanks

to a lot of hard work — it's about time I gave these foes of ours another bang.

The next 'bang' Tomkinson gave the enemy was produced by Captain R. 'Tug' Wilson, Royal Artillery, and his commando marine corporal, who had joined *Urge* for this demolition expedition in the Tyrrhenian Sea. Their orders were to act as they pleased for the confusion of the King's enemies.

Late on the night of 29 March the Folbot party landed in a mizzle of rain and poor visibility to investigate a promising railway line in the Gulf of Policastro. Within forty-five minutes they were back on board, having laid their charges on the track. At 0055 on the morning of the 30th a southbound train was blown up, the front end rolling down the embankment. Meanwhile an armed merchant vessel had entered the bay and Tomkinson turned his attention to her. He fired three torpedoes at 3,500 yards range, which missed, so *Urge* went to gun action. The enemy returned as good as she got; when one of her rounds soaked those on the bridge, Tomkinson decided to dive.

On 1 April, unaware of the catastrophe unfolding at Lazaretto, *Urge* scored a double hit on the Italian cruiser *Giovanni delle Bande Nere*. She had already been damaged by Rear Admiral Vian's ships in The Second Battle of Sirte and was returning with her escort of two destroyers to the repair yards of Spezia. Ironically, Tomkinson had first identified the warship as one of the larger classes of cruiser and had altered the depth-settings of his torpedoes accordingly: from ten feet to twelve and sixteen feet to eighteen. As Captain (S)10 remarked later, torpedoes with such a setting would not normally have hit a 6-inch cruiser, but would have run harmlessly underneath her. Only because of the earlier damage was she drawing a deeper draught than usual.

On 6 April *Urge* returned to Lazaretto to find that two more submarines had been sunk in harbour; nor were they the only casualties.

Pandora (Lieutenant R. L. Alexander) had arrived in Malta on the night of 31 March and discharged her cargo of white oils in Marsamxett Harbour at once. She had brought other stores to be unloaded in Grand Harbour and at dawn on 1 April she moved to Hamilton Wharf. Because of the urgency, men worked on her constantly, even when the air raid began. Beside her on the wharf was the Greek submarine *Glaukos*. In the dry dock opposite the jetty was the destroyer *Lance,* of Force K fame, who was having her rivets and rudder repaired.

Four of *Lance's* officers had been left behind as a maintenance party while the rest of the ship's company took a break − her first lieutenant, Godfrey Style; her 'Chief', Frank King; her navigating officer, Peter Dallas-Smith; and her Number Two, David Morgan. As Style here records, all four men were on her upper deck when the Ju 87s and 88s appeared:

> The dive-bombers were very high. Then, as we watched them peel off one by one, we *knew,* as they came down towards us, that the submarine and *Lance* were their target.
>
> We saw them dropping two 'sticks': the first bomb landed on poor Senglea, the village on the hillside, which was already pulverized. The second bomb hit *Pandora*. It was a ghastly sight. Her conning tower must have been open, because out of it spouted a great mass of roaring flame, as if powered by a blow lamp: a sight I shall never forget.

Four minutes later *Pandora* had sunk. Two officers and twenty-three ratings had been killed. Style and his companions were still racing across the jetty to see if they could help when the next wave of bombers arrived:

> I had the impression that the leading Ju was coming straight for me. He was so low that I could see the pilot's face through the perspex of his cockpit. Then he let go his 1,000lb bomb . . .
>
> Peter Dallas-Smith lay there with a large splinter through his badly smashed leg. It developed gangrene and was amputated in St. Paul's Hospital. The Chief had a large slice of his bottom carved off. David Morgan's left arm was slightly injured.
>
> I was conscious of my fore-arm being knocked straight off and a fountain of blood when my artery was cut. My head was in the badly wounded part of the poor Chief's behind.
>
> Each officer, in those days, carried a syringe and a phial of morphia in his uniform. So David Morgan extracted his syringe and, carrying out the correct drill, shoved the needle through

my uniform . . . then tied a label onto me which recorded how much morphia he had given me. But he made a 50% error and in fact had only given me a half dose.

We were taken to the tunnel where a naval doctor took care of us. I was given no more morphia because of his mistake on the tally, so my journey to the 45th General Hospital in the ambulance was an uncomfortable ride.

An extraordinary relief overwhelmed us when we arrived at the hospital; it was marvellous to reach the operating theatre and pass out.

We were in a rare old mess. A hunk of steel through my thigh almost took off my left leg. Another hunk went through my chest. Both my eardrums were blown out, but mercifully I've been left with only one permanently deaf ear.

But, Style concludes, he was 'very lucky'. He was alive. One of his visitors in hospital was Shrimp Simpson, an old friend of his — 'we had served together in *Sussex* in '34' — who later arranged for Style to return home in the store-carrying submarine *Clyde*.

Style's beloved *Lance* survived only a few days more. Like the Greek submarine *Glaukos,* she received minor damage, but was then sunk in another raid on 4 April.

At the same moment as the Ju 88s were attacking *Pandora,* another batch was blitzing Lazaretto, remembers Fred Matthews, Stoker Petty Officer of *P 36*. She was alongside at the wardroom berth, having returned from patrol and being in need of repairs 'after a six-hour attack on us by destroyers dropping about 300 depth charges'. Matthews recalls:

When the first bomb dropped and holed us, the coxswain and I were drinking a couple of tots of rum in our mess, having temporarily ignored the air raid warning orders to take to the shelter. We made it to the conning tower and over the side in about ten seconds flat, past a gaping hole.

Unlike Matthews, Kenneth England was obeying orders in remaining on board, for he and the torpedo officer had been detailed to stay behind as a maintenance party, while the rest of the crew were at rest camp at Ghain Tuffieha. England, the Outside ERA, writes:

> I shall always remember watching three bombs leave the bomb bay of a diving Ju 88 as I looked up through the conning tower hatch. As the bombs grew larger and larger, I was quite sure that they would come straight through the hatch and into the control room. They straddled the boat, moved it some twenty feet along the jetty and blew the bottom in, as well as doing major damage inside the boat.

The torpedo officer and England had fortunately escaped serious injury, but as the poisonous chlorine fumes swirled up from broken batteries the two men 'baled out very rapidly indeed'. Despite efforts to save *P 36,* she sank eighty feet on to a ledge, clearly visible from the gallery outside the wardroom where officers often sat having a drink. She remained there until 1958, when she was raised, towed out to sea and sunk in deep water.

Unbeaten was caught in the same blitz, having attempted to dive as soon as the raid began. She was near-missed by a couple of 'sticks', one bomb twisting her bow-shutter gear and distorting her tubes, but by 9 April she was patched up again and operational.

Another near-miss on *Penelope,* trapped in Grand Harbour since the Second Battle of Sirte, caused such shrapnel damage that her crew nicknamed her 'HMS *Pepperpot'.* Within days she managed to escape and reached the comparative safety of Gibraltar on the 10th.

According to George Taylor, liaison officer in *Sokol,* he ran into Simpson on the morning of 3 April when Simpson scribbled a note for Taylor to give to *Sokol's* CO, Boris Karnicki. Shrimp had a hunch that the German pilots would come back for her and, if she stayed where she was, she would surely be sunk. He therefore issued orders that *Sokol* be moved to one of the creeks and covered with camouflage.

Thus began a fortnight of constant movement for the Polish submarine. Every day the raiders would come, apparently seeking her out, and almost invariably they would pinpoint her position and drop their bombs. Somehow she survived them all.

Every night she would move again, while repair work continued on her batteries, and then the camouflage would cover her again by day. On the 8th, when all the surrounding barges and buildings were flattened by the bombs, *Sokol* was damaged, but again that night she was moved and the camouflage replaced. By the 13th she was functioning sufficiently to be able to dive in harbour, but on the 15th she fouled the booms at the mouth of Grand Harbour and broke a propeller. This mishap prompted the decision 'that we should try to leave Malta for Gibraltar,' writes George Taylor, 'where we could be efficiently repaired for return to the UK'. It would be a slow and hazardous passage, with only one battery operating and only a single propeller, but Boris Karnicki was confident his boat would make it. To by-pass the damaged batteries, Chief E. R. A. Sienkewitch connected the generators directly to the main electrical system, a dangerous procedure never before attempted in the *Us*. His gamble succeeded.

Finally, on 16 April, a strangely quiet day, *Sokol* surfaced in daylight and prepared to leave Malta. Thanks to Captain (S) 10's prescience, and the hard work of her ship's company and all who kept her afloat, *Sokol* had eluded the enemy. Taylor writes:

> The only casualty suffered by *Sokol* had been during an air raid on Birkirkara, when one of our seamen was literally picked up by the blast of an exploding bomb and hurled against a stone wall. This had a profound effect upon our ship's company and upon Boris, who regarded all his crew as his own personal chums. The only other casualty during the whole of this blitz was our cat. We had captured this fine animal when we boarded the Italian schooner *Guiseppina* in the Gulf of Gabes; we brought the cat back as our personal prize. She took up residence near the billiard room in the base, and subsequently departed this world when the billiard table fell on top of her during a bombing raid.

The cat had used up all her nine lives, but *Sokol* had not; she would return to Malta again.

At the end of March, Admiral Sir Andrew B. Cunningham, Commander-in-Chief Mediterranean, 'ABC' to his sailors, was appointed representative for the British Chiefs of Staff on a Washington committee. Later in the year he would return to the Mediterranean, but in the meantime, until his successor arrived, Vice-Admiral Pridham-Wippell was Acting Commander-in-Chief. On 5 April Pridham-Wippell was asked by the Admiralty to consider the advantages of moving an old depot ship, *Lucia*, from Colombo to Alexandria, so that the Tenth Flotilla could be evacuated forthwith from Malta. (On the same day as the proposal was forwarded, *Lucia* was sunk by the Japanese). Simpson was, of course, consulted. He believed that with Malta's aircraft barely able to function, his flotilla was the last remaining weapon to wield against Rommel's umbilical link with Italy. Not only that, but the submarines were the only defence against the likely bombardment of the island by Italian ships, prior to the expected invasion. More over, the people of Malta regarded the *Us* with proprietorial affection; how would they feel if their valiant little submarines deserted the island?

No: the Fighting Tenth would carry on, at least for the moment. But the elaborate precautions to protect the submarines would have to be even more stringently enforced. While any submarine was on the surface she was in imminent peril of destruction; even submerged in harbour she was not safe, for Kesselring's pilots were systematically bombing the water. Thus the new orders were for submarines to stay submerged by day *outside* the harbour, in deeper water, despite the fact that they would be out of communication. Meantime, the boats were surely better off on patrol.

The German and Italian planners were still frenziedly making arrangements for Operation 'Hercules', the intended invasion of Malta. According to Cajus Bekker's book *The Luftwaffe War Diaries,** 'The Italian leader of the operation, Marshal Count Cavallero, had at his disposal 50,000 men for the air landings alone — equivalent to the whole British garrison' — and the seaborne landings would involve 'no fewer than six Italian divisions totalling 70,000 men.'

Kesselring himself flew over Malta in the second week of April

* Macdonald & Co, 1966 (first published in German, 1964).

to inspect the damage his pilots had wrought. He afterwards reported to his master that the bombing had 'eliminated Malta as a naval base'. Nevertheless, he added:

> I intend to continue the attack, if weather permits, until April 20th, and then, by harassing raids, to prevent the enemy from repairing the damage.

Now was surely the time for Hitler to launch the invasion. But he remained as anxious about crossing the sea to invade this island as he had been hesitant in crossing the English Channel in 1940. 'On land I am a hero,' he confided to Admiral Raeder, 'but at sea a coward.'

Back-pedalling once again, Hitler postponed Operation 'Hercules' until after Rommel's great offensive, planned for May. When Rommel reached the Egyptian frontier, Hitler promised, the Great Plan could commence.

P 31 (Lieutenant Kershaw) returned to Malta on 8 April after a quiet patrol north along the Italian mainland as far as Civitavecchia, where he surveyed the swept channel. With the new routine in force, all but a maintenance party were immediately sent to rest camps at Ghain Tuffieha and Mellieha, while the boat was obliged to sit all day long on the sea bottom. Even the rest camps were dangerous places, as our spare crew telegraphist noted in his log:

> 7 *April*. Rest camp machine-gunned by a crashing Ju 88. Plane landed in sea. Machine-gunned by Mes when swimming.

On Easter Sunday, the 5th, Pat Norman, in *Una* fired a salvo at the transport *Palestrina* (5,335 tons) and scored two hits; within ten minutes she had sunk. As Norman says: 'Retribution was very considerable.' The Italian ship had been escorted by two destroyers, one of whom came uncomfortably close with her counter-attack — though not as close as she imagined.

Years later, after the war, Pat Norman was first lieutenant of the battleship *Vanguard* when she paid a call on Taranto. He invited his opposite number in the Italian battleship *Duilio* over for a drink, and naturally both men fell to reminiscing about the war. The Italian told a remarkable story about how he had sunk a British submarine under difficult conditions, and ended up being decorated. 'And here is my medal,' the proud man announced, displaying it for Norman to admire. But Norman had been leading him on. 'We had a lot of information on our sinkings,' he writes. Knowing the answer in advance, he asked his visitor if the ship that the submarine had attacked was the *Palestrina*:

> It was lovely to watch his horror when he found that he'd been decorated for sinking me, and there I was talking to him! He asked me: 'Please, never tell anyone about this.' 'I won't for some considerable time,' I told him.

That was in 1949.

P 34 was on patrol off the tip of Italy's heel, with Lieutenant J. W. D. ('Basher') Coombe in command to give Harrison a rest. At 0924 on 12 April a shattering explosion blew her to the surface. All lighting aft in the boat was extinguished, but on inspection only minor damage was apparent. As no aircraft or ship had been in the vicinity, the explosion was presumed to have been caused by a detonating mine. Later that day, when preparing for an encounter with enemy warships, *P 34's* torpedoes were found to be jammed in their tubes. She returned to harbour forthwith, arriving in foul weather on the 16th. At least the poor visibility deterred the German raiders.

Upholder had sailed from Malta on 6 April for her final patrol before returning to the UK. On board were two Arab agents and Captain 'Tug' Wilson, Royal Artillery, with his Folbot. Wilson was to ferry the two agents ashore in the Gulf of Sousse. On the night of 9/10 April, the operation completed, Wilson returned safely to the submarine. Wanklyn signalled, 'Operation successful.' Wanklyn's orders were now to rendezvous with *Unbeaten* (Lieutenant-Commander Woodward), in order to transfer the army officer.

Unbeaten, patched up after her near miss, was returning to Britain ahead of *Upholder* and Wilson would go with her. The transfer was to take place off the flat-topped islet of Lampione, one of the Pelagie group, in the early hours of the 11th. The two submarines duly made contact, but because of rising winds Wanklyn suggested that Wilson might prefer to stay on board *Upholder*. But Wilson was an old hand with the canoe and made the transfer safely. *Unbeaten* proceeded towards Gibraltar and ultimately to England; *Upholder* continued her patrol, heading south towards Djerba Island and then East towards Tripoli.

On 12 April Simpson had received reports from reconnaissance aircraft that an escorted convoy was sailing south from Taranto. Anticipating the enemy's route, he signalled to *Upholder* to join a patrol line with *Urge* and *Thrasher* (Lieutenant H. S. Mackenzie), to the northward of Tripoli. Both Tomkinson in *Urge*, Wanklyn's great friend, and Rufus Mackenzie in *Thrasher* reached the line on the 13th, but failed to make contact with *Upholder*.

Upholder did not return from patrol. On 18 April, 1942, she was posted missing, presumed lost.

It is not known to this day how this most famous of submarines and her gallant company met their end. One possibility is that she was mined off Tripoli during the night of 11/12 April, but this seems unlikely. Although the enemy's records showed, after the war, that a submarine was sighted at 1900 on the evening of the 11th just north of the Tripoli minefields, their own investigations revealed no evidence of a submarine sinking. In any case, a Commanding Officer of Wanklyn's competence would never have taken his boat into such a well-known minefield.

A second possibility is that *Upholder* was a victim of anti-submarine patrols on the 14th. Again, German reports show that a British submarine was sighted off Misurata on the 13th, and on the 14th both *Urge* and *Thrasher* heard underwater explosions to the north-west. But against this theory is the fact that the enemy records showed no anti-submarine action for the time and place in question. The explosions heard by the two British submarines might have resulted from an RAF attack on the same Tripoli-bound convoy that they had been sent to destroy.

Thirdly, it is possible that *Upholder* was sunk by the Italian torpedo boat *Pegaso*, part of the escort for that convoy. *Pegaso* was alerted to the presence of an enemy submarine on the afternoon of the 14th by the convoy's seaplane escort, which dropped a smoke marker in position 34° 47′N, 15° 55′E. This modern *Orsa-*class torpedo boat, 850 tons, had only two days previously completed her refresher training on the new German asdic with which she had been fitted in the New Year. Her Commanding Officer has recorded:

> *Day 14.4.42. 1615 hours.* As a result of white smoke from escort seaplane and distant reading on echo-direction finder, I carry out the prescribed alarm signals for the submarine and begin the attack by dropping a pattern of depth charges.
>
> *Day 14.4.42. 1630 hours.* Receiving no further echo on echo-direction finder, I call off the attack and rejoin the convoy, resuming escort duty.

If the submarine that the seaplane had sighted and *Pegaso* had found on her asdic was really *Upholder,* she was *some one hundred miles** north-east of her ordered position in the line with *Urge* and *Thrasher.* But it is not inconceivable that Wanklyn, known for his dash and initiative, had altered course in order to intercept the enemy convoy more directly.

The truth is that no-one will ever know what happened to *Upholder.* During her fifteen months in the Mediterranean she had safely completed twenty-four patrols; this was her twenty-fifth, her last before returning to the UK. Thenceforth 'the last patrol before going home' was regarded with superstitious caution. In total, she had hit with thirty-one of the ninety-eight torpedoes she fired. According to Admiralty estimates later, she had sunk '3 U-boats, 2 destroyers, 1 armed trawler and 15 enemy transports and supply ships'.

It was a long time before the Tenth Flotilla could absorb the unbelievable news.

Upholder's original first lieutenant, M. L. C. ('Tubby') Crawford, had left her in November, 1941, in order to return home for his 'perisher'. He handed over to Lieutenant Brian Band, who was killed only days later in the raid on Lazaretto. Band's successor was Lieutenant P. R. H. Allen, who was *Upholder's* first lieutenant when she was lost. Captain Crawford has written a history of *Upholder* in which he notes:

---

* A *U's* 24-hour Mean Line of Advance was 90 nautical miles.

However *Upholder* was sunk, the Navy lost not only an out-standing submarine commander, but an officer who had all the qualities necessary for the highest appointments in the service. One must not forget that the Navy also lost a very highly trained and experienced team of officers and ratings, for, of those that were lost, all but a handful had been with Wanklyn throughout the life of *Upholder*.

With Wanklyn were lost his three officers and twenty-eight men.

It was a cruel blow for everyone in the service, but most keenly felt by those in Lazaretto, especially Captain (S). Wanklyn had been Simpson's first lieutenant in *Porpoise* before the war and they had been firm friends ever since. Simpson later recalled how Wanklyn had first had difficulty in hitting his targets, then 'suddenly he got the knack':

> He was not a better attacker than many others in normal circumstances, but two things happened. Wherever Wanklyn was sent the enemy appeared, and noteworthy targets too; this gave him much practice and increasing confidence, which made him turn fleeting opportunities into complete success.

And yet, as Simpson added, 'His modesty made him loved and respected by all.'

To keep the news from the enemy, the Admiralty did not announce *Upholder's* loss until much later, and then they issued this unique statement:

> It is seldom proper for Their Lordships to draw distinctions between different services rendered in the course of naval duty, but they take this opportunity of singling out those of HMS *Upholder*, under the command of Lieutenant-Commander Wanklyn, for special mention. She was long employed against enemy communications in the Central Mediterranean, and she became noted for the uniformly high quality of her services in that arduous and dangerous duty. Such was the standard of skill and daring that the ship and her officers and men became an inspiration, not only to their own flotilla, but to the fleet of which it was part, and Malta, where for so long HMS *Upholder* was based. The ship and her company are gone, but the example and the inspiration remain.

17

APRIL/MAY, 1942

On 15 April, 1942, the Governor of Malta, General Sir William Dobbie, announced that he had received a communication from the Secretary of State for the Colonies. He had been commanded by the King 'to convey to you the following message':

> To honour her brave people, I award the George Cross to the island fortress of Malta, to bear witness to a heroism and devotion that will long be famous in history.
>
> GEORGE R.I.

Ever since, the invincible 'island fortress' has borne its battle honour with pride: Malta, GC.

It was a unique and splendid award, and an undoubted morale-booster. But it did not stop the bombs from falling. In February there had been 236 raids, during which 1,000 tons of bombs had been dropped. In March there had been 2,000 tons of bombs. By the end of this month, there would have been 6,700 tons of bombs dropped on the island.

Our spare crew telegraphist noted in his log, after spending two days at the rest camp at St Paul's Bay:

> *18 April.* Returned to S/M base.
> *19 April.* Battery of 3.7" AA guns on our island [Manoel Island] wiped out. Three hours continuous dive bombing. Many casualties in Royal Artillery.
> *20 April.* Manoel Island guns and gun crews replaced. Sent to rest camp at St Paul's. The position in the S/M base now is so bad that washing can only be hung up under cover; white caps

are not to be worn in the base. Jerry bombs any place that is inhabited and looks big enough for a S/M base. Spitfires put up a good show for first time since arriving on the island.

21 April. Returned to S/M base. Took over S/M *P 31.* Worked all night, then stand off.

22 April. Took over *P 31* from Duty Watch at 2100. Dived between Inner Baffle and Outer Boom – 62 feet.

24 April. Took over *P 31* at 2100 alongside Torpedo Depot. Three torpedoes out; three new ones in. Dived outside boom at 0500. Depth 105 feet. Celebrated 2,148th alert.

The Spitfires which our telegraphist mentions on the 20th had arrived only that day. Forty-seven had been embarked on the American carrier USS *Wasp* in the River Clyde, and all but one reached the island safely.

Simpson had been informed on the 17th that the Spitfires were coming, but, after discussions with his opposite number in the RAF, he was convinced that even these valiant Spitfire pilots would be no match for the aerial barbarians. The enemy would destroy the 'Spits' immediately on landing. He made up his mind: the flotilla would have to move.

Two days later, an aircraft from Alexandria brought an unexpected visitor for Simpson: Captain Phillip Ruck-Keene, who, as Captain (S)1, was the man to whom Simpson was responsible. With him Ruck-Keene had brought a message from FOS, Sir Max Horton, which said in effect that the Tenth Flotilla would have to leave Malta very soon. FOS could not replace such losses. In consultation with Ruck-Keene and Leatham, the Vice-Admiral, Malta, at Lascaris, Simpson made it plain that he too thought the Tenth could no longer stay. But he would give the Spitfires a chance. If the RAF pilots could somehow work a miracle, perhaps the awful moment could be staved off.

On 19 April, almost before the forty-seven 'Spits' flown off from *Wasp* could touch down, Kesselring's airmen pounced. The Ju 88s and Me 109s swooped over the three RAF airfields, Ta Qali, Hal Far and Luqa, and shot up most of the Spitfires on the ground, before they could reach their pens. By dawn of the next day, 21 April, only twenty-seven Spitfires remained. By that evening, only seventeen. (By the end of April there were seven.)

The following morning Simpson left Lazaretto, took a *dghaisa* across the harbour and climbed the steep alleyways to Lascaris. Here he sought out Vice-Admiral, Malta, and announced his decision: the Tenth Submarine Flotilla would evacuate the island as soon as possible.

Admiral Leatham approved the decision and informed Pridham-Wippell, the acting Commander-in-Chief, Mediterranean, accordingly.

There were now only five *U* survivors at Malta: *Urge, Una, P 31, P 34* and *P 35*. At the time Simpson was making his sad decision, three were in harbour, *Una, P 31* and *P 34,* while the other two were out on patrol. *Urge* was patrolling between Lampedusa and Pantellaria, where she had sighted a two-ship convoy on the 12th. Her attack was thwarted when the flying boat escort saw Tomkinson's torpedo tracks; the convoy stopped to let the 'fish' pass. She returned to Lazaretto without further incident on the 22nd.

To the south of *Urge, P 35* had a little more luck. On the 19th Lynch Maydon damaged a 6,000-ton northbound supply ship and, later that afternoon, off the Kerkenah Banks he sighted another northbound ship, the *Assunta de Gregori* (4,219 tons), escorted by one destroyer and two aircraft. Though firing only two torpedoes at a range of 11,000 yards, he hit with both. The ship went to the bottom and the counter-attack was negligible.

P 34 had gone straight into the dockyard as soon as 'Basher' Coombe brought her back from her close encounter with a mine off the heel of Italy. As soon as her damage had been tended, she slipped round to Marsamxett Harbour, Lieutenant Harrison having resumed command. Now, with half his crew, he prepared his boat as swiftly as possible for her departure from Malta. As usual, the enemy raids made it impossible to stay surfaced during the hours of daylight, so at dawn on the 24th the submarine dived. On board, 'to support my very inexperienced fourth officer', was her CO himself. *P 34* 'bottomed at about ninety feet between two baffles', Harrison recalls, referring to the net barriers across the harbour mouth, 'and quite close to the Lazaretto base'. Harrison found it unnerving to be sitting passively on the harbour bottom while huge 1,000kg bombs crashed down all around: 'One got absolutely no warning, unlike depth-charging, of the loud detonations which went on at intervals for much of the day.' But at last the night was falling; it was time for *P 34* to surface. To Harrison's exasperation, the submarine would not respond:

> After any amount of blowing ballast tanks, the depth gauges continued to show the submarine at ninety feet. I thought that, as a result of near misses, the submarine had been caught under one of the baffles, so I made considerable use of the submarine's propellers — ahead and astern — to try and free her. But the depth gauges continued to show the submarine at ninety feet. It was not until some time later, when a member of the base staff jumped on to the bridge of the submarine and worked the engine room telegraphs that I realized that the submarine was in fact on the surface.

The base staff, including Simpson, had seen the submarine surfacing after dark, but then remaining motionless as if in trouble. He and Sam MacGregor pulled across in a skiff and found her caught by a thick wire hawser, taut across her conning tower. MacGregor took his hacksaw to the wire and suddenly it parted with a crack! The boat sprang to the surface.

While Simpson and his *U*s prepared to leave Malta, two of the gallant large submarines arrived: the River-class *Clyde* from Gibraltar and the minelayer *Porpoise* from Alexandria. Both were stuffed with stores: everything from munitions to mail, as Lieutenant J. R. H. Bull remembers. Bull was fourth hand in *Clyde* (Commander D. C. Ingram), after she underwent conversion at Gibraltar so that she could carry stores: 'We sailed for Malta on 10 April,' writes Bull, 'with 88 tons of petrol, 30 tons of kerosene and 70 tons of ammunition' which was 'not a popular cargo because it involved a lot of "no smoking" after embarkation'.

When *Clyde* arrived in Malta she soon discovered why the Tenth was being forced to leave. Because of the bombing, she was obliged to spend the entire day on the harbour bottom, and even there the bombs were dangerously close. One large bomb exploding in the water overhead gave the boat a severe shaking, but no serious damage was found.

Having unloaded her stores, *Clyde* now embarked 'a large quantity of rough copper slabs', writes Lieutenant Bull, 'to compensate for the loss of weight after we had discharged the ammunition'. The space where a section of battery was removed 'came in handy for the accommodation of officer passengers, some of them sick or wounded, who were being evacuated from Malta.' At first light the following morning, the submarine sailed from Marsamxett Harbour and was immediately forced to dive by German aircraft swooping out of the sky. But something was wrong: the submarine plunged to the seabed, then hurtled back to the surface, not once or twice but three times. Each time she surfaced the German aircraft opened up with their machine guns.

Somehow the submarine managed to return to harbour, to the dubious safety of Lazaretto Creek, where a diver was sent down to investigate. The problem, he soon reported, was that the after hydroplanes were jammed at 'hard-a-dive'. To linger in Malta's dockyard for proper repairs was asking for trouble, so the Lazaretto staff lashed the after planes amidships with wires. David Ingram decided that *Clyde* would have to manage with only her fore planes. The following morning she set sail again. This time she managed to get as far as the coast of Sicily, writes Lieutenant Bull:

> I was lying on my bunk in the wardroom when I was suddenly aware of the sound of waves breaking on rocks. I rushed to the control room and told the captain . . . He pooh-poohed my statement, but then there was a distinct bump: the boat's bow rose and the asdic went dead. David ordered periscope depth.
>
> On putting the periscope up on what he thought was the bearing of the land, he could see nothing. He again pooh-poohed my anxiety and swung the periscope around on a sweep. Suddenly, he stopped and swore: all he could see was the light of a lighthouse, so close that he could see the keeper.

The Italian lighthouse-keeper failed to notice her and she crept back out to sea 'minus the asdic dome which had been swiped off when we grounded'. *Clyde* reached Gibraltar safely, after a long, slow and very careful passage, on 26 April.

Porpoise (Lieutenant L. W. A. Bennington) and her cargo of stores arrived from Alexandria on the 26th, and after embarking passengers for evacuation to Egypt she left again on the 29th.

By this time the first two *Us* had also left Malta. *P 31* had sailed for Alexandria on 26 April, followed on the 27th by *Urge*. Half an hour after *Porpoise P 34* also left. The base staff were being evacuated too, leaving only a care and maintenance party behind. Captain (S) would stay until *Una* and *P 35* were ready to go, then he too would leave.

German E-boats had started to appear off Malta's coast, sowing mines in the approach channels. Such minesweepers as remained to Vice-Admiral, Malta, were prevented from operating by prowling Me 109s. Any day now the submarines and surface ships alike would be trapped in their own harbours by enemy mines. The warships would eventually be picked off by the Luftwaffe.

The submarine base was in ruins. The dockyard was so thoroughly ravaged that it was barely functioning. The airfields were in a similar state, and the people of Malta were very nearly starving. Everyone was sure the invasion was about to begin.

At the end of April Mussolini went to see Hitler at his 'Eagle's Nest', the Berghof. Admiral Raeder's representative, Captain Junge, attended the meeting and afterwards wrote to a certain Captain Wangenheim at Operations Division in Berlin, his letter dated 1 May 1942. 'Here, in haste, is my latest news of the Mussolini discussion at the Berghof,' he wrote. 'General impression: most satisfactory.'

> Agreements were finally reached on the Libya operation and on Malta. First Libya: end of May or beginning of June. Then Malta: mid July, since to attempt both simultaneously would cancel out each, particularly as regards air cover.

Hitler was still postponing 'Hercules' in favour of Rommel's planned offensive. Now that Malta's threat to the supply convoys between Italy and North Africa had been, in Kesselring's opinion, eliminated, Rommel was obtaining all the troops, tanks and ammunition he wanted. He was ready and raring to go, and he had Hitler's backing.

It was Hitler's insistence on every possible support being given to Rommel that caused the Fliegerkorps to be moved from Sicily to Libya. Almost overnight, Malta's fate began to improve. Although the Regia Aeronautica continued the bombing, the raiders were fewer in number, less determined, more easily deterred. And more help was on the way from Britain, in the form of Spitfires.

But before the aircraft reached Malta, the Tenth Submarine Flotilla would be in exile.

Phase III

Exile

MAY – JULY, 1942

18

The bitterness of exile for the Tenth Submarine Flotilla in Alexandria was compounded even as it began by the tragic, inexplicable loss of one of them.

Urge had left Malta on 27 April, taking the same route to Alexandria as *P 31*. On the 28th she had been followed by the faster *Porpoise*, as well as *P 34*. All the other submarines arrived at Alexandria in due course, but by 6 May it was clear that *Urge* was missing. A U-boat was known to be lurking in the area, but *Porpoise* sighted her on the evening of 2 May and immediately passed a warning to *Urge*, at that stage presumed to be some fifty miles astern. It is therefore unlikely that Tomkinson was caught unawares by the enemy boat. A more probable explanation is that *Urge* had been mined within about forty miles of Malta, caught by the dense new minefields being laid by the E-boats in the approaches to Malta's harbours. *Urge* was not fitted with a mine detection unit (MDU), but even if she had been it would have made no difference. Because the device emitted a distinctive pulse, readily detectable by a listening enemy, even those *U*s so fitted seldom used it.

Lieutenant-Commander E. P. Tomkinson and his company had survived their comrades in *Upholder* by just two weeks. 'Tommo' and 'Wanks' had been particularly good friends, and both had been exceptional commanding officers. Simpson later wrote to his senior officer, Ruck-Keene:

> Lieutenant-Commander Tomkinson was an outstandingly able leader, whose strict disciplinary methods were mellowed by a great sense of humour, charm and understanding.

The chief difference between Tomkinson and Wanklyn was that the former suffered fools less gladly. The determination, forethought and excellent eye of both officers produced results of an equally high order of merit.

In eighteen patrols *Urge* had carried out nineteen attacks, scoring nineteen hits with sixty-one torpedoes. She had sent one enemy cruiser to the bottom and damaged another, hit an enemy battleship, sunk and damaged 52,635 tons of Rommel's shipping, wrecked two trains and carried out several special missions. And before she even reached Malta she had sunk the Axis tanker *Franco Martelli*.

Once again Simpson found himself writing one of those heartbreaking letters, this one being to his friend's young wife. 'His great determination was twofold,' Simpson wrote, tapping out the letters personally on a borrowed typewriter, 'to beat the enemy and to rejoin you.'

Simpson was still in Malta when it became known that *Urge* was missing. Some of the Lazaretto base staff still remained to be evacuated, and two more of the *U*s had yet to leave: *Una* and *P 35*. As *Una*'s captain, Pat Norman, recalls, although the *U*s were 'not very big' (the wardroom was designed for only four officers) when he finally set sail for Egypt on 4 May.

> I had eighteen in the wardroom, including CPOs and ERAs; there were about forty extra hands on board, plus all their tools and gear. So, en route to Alexandria, it was difficult to breathe at the end of a day's dive.

Meanwhile Malta was about to lose an old and much loved friend, General Sir William Dobbie. Worn out by the strain of the past two years, his health had broken and now he was retiring. He and Lady Dobbie left the island on 8 May in the same Sunderland aircraft that had brought the Governor's successor, Field-Marshal Lord Gort VC.

On 5 May *Olympus* (Lieutenant-Commander H. G. Dymott) arrived at Malta with a precious cargo of supplies from Gibraltar, including aviation fuel and stores for the half-starved islanders. It took two full days to unload her cargo, but on the 8th she was preparing to sail again. This time, returning to Gibraltar, she was taking a human cargo: six officers and thirty ratings, all survivors from *Pandora, P 39* and *P 36*. That night she sailed, and while still on the surface in the swept channel, only six miles from St Elmo Light, she struck a mine. The tragedy was revealed the following day when a few exhausted men stumbled ashore. Although most had survived the mine explosion, all but a dozen perished during the ensuing seven-hour swim to shore. Among the dead were the captain of *Olympus*, Lieutenant-Commander Herbert Dymott, and those of *P 36* and *P 39*, Lieutenants Edmonds and Marriott.

Aghast at this further loss, so soon after *Urge*, in London Sir Max Horton, as FOS, was trying to persuade the Admiralty to adopt new anti-mine measures.

> Though I feel sure V. A. Malta [Leatham] with his limited facilities is taking every precaution to safeguard submarines, it is suggested that where it is not possible to sweep submarines in and out of the harbour, they should be preceded by a vessel acting as a 'mine-bumper', as was the custom in the Home Fleet at Port X during the winter of 1939-1940.

Leatham did indeed have 'limited facilities'. He could not spare any ships to act as 'mine-bumpers' and the minesweepers were working at full stretch. In any case, by this time there were virtually no submarines left at Malta.

The tragic news of *Olympus*'s loss on 9 May cast a deep pall of sorrow over the island, only partially relieved by the growing roar of Supermarine engines – the first of another batch of Spitfires brought by USS *Wasp* and HMS *Eagle*. Thanks to the determination of Winston Churchill to hold on to this fortress island, and the generosity of President Roosevelt in making the carrier *Wasp* available for a second time, Malta's airfields were busy again. In all, sixty-five Spitfires now arrived, immediately dispersed between the three bases at Ta Qali, Luqa and Hal Far, and this time they knew what to expect. The enemy would meet far stiffer opposition now. 'Who said a wasp couldn't sting twice?' commented Churchill.

The following day, the 10th, more relief arrived for the island in the shape of *Welshman* (Captain W. H. D. Friedburger). This fast minelayer, capable of 40 knots, had adopted the disguise of a *Leopard*-class French destroyer, and, after hoisting the Tricolor and embarking foodstuffs, ammunition and other stores at Gibraltar, she ambled westwards at low speed, under the suspicious noses of enemy aircraft. Only when she turned in to Malta's Grand Harbour did the enemy realize he had been fooled and the German aircraft plunged out of the sky to sink her. But *Welshman* shrouded herself in smoke and the Jus and Me 109s were surprised by a sudden counter-attack from the newly arrived Spitfires. By the end of the day the RAF had shot down eleven bombers and nine fighters and damaged many more. Not surprisingly, this Sunday was to go down in RAF annals as 'the Glorious Tenth of May'.

It was the turning point in the battle for Malta. By a sardonic twist of fate, only one day earlier, on 9 May, the Captain of the Tenth Submarine Flotilla and his Engineer Officer, Sam MacGregor, had flown out of Malta bound for Alexandria in an RAF Hudson.

The passage from Malta had been not without incident for two of the four surviving *Us. P 34* continued to suffer problems resulting from her near-miss with the mine during her last patrol, and two days before reaching Alexandria there was a fire in her motor room. The main motor heads had burnt out because a damaged cable short-circuited against the pressure hull. On 6 May *P 34* at last limped into harbour.

P 35 had barely left harbour, on 10 May, when she sighted two unidentified ships off St Elmo. Neither ship responded to her challenge and the submarine was compelled to open fire. As it turned out, the ships were our own minesweepers and the situation was resolved without further ado. *P 35* finally arrived at Alexandria on the 19th.

Una's captain, Pat Norman, was much relieved to reach the Egyptian port safely with his extra load of base staff, as he relates here:

On arrival on 14 May at Alexandria, I could not resist stopping in the Great Pass on our way up-harbour before going alongside

Medway [the First Flotilla's depot ship] to pick up some seaweed which was floating in the water. We tied it to the object glass of my periscope. We went alongside with this enormous bit of seaweed blotting out the object glass of the periscope.

'Norman, what on earth is that?' Captain Ruck-Keene asked.

'Well, sir, it's just grown there,' I replied. 'We've just done seventy-five consecutive days dived by day.'

It was true enough that the Tenth Flotilla's submarines had spent so much time underwater because of the enforced dives in harbour. As a result, all four boats were in extreme need of attention. As soon as they reported their safe arrival to Captain (S)1 at Alexandria they were sent on to Port Said for slipping, scrubbing and anti-fouling, as well as more thorough maintenance and repairs than had been possible in Malta.

After the frenzied activity and constant tension, The Tenth's ships' companies were able to enjoy a well-earned rest, though it would not last for long.

On 21 May Admiral Sir Henry Harwood arrived in Egypt as the new Commander-in-Chief, Mediterranean, and was immediately embroiled in plans for the relief of Malta. With the Mediterranean Fleet now acquiring reinforcements, arriving via the Cape of Good Hope through the Suez Canal, and with further Spitfires on their way, Admiral Harwood would have considerable forces with which to cover the supply convoy, codenamed Operation 'Vigorous'. Simultaneously, there would be another convoy for Malta heading east from Gibraltar: Operation 'Harpoon'.

As further cover for these two convoys, every available submarine was to be sailed, including those based at Gibraltar with the Eighth Flotilla — one of their number being *P 211*, the first of the new *S* class. And, destined eventually to join the Tenth, three new *U*s were entering the Mediterranean — *P 42, P 43* and *P 44*. Their first task would be to patrol the waters between Sardinia and Marttimo, west of Sicily, to prevent the Italian battlefleet from leaving the Tyrrhenian Sea to threaten 'Harpoon'.

The four surviving *U*s at Alexandria would join the First Flotilla's *T*s in the eastern basin of the Mediterranean. After discussing tactics with Admiral Harwood's Chief of Staff, Rear-Admiral

Edelsten, Captain Simpson and Captain Ruck-Keene decided to position their submarines in a line across the southern Ionian Sea, with the *U*s at the western end of the line. The *T*s, with fifteen knots as against the *U*s' ten, would take the eastern end, should it become necessary to double back towards Alexandria. All boats were to be in position by sunset on 14 June. As soon as the RAF's reconnaissance planes reported that the Italian battleships were leaving Taranto, the whole force was to steam slowly westwards. 'Harpoon' comprised seven supply ships, 'Vigorous' eleven.

Rommel had launched his Libyan offensive on 27 May, his object being to take Tobruk. With his fast Panzer army he quickly skirted the defensive positions prepared by the British and took them by surprise. By the end of the first week of June the Afrika Korps had gained the upper hand, thanks partly to Rommel's skilful tactics, partly to his superior tanks and weaponry. Auchinleck's Eighth Army prepared to evacuate Tobruk.

To Rommel's fury, just when he most needed air support, the Luftwaffe flew off to attack the Allied convoys.

On 11 June the 'Harpoon' convoy sailed through the Strait of Gibraltar. On the 12th all seemed well, but the convoy had been spotted by enemy aircraft. On the 13th the first bombers arrived; one supply ship was sunk at once and one of the escort, *Liverpool*, was so badly damaged that she had to be towed back to Gibraltar. That same afternoon, *P 43*, one of the new *U*s, reported that an enemy squadron had left the Sardinian port of Cagliari and was heading east; but the warships managed to elude the submarines and slipped into Palermo on the morning of the 14th, then headed south, clearly intending to intercept the Allied convoy somewhere in the Narrows. Suddenly the German bombers stepped up their attack.

The westbound convoy, 'Vigorous', was faring no better. Again, almost as soon as it sailed the convoy was spotted by enemy aircraft. One vessel was bombed and forced to return to port. On the 14th another vessel was sunk. Now the enemy fleet moved out from Taranto, and the submarines, alerted by the RAF's Marylands prepared to intercept it.

Early on the morning of 15 June *P 31* sighted the enemy warships from afar, as her fourth hand and navigating officer, Lieutenant Donald Wilson, RANVR, remembers:

> There was this magnificent-looking battleship, accompanied by two cruisers and many destroyers. They looked wonderful, approaching at about 28 knots, and you can imagine the feeling in the boat!

But the enemy battle fleet was too distant for an attack: 'I think that the closest we got to them was about six miles,' Wilson writes.

P 35 had also sighted the enemy. Before dawn Lynch Maydon had sighted aircraft flares being dropped to guide the enemy warships, and these gave Maydon an approximate course. After a successful star fix, *P 35* dived at first light and shortly afterwards picked up loud HE to the north-west. Maydon made a periscope sighting and identified two battleships, with two cruisers in line ahead. He grouped up to close the targets at full speed. A full salvo of torpedoes was ready for firing. To his amazement, the sea around the leading battleship suddenly spouted a curtain of splashes which blotted out his target. A high-level bombing attack was being carried out by the RAF.

The battleships, by now identified as *Vittorio Veneto* and *Littorio*, turned to starboard, while their escort of cruisers and eight destroyers milled around in confusion. When the general mayhem subsided and the spray settled, *P35* sighted only one damaged cruiser, *Trento*.

The battleships having turned full circle, they steamed past *P35* and Maydon fired four torpedoes at 5,000 yards at the leading *Littorio*. Three explosions were heard and Maydon thought there could have been one hit. RAF reconnaissance later reported that the *Littorio* had been damaged and forced to return to Taranto. A Malta-based Wellington torpedo-bomber scored another hit on *Littorio*'s bow.

Now *P 35* went deep to reload, while stalking *Trento*. The damaged cruiser was surrounded by destroyers carrying out a full anti-submarine search; though one of them passed directly above *P 35*, she was not detected. At a range of 4,000 yards Maydon fired two torpedoes and as he went deep he heard two hits.

P 31 and *P 34*, at full speed, were also closing in for the kill. In *P 34* Harrison was observing *Trento* lying stopped with a small fire burning around her forward funnel; her crew were lounging on the guard rails, when she suddenly blew up. The scene is recalled by our spare crew telegraphist, who had been drafted to *P 34*.

> *15 June*. Dived at 0545 as per usual routine. Fifteen minutes after falling out Diving Stations, loud explosions were heard; on coming up to periscope depth from seventy feet, an amazing spectacle was taking place. The Italian battle fleet consisting of 2 BS, 3 Crs, 9 Drs, was being attacked by torpedo bombers of the RAF, the Fleet Air Arm and Liberator aircraft of the American Army Air Corps. Our position at this time was 035° 50' North, 019° 00' East, this position being in the centre of the enemy. During the continuous aircraft attacks, we were cruising round at periscope depth, taking photographs*. At 1015, a very loud explosion was heard. An 8-inch cruiser was sinking.

The submarines all went deep and returned to their position in the line.

But their task now was to cover the convoy's retreat. Admiral Harwood, seeing the enemy's overwhelming superiority in the air, knew that his convoy could not get through. By the 19th the *U*s had been recalled to Alexandria.

'Harpoon' had ended in disaster. Backed up by German bombers, the Italian squadron from Palermo attacked and sank or damaged all but two of the merchant ships and two destroyers. Only two supply ships arrived safely in Malta.

It was a serious tactical defeat for the Mediterranean Fleet. Not only had we failed to revictual the besieged island, but we had lost one cruiser, three destroyers and two merchant vessels. Malta's plight was now critical. Under Churchill's leadership, the War Cabinet decided to make one last, all-out effort. 'The Navy would never abandon Malta,' Churchill asserted and, almost immediately, the planning began for Operation 'Pedestal.'

---

* In those days there was no periscope camera; to take photographs, the camera had to be held against the periscope's eyepiece and the shutter operated manually.

All four Us had returned to Alexandria by 28 June to hear the unbelievable news that Tobruk had fallen. The port that had been the focus of such enormous effort, both for the garrison that held it and the fleet that supplied it, was in German hands. But there was no time to dwell on the loss while Rommel's Panzer army thrust on towards the Egyptian frontier.

Already the Mediterranean Fleet was preparing to evacuate its base, some ships heading south through the Suez Canal, others — including the submarines — north to Palestine and Syria. Then, on 28 June, Mersa Matruh fell to the enemy. The Germans now had an airfield from which to launch bomber raids on Alexandria. 'This was when the real panic in Alexandria occurred,' writes Pat Norman, *Una*'s captain. On the following day, Sunday the 29th, all remaining ships evacuated the Egyptian port 'having sent parties ashore to break up all stores and gear, so that they wouldn't fall into German hands. Everyone was absolutely convinced that the Germans would be in Alexandria within forty-eight hours.'

It was not until later that the signal arrived from *Thrasher* (Lieutenant 'Rufus' Mackenzie): She had sunk Mussolini's yacht *Diana*★, who was being used to transport a working party of 294 officers and men to Tobruk, to open up the port to Axis shipping. But this was the only good news to arrive at this bleak time.

On the evening of the 29th all remaining ships prepared to evacuate Alexandria. First to go was the Greek depot ship *Corinthia*, serving the four Greek submarines *(Katsonis, Triton, Papanicolis* and *Nereus)* who were attached to the First Flotilla; then *Medway*, the mother ship of the First Flotilla; then the escort comprising the cruiser *Dido* and seven destroyers. As Captain (S)1, Ruck-Keene remained with *Medway*, while Simpson sailed in the destroyer *Sikh*.

The following morning *Medway* was torpedoed by *U372*. It took twenty minutes for this magnificent depot ship to plunge to the bottom of the Mediterranean and with her went ninety torpedoes and all the spare machinery the First Flotilla had been able to remove from Alexandria. Miraculously, out of a ship's comp-

---

★ Rommel was depending on her cargo of cased petrol for his tanks. Her loss was a critical factor in meeting this advance.

lement of 1,135, only thirty ratings were lost, while forty-seven of the torpedoes floated clear and were able to be salvaged. Among the survivors was Third Officer A. S. Coningham, WRNS, who was later Mentioned in Dispatches for handing over a lifebelt to a sailor in difficulties. Another survivor was Captain Ruck-Keene, and a third was Paymaster Sub-Lieutenant George Hardinge, for whom this was the second ducking in two months: he had been in *Naiad* when she too was sunk by a U-boat. Hardinge was later invited to become Simpson's secretary and he elected to travel to Malta by submarine when the flotilla finally returned.

Medway's loss was a bitter blow, marking the nadir of our fortunes in the Mediterranean. Rommel and the Afrika Korps had been halted at the Egyptian border, only sixty miles from Alexandria; and the place where the Eighth Army had chosen to make its stand was called El Alamein.

Gradually the submarines from the Tenth and the First Flotillas arrived at Haifa, where *Cleopatra* became their temporary mother ship, while negotiations continued with the Free French. Beirut was considered a more suitable base for the submarines, but Beirut was in the French Mandate of Syria and permission had first to be sought from General de Gaulle and his advisers in London.

Haifa was no substitute for Alexandria, and en route the four *U* captains decided to take their boats in to Port Said for scraping 'because of our dreadful state from barnacles' writes *Una*'s CO, Pat Norman.

> After leaving Alexandria we made a surface passage to Port Said, most of it in daylight. We were attacked by a Swordfish torpedo bomber (Stringbag). All recognition signals during those panicky days seemed to have gone by the board. The only way I could get rid of him was to flash at him '**** off!'

After Port Said the submarines headed north to Haifa to rejoin Simpson and the survivors from *Medway*.

At Haifa Simpson worked hard to establish a temporary base for the Tenth Flotilla, and his COs and their officers and men took their cue from him. Already the word was spreading that Rommel had outreached himself. By storming eastwards in pursuit of Eighth Army he had stretched his supply line almost to breaking point. Probing the Allied defences along the Egyptian border, he found them well dug in at El Alamein where, under General Auchinleck, the Allied troops gave his Afrika Korps a severe mauling. Although this, the first battle of El Alamein, was not concluded until 25 July, Rommel was learning that the Eighth Army had plenty of fight left in it yet.

Further good news, and of more immediate significance to the exiled submariners of the Fighting Tenth, eager to get back to Malta and the battle, came from Admiral Leatham who signalled on 5 July that all approach channels to the island had been swept. The one small success of the two failed convoy operations had been the arrival in Malta of Commander Jerome in *Speedy*. He had led his three up-to-date fleet minesweepers round Cape Bon during the night of 14/15 June, unnoticed by the enemy who were concentrating on 'Harpoon' and the supply ships. The sweepers slipped safely into harbour. Their hard work and courage in the face of constant danger meant that the Tenth's submarines could now return to their home base.

It also meant that the *U*s would soon meet their new sisters, currently straining at the leash in Gibraltar. *P 42*, *P 43* and *P 44*, after their duties during the two ill-fated convoys, had returned to the Eighth Flotilla's base to continue patrols in the western basin of the Mediterranean. They now had been joined by two more *U*s, *P 37* and *P 46*.

Thus, while the First Flotilla started moving north to Beirut, Ruck-Keene leaving Simpson in charge at Haifa, the *U* crews and COs made the most of their enforced rest. Simpson reports on these relaxed days:

> That transit camp at Haifa . . . was in a most unkempt state, but was potentially quite a good place, having adequate galleys, bathrooms, cricket field and sea bathing, also a canteen and small theatre. In a few days the naval quarters were ship-shape and clean, and survivors [from *Medway*] were settling down and were temporarily kitted up with khaki and forage caps. The behaviour of personnel throughout these uncomfortable times

was excellent. Shore-going attractions were considerable but prices so exorbitant, except at NAAFI canteens, that the men could not take much advantage of the distractions. The men had a real change and an interesting time, taking part in camel and donkey races and on at least one occasion a moonlight feast with Arabs where whole sheep were roasted and eaten. I feel that if Palestinian troubles revive after the war (which is locally regarded as inevitable) the submarine sailors from the First and Tenth flotillas would prove pro-Arab.

One of those enjoying the Palestinian hospitality was our telegraphist, still serving with *P 34*. In his log for 3 July he notes the loss of *Medway*, and adds feelingly: 'Another kit gone west.' But on the 10th he was off to Jerusalem for five days' leave, with a group of others who were 'guests of the Palestinian Police Force at Mount Scopus, half a mile outside Jerusalem'. He visited all the sights − the Wailing Wall, the Church of the Holy Sepulchre, 'saw Calvary and Tomb' − but the log contains no comment on the impressions they left on him. His next relevant entry is on 17 July, when his log reads: 'Stored ship. To sea at 1950, bound Malta.'

Phase IV

Return Match

JULY, 1942 – OCTOBER, 1943

19

The Tenth Submarine Flotilla was back at Malta. Simpson flew with his staff from Cairo, touching down on Maltese soil on 22 July. The exile had lasted just over ten weeks.

The first of the *Us* to return was *P 34*, arriving at Lazaretto at 1230 on 31 July, 1942. She was followed by *P 31* and *Una* on 1 and 2 August respectively, and by *P 35* on the 12th. All four had completed patrols on passage to Malta, in the Aegean and off Crete, but without incident. *Una's* captain, Pat Norman, remembers the moment of his return, 'getting to the 100-fathom line and surfacing to see a lovely minesweeper which I followed all the way into harbour'. It was, he says, 'all very satisfactory.'

The pleasure of returning to Lazaretto was enhanced by meeting old friends, such as Commander Hubert Marsham and his care and maintenance party. They had not been idle while the *Us* were away. New sleeping quarters, sick bay, dental surgery, operations rooms and offices had been hewn out of the rock. New bathrooms had been built closer to the messdecks, and the cinema was working again. Only the 'under-rock repair shop, 60 feet by 25 feet by 15 feet' was not yet completed, Simpson wrote in his monthly summary for August, and this was expected to be functioning 'by mid November'. In the harbours, divers had worked without stop to salvage whatever possible from sunken submarines, and, supervised by Lieutenant 'Wiggy' Bennett, the flotilla's torpedo officer, were hoping to extract the torpedoes still on board the wrecked *Pandora*. One of the divers had been a member of *P 34's* ship's company, Alex McCandlish, whose skills with the DSEA set made him particularly valuable to the salvage workers. Among his tasks was the recovery of gear dropped into the sea by Malta's only spy, Carmelo Borg Pisani.*

It was a relief to the Us to find that the RAF pilots, now under the direction of Air Vice-Marshal Park, of Battle of Britain fame, were regaining control of Malta's skies, and gradually the raids were becoming fewer and less effective. Proudly the Spitfires kept a tally of their kills, which totalled 160 enemy planes shot down during July. But it was a shock to see the widespread hunger in the island, many people being kept alive only by soup kitchens run by the Civil Administrator, Wingrave 'Gravy' Tench. Everyone was thinner, weaker and, though still as staunch as ever, less able to sustain hard labour in the docks and workshops.

Simpson wrote in his August summary that an 'increase in bugs, fleas and flies is noticeable and the result of their depredations an unpleasant sight':

> Nevertheless, except for some increase in tuberculosis, diphtheria and a few cases of lock-jaw, the health of the island has remained remarkably good, with no epidemics except for scabies, which is rampant; though in this Flotilla we have had only ten cases since 1 July and it is on the decrease.
>
> With the imperative need for strict rationing and the added difficulty at this time that local produce, particularly vegetables, is very scarce and there are no potatoes, the menus are perforce restricted. The patrol menus have been maintained at a satisfactory standard of bulk and the Superintendent, Victualling Yard, is eking out the last of the potatoes exclusively for submarines at sea.

But the Tenth Flotilla, as we have seen, had started its own pig farm — and not only pigs, but rabbits and cauliflowers to supplement the monotonous diet of tinned and dried foods. In his August summary Simpson added:

> Ever since last February, the entire base has had hot roast

---

* Pisani had been brought to Malta by an Italian MTB and landed below an unscaleable cliff where he was found by an RAF team on 18 May, 1942. He was hanged on 28 November, 1942.

pork for Sunday dinners and cold in the evening, free of charge, from our farm, and we have enough in cold storage to last about three months. The herd has had to be reduced to one boar and two sows, with eighteen growing pigs, due to the lack of offal for feeding, but we are well placed. Both sows farrowed this month, one producing nine, whilst the second, who is very victory-minded, gave birth to twenty, which were unfortunately so weakly that only four survived.

By comparison with the rest of the island, the submariners were indeed doing well; but it was not easy for young active men to adjust to this life of rationing and shortages, especially after the relative abundance of Haifa and Alexandria. They had their priorities right, as the log of our spare crew telegraphist shows. On 2 August he noted that 'except for a shortage of food and absolutely no beer, we are not doing so bad. The raids have slackened off to what they were in January.'

But the principal change at Lazaretto was the presence of the new submarines.

The first of the new Us had arrived at Malta before their exiled sisters were able to return. The leader of the pack, arriving on 20 July, was P 42 (Lieutenant A. C. G. Mars), followed on the 21st by P 44 (Lieutenant T. E. Barlow) and on 2 August by P 43 (Lieutenant A. C. Halliday). Two more Us were still at Gibralter, P 46 and P 37, but would soon be joining the Tenth and, even before then, would arrive an old friend returning from her refit in the UK — Utmost.

The first task for the newly reinforced Tenth Flotilla was to help provide cover for Operation 'Pedestal', the climax to the determined attempts to revictual the starving island. The fourteen supply ships assembled in the River Clyde on 3 August had passed through the Strait of Gibraltar during the early hours of 10 August. Their mighty escort included the two battleships, Nelson and Rodney, and three carriers, Victorious, Indomitable and Eagle, which between them had seventy-two fighter aircraft to provide the convoy with an aerial umbrella. While Admiral Harwood headed a diversionary convoy from Egypt, and Admiral Vian led a spurious bombing raid on Rhodes, it was hoped that 'Pedestal' would manage to escape the attention of enemy aircraft.

Altogether, eight submarines would also be involved, with orders to make themselves as conspicuous as possible in order to deter enemy fleet movements. Accordingly, there was much deliberate signalling while the boats took up their positions. Three boats from Malta formed a line south of Pantelleria, *P 31, P 34* and *P 44*, with our old friend *Utmost* and new boy *P 46* from Gibraltar, plus another boat from Gibraltar, one of the new S-class, *P 222* (Lieutenant-Commander A. J. Mackenzie). *P 211* (Commander Ben Bryant), another of the *S*s who would later be attached to the Tenth Flotilla, took up a position off the north coast of Sicily, backed up by *P 42* off the Lipari Islands north-west of Messina.

A ninth submarine, *Una,* had a special operation of her own to carry out, Operation 'Why Not?' The object of this raid was to strike at the enemy's airfield at Catania, on the east coast of Sicily. Lieutenant Tom Lancaster, navigating officer, well remembers this patrol, for he had just arrived from Haifa on a 'magic carpet' run with *Otus* — 'bringing a cargo of dried milk urgently needed by the Maltese mothers and children'. He was transferred to *Una* and told he would be sailing the next day:

> It was intended that *Una* should sail after dark on 9 August and that the attack should take place at 0200 on the 12th. Nine commandos of the Special Boat Section were embarked with their Folbots, plus equipment. In addition, we carried a doctor and a small brown dachshund bitch with white feet, appropriately named Socks. She belonged to one of the commando officers, Lieutenant Desmond Buchanan, Grenadier Guards, to whom she had been given by the Princess Ali Khan.
>
> The normal complement of the submarine was four officers and twenty-eight men. Now we had eight officers and Socks using the tiny wardroom, while the rest of the commando and their gear grossly overcrowded the vessel. When not on watch, I slept on the bare floor of the submarine under the wardroom table, with Socks for company. One obvious problem was what to do with Socks when the calls of nature had to be obeyed. The sailors rallied round and spread old newspapers over the control room floor; though little Socks was very shy, she soon got the general idea.

In the few hours before disembarkation off the Sicilian coast, on the night of 11/12 August, the commandos cleaned their weapons, checked the Folbots and prepared their stock of explosives. Each man carried his own choice of hand-gun which included a Mauser machine pistol, 9mm Beretta, .38 Smith & Wesson revolver and a .45 Colt revolver, in addition to Thompson sub-machine guns. Other 'toys' included fighting knives, unholy-looking brass knuckle-dusters and coshes made of rubber hose filled with lead. We were regaled with gruesome descriptions of previous raids they had carried out.

The commandos wore a wide variety of apparel, each to his own taste. Uniform was *out*, but some regular military insignia had to appear somewhere: in the event of capture it could then be proved that they were *bona fide* Service personnel and not partisans. One officer considered that a single uniform button was sufficient for this purpose.

Due to a choppy sea, a couple of Folbots were damaged while the commandos were embarking, so that only six men continued with the operation. Once they were clear, at 2300, 12 August, *Una* dived and patrolled in the vicinity; she surfaced again at 0330 on the 13th to recover the commandos as had been arranged.

Unfortunately, there was no reply to our signals or any sign of the Folbots. *Una* patrolled in the area and proceeded to the alternative rendezvous forty-six hours later, within one mile of a prominent rock at the south of the bay. But without success. She then returned to Malta with a very sad ship's company.

On reaching Catania airfield, the commando had found the whole area floodlit and a German sentry armed with a sub-machine gun standing by every aircraft. It was doubtful whether even one aircraft could be destroyed, so it was decided to blow up a large pylon carrying electric power to the airfield. This was achieved, but the commando was spotted and one man was killed. The remainder escaped to sea but because of the bad weather they missed the submarine. As the wind and sea increased it was evident the Folbots could not be kept afloat for long, so it was decided that Lieutenant Buchanan (a strong swimmer) should swim to the shore and get help of some sort. Accordingly, he stripped off his clothes, leaving only a Grenadier Guards' button tied round his neck. On his way inshore he saw a fishing boat, swam to it and directed it to the Folbots. The crews were picked up and, in Buchanan's own words, 'We were taken ashore and I had the odd experience of being marched through the town of Catania with only a Grenadier's button round my neck — and I must say, I hated it.' The commandos were made prisoners of war, although Buchanan escaped subsequently. Among these brave men was Lieutenant Eric Newby, the well known author. He escaped from his POW camp with the help of the lady whom he married later.

Lieutenant Buchanan had left a note with Lieutenant Norman (Pat Norman, the CO) concerning the disposal of his effects in the event of his failure to return from the operation. *Inter alia* his gramophone and records were to be given to *Una's* wardroom and Socks was to be sent to the Princess Ali Khan at the Hotel Angleterre at Beirut. Having had experience of life in a submarine, Socks took passage to Beirut in *Parthian*.

Meanwhile, another of the *U*s was on an unorthodox mission. *P 42*, commanded by Lieutenant Alastair Mars, had taken up her position off the Lipari Islands by 6 August when he sighted a supply ship and launched an attack; in vain. On the 8th he missed another supply ship. He now had only one salvo of four torpedoes remaining for the enemy battle squadron, should it sally forth to attack the 'Pedestal' convoy. But on the evening of the 8th, surfacing in the Gulf of San Eufemia, *P 42* went to gun action on the coastal railway line.

P 42 was the first *U* to be fitted with the new 3-inch gun, and this was the first time it had been in action. It was considerably more successful than the 12-pounder which was regarded as little better than a pop-gun. Jack Michell, of *Upright*, once examined the plaque on the side of one 12-pounder, which read:

Imperial War Museum
EURYALUS, Second Class Cruiser:
12-pdr gun, landed and put on trunnions
and used in the relief of Ladysmith, 1899.

As Jack Michell remarks, 'So these 12-pounder guns had been dredged up from museums, dumps, scrap metal yards, and fitted to our early *U*s *faute de mieux!*'

But this new 3-inch gun cut a train in half with its first shell, and the next ten rounds brought down power lines and destroyed the rest of the train. *P 42* withdrew to the southward, thoroughly pleased with her success.

During the forenoon of the 10th, off Sicily's Cape Milazzo, *P 42* came under sudden, inexplicable attack when fifty-three depth charges were dropped around her. That evening she met similar unprovoked aggression. Mars, guessing that the enemy must have laid down offshore hydrophones, moved to a new position west of Stromboli: 'a very clever selection', Simpson commented later: 'At about midnight on Wednesday 12 August,' writes Lieutenant Paul Thirsk, RNR, who was then *P 42's* third hand and navigator, 'we received a signal: "Enemy cruisers coming your way".' Thirsk continues:

> At breakfast time on the 13th ... I was on watch in the control room. The weather was fine, the sky blue and almost cloudless; a slight chop on the sea helped use of the periscope and would make our outline, submerged, less visible from the air. As was usual at Watch Diving, the boat was quiet and peaceful. Most of the ship's company were sleeping before breakfast.
>
> In the control room, the helmsman and the two planesmen controlled the boat's course and depth. The asdic operator maintained a listening watch: an ERA presided over the telemotor pump, blowing panel and watched also for my signals to raise and lower the periscope. In such conditions, the large periscope was used in a pre-ordained fashion. First, a quick all-round look in low power, searching the horizon for surface craft and some 30° of sky for aircraft. A few seconds later, 'up periscope' again; a careful search of the horizon for 90° from right ahead to each beam in turn, in high power (i.e. 4 magnifications). Again, a few seconds later, another all-round sweep in low power, followed after a pause by a high-power search of the next quadrant of the horizon ... and so on, until one's two-hour stint was up.
>
> At 0743, suddenly this peaceful routine was shattered. The asdic operator reported Hydrophone Effect almost dead ahead. There was nothing in sight on the bearing, but a listen on the headphones left me in no doubt that heavy units were approaching. I immediately ordered Diving Stations and *Unbroken*★ sprang to life. I had just time to sight the white top-masts of the

★ *P 42* like all the Us, later acquired a less impersonal name, as we shall see.

cruiser force before handing over the periscope to the captain, Lieutenant Alastair Mars. The whole attack was over in some fifteen minutes.

The force was steaming at 25 knots, a speed which just gave us enough time for a retiring turn to get off-track. We went to fifty feet, and grouped up to our full speed of 8 knots to reach our firing position. Even so, we would be desperately close to the enemy's line of advance, with its four cruisers, eight destroyers and two seaplanes. ... Two of the screening destroyers passed alarmingly close and a third, for which we should really have gone deep, literally thundered over our fore-casing, missing the conning tower by only a few feet. Then one bow salvo of four torpedoes was on its way and we went deep with a drastic alternation of course.

Two hits were heard: one severely damaging an 8-inch cruiser and the other a 6-inch cruiser. Neither of them played any further part in the war.

The destroyers were soon after us and the counter-attack was heavy, lasting from 0900 to 1900, when we surfaced and were ordered to return to Malta.

Later, we learnt that the 8-inch cruiser which we hit was the *Bolzano*; the 6-inch, the *Muzio Attendolo*. *Bolzano* was hit in a fuel tank and fire gutted the ship before she was beached. *Attendolo* lost sixty feet of her bows, but managed to reach Messina where she was patched up and sent on to Naples for more repairs. *Bolzano* was finally sunk in Spezia in June 1944 by two British human torpedo crews.

As Lieutenant Thirsk comments at the conclusion of his account, 'Nothing seemed so sweet as seeing the stars and breathing the fresh air when we surfaced that evening.'

Lieutenant Mars had made a very skilful attack, particularly in view of the fact that he had only one salvo of torpedoes left, as well as having to attack while the destroyers were about to ram him. On 18 August he brought *P 42* safely back from patrol★.

The following day *P 44* arrived back from her patrol and had to go straight into the dockyard for major repairs. She had been diverted to finish off an enemy ammunition ship (later identified

★ Alastair Mars has written an excellent book describing *P 42's* exploits in the Mediterranean; *Unbroken: The Story of a Submarine* (Muller, 1953)

37. Another of *Unruffled's* victims: *Una*, supply ship, sinks off Capri on 11 October, 1942. The photograph was taken by holding a camera against the periscope eyepiece.

38. *Unbroken* (*P.42*) (Lt B.J.B. Andrew) salutes the Captain of the Tenth Submarine Flotilla as she sails for home. Flying her Jolly Roger, she has carried out fifteen war patrols, the majority having been under the command of Lt. A.C.G. Mars.

39. The 10,000-ton cruiser *Bolzano* was torpedoed and damaged by *Triumph* (Cdr W.J.W. Woods) on 26 August, 1941; torpedoed again on 13 August, 1942, by *P42* (Lt Alastair Mars), she was beached on the island of Panarea and finally sunk during the night of 21/22 June, 1944, by a British 'chariot'.

40. *Unbending* (Lt E.T. Stanley) in her berth at Lazaretto. During her nine patrols, she sank 13,316 tons of shipping and damaged a further 10,000 tons.

41. *Unbending* airing bedding, drying clothes and maintaining the gun. Note her QV 4 radar warning receiver aerials on port side of conning tower.

42. Bullet-riddled *Una* (Lt J.D. Martin) returns in February, 1943, to the UK. Note the anti-tank shellholes, a souvenir from Tunisia, when she was under the command of Lt C.P. Norman.

43. *Unison*'s ship's company. Officers, from left to right:- Sub-Lt D. Palmer, Third Hand; Lt A.R. Daniell, Commanding Officer; Lt John King, RNR, navigating officer; Lt J. Haward, first lieutenant.

44. Her diesel exhausts still smoking, *Unison* clears the inner boom outward bound for her next patrol. Taunting her from the Valletta side are the three entrances to the unfinished submarine pens.

45. CPO 'Happy' Day, *Unison*'s cox'n, issuing cigarettes in the fore-ends.

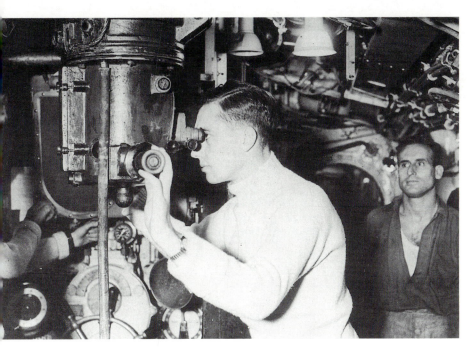

46. Lt J.C.Y. Roxburgh, captain of *United*, at her search periscope. The Third Hand is working the Fruit Machine mounted above the steering wheel, and on the division which separates the wardroom from the control room.

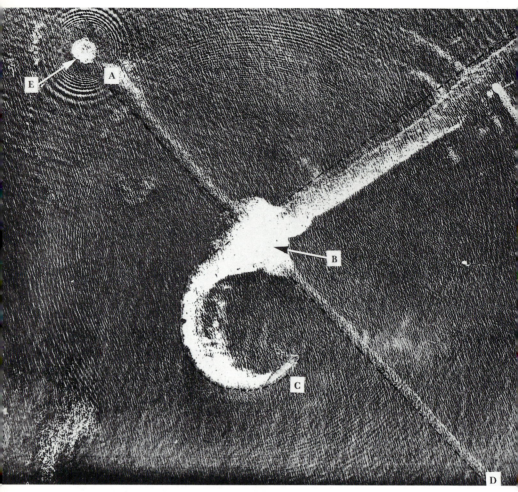

47. A PRU Spitfire from Malta photographed this attack by *United* (Lt J.C.Y. Roxburgh) on the ex-Norwegian liner, *Ringulv*, 5,153 tons.

A: the submerged *United*'s four torpedo tracks.
B: two torpedo hits.
B-D: tracks of two torpedoes which missed.
C: target is turning disabled, about to sink.
E: a bomb from an unobserved aircraft escort.
Note: shock-wave ripples from the explosions; oil pollution from the crippled ship; the wake from the escorting destroyer at bottom left.

48. The Cox'n, CPO J.R. Wickens, and First Lieutenant, (the author) on the bridge of *P 44* (*United*).

49. *Unrivalled* clears the boom on return from the Adriatic. When the Italians capitulated, she hustled eight ships from Bari before the Germans arrived. She escorted her motley convoy back to Malta.

50. Captain G.C. Phillips, Captain of the 10th Flotilla, visits *Unruffled*. He is saluted by the First Lieutenant, Lt O. Lascelles, in shorts, and by her Captain, Lt J.S. Stevens, who is in khaki.

51. The ever-cheerful Commanding Officer of *Unruffled*, Lt J.S. Stevens (right), sails for patrol with Surgeon-Lieutenant Crowley as an observer. British submarines never carried medical personnel. All illness was dealt with by the Cox'n.

as *Rosolino Pilo*, 8,325 tons) which the RAF had bombed and was still afloat off the Tunisian coast. In the small hours of the 19th her captain, Lieutenant T. E. Barlow, sighted an indistinct shape ahead. Cautiously he edged forward on the surface. 'It was very dark,' he remembers, 'one of those calm but murky Mediterranean nights when sea and horizon merge into one, and it is hard to see anything clearly.' At last he felt confident of his target and fired one torpedo at a distance of 800 yards. Barlow goes on:

> I could see the torpedo track running true and altered course away. The submarine had hardly begun to turn when the whole firmament around us seemed to ignite with a colossal explosion and an enormous burst of flame. For a moment, I thought we had blown ourselves up ...

P 44's gunlayer, Leading Seaman Cyril Balls, remembers that moment too:

> The skipper was calling *'Dive, dive, dive!* from the bridge, but so much water was pouring through the hull that we had to advise him very quickly. ... Numerous hits had pierced the hull, one a four-inch gash. We were unable to dive at all. Water had poured into the motor room, causing all sorts of spectacular sparks and the switch gear was hazardous to the touch.

On the bridge, Barlow, in his anxiety to dive the boat, watched in exasperation as his third hand, Sub-Lieutenant Evatt, RANVR*, who was the nephew of the Australian External Affairs Minister and whose first patrol this was, slowly reacted to the diving hooter and finally followed the lookouts down the conning tower ladder: 'He was a tall chap and I thought I would never see the end of him going down the hatch, before I could follow him and shut the lid on the blaze.'

But Barlow was greeted by 'sparks and flashes' as water entered the electrical circuits, 'making the place look like a Brocks benefit night'. Despite the danger of surfacing after an

---

* The Hon Philip George Evatt, DSC, QC, retired in 1987 as Judge of the Supreme Court of Norfolk Island and the Northern Territories, Australia.

attack, and then lying immobile while battery fuses were removed, Barlow knew this was what he had to do.

> Working by the light of the miners' lamps which we carried for emergency, Peter Beale, my First Lieutenant, and his team of electricians got on with it. I was up on the bridge again and preparing for any Italians who might come to greet us.

Cyril Balls takes up the story:

> It was soon evident what had happened. A twelve-foot girder from the target had hurtled through the air and embedded itself in the side of the conning tower. It was a miracle that those on the bridge survived. The W/T gear, periscopes, the binnacle, and upper steering had all been wrecked and the jumping wire parted.

And so, in almost total darkness pierced only by the few miners' lights, the Chief ERA, Balls and the others cleared away the shambles on the slippery casing and the bridge:

> The girder was cut away and gently lowered over the side, with a similar operation for the jumping wire. At the same time, wooden wedges and cotton waste were hammered into the holes in the hull from above. Communications were restored and we were finally ready to test the skills applied ... Breath held, fingers and everything else crossed, we slowly dived, and miraculously achieved a depth of seventy feet with no inflow through the makeshift repairs. And so to Malta for docking and full attention.

Barlow was nervous about 'how Captain (S) would treat the matter of a somewhat bent submarine'. Fortunately, 'Shrimp was philosophical'; he was simply glad to have his boat back, particularly at this time, for sad news had arrived from Haifa that one of the First Flotilla's *T*s had been lost — *Thorn* (Lieutenant-Commander R. G. Norfolk). It is thought that she had been sunk off Crete on 6 August by the Italian destroyer *Papa*. There were no survivors.

The 'Pedestal' convoy had run in to trouble. Enemy aircraft

had spotted it on the morning of 11 August. *Eagle*, the veteran aircraft carrier that had come to Malta's aid and flown off so many Spitfires, was sunk that same afternoon. *Indomitable* was damaged and the destroyer *Foresight* was sunk on the 12th, with two of the merchant ships.

The battleships and the remaining fighters responded with everything they had, but the German and Italian pilots made repeated and determined attacks. That evening, a double U-boat attack sank one cruiser (*Cairo*) and damaged two others (*Nigeria* and *Kenya*). Early on the morning of the 13th, yet another cruiser (*Manchester*) was sunk by an Italian E-boat, and E-boats also accounted for the loss of four more merchantmen. Another two of the supply ships were lost south of Pantelleria. Only three survivors sailed into Malta that evening, followed the next day by the severely disabled *Brisbane Star* and finally, on the 15th, by the even more disabled tanker *Ohio* with her vital cargo of oil.

The cost, both in merchantmen and in warships, was tragically high, and this proved to be the last of the huge convoys. It seemed like a disaster at the time, particularly to those in Malta; but at least one observer guessed that this was not the 'big victory for the Axis' that it seemed. He was the German Vice-Admiral Weichold, who wrote:

> Thanks to these new supplies, Malta was now capable of fighting for several weeks, or, at a pinch, for several months. The main issue, the danger of air attack on the supply route to North Africa, remained. To achieve this objective, no price was too high, and from this point of view the British operation, in spite of all the losses, was not a defeat but a strategical failure of the first order by the Axis, the repercussions of which will one day be felt.

Weichold was right. Thanks to the *Ohio's* oil, Malta's aircraft would remain operational and the Us and the strike aircraft could now cooperate in our offensive against Rommel's shipping routes. A fitful glimmer of hope appeared on the horizon.

20

AUGUST/SEPTEMBER, 1942

General Erwin Rommel had reached the peak of his career when he took Tobruk in June. His was a brilliant military success, rewarded with immediate promotion to Field-Marshal. But by July he and his Afrika Korps were facing problems; they had swept so far east, and so fast, that their supplies could barely keep up with them. Hitler, seeing Rommel's progress as evidence that Operation 'Hercules' was an unnecessary diversion, threw into North Africa the men and *matériel* originally destined for the invasion of Malta. But Auchinleck's Allied troops had turned the tables, holding out against the swift Panzer army with its technically superior tanks. Then on 12 August, Montgomery arrived in Cairo to take over command of the Eighth Army.

At first Rommel was content merely to check the Allied lines, probing here and there, but gradually he became more impatient. Rome and Berlin promised him more troops, more ammunition, more fuel, but none of it was forthcoming. Some had been diverted to the Eastern Front, but the rest was sitting uselessly in Italian ports, waiting to be ferried across to Libya. Unfortunately for Rommel, the supply line was simply drying up, directly as a result of interference from the Malta-based forces.

The Italians were loath to sail convoys without escorts, but the GAF was too busy in North Africa and Greece to give the requested support, and so the Italian pilots were increasingly relegated to the back-up role their German counterparts disdained to take. Ill feeling between the Italians and the Germans had increased after the Luftwaffe refused to coordinate their attack on Operation 'Pedestal' with that of the Italian fleet. Hitler was becoming exceedingly dissatisfied with Mussolini, as Admiral

Raeder knew. Raeder had met Hitler on 26 August to assess strategy and afterwards reported that he had told Hitler:

> I continue to regard the possible attempt of the Anglo-Saxons to occupy north-west Africa and get a foothold in north Africa, with the aid of the French, as a very great danger to the whole German war effort. They would attack Italy from there and endanger our position in North-East Africa. Therefore, Germany must maintain a strong position in the Mediterranean.

Not surprisingly, Hitler agreed with this kind of talk, and stepped up the pressure on his favourite Field-Marshal to break through the Allied Lines.

Accordingly Rommel launched an all-out offensive on 31 August. Edging round the Allied positions at El Alamein, he wanted to penetrate the ridge of Alam Halfa. If all went well, he hoped to be in Alexandria within three days.

To the Tenth's other successes in August was added one final hit. On the 27th *P 35* was in the western approaches to the Anti-Kithera Channel, between Greece and Crete, when she sighted a small escorted convoy and promptly sent one supply ship to the bottom – *Manfredo Camperio* (5,465 tons). The escorting destroyers, instead of picking up survivors as usual, immediately launched a hunt for the submarine, but *P 35* escaped unscathed.

In Malta the month of August ended with weary resolve to pull the belt in another notch and see how far the meagre stocks could go. The 32,000 tons of supplies delivered by the five lonely merchantmen from Operation 'Pedestal' were a welcome contribution, but they would not last forever. The store-running submarines had been busy this month, both *Rorqual* and *Clyde* each ferrying petrol and personnel; but in September they would have to make yet more 'magic carpet' runs, bringing food, petrol, ammunition, smoke canisters and torpedoes to keep the island in action.

The Luftwaffe seldom appeared now, but the Regia Aeronautica continued to pay sporadic visits whenever the Spitfires allowed them to, as Simpson indicated in his monthly summary for September:

Extremely few bombs have been dropped on the island during the month, and none in the vicinity of the base or dockyard. An average of three air raid alarms are sounded daily, but as a rule the enemy are met by our fighters in time to prevent them from crossing the coast. Work in the flotilla is not severely interrupted and a most efficient smoke screen has been evolved from canisters all round Lazaretto Creek, to prevent aerial photographs or accurate bombing.

Simpson also wrote approvingly of progress in repairing blitzed buildings. Extra accommodation was now being made available to house the increasing numbers of personnel flown in or brought in by submarine since July. He also noted:

> The Lazaretto farmyard is getting into its stride again; rabbits are breeding, turkeys fattening, a 'shoat' bleating. A sow with a litter of twenty lost all but one, due to loss of suction; but it is hoped that more scraps can be saved with the institution of the new Dining Hall, and further tragedies of this nature can be prevented.

The same report contained a typically dry report of a lecture Simpson was invited to give at military headquarters on the subject of 'The Role of Submarines in Co-operation with Land Forces':

> It appeared to be happily received and question time was not difficult since the lecture preceded a military dance, to give the girls of Citta Vecchia a treat; and as there was a seven-mile bicycle ride in prospect for many of the audience, they had no breath to waste. The lecturer also had the pleasure of attending this party, where a really good dance band and a cabaret of popular songs by Welsh miners all combined to provide a grand evening. So, although social activity in Valletta and Sliema is negligible, there is still a certain amount of hunting in the shires.

In September the flotilla acquired a new Commander (S), for on the 13th Hubert Marsham left. He had made a magnificent contribution to the Fighting Tenth's ability to fight, staying on to hold the fort while the submarines pursued the course of greater discretion and withdrew. His successor was Commander Christopher Hutchinson, DSO. Hutchinson had earned his decoration on 9 April, 1940, when he was Commanding Officer of *Truant* and made a successful attack on the cruiser *Karlsruhe*, sinking her in the Skagerrak. 'Hutch', as he became to the Tenth, remained as Commander (S) 10 until the flotilla was finally disbanded, outlasting not only Simpson, but Simpson's two successors.

Hutch pays tribute to Sam MacGregor, the flotilla's Chief Engineer, and MacGregor's successor Commander Tom Sanders, who 'worked wonders in the workshops', as well as the Maltese naval ratings and the AA gunners who were 'splendid'. But Hutch himself had a difficult job, one of the saddest aspects being 'the collection of personal belongings of those men who would not return'. He also had responsibility for ensuring that discipline and security was maintained on the base, and writes:

> Our COs were mostly young, raring to go, brilliant at sea and full of high spirits in harbour. Sometimes I had to make myself unpopular when they overstepped the mark, with pistols and flash crackers coming into their games. I was very conscious of these dangers, as we had lost one Maltese sailor and one Polish Petty Officer due to monkeying around with firearms.

But at sea the first half of September was frustrating.

Like their confrères in the First and Eighth Flotillas, the Us were making disappointing progress. Claims to hits were often disproved, the reason being partly that attacks were now made under much greater pressure. With new asdic equipment and better training, the enemy's pursuit and detection techniques were rapidly improving. Thus our COs were often unable to verify through their periscopes the result of their attacks.

The Tenth, with eight submarines now (*P 31* having sailed home for her refit after 'Pedestal'), countered this new threat by dispersing patrols over as wide an area as was feasible, in order to dissipate the enemy's anti-submarine forces. Increasingly, therefore, the Us would find themselves in unfamiliar waters, which added to the risk they faced.

On 7 September *P 34* was sailing across the Ionian Sea for her last patrol off the Greek island of Cephalonia when she was diverted to attack a three-ship convoy escorted by *eleven* destroyers. Such a sizeable escort indicated a truly worthwhile target and Lieutenant Harrison fired one full salvo. He thought he obtained one hit, but could not be sure as he at once faced the escort's very determined counter-attack. Two depth charges were extremely close, and the submarine plunged to 270 feet. Leakage from the stern glands flooded the bilges to the level of the bottom of the main motors, but bilge pumps could not be used as the noise they made would reveal her position to the hunting destroyer. The port motor suffered extensive damage, but the starboard motor was sufficient to take Harrison and his crew safely back to Malta.

This had been *P 34*'s thirteenth and last patrol before returning to the UK for her refit. Patched up in Malta's dockyard, she was at last able to sail on 25 September, but will reappear later in our story.

P 42 was once again involved in a special operation during September. Her orders were to advertise her presence as widely as possible, and so she was due to make attacks either by torpedo or with her 3-inch gun in places as far apart as the Gulf of Taranto and Sicily. She also landed a two-man commando party in Crotone harbour, where a new type of limpet mine was to be used on enemy ships. But the soldiers were captured. Captain Wilson, Royal Artillery, and Bombardier Brittlebank were well known to the submariners at Lazaretto and were sadly missed.

Utmost, who had returned from her refit during August, was now under the command of Lieutenant J. W. D. 'Basher' Coombe. In mid-September she was ordered to take up a position east of the minefield known as QBB/55, straddling the Sicilian Channel, while two submarines approached from Gibraltar: *P 211* (Commander Ben Bryant) and *Talisman* (Lieutenant-Commander M. Willmott). *P 211* was new to the Mediterranean, but this was to be *Talisman*'s second commission with the First Flotilla. She was off the Algerian coast on 15 September when she reported a U-boat, but after that nothing is known of her fate. It seems likely that she was mined while picking her way through the Sicilian Channel. *P 211* arrived safely at Lazaretto on the 19th, while *Utmost* was sent to investigate shipping movements at Porto Empedocle on the south-west coast of Sicily; nothing was found except fishing boats, and the rest of her patrol was uneventful.

P 35 was patrolling off the Ionian island of Zante when she was diverted, on 27 September, to intercept another two-ship convoy with a large escort, this one comprising five destroyers and numerous aircraft. Lynch Maydon fired a full salvo at 6,000 yards and obtained one hit on the *Francesco Barbaro* (6,343 tons); a sighting by periscope showed her down by the stern with smoke pouring from her. But when *P 35* started reloading to finish her off, the noise in the fore-ends was picked up by the enemy's escort, which triggered off a very accurate counter-attack.

But Maydon was not finished yet: he took the boat deep and waited. At 2230, six hours later, he surfaced and persisted with his attack. Again he obtained one hit, but still the stricken ship refused to sink. All that night *P 35* dodged the destroyers and at 0603 the next morning she came up to periscope depth. The enemy ship had finally sunk.

Lieutenant J. S. Stevens, known as 'Steve', has written a book about his exploits in submarines, *Never Volunteer*, in which he includes a description of *P 46*'s successful patrol in late September, 1942. *P 46* had by now been fitted with one of the successful new 3-inch guns, and according to Stevens the gun was the object of devoted attention from gunlayer AB Sandy Powell, who 'spent long hours polishing and oiling the metal work with loving care'. *P 46* was off the Tunisian coast one night when 'a darkened vessel was sighted on a southerly course':

> She was a large motor schooner, undoubtedly taking a cargo to an African harbour that would comfort Rommel. 'Open fire!' came the order. After eight rounds she was ablaze; her crew abandoned her and we withdrew.
>
> Very soon afterwards I was astounded when the Officer of the Watch pointed out the navigation lights of a ship to the north. Tunisia was under the Vichy regime and neutral, but we were well off shore, so investigation was called for. At full speed we closed this mystery ship. A medium sized freighter, the name *Liberia, Vichy* was boldly displayed and illuminated on her side. The status of such a ship was uncertain so I went below to make a quick study of C-in-C Mediterranean's orders on the subject. These stated clearly that Vichy shipping was to be sunk

at sight if (a) under way after dark; or (b) outside the three-mile limit of territorial waters. She fulfilled both these conditions.

Having let her pass unmolested while clarifying the situation, we overhauled her and fired two torpedoes at her from close range. One hit her, and she sank by the stern in a quarter of an hour. In the weather conditions prevailing, her crew should have had little difficulty in getting ashore safely.

P 46 had been surfaced throughout; the second torpedo circled, indicating a gyro failure, and narrowly missed us at least once. The thrill of this first torpedo success enabled us to ignore the dangers of the 'circler' with equanimity.

The following evening, the Gun Control Officer, Lieutenant Lascelles, was Officer of the Watch when he sighted another supply ship and called Stevens to the bridge:

She was tracked for some time to establish her course and speed; then we turned towards her and soon the phosphorescent tracks of the three torpedoes aimed at her were clearly visible on the calm sea surface. These missed, and fire was opened from the 3-inch gun. She replied with rapid and accurate gunfire; we dived to avoid this . . . I waited an hour for moonset before attacking her again. One torpedo struck her amidships; she exploded into a pillar of fire which burned for some time, indicating a cargo of petrol. She was the *Leonardo Palomba* of 1,100 tons.

For one month during the autumn of 1942, Sub-Lieutenant Paul Thirsk, RNR, was asked to assist Captain Simpson in the Operations Room at Lascaris. 'I was full of apprehension about working for such an august master,' he later wrote, '(but) I need not have been. His mixture of cheerful bonhomie and infectious humour soon put me at my ease and he was a delight to be with.'

Our day started after breakfast when we went over by *dghaisa* from Lazaretto to Lascaris. My job, each morning, was to prepare a map or plan of the central Mediterranean, showing the patrol areas, or last known positions from signals, of all Tenth Flotilla boats and of any boats on passage or boats of other flotillas operating in the area. While I was doing this Shrimp would pore with rapt concentration over the night's crop of signals . . . Against the background of each morning's concentrated study, he would proceed to write or dictate signals to make whatever adjustments to his submarines' dispositions he thought necessary . . . It was typical of him, and well appreciated by his Commanding Officers, that his first consideration was to engage the enemy more closely and do as much damage as possible. But it was equally well realized that he had a masterly grasp of operating conditions and would never unnecessarily hazard a submarine or put her into danger.

It appeared to me that this total rapport between Shrimp and his COs was the basis of a mutual trust and respect which was reflected in the Flotilla's achievements.

Amid all the death and destruction in the central Mediterranean in those days, his light-hearted touch was irresistible. Paperwork in the Flotilla was at an absolute minimum due to the continuous bombing of Malta. Instead of voluminous sailing orders, Bob Tanner, Staff Officer Operations, had a supply of old return railway tickets. On these he would simply write 'Naples and return', 'Tripoli and return', etc. Naval Store Depots in the UK were totally out of luck over intricate and bureaucratic paperwork. If any got through at all, Sam MacGregor would either write on it: 'Not known at this address' or simply throw it away. Standards of dress and drill were relaxed, but the underlying discipline, bearing and morale of the Flotilla under Shrimp was superb.

Morale was certainly improving this September of 1942, partly because of the good news from Alexandria as the Eighth Army continued to hold out on the Egyptian frontier.

After the week-long battle of Alam Halfa ridge, at the beginning of the month, Montgomery had Rommel wondering where next to turn. The Allies, with their short supply line from Alexandria, were rapidly being reinforced while the German army remained dependent on that long, wavering supply line from Italy. The job of the Tenth Submarine Flotilla was to constrict that supply line until nothing further could pass through, and thus starve Rommel out of North Africa.

To aid the flotilla in its task, London was sending out every new submarine that slid down the slipways and survived its working-up patrol. Not only Us were coming now, but the new-construction Ss as well. New arrivals during September included *P 211*(Commander Ben Bryant) and *P 46* (Lieutenant J. S. (Steve) Stevens) as we have seen, and *P 37*, (Lieutenant E. T. (Otto) Stanley) as a replacement for *P 34*, now on her way back to the UK. Another two *S*s would arrive in October: *P 212* (Lieutenant J. H. Bromage) on the 9th and *P 247* (Lieutenant M. G. R. Lumby) on the 19th, all arriving from Gibraltar and crammed to the limit with stores.

Although they did not yet know it, the submarines of the Tenth would soon be providing essential back-up, not only for Montgomery's offensive at El Alamein, but also for the greatest Allied operation the war had yet seen: Operation 'Torch', the landings in north-west Africa.

21

OCTOBER 1942

October, 1942 would prove to be the Tenth Submarine Flotilla's busiest month, and one of the most successful.

The innings was opened with a flourish by the newcomer, *P 37*, who had been 'allocated an area off the southern part of the Tunisian coastline' remembers her CO, 'Otto' Stanley. On the 8th a target vessel was sighted and two torpedoes fired. They missed. The submarine now surfaced and opened up with her 12-pounder, which at least caused the crew to abandon ship. But, as Stanley writes, 'A ship without a flammable cargo would stand a lot of hits'. He decided to manoeuvre alongside the vessel in order to board her and place demolition charges. 'In the excitement of this, my first encounter,' he admits, 'I forgot to turn in the fore-planes'.

> We struck the target unduly hard at a sharp angle and bent our bows, though luckily not so badly as to mask the torpedo tubes. Demolition charges were placed, the fuse lit. Some trophies were collected, including a nice pair of binoculars. It was sad to see red wine flowing through splinter holes from two large wine casks upon the upper deck.

The vessel, by now identified as *Lupa* (340 tons), finally exploded and sank.

The following day *P 37* found another small vessel and again used her 12-pounder to persuade the crew to abandon ship. This time the coxswain, Petty Officer W. J. Booty, took the submarine alongside. Apparently *P 37* was running out of demolition charges, for Stanley remembers the torpedo gunner's mate,

Petty Officer Kissane, pouring shale oil all over the decks and then setting light to it. 'The ship burnt satisfactorily,' Stanley adds. But his first exciting patrol was still far from over. That same night he woke from a nap on the bridge:

> Putting the Italian binoculars to my eyes, I immediately saw a ship to the northward. The night was dark and the Officer of the Watch and look-out could not see it for what seemed an interminable time. I have always thought it a classic case of extrasensory perception, which other ships' captains have occasionally reported.
>
> We closed for twenty minutes after sighting, then fired two torpedoes at an estimated range of 1,500 yards. We heard no explosion, but an enormous pillar of flame flared upwards. The target was the *Helgar,* 1,851 tons, and was probably laden with petrol.

Helgar was still blazing away at dawn as *P 37* moved north, following orders from Captain Simpson to take up a new billet off the Tunisian island of Kuriat.

For four days all was quiet, but then there was another surge of activity. Simpson had received word that an enemy convoy was heading southward, and he redisposed his boats accordingly. Stanley remembers:

> At 1700 on the 17th we were moved to a position south of Pantelleria, as centre submarine of a north-south line of five boats: *Utmost, P 211, P 37, P 42* and *P 44*. We were in position by 0600 on the 18th . . . At 1153 [on the 19th] the mastheads and smoke haze of the convoy were sighted due north. As they approached, I could distinguish four merchant vessels in two columns . . . The first torpedo was fired at 1249 from a range of about 1,000 yards. I aimed one half-length ahead of the leading ship of the port column, and subsequent torpedoes were fired at thirteen-second intervals, to produce a spread of two ships' length.
>
> I hoped that the torpedoes missing ahead or astern would hit the leading ship of the further column. Explosions were heard at one minute fifteen seconds, and two minutes five seconds, after the first torpedo was fired. Hits were obtained on SS *Beppe*★

★ The same ship hit by *Ursula* in October, 1941 (see p.114.)

4,859 tons, and the *Giovanni da Verazzano,* a 2,010-ton *Navig-atori*-class destroyer.

P 37 had no more torpedoes left and so returned to Malta on the 21st. Stanley was delighted to find his hits had been confirmed by enemy signals intercepted by Bob Tanner, the flotilla's Staff Officer, Operations. As Stanley himself commented, 'Two days later the Eighth Army struck at El Alamein. It was agreeable to think that we had helped to limit the enemy's stocks of fuel and ammunition for the forthcoming battle.'

Unfortunately, Stanley's hopes were not justified; the enemy tanker in the convoy managed to get through, as we shall see.

P 46 sailed for the Tyrrhenian Sea during the first week of October, where Lieutenant Stevens reports that he began by attacking a small coaster. His two torpedoes missed, though not by much: 'That we were close was confirmed by glimpses, through the periscope, of startled expressions on the faces of two Italians on the coaster's bridge.'

Sailing close around the volcanic island of Stromboli, *P 46* crossed the Gulf of Santa Eufemia and made for the Calabrian coast. Her objective was to launch an attack on the coastal railway line, on which she was going to use her 3-inch gun in a night attack. As the gun's effective range by night 'was no more than 1,000 yards', 'Steve' reports, he took the submarine as far inshore as he dared and then stopped while the gun crew manned their gun. The crew comprised the gunnery control officer, Sub-Lieutenant 'Olly' Lascelles, with gunlayer, Sandy Powell and trainer, Preece.

For four nerve-racking hours the submarine waited in the dark, on the surface, close inshore, for a southbound train to appear, which it finally did. The gun's crew opened up and the train 'rolled to a halt, half a mile down the line', Stevens reports.

> Feeling that we had at least tweaked Mussolini's tail by giving some of his soldiers a delayed and uncomfortable return from their weekend, we withdrew discreetly to seaward. Leading Signalman Ron Hiles was invited to add a suitable railway emblem to the Jolly Roger.

Two days later, on 11 October, *P 46* made a long-range torpedo attack on a 1,400-ton supply ship, 'the Yugoslav-registered *Una*' according to Stevens . . . missed. However, as he goes on:

> Having sighted bubbling torpedo tracks, she took fright and reversed course, probably to return to Naples. This enabled me to close the range and, half an hour later, I aimed the only torpedo ready for firing.
>
> Petty Officer Tommy Farr, torpedo gunner's mate, despatched it at 1,500 yards range to hit the target amidships. She caught fire and sank later. Very soon destroyers and corvettes were sweeping the area with asdic, but luck was with us. Slowly and at depth, we withdrew unmolested.

Before returning to base *P 46* made one further attack, sinking the '1,055-ton *Loreto*, off Cape Gallo, Palermo'. Another very satisfactory patrol thus came to an end.

As a postscript to his account of this patrol, 'Steve' adds that his first lieutenant, Gordon Noll, now left Malta to fly home for his 'perisher', his place being taken by Max Seaburne-May, while John Fenton joined as navigator.

While *P 46* was loitering nervously in the Gulf of Santa Eufemia on the night of the 9th, *Utmost* was having trouble with the two Italian spies whom she was supposed to land in the Gulf of Gaeta, north of Naples. At the last minute, when the boat was close inshore, they lost their nerve. After three and a half hours of persuasion, they were finally man-handled into the two Folbots. This delay forced *Utmost* to lie bottomed for nineteen and a half hours. Surfacing to renew her air by using only her ship's ventilation, *Utmost* then bottomed again for another fifteen hours, with all lights and machinery switched off. Much physical unpleasantness was endured, including vomiting and severe headaches. And all in vain. The two spies, it is thought, were captured and executed.

Simpson had a few rough words for Lieutenant Coombe when he explained what had happened. In Captain (S) 10's opinion, the boat was more important than the two spies, and the boat and her crew could easily have been lost.

On the lighter side, *P 211* was having some fun in the Adriatic with dummy periscopes. According to Ben Bryant's book* these were 'a brainwave of Shrimp's':

> They were perfect copies of a periscope, but made of wood and weighted so as to float vertically, showing about three feet. The idea was that they would be seen and reported and the Italians would waste much fuel and energy in rushing to attack them. The sailors had painted on extremely rude messages to Mussolini. Had he obeyed the exhortations, even that amply proportioned man must have suffered intolerable discomfort.

In between the fun and games, however, *P 211* managed to sink the 895-ton *Veglia* off Sibenik on 2 October, using a combined gun and torpedo attack, and then, on the 5th, she turned her sights on 'a small steamer of under 1,000 tons, her decks crowded with soldiers':

> She was on the small side for a torpedo target, and at 1021 we came up on her quarter at 1,000 yards range. The first shell was away about forty-five seconds from breaking surface, but to my surprise there was an extremely alert shore battery . . . and very soon shells were pitching all around us.
> Our shells, however, were all hitting about the water line and, as our target turned stern on, three went in around her rudder; she ran up on the reefs of Trava Island. Men were leaping off her into the water, which was black with bobbing heads. By this time the shore artillery was putting up a very creditable performance and we secured and dived.

P 211 had also put up a very creditable performance, having 'got off twenty rounds, all hits', as Bryant writes, in less than three minutes. He concludes his account of this incident with a half-affectionate sideswipe at his wretched gun, which was after all 'designed to shoot at Zeppelins in World War I'.

Both *P 211* and *Utmost* took part in the five-boat patrol line across the enemy's path on 19 October, in which *P 37* had such spectacular success. *Utmost* made a two-torpedo attack but missed, then passed a valuable enemy report, while *P 211* finished

* *One Man Band* (William Kimber, 1958).

off a stopped ship, the *Titania* (5,397 tons), early on the 20th, despite the presence of two destroyers.

P 42, having received *Utmost's* report, was able to intercept the tanker with two other supply ships and, as suggested by Simpson, fired off a fanned salvo. This was one way to confuse the escorting aircraft. Although she might have made two hits and caused some damage, Simpson later suggested to Alastair Mars that he ought to have concentrated on the tanker. He was also mildly critical of Mars for his evasive tactics during the ensuing counter-attack, when several very near misses from depth-charges resulted in serious damage to the batteries. Even-handed as ever, Shrimp praises 'the good work of Lieutenant Haddow and Chief ERA Manual' and particularly 'the incident of Able Seaman Jones requesting to revert to General Service by way of a diversion in the midst of this attack. This showed 'the right spirit', said Captain (S)10.

Paul Thirsk, *P 42's* navigating officer, adds that, when she finally limped into harbour on the 20th, the fumes (chlorine gas) from the damaged battery were so bad that 'most of the ship's company remained on the casing, with the watchkeepers below wearing DSEA sets'. *P 42* now went into drydock for a lengthy spell.

In the very early hours of the same day that *P 42* limped home, the fifth boat in this patrol line finally had her chance to intercept the convoy — *P 44*. The author was Officer of the Watch that night and vividly recalls:

> Plugging through the seas, with spray drenching us all on the bridge as we closed our prey. Suddenly we plunged into a swirling bank of black, acrid smoke . . . and emerged to see the convoy dead ahead of us. The tanker was at 5,000 yards on a 140° track, with a destroyer in between, at about a mile. The generators were stopped; the tubes were brought to the ready; Tom Barlow was crouching over his torpedo sight. Three torpedoes were fired and two explosions heard; later we reported that we had hit the *Petrarca* (3,329 tons), but the hit was never confirmed.

So ended this co-ordinated attack on the convoy. The tanker and its cargo of fuel for Rommel's tanks was sighted, with the other small merchant vessel that escaped the attack, in Tripoli the next day. It was not an unmitigated success, but as Simpson remarked, 'The results certainly rattled the enemy.'

In the middle of the month there was a sudden renewal of the mass bombing raids. Kesselring was staking all on one last throw of the dice. With our submarines even now strangling the German supply line to Libya, he realized his mistake: Malta had not been neutralized at all. The invasion which Hitler had kept postponing was now impossible and the obstacle to German ambitions in North Africa was growing more menacing by the day. Summoning every aircraft available, both German and Italian, he managed to launch 300 bombers and 200 fighters from the Sicilian airfields, day after day, from 11 to 20 October. But Kesselring's gamble failed. Now Malta could send up over a hundred Spitfires and they and the AA batteries gave the enemy pilots a last hard lesson. The siege of Malta was nearly over.

Life in harbour was considerably easier now that Malta's skies were defended, but still the occasional raider appeared and precautions had to be kept up. Tom Lancaster, first lieutenant of *Una*, remembers that a smokescreen was one method of deterring the enemy:

> Submarines in harbour had smoke canisters placed on their casings, one right forward and another aft. In the event of a 'Red' warning, these were ignited and the whole harbour became full of smoke, which took a long time to clear.

Lancaster also recalls the fear of 'sprites', the term used for enemy frogmen. He quotes the public notices advising anyone who saw such intruders to raise the alarm by crying, 'Beware of sprites!' and then tossing grenades into the water to 'cause them to be dead'; he says, 'The stilted phraseology has stuck with me to this day.'

Shortages of every kind dominated life ashore, from soap to silver currency, according to Tom Lancaster. *Una* had acquired a case of 'pusser's lard' while in exile and kept it under lock and key; but one day the lock was broken and the case disappeared.

Silver coinage, too, was disappearing, as nervous islanders hid it away; naturally the authorities tried to discourage the practice but in vain. Postage stamps now had to be used, and Lancaster remembers paying his sixpenny ferry fare, on the *dghaisa* taking him across the harbour, with 'half a shilling stamp, cut diagonally'.

Food was the dominant concern, both on patrol and ashore. Stevens writes that tinned potatoes were the only kind available, and these were 'reserved for aircrew and submariners at sea', but even tinned potatoes were restricted to 'only one meal per patrol'. Ironically, as Tom Lancaster points out, back home in Britain there was a glut of potatoes in the autumn of 1942 'and the Government went to great lengths in its "Potato Pete" campaign to persuade the populace to eat more'.

Much was dependent on the skills and inventiveness of the submarine's so-called cook. Stevens and the crew of *P 46* were fortunate to have AB Bennett on board, who 'had been a baker before his call up. A willing and cheerful Mancunian, he certainly improved our gastronomic lot'. In *Una* Lancaster remembers another young AB 'who in peacetime was a lorry driver' but who 'worked wonders' with dried egg and dehydrated vegetables: 'His omelettes were superb.'

Lancaster also notes that submarine crews were given various nutritional supplements, such as 'halibut oil capsules, ascorbic acid tablets and Service lime juice', which undoubtedly helped to maintain their health. By coincidence, it was Lancaster's own boat, *Una*, who went on patrol that October with a doctor on board. But he was not an ordinary medical doctor; he was Surgeon-Lieutenant A. F. Crowley, RNVR, a psychiatrist.

Crowley had been flown out from England to observe morale and to offer help where necessary. His presence was not unanimously appreciated, nor was his speciality entirely understood. Tom Lancaster remembers 'one sailor who had dallied with a maiden' and discovered the consequences only while at sea. He went to the coxswain and the coxswain, interrupting Crowley and the officers at breakfast in the wardroom, asked if the doctor would see the patient.

The reply was in the affirmative, whereupon the Swain drew

the curtains fully open to reveal the most sorry-looking customer, to whom he gave the command: 'Flash!'

The subsequent action hardly stimulated the appetites of the astonished observers.

Una's patrol, from 12 to 23 October, included one special operation, launching a Folbot party off the Calabrian coast, and one attack on a tanker. The former passed off successfully, but on the night of the 17th/18th, as Pat Norman was about to fire his salvo, the convoy altered course straight for him, forcing *Una* to go deep. Then the tanker's escort of three destroyers began a fierce and very accurate counter-attack with depth-charges, three of which dropped unpleasantly close.

After the patrol, Crowley summarized his impressions thus:

> The cramped accommodation, close contact with messmates and lack of exercise all play their part in setting up a state of nervous tension. Though this is slight at first, it increases as the days go on, and may prove to be the 'last straw' when a more severe nervous strain is superimposed. This condition is somewhat offset by the increased amount of sleep which submarine life imposes and also by the welcome diversion which mealtime provides. Again and again, I have noticed how all looked forward to meals and how any default in the bill of fare was met with grumblings and general lowering of morale.
>
> Atmospheric conditions, once the initial discomfort has been overcome, appeared to be quite adequate for the amount of work required, but considerable discomfort was caused by excessive respiration due to the raised atmospheric temperature while dived. Towards the end of the dive, when oxygen content had decreased and carbon dioxide increased, there was a noticeable slowing of the mental processes, together with creating irritability and shortness of temper.
>
> During a depth-charge attack, it was observed how calmly each person behaved. This was partly due to the fact that atmospheric conditions had probably slowed down the intellect. However, when the second attack followed some time later, there was a noticeable increase in excitability, as evidenced by the holding of any available fixed object in an endeavour to steel oneself for the impact and its consequences. When the action was over, the effect was seen in the form of increased excite-

ment and excitability and, in myself at least, physical exhaustion. The result of a prolonged attack can be imagined.

Submarine patrolling is probably the most exacting of all types of modern warfare. From the foregoing, it will be seen that, apart from the ordinary hazards of life, the submariner's chief enemy is nervous strain. This should be combated by allowing each man a complete change after patrol, together with the granting of all amenities possible, e.g. good food and reading material whilst on patrol.

Needless to say, Crowley's conclusions were taken with a good-humoured pinch of salt.

Another visitor to Malta this month was Commander Devlin from HMS *Vernon,* the Royal Navy's torpedo school. He brought with him a CCR (compensating coil rod) torpedo pistol, the function of which was to detonate the warhead of the torpedo beneath the target's hull and without actual contact. Trials had proved it to have devastating results. Devlin's intention was to instruct the ships' companies in the fitting and use of this pistol, but unfortunately the flotilla was so busy that his training had to be done piece-meal and partially.

The flotilla's torpedo officer, Lieutenant C. J. 'Wiggy' Bennett, was anxious about the supply of torpedoes, especially now that the boats were so active. In his summary for October he noted that, in thirty-three attacks, ninety-seven torpedoes had been fired — a monthly record — and his stock of Mark VIIIs in particular was rapidly diminishing. Although he and his divers were still trying to retrieve torpedoes from the sunken *Pandora,* it was disappointingly slow progress.

Overall, the month's progress was highly satisfactory, rounded off by a double attack on 23 October by *P 35.* Despite harassment by two schooners, a tug and an A/S trawler, Lynch Maydon took *P 35* into the Khoms roads and put two torpedoes into the already damaged *Amsterdam* (8,670 tons) and then one torpedo into the tug *Pronte* (182 tons) who quickly sank. Italian attempts to salvage *Amsterdam* were finally abandoned on 23 January, 1943.

On the same night that Maydon and *P 35* found success off

Khoms, Montgomery's artillery thundered into action at El Alamein. It was the prelude to an epic battle that swayed to and fro for eleven days, until the New Zealand Division punched a gap through enemy lines on 3 November and burst through.

Rommel was ill. At the end of September he had flown back to Germany, both to consult the doctors and to discuss matters with the Führer. On 24 October, when Rommel was still in hospital, Hitler personally telephoned him with the bad news from El Alamein. Two days later, although he was still a sick man, he had returned to his Afrika Korps. Now it was they who were retreating, pursued by a triumphant Eighth Army.

Meanwhile, the great Allied armada was converging on northwest Africa. Operation 'Torch' was about to begin.

22

NOVEMBER, 1942

Operation 'Torch' had been planned during the summer as a joint Anglo-American action to land 90,000 men in north-west Africa. Three landing areas were chosen: at Algiers and Oran on the Mediterranean coast and at Casablanca on the Atlantic coast of Morocco. The Allied Commander-in-Chief was to be General Eisenhower, while overall naval command lay in the hands of Admiral Cunningham, 'ABC' himself. Months of meticulous planning were about to come to fruition. The operation would start on 8 November.

For the last few days of October the submarine crews of the Fighting Tenth enjoyed a welcome rest. For a change, there were no bombing raids. It was a chance to relax, check the boats and prepare mentally for the task ahead. Operational orders had been issued weeks ago, and the submarines of the Mediterranean Fleet all knew what they had to do.

The Eighth Flotilla would be operating west of Longitude 8°E, with the specific duties of containing the Vichy French fleet at Toulon and providing beach reconnaissance and beacons off the African coast. The First Flotilla, having loaned two submarines to the Tenth, would prevent Axis forces from moving westwards from the Aegean. The Tenth, for its part, would operate all submarines between Longitudes 8°E and 19°E. This area was subdivided by a line between the western tip of Sicily and the Tunisian headland of Cape Bon. In the western half of the area, Captain (S) 10 was responsible to the Naval Commander of 'Torch', technically the Allied Naval Commander Expeditionary Force (ANCXF), better known as Admiral Cunningham. In the eastern half his orders would come from the Commander-in-Chief Mediterranean, Admiral Harwood.

The Tenth Flotilla's specific orders were to prevent the Italian fleet from interfering with the landings.

During the first week of November the submarines of the Tenth gradually left harbour to take up their appointed positions. *Una* and *Utmost* would patrol south of the Strait of Messina, off Cape Spartivento in southern Calabria. North of the Strait would be *P 37*, *P 35* and *P 43* with the three *S*s that had temporarily joined the Tenth during the last six weeks, *P 211*, *P 212* and *P 247*. The other two *U*s would form a five-boat patrol line extending north-west from Cape San Vito in north Sicily, at intervals of five miles, with *P 46* nearest Sicily and her sister *P 44* nearest her. Another two submarines, on loan from Beirut, *Parthian* and *Turbulent*, would patrol the south-east corner of Sardinia, off the Cavoli light.

Such were Captain Simpson's plans. On 1 November *P 46* (Lieutenant Stevens) was due to sail when the stern wire fouled her port propeller and, while divers worked to clear the wire, her patrol position was taken by *P 37*. *P 46* then sailed the following day for *P 37*'s position.

Our spare crew telegraphist had been drafted to *P 43* who left Malta on the 1st. On the 6th his log records that *P 43* had reached her appointed position:

> Arrived on billet in Straits of Messina. Fired four torpedoes at German U-boat off Stromboli. Missed. Reloaded in afternoon. Changing billets with *P 35* every forty-eight hours.

This was not the only U-boat that had a lucky escape on this day. *P 46* fired a full salvo at one, missed, and then sighted another; but the second one was at extreme range and, because our submarines had orders to conserve torpedoes for bigger game, *P 46* allowed the enemy boat to pass. *Utmost* also sighted a U-boat and fired a salvo. Because of the bad weather and her bulbous bows, the salvo was fired with a 20° bow-down angle, to prevent a break-surface when the torpedoes left their tubes, whereupon the torpedoes passed under the enemy boat who was only 250 yards distant. The U-boat occupied the whole field of vision in 'Basher' Coombe's periscope, and the look of apprehension on the faces of the bridge personnel was clearly visible as *Utmost*'s torpedoes approached. It was the most bitter disappointment.

On the morning of 8 November the patrolling submarines received news that the Allied landings had begun.

P 46 had already allowed an enemy U-boat to pass, followed shortly afterwards by a 3,000-ton tanker and two destroyers – all ignored because she had to conserve her torpedoes.

On the morning of 10 November, off Cape San Vito, Stevens sighted the cruiser *Attilio Regolo,* accompanied by six destroyers and three aircraft. In his book *Never Volunteer* he describes how he made his attack:

> Passing between two screening destroyers without molestation we arrived in position to fire a four-torpedo salvo at 1,500 yards range. With the strong escort there was no question of staying at periscope depth to watch for a torpedo hit; as soon as the last torpedo was on its way, we were on our way to the depths.

P 46 was then subjected to a persistent but fortunately inaccurate counter-attack, and after 'creeping away, silent and deep, to the west' her CO decided to surface in order to pass a W/T signal to Lazaretto. Having expended all her torpedoes he intended to return to base.

> Five hours after firing, in mid-afternoon, we surfaced. Through binoculars I could see mast tops of destroyers circling the cruiser and laying smoke screens.
>
> Aircraft were patrolling the area but failed to sight us. As our presence was well compromised, it was gratifying that Malta W/T answered our first radio call; it was not unknown for ships to blaze away into the ether at full power for long periods and then to be answered by Bermuda or Whitehall W/T.

The plume of water caused by *P 46*'s hit had been sighted by *P 44,* although the cruiser was not visible. Tom Barlow immediately went to Diving Stations and *P 44* was already under way when a signal arrived from Captain (S) 'ordering us to close the enemy. *P 44* was forced to go deep, as the glassy calm up top meant that circling aircraft would have spotted the tell-tale swirl of propellers'.

For five hours *P 44* stalked her prey, as the author well remembers, this being his second patrol as understudy to Peter Beale, the first lieutenant:

> Five long hours of tension as Barlow inexorably reduced the range. He was using the porpoising technique with fifteen-minute bursts of full ahead, grouped up. In between bursts Peter Beale stopped the motors to plane the boat up to periscope depth for the captain to have a lightning 'look'. And at each rapid squint the target became more visible: first the white crosstrees of her mast, the director, her foremost funnel, then the after funnel . . .
>
> If Tom Barlow felt the tension he did not show it. As we came up to periscope depth one last time, our batteries very low and all tubes ready, Barlow had another quick look. Instead of the damaged cruiser moving slowly south, she was now moving stern-first and northwards. We could never have caught up with her.

P 211 was to be equally frustrated, as Ben Bryant explains in his book, *One Man Band*. Just over the horizon, he too had seen the smoke caused by Stevens' torpedo hit and then heard 'not so enviously' the ensuing counter-attack. Bryant goes on:

> It was a Sunday and that evening as we were having our Sunday service in the control room, Paris, the Petty Officer Telegraphist, brought me a signal from Shrimp Simpson. It read: *Damaged enemy cruiser NE of Cape St Vito in tow with eight destroyers, six E-boats and aircraft in company. P 44 close immediately. P 211 proceed to C. Gallo to intercept* . . .
>
> It was nice to be released from the boring patrol line, but the prospect of being mixed up with this party on the surface at night in inshore waters was a bit sobering. I reckoned that our interception could wait a few minutes whilst we finished the service and maybe a little more fervour went into the prayers.
>
> I dare say that many services have been held in stranger places, but no one in *[P 211]* would have missed our little Sunday service in the control room; the officer of the watch scanning round on the periscope, the planesmen controlling the depth, the helmsman his wheel, an occasional trimming order. One particular prayer — it is not to be found in any prayer book and

I forget where I found it, though I believe it is called the Knight's Prayer — was particularly pugnacious and that we looked upon as our own.

Everyone who could crowd into the control room, oil-stained and unshaven, and just outside, the Roman Catholics, the only denomination who could not join in, would collect for the sermon. I regret to say that this was a bit secular; it covered what we had done the previous week, the mistakes we had made and what I intended doing the following week, together with any general information. On this occasion I read out Shrimp's signal, which was greeted with the usual imperturbability. We then surfaced and worked up to full power as we made for Cape Gallo near Palermo.

Despite a skilful and close approach, dodging and weaving through the escorting ships, *P 211* eventually had to admit defeat. As Bryant says, it had been a strenuous chase: 'Our eyes were nearly hanging out; failure is so often harder work than success'.

There is a postscript to the story. According to Stevens, the cruiser was later sighted 'minus sixty feet of her bow part' and had to be towed back to Palermo. Stevens then became a public hero, much to his own amusement, as he explains in his book:

> The success of the landings and the lack of enemy activity made for a dearth of sensational items for General Eisenhower's first press conference as Supremo at his Gibraltar HQ. So in *P 46* we hit the British headlines. 'I'll tell you about the maddest submarine captain in the British navy,' the General was reported as saying. 'He is Lieutenant J. S. Stevens, who saw an Italian cruiser through his periscope, fired a torpedo and badly crippled her, then prepared to finish her off but found that he had been fighting so hard that he had run out of torpedoes and ammunition. He then surfaced and radioed his location for other units to take care of her.'
>
> The British press fastened on to the 'maddest' epithet with gusto, and used it for some time to come. General Eisenhower was, of course, using the word in its usual American sense of 'annoyed' or 'frustrated,' but the press did not choose to stress this.

Following the successful landings at Oran and Algiers, the submarines that had been patrolling off the Algerian coast were now released, some to join the Tenth in the central basin. *Ursula* had returned to the Mediterranean after her refit just in time to share the excitement at Oran and now she was heading east for a patrol off Marittimo. With her went two new U's, *P 48* and *P 45,* while a third, *P 54,* stayed temporarily with the Eighth Flotilla.

The Eighth Flotilla boats received a signal on the 11th from their Captain (S), Captain Fawkes, noting that the French battle fleet had been reported leaving Toulon and adding that an appeal had been made to the French fleet to join the Allies in the North African ports. The submarines off Toulon still had a watching brief, but events were now moving at perilous speed. Within three days the Germans were to have invaded southern France, up till now the so-called 'Unoccupied Zone'. The question that the British and American leaders were asking themselves was, 'Which way would the French fleet jump?'

That same day *Turbulent* (Commander J. W. Linton) achieved a very notable hit. Off the Sardinian coast she sank the *Benghazi* (1,554 tons), the depot ship for German U-boats based on Cagliari. To the bottom went forty torpedoes of the latest electric type, diesel and lubricating oils, and 'perks' for the U-boat flotilla. It was satisfactory vengeance for *Medway.* Two days earlier, on the 9th, *P 247* made a direct attack and sank the 630-ton Italian U-boat *Granito. P 247*'s CO, Lieutenant Lumby, remembers: 'It was on the surface, steering a westerly course right across our track'. Lumby fired a full salvo 'at a range of less than 800 yards and three of them hit. There were no survivors and only three seat lockers and a large patch of oil marked the spot'.

Although it did not become known to the Tenth for some time, that same Armistice Day, 11 November, 1942, also saw the loss of one of their sister Us in *Unbeaten.* Teddy Woodward had sailed her home for major repairs in April, the last submarine to work with Wanklyn's *Upholder,* and now, her repairs completed, she was heading back south. As Woodward, promoted to lieutenant-commander, was then running the 'attack teacher' course for the COQC at HMS *Dolphin, Unbeaten* had acquired a new CO in Lieutenant Donald E. Watson. En route south, she was to land a commando party in the Bay of Biscay, its objective being to destroy shipping in French ports; but on completion of this operation, at 0230 she was attacked on the surface in bad weather by an RAF bomber. The aircraft's radar set was playing up and the Wellington's pilot had received a signal warning of a U-boat sighted in this area. He and his crew cannot be blamed; such tragedies are inevitable in wartime.

On 12 November, a signal was sent to 'All British ships and authorities in Operation "Torch" and Vice-Admiral Malta'. It came from Admiral Cunningham, who had established his new base at Algiers:

> An armistice has been signed in North Africa, but German air and ground units are infiltrating into Tunisia. Our forward troops reached Bone today, Thursday. The ports of Algiers, Bougie, Arzeu, Mers-el-Kebir and Fedala are working. Ships have been sunk in ports of Oran and Casablanca which interfere with port working, but this I hope will only be temporary. The assaults went with a swing, a fact of which we may well be proud. Our task is not yet finished. We must assist the allied armies to keep up these assaults and re-establish our control of the Med.

The first phase of 'Torch' was over. The next phase would centre on Vichy-controlled Tunisia. The submarines were therefore redisposed and ordered to resume the offensive against shipping between Sicily and Tunisia.

On 11 November, while the British submarines were elsewhere engaged, three Italian battleships sailed from Taranto. Slipping through the Strait of Messina, they were making for Naples. *Littorio, Roma* and *Vittorio Veneto,* escorted by an entire destroyer flotilla, had managed to escape detection until the following day. But *P 35* was in position, as Simpson had redirected her to the Gulf of Santa Eufemia; with a party of commandos, she was to blow up more southbound troop trains. *P 35* sighted the heavy ships off Cape Vaticano. She 'manoeuvred into position for an ideal beam shot,' according to Simpson's book, and fired a full salvo of torpedoes — which missed.*

---

* Five days later, *P 35* torpedoed and damaged *Piemonte* (15,209 tons). She was beached but refloated.

What exactly went wrong is not clear. In his book Simpson praises Lynch Maydon as 'a cool-headed expert,' and goes on:

> My explanation is that the loud beat of these three giant ships gave an impression to the asdic operator of a double effect, and 240 revs were reported instead of 120 . . . So passed the flotilla's fourth and last opportunity to sink a battleship and in bitter disappointment I wrote in my remarks to *P 35*'s patrol report 'but on consideration these battleships have never done anyone any harm'.

In retrospect, it is clear that this move by the Taranto battle fleet was part of a general regrouping of Axis forces, prompted by the realization that Hitler's Grand Plan had failed.

It was now clear to both sides that, if the Afrika Korps was going to survive, every effort must be made to keep open the two remaining supply routes — to the Tunisian ports and to Tripoli. From now on the enemy's anti-submarine forces, both surface ship and air, would concentrate on these two routes. The confrontation between our submarines and the enemy's A/S forces was about to intensify dramatically.

Simpson and the Fighting Tenth were preparing to resume the offensive against shipping between Sicily and North Africa. But it was two of the borrowed *S*s who were first sent south to the Tunisian coast — *P 211* and *P 212*. As we have seen, *P 35* was in the Gulf of Santa Eufemia; *Utmost* and *P 46* were both returning to base to reload torpedoes; *P 44* and *Una* had both been recalled, while *Ursula* and the two new *U*s were still off Marittimo.

P 212 (Lieutenant John Bromage) was off the island of Kuriat, soon after dark on 14 November, when she sighted a ship, later identified as the *Scillin* (1,580 tons). She went to gun action at a range of 1,500 yards and the ship was brought-to. Then, when the target ship started transmitting an SOS, a single torpedo was fired at a range of 750 yards. It hit abreast the engine room and the ship sank in less than a minute.

Closing her victim to discover whether there were any survivors, *P 212* found herself sailing towards an unusual number of swimmers in the water. Obviously the ship had been carrying far in excess of her steaming complement. Then the cry was heard from the water: *'British prisoners of war!'*

Fortunately the weather was fine and the sea relatively calm. Over the next half-hour *P 212* managed to recover sixty-one survivors. It was an amazing feat, performed by her first lieutenant, Lieutenant M. M. Melson; her engineer officer, Mr D. J. Thomas, Warrant Engineer; and five able seamen. They hauled the shocked survivors up on to the casing, then passed them down the gun tower and conning tower hatches. Bromage later praised not only his own crew but also the 'exemplary behaviour' of the British POW survivors:

> Whilst in the water, unlike the Italians, they patiently took their turn to be rescued, though weak from wounds and lack of food; and it was typical that in response to a call from the casing, 'Are there any Englishmen in the water?' the reply from the last man should come back, 'No, but there's a Scotsman!'

But many men still remained in the water when *P 212*'s HSD reported asdic impulses astern and very soon a bow-wave was sighted on the bearing of the impulses. Regretfully, but correctly judging that the safety of his boat came first, the CO was forced to abandon the remaining survivors as *P 212* set course for the open sea.

From the survivors (twenty-six British, thirty-five Italian) it was discovered that the *Scillin* had sailed from Tripoli with 810 British prisoners of war on board and 200 Italian troops, bound for Sicily. *P 212*'s torpedo had blown out the bottom of the hold in which the British POWs were herded. In his report on the incident Simpson wrote:

> It was naturally a cause of deep regret to Lieutenant Bromage that there were only twenty-four [sic] British survivors out of 810 prisoners packed on board, the remaining survivors being the Italian crew. This in no way detracts from the fact that this night attack was very well executed. Furthermore, that during the disorder consequent upon such an influx of prisoners who were sick and wounded, the utmost vigilance was maintained and the enemy torpedo boat both heard and seen before it could gain contact.

Simpson also singled out for praise 'the excellent work of the Coxswain, Chief Petty Officer Flack,' who had cared for all the wounded men pulled from the water. Captain (S) 10's report continues:

> *P 212* returned to Lazaretto to disembark survivors at 1345 on 15 November. A working party was promptly put on board to scrub out and disinfect the submarine, since most of the survivors had dysentery, and at dawn the next morning (16 November) *P 212* sailed for patrol in the Gulf of Sirte.

The incident had been another of those unavoidable tragedies of war.

By the time *P 212* returned to base, her sister, *P 211,* was already on her way south to the Gulf of Sirte. Off the Tripolitanian coast she sighted a steamship escorted by a *Crotone*-class torpedo boat and circling aircraft. Ben Bryant decided this steamship was worth an attack. For hour after hour *P 211* pursued his target, dodging the torpedo-boat and aircraft, but time and again she was thwarted, until finally the enemy nipped into port at Zuara and hid behind Djerba Island. The full story is told in Ben Bryant's book, *One Man Band,* but the episode ends with *P 211* hitting with a single torpedo.

> It was most satisfying to see our steamer stopped and down by the stern. As I watched, her bows reared up till they were above her funnel and she slid under by the stern. It had been a very lucky shot, but I think well earned. We had started to attack her twenty-seven and a half hours before. It was the longest attack I ever did.

It was also a lesson to the Tenth Flotilla that life was going to become even more difficult. The enemy was getting desperate and the stakes were high, for the survival of all the Axis forces in North Africa depended on these supply routes being kept open.

Belatedly, German High Command was supplying the troops, tanks, ammunition, petrol and food that Rommel had needed months before. Such was the importance attached to the supply runs that even troop-carrying German aircraft like the Ju 52s were diverted to become anti-submarine escorts. Every convoy would also have a heavy escort of surface ships — destroyers, torpedo boats and E-boats. Minefields were extended and regularly re-sown.

In future the *U*s of the Fighting Tenth were going to meet an even more determined foe.

23

NOVEMBER/DECEMBER, 1942

The second half of November was a difficult time for the Tenth Flotilla, because of the enemy's augmented anti-submarine measures. Despite the presence of the three Ss and the new Us, the total tonnage sunk during this period was well down on October. But good news had arrived in the form of two fast minelayers, one from each end of the Mediterranean — *Welshman* from Gibraltar and *Manxman* from Alexandria. Covered by Operation 'Torch', both ships reached the island intact, laden to the gunwales with aviation spirit and enough provisions to keep the islanders going for a few weeks more. Supplies were also brought from Alexandria by four of the store-carrying submarines, but it was clear that another full-scale convoy was needed.

In mid-November, operational responsibilities for the three submarine flotillas were revised, with the Eighth Submarine Flotilla now moving, complete with its mother ship *Maidstone,* from Gibraltar to Algiers. In future Captain Fawkes would operate his flotilla as far east as Cape Bon. Captain (S) 10 would operate any of the Eighth Flotilla boats that ventured east of Longitude 8°E and north of Sicily. Captain (S)1, in Alexandria, would continue to operate the submarines of our Greek allies, who had kept the enemy occupied in the Aegean and eastern Mediterranean throughout 'Torch'.

On 16 November the Greek submarine *Triton* (Lieutenant-Commander E. Kontoyannis) was attacked by a German submarine chaser. *Triton* had already completed a useful patrol by landing secret agents in occupied Greece and then attacking an important convoy in the Aegean. But *U-Jager 2102* proved an implacable adversary; after carrying out four counter-attacks and dropping forty-nine depth-charges on *Triton,* she forced the submarine to the surface. *Triton* courageously opened up with her gun, but was then rammed and sunk. The CO and thirty-two survivors were picked up, including her British liaison officer.

The last convoy had formed, the final effort to lift the siege of Malta. Codenamed Operation 'Stonehenge', four supply ships arrived through the Red Sea and assembled in Alexandria, ready for departure on 17 November. Escorted not only by the battle-scarred 15th Cruiser Squadron under Rear-Admiral A. J. Power and seven destroyers, but also by RAF fighter cover from recaptured Libyan airfields, the convoy arrived without loss at Grand Harbour on the 25th. Enemy aircraft made repeated efforts to stop the convoy. The cruiser *Arethusa* was hit and 155 of her brave company perished. They were, however, the last casualties in the struggle to keep the island fortress alive.

The siege of Malta had been lifted after two and a half years. It had been a very near thing. If these supplies had not arrived the island would have been forced to surrender by the second week of December.

One consequence of Malta's renewed offensive potential was that Admiral Cunningham's fleet was to be busier than ever. Not only did his ships have to keep Montgomery's advancing army supplied by ferrying reinforcements to Tobruk (recaptured on 13 November) and to Benghazi (on the 20th) but Force K was now reconstituted as a surface force working from Malta.

But the French fleet at Toulon had not heeded the call to join the Allies. Although Admiral Darlan had agreed to support the Anglo-Americans, Admiral Godfroy was still considering his options. At the end of the month he finally threw in his hand with the Allies, but by then the rest of the French fleet had scuttled itself in harbour.

Una had a new CO – John (Joe) Martin, who had been the spare CO. Simpson decided that Pat Norman had done enough and should go home. But it was some weeks before he could go and, because Bob Tanner's replacement as SOO, Bill King, was ill, Norman spent the next few weeks standing in for him at Lascaris. Eventually, he writes, he was offered a place 'in the bomb bay of a Hudson aircraft'.

> We made a non-stop flight to Gibraltar, very uncomfortable, very cold, and we were fired on over the battlefield in Tunisia. At Gibraltar I hitched a ride in a 'four-stacker', an American lease-lend destroyer which was due to escort a six-knot convoy out to 15°W in the Atlantic before arriving in the UK. Eventually I arrived in Milford Haven in the middle of the night. I borrowed a skiff from the destroyer, rowed ashore and cadged a lift in a lorry to some mainline junction in South Wales.
> I had been away for almost two years. I met my daughter for the first time when she was eighteen months old.

Thus it was not Norman but Martin who took *Una* to sea late that November on what was to become known as 'the Tunis run'.

One after another the *U*s would be dispatched to the northern coast of Tunisia, around Bizerta, Cape Bon and the Gulf of Tunis itself. Lumby, captain of *P 247,* described it as 'quite the nastiest patrol area I had ever endured'.

> The weather seemed always to be bad, visibility was not good and there was a permanent easterly set of at least two knots . . . Our only navigational mark was the Cani Rocks north-east of Bizerta, which were only visible at odd moments.

And the more the enemy's supply lines were squeezed, the more desperate he became to keep them open – and the more intensive his anti-submarine measures were.

The one consolation for our submarines was that on 21 November, at long last, the Admiralty lifted all restrictions in the Mediterranean; save for the ships trading between Spain and Algeria, and vessels in Turkish waters, all shipping could now be sunk at sight.

Utmost had sailed from Malta on 17 November. On the 23rd she made an attack, later thought to have been on the Italian armed merchant cruiser *Barletta,* escorted by the torpedo boat *Groppo.*

That evening Coombe signalled Malta, reporting success and saying that he was returning to reload torpedoes. But *Utmost* never arrived. She might have been mined; she might also have been caught, coincidentally, by *Groppo*.

According to Italian records, at 1210 on the 25th, *Groppo* was escorting another convoy south around Marittimo, when her captain saw a circling aircraft drop a bomb some 4,000 metres off – the warning that a submarine had been sighted. *Groppo* now joined the hunt and, getting a contact, launched an immediate attack. Her captain reported at the time that he had been successful, but his superiors judged that his claim was dubious. As is so often the case, those left behind can only wonder.

Una was in the same area, though a little to the south of *Utmost*'s position. With Joe Martin in command she was patrolling off the Gulf of Tunis. Late on the 26th, according to her third hand, Tom Lancaster, Martin decided to take her into the bay:

> The sea was calm; moonlight and a fairly clear sky gave excellent visibility. About midnight a vessel was sighted on a southerly course. Because of the sea and light conditions, it was decided to carry out an attack submerged. The target [never identified] was hit and blew up at 0047/27 November.
>
> The explosion was so violent that many of the electric lamps were broken throughout the submarine and the thick plate-glass front of the 'fruit machine', which I was operating, was completely shattered.

Fortunately, *Una* was not badly damaged and retired to safety outside the bay, where, like *Utmost,* she surfaced to transmit a signal reporting success and indicating her intention to return to base. Tom Lancaster's record continues:

> No sooner had this signal been made when one from base informed us of the loss of *Utmost* and warning all submarines to alter course while transmitting by radio. . . . I was on watch on the bridge shortly after the signal had been received from base. The sky had clouded over by this time, although there was some faint light ahead. Before long I detected through binoculars a number of small dark objects on the horizon, evenly

spaced and covering an arc of about 30°. These were judged to be a group of anti-submarine vessels disposed in line abreast and coming down our grain, searching for us. Evidently, the enemy direction-finders in Sicily had fixed our position (they were most efficient in this field) and had directed the hunting craft on to us. *Una* dived and went deep, maintaining her course, thus presenting a small target to the hunters. Before long the sound of propellers was heard passing overhead but no contact was made.

Luck was with *Una* that day, and she returned safely to Malta on 3 December.

Much further south was *P 44* who had sailed from Malta on the 18th to patrol the western side of the Gulf of Sirte. The author, by now first lieutenant, remembers this patrol as particularly trying: 'Not only was the area notorious for shoals and a featureless coast, but this was a full moon period which did not help concealment while we were battery-charging on the surface. Our objective was to investigate RAF reconnaissance reports that coastal craft and cargo-carrying U-boats were creating a supply dump for the retreating Afrika Korps at Burat-el-Sun.'

P 44 was just outside this little port at dawn on 21 November when an Italian U-boat approached from the eastward. Our torpedo salvo missed ahead and Tom Barlow was just considering whether to pursue her into harbour when we touched bottom. Loitering outside the harbour, we hoped to catch her leaving later but at 1340, when she did emerge, we were in the wrong position to attack. As Shrimp Simpson put it in his report, 'Nettled by this lack of success, Lieutenant Barlow entered harbour and engaged a schooner, scoring twelve hits with her 3-inch gun.' We opened up on the shore installations, until the breech mechanism jammed, and we were obliged to withdraw.

Two days later, off Misurata on the 23rd we had more problems with the gun, as our gunlayer, Leading Seaman Cyril Balls, remembers. 'The gun was a very effective weapon in the right circumstances,' he writes, but on this patrol it was playing up. It was Balls himself, with his exceptional eyesight, who sighted 'seven objects against the landfall':

> Lieutenant Barlow thought that they were shapes ashore but I
> noted that one appeared to be moving faster than the rest. We
> approached from astern on their starboard quarter and, with
> the gun closed up, I waited for the order to fire at the last
> vessel in line. I got one round away and the gun jammed,
> which was probably just as well. The whole lot opened up on
> us (they were ack-ack barges!) with tracer peppering the conn-
> ing tower.

It was always a scramble to 'clear the gun' on such occasions,
for not only the gun's crew but the whole chain of men passing
up ammunition had to 'get below in double-quick time':

> The first vertical ladder to the lower hatch was slithered down,
> with shins and knees bashing the coaming. Down the second
> ladder, tab-holes were clobbered by hefty boots, and fingers
> trodden on. Woe-betide anyone who had Stoker Sidney above
> him. He rowed around in what must have been size twelves.

On this occasion Balls clambered into the conning tower and,
while waiting his turn down the ladders, heaved all the 'ready'
shells over the side.

> An E-boat, the faster one I had earlier reported, was belting
> towards us as the Skipper slammed the hatch. Q tank should
> be blown very soon after diving, but wasn't, and we zoomed
> to about 200 feet in thirteen seconds. Fortunate, again, as the
> first depth charges crashed well above us.

Continuing westwards, in the early hours of the 26th *P 44* was
confronted by an enemy vessel escorted by one torpedo boat
ahead and one astern. In the bright moonlight she had no option
but to dive and make a submerged attack. Simpson later criticized
this torpedo attack for being a quarter of an hour too late and
for having earlier, on the 23rd in full moon conditions, chased
the enemy on the surface. 'What could possibly have been
achieved is not understood,' he wrote on the patrol report, 'since
the target and both torpedo boats were in any case faster than

the submarine. It is not surprising that at 0255 *P 44* lost touch after accepting an unnecessary hazard for forty-five minutes.'

But *P 44* arrived back at Malta safely on the 30th.

The *S*s had been joined by another of their class, *P 228,* whose commanding officer was well known to the Tenth — Lieutenant Ian McGeoch. *P 228* and another *S*-class, *P 221* (Lieutenant M. F. R. Ainslie), were operating under Captain (S) 8 for the moment, but the former would soon be in Malta. Her first strike was made in combination with *P 247* on the convoy to the west of the Cani Rocks, where she sank the Italian destroyer *Aviere* (1,620 tons).

P 247 had attempted one attack herself, on a small unescorted merchant vessel, but something went wrong, as Lumby here recalls:

> We fired three torpedoes and went deep. There was no bang. But as we went down we heard a noise like cannon fire, which seemed surprising. Later it became apparent that it was a 'circler'. The gyro in one of the torpedoes had been upset by the rough sea and it was running in circles over our heads. This was an unusual event. The Mark VIII torpedo was a marvellously reliable weapon and, in over fifty fired by *[P 247],* this was the only one to give trouble.

Lumby adds that the Mark VIII 'was still going strong in 1982: viz, the sinking of the *General Belgrano*'.

At the end of the month Simpson dispatched *Traveller* (Lieutenant-Commander D. St. Clair Ford) to the Gulf of Taranto, partly to intercept shipping off Crotone and partly to reconnoitre for an important series of special operations to be undertaken by her sister *T*s. Drummond St. Clair Ford was captain of *Parthian,* but since Lieutenant Michael St. John, *Traveller's* own CO, was ill, St. Clair Ford relieved him for this patrol. *Traveller* left Malta on the 28th and never returned. She is thought to have been mined, probably in the approaches to Taranto on about 4 December. St. John then took over *Parthian.*

This terrible blow was followed by another very soon afterwards. *P 222* (Lieutenant-Commander A. J. Mackenzie), operating under Captain (S) 8, was sunk off Naples on 12 December, by the torpedo boat *Fortunale*. There were no survivors.

It would have helped morale in the Tenth Flotilla, mourning the loss of these two submarines, if anyone had read the letter which Hitler wrote to Mussolini on 28 November, urging him to re-animate his convoy escort organization.

The Führer had just learned that Tripoli harbour had been blocked for fourteen days and supply vessels were unable to leave because of the patrolling British submarines. Moreover, 'the supply route to Tripoli via Tunis cannot be used' and 'the Italian navy maintains that it has no escort craft to provide protection for the voyages to Tunis and Tripoli. Tripolitania cannot be held under these conditions.'

Rommel was summoned back to Germany at the end of November and now faced the full wrath of a man who thought he had been robbed. The Afrika Korps was clanking to a halt in the sand; with every day that passed the supply situation became more perilous, until by 16 December the Panzer army was com-pletely motionless in the desert — 153 tanks without a drop of fuel.

Mussolini was on the point of giving up. He had confided to his staff on 14 September that the naval war was as good as lost, and now the Anglo-Americans looked likely to sweep across the whole of North Africa. Perhaps they would next turn their eyes north to Italy? His nervousness was not helped by his ally's fury, not only at obstacles in the Mediterranean but at the latest turn of events on the Eastern Front, where the Russians had launched an unexpected counter-offensive at Stalingrad. Mussolini could see the writing on the wall.

24

DECEMBER, 1942

While the net tightened around Rommel's troops in Libya, the American First Army was making for Tunis. Montgomery's Desert Rats were reaching out for the prize of Tripoli, as the submarines in Malta were preparing for an unusual new offensive — Operation 'Principal'.

As we have seen, back in December, 1941, the battleships *Valiant* and *Queen Elizabeth* had been sunk in Alexandria harbour by an intrepid team of Italian frogmen. Churchill was so impressed that he immediately chivvied the Royal Navy into developing similar teams; the result was the 'chariots'. Each two-man chariot was twenty-five feet long with an explosive charge of up to 700lb carried in the bow, which could be detached and slung beneath the target ship.

Battery-powered, the chariot had a top speed of 20 knots, but a range of only twenty miles; it would have to be transported on specially adapted submarines to within that distance of its target. The crew sat astride the torpedo, behind protective shields, wearing special breathing apparatus that left no bubbles; the disadvantage was that it could only operate at a maximum depth of thirty feet. These men needed a special sort of courage and it is small wonder that they and their colleagues in midget submarines won a total of four Victoria Crosses.

For months now the charioteers had been in training in Scotland, supervised by Commander G. M. Sladen and Captain W. R. Fell. Sladen was an experienced submarine officer, who had been CO of *Trident* operating in Arctic waters, and a strong personality. He flew out to Malta during the first week of December, followed shortly afterwards by the three specially adapted submarines carrying the chariots and charioteers: *Thunderbolt* (Lieutenant-Commander C. B. Crouch), *Trooper* (Lieutenant J. S. Wraith) and *P 311* (Lieutenant-Commander R. D. Cayley).

The first of these three was the former *Thetis,* who had sunk in a tragic accident during trials in Liverpool Bay in June, 1939, with the loss of ninety-nine men. Salvaged and renamed, she was ready at last to enter the fray. Simpson later wrote that 'Crouch was a splendid man whose leadership restored the ill-fated *Thetis* . . . into the confident, offensive *Thunderbolt.*' Simpson was also delighted to see his two old friends back — John Wraith and Dick Cayley. He met 'the effervescent roly-poly figure of Cayley on the landing steps':

> 'Hello, sir,' he said. 'Looks as if you've had the house-breakers in! It's good to be home again.'

The objective of Operation 'Principal' was to sink the Italian fleet. But before the new submarines and their chariots could start work they needed very precise information about the fleet's whereabouts. This would be an extremely perilous series of attacks, risking both the chariot and the submarine. The risk had to be worthwhile. So, as the submarine crews and charioteers made last-minute preparations, the Tenth Flotilla boats continued their own offensive.

P 35 (Lieutenant Maydon) scored the first success during this month. She was on the surface on the night of 2 December in the Gulf of Hammamet when she sighted a convoy of ships heading north. Maydon picked his target, the *Sacro Cuore,* but, fearing that she might be carrying British prisoners of war, ordered his gunlayer to aim at the rudder and at the bridge. According to Captain (S) 10's report later:

> Unable to comply with such precise instructions, the gunlayer aimed halfway between the two and, at 300 yards range, the second round severed the main steam pipe in the engine room which stopped the ship. The crew immediately lowered a boat when the second shell hit the bridge.

Now that Maydon was sure there were no POWs on board, *P 35* circled the ship while the gunners shot holes along her waterline. It was a novel technique, but successful; the ship sank.

From the Luftwaffe survivors in the lifeboat, Maydon selected ten, leaving the remainder to pull for land. Arriving back in Malta on the 4th, *P 35* disembarked her prisoners, who were so astonished to find the island still surviving, and particularly to find themselves provided with new boots, that they were easily caught off balance. During interrogation they supplied some very useful information. *P 35* sailed the next day to continue her patrol.

The weather was deteriorating as she closed the harbour entrance of Hammamet on the night of the 8th; rain squalls reduced visibility and the submarine was rolling so heavily that the sounding machine could not be wholly relied upon. Leaving the Officer of the Watch, the first lieutenant, Jimmy Launders, on the bridge, Maydon descended to the control room to check his chart and soundings. The submarine went hard aground.

It was only an hour or two before dawn and she was stuck hard on a lee shore opposite the harbour entrance. Captain (S) 10 later criticized her CO for having proceeded at excessive speed, given the conditions, but added that 'subsequent events reflect great credit on Lieutenant Maydon'.

Petty Officer Telegraphist Fred Buckingham remembers that morning well. He was in his wireless office when *P 35* ran aground.

> The boat gave a violent lurch and stayed at an angle of 20°. I waited with bated breath for another wave to batter us still further over, though I knew that, with the weight of batteries and machinery, it was almost impossible to turn a submarine over.
>
> Phil Murray (the Outside ERA) arrived to tell me that we were high and dry on a sandbank, a short distance from the shore. It was still dark so we stood a chance. The tide was coming in, so perhaps we would be lifted enough to enable us to slip off the sandbank by going full astern.

Maydon had immediately flooded main ballast to prevent the boat from being swept beam-on to the seas, but nothing he did thereafter seemed to make much difference. Daylight was creeping into the sky. Soon the boat would be visible to the only port in thirty miles of barren coast. Maydon warned the ship's company to prepare to abandon ship. While one man was to fix demolition charges to *P 35*'s torpedoes, then swim for his life, the rest would swim ashore with the few rifles and pistols kept on board and, splitting into three groups, would attempt to fight their way through enemy lines, to join the American First Army.

Buckingham recalls that the man appointed to fix the demolition charges refused point-blank to do so:

> It must be said in his defence that, for some reason, he was a non-swimmer. 'Then I must have a volunteer,' Maydon said. The youngest officer on board was a South African, and he immediately volunteered.

Like the others, Buckingham was 'trying to prepare myself mentally to becoming a prisoner of war'. He did not give much for his chances of fighting through enemy lines. They started looking around for 'insurance':

> We had quite a few things of value, such as the chronometer, deck watch and test instruments. They might come in handy for bartering if we did not get through; or they might make a bob or two if we did.

'At last the time came for desperate measures,' Buckingham goes on. 'The captain gave the order to let go the drop keel.' This was a three-ton chunk of the keel which could be dropped in an emergency by releasing levers inside the boat. *P 35* slid backwards off the sandbank and retired to open sea:

> All of us were a little bit older, with a few more grey hairs. As soon as we had enough water under us, we sank beneath the waves — safe once more — and after some time, succeeded in catching a new trim.
>
> We finished the patrol and returned to Malta where I think we had three tons of ballast put in the bottom of the boat to compensate for the loss of the drop keel.

Fred Buckingham forgets to mention that *P 35* made another

attack before finishing the patrol, having sighted a small coast-hugging ship escorted by three aircraft. At a range of 4,500 yards *P 35* fired three torpedoes and obtained one hit. The target was blown out of the sea, vanishing in a huge pall of smoke; obviously she had been an ammunition ship. What intrigued Maydon was that, after his hit, he could see only two aircraft through his periscope. Simpson's report says:

> *P 35* feels inclined to claim one aircraft from the explosion, though the torpedoing of an aircraft at 1,000 feet seems more like the story of a rear-gunner in a bomber aircraft.

This had been *P 35*'s penultimate patrol before returning to the UK. For her last patrol she had to sail without her regular 'PO Tel', as Buckingham was suffering serious ear problems caused by chronic leakage of compressed air in the boat's high-pressure air lines. 'I felt a bit of a fraud,' he writes, but he would continue to suffer from the same problems in future years. He was particularly relieved to see *P 35* return safely from her final patrol, and then he embarked on her once more to return to England for the refit.

P 44 acquired a new CO during December. Tom Barlow had been appointed Assistant SOO to help Simpson at Lascaris, and his place was taken by Lieutenant J. C. Y. Roxburgh. Roxburgh was the youngest CO in the submarine service and his sole experience in command to date was in a training boat, *H 43*. *P 44*'s gunlayer, Leading Seaman Cyril Balls remembers:

> When we first saw him, I think that all our hearts sank: he looked so young and was, in fact, only twenty-three, just a few months older than myself! Our first patrol with him, starting on 11 December, proved very eventful and we soon realized that there was a new name over the door and that we had a cool customer in charge.

In his patrol report for *P 44* Captain (S) 10 later wrote:

> There was a vital need to keep submarines on the Palermo-

Bizerta route and, though I felt that it was asking a lot of Lieutenant Roxburgh to carry out his first patrol in this area, he was keen to do so . . . This patrol from beginning to end was full of events, eleven merchant ships, all escorted, twenty-five destroyers, a large number of anti-submarine craft and almost continual overhead air traffic being encountered in the ten days that *P 44* was in her patrol position.

Those ten days were a constant round of activity as *P 44* nipped and ducked between the streams of enemy ships and dodged the A/S craft. All too often she had to take swift evasive action, as when she surfaced at 2345 on the 18th to find 'six E-boats stopped on a north-south patrol line at about half-mile intervals . . . presumably listening' (as the patrol report says).

Bad weather also helped to foil one attack that Roxburgh attempted on the 19th, following which the target ship passed just *seven feet* overhead. The convoys were so heavily escorted that any attack now was interrupted by sudden forced dives, alterations of course and other evasive tactics.

In the early hours of the 22nd Roxburgh was manoeuvring to attack an Italian supply ship when the accompanying destroyer apparently detected the submarine. Just as Roxburgh gave the order to fire, 'the destroyer dropped a charge right on top of the submarine and very close. As a result the order to fire was not heard, and when the remaining two torpedoes were eventually fired it was some fourteen seconds late' (the patrol report again).

As Captain Simpson concludes in his report, 'This patrol did not result in the sinking of any ships but, for continual activity and strain on personnel, it can have few equals.' He added that Roxburgh had shown commendable 'determination and good submarine sense which brought him safely through his first patrol'.

Recalled to base on the 23rd, *P 44* arrived back at Lazaretto on Christmas Eve, 1942.

Like her sister Ss (*P 211* and *P 212*), *P 247,* who had been operating with the Tenth Flotilla boats during 'Torch', was recalled for Christmas to the Eighth Flotilla base at Algiers. Her CO, Lieutenant M. G. R. Lumby, writes that she arrived off Algiers at dawn on Christmas morning to be greeted with this signal: 'Welcome to Algiers. Merry Christmas. All shore leave is cancelled.' Lumby explains:

> In due course, we were safely tied up alongside the depot ship, *Maidstone,* and were being welcomed by Captain Barney Fawkes, the Captain S of the Eighth Submarine Flotilla. Leave was cancelled because of tension ashore, the French Admiral Darlan having been assassinated on Christmas Eve.

The assassin was a lunatic, but the murder has remained a mystery. The crime naturally heightened anxieties for a few days.

In Malta, by contrast, Christmas looked as though it was going to be a time of relative peace. The enemy still attempted sporadic air raids but seldom managed to penetrate the efficient RAF defences. The siege had been lifted, and another five supply ships had arrived from Alexandria. Force K was making useful forays against the enemy convoys, as were the RAF's aircraft; and, if the Tenth Flotilla's tally was slightly disappointing, that was due partly to the success of others.

As before, Captain Simpson tried to keep as many as possible of his submarines in harbour for Christmas. The *S*s were, as we have seen, at Algiers, but the newly arrived *T*s were at Malta now, and the Tenth had been joined by two new *U*s − *P 48* (Lieutenant M. E. Faber) and *P 51* (Lieutenant M. L. C. Crawford). It was the two newcomers who would spend Christmas out on patrol, along with *Ursula* who had returned for her second commission in the Mediterranean during Operation 'Torch'.

Following her refit in England, *Ursula* had found a new captain, Lieutenant R. B. Lakin, and a new base − Algiers. She had completed two successful patrols for the Eighth Flotilla since her return. She spent Christmas Day on her billet north of Marittimo, and on the 28th torpedoed and sank the German-manned *Gran* (4,140 tons). It was a fine start to her third patrol, and then two days later, she attacked a convoy of three ships and four destroyers. It was a bright moonlit night when she made her approach off Cape San Vito, and this may have caused her to overestimate the range and the zigzag.

The target ship rammed her and both the periscopes and

standards were 'wiped'. Such was the damage that she had to
return to England. It had been the gallant *Ursula's* last Mediterranean patrol.

P 48 had also been operating with the Eighth Flotilla out of
Algiers during Operation 'Torch', but her captain was worried
at her lack of success. She had completed three blank patrols and
Michael Faber, a friend of the author's since schooldays, confided
that he felt responsible; he had an outstanding first lieutenant in
Stephen Spring-Rice ('Sprice' to everyone) and a fine ship's company, and Faber was concerned about letting them down. 'We
talked far into the night on 10 December: it was clear that Faber
was suffering all the stress that goes with bolstering the morale
of others while he was suffering from a lack of self-confidence.
That was the last time I saw him.'

P 48 sailed on 21 December for the billet recently vacated by *P
44* in the mouth of the Gulf of Tunis. She never returned. We do
know how she met her end, however, from the Italians' records:

> The torpedo boats, *Ardente* and *Ardito,* of the *Fortunale*-class,
> sailed from Palermo on 24 December, escorting two merchant
> ships, *XXI Aprile* and *Carlo Zeno.* At 1120 on Christmas Day,
> twelve miles north-west of the island of Zembra in the Gulf of
> Tunis, a submarine asdic contact was obtained at 2,600 metres.
> Twelve depth-charges were dropped. The senior officer in
> *Ardente,* after waiting for a quarter of an hour for the disturbed
> water to subside, then regained contact . . .
>
> After the third attack with another twelve depth charges, the
> bridge sighted a confused 'boiling' on the sea. Thinking that the
> submarine was about to surface, all guns were trained on this
> spot. But the boiling slowly subsided and when the echo from
> the submarine was again obtained, the target's position was
> stationary at a depth of 200 metres.
>
> To make doubly certain, *Ardente* carried out a fourth and final
> attack, dropping a further twelve depth charges. Being certain
> of a kill, *Ardente* and *Ardito* then rejoined their convoy and
> escorted it to Bizerta.

There were no other British submarines in the Gulf of Tunis that
Christmas Day of 1942; *Ardente's* 'kill' was certainly *P 48*.

Because *P 48* had not been due to return from patrol until early

January, her loss was not immediately apparent. Christmas at Lazaretto was a chance to relax, shake off the tension and enjoy what few pleasures were available. Tom Lancaster, *Una*'s third hand, remembers that some of the men 'who had tarried at the wine somewhat liberally' were diving into the harbour from one of the larger boat's periscope standards.

'One of them struck the edge of one of the saddle tanks. His friends lashed him in a Neil Robertson stretcher and swam for the shore, towing their half-submerged charge behind them'. Fortunately, as Lancaster goes on, 'The distance was short and the injured man suffered no serious harm.'

Lancaster also remembers the 'practical, if not elegant' solution that Sam MacGregor and 'Creedy', Mr L. A. Creed, the Commissioned Engineer, had found to the shortage of drinking vessels. They had discovered that 'winding an electrically heated red hot wire around the shoulders of an empty beer bottle and plunging it into cold water produced a clean break'.

In the New Year's Honours List Sam MacGregor received the OBE, Tom Lancaster notes, along with 'two well-known showbiz personalities', which prompted his gruff retort to those offering congratulations: 'I'm not so keen about being teamed up with a couple of comedians.'

By the New Year the submarines also received a mark of recognition from above, though of a rather different kind. For some weeks now the Prime Minister had been fretting about the fact that our submarines bore 'no names'. He wanted them to receive proper names instead of numbers. It was typical of Winston Churchill that he could take a personal interest in such a seemingly trivial matter. On 5 November he had written to the First Lord of the Admiralty, Alexander, recommending that names be found:

> I have no doubt whatever that names should be given, and I will myself make some suggestions that may stimulate others.

On 19 December he was needling the First Sea Lord, Sir Dudley Pound:

> I am still grieved to see our submarines described as *P 212*, etc.

259

in the daily returns. I thought you told me that you would give them names. It is in accordance with the traditions of the Service and with the feelings of the officers and men who risk their lives in these vessels. Not even to give them a name is derogatory to their devotion and sacrifice.

Eight days later, on 27 December, he was again writing to Alexander:

These names for submarines are certainly better than the numbers. Please see my suggestions. I have no doubt a little more thought, prompted by the dictionary, would make other improvements possible.

Now do please get on with it, and let them be given their names in the next fortnight.

According to Simpson, Dick Cayley joked that his *T*-class boat, *P 311*, ought to be called ' "*Two Tank Amen*", or its abbreviated form, "*Tutankahmen*" ', a reference to the two huge cylindrical containers for the chariots, attached to her fore- and after-casing

The first chariot operations took place at the turn of the year. It had been decided that because the big *T*-class parent submarines would be so very vulnerable, the *U*s would be taken off patrol duties to recover the chariots. Accordingly, when *P 311* sailed for Maddalena on 28 December, she was followed two days later by *P 43*, or *Unison* as her name was now.

P 43/Unison had just found a new captain, as our spare crew telegraphist noted in his log: 'Lieutenant A. R. Daniell, ex-first lieutenant of S/M *Upright*. He has just arrived by plane from UK.' Anthony Daniell and *P 43/Unison* had spent one day on exercises, getting to know each other, then disembarked two torpedoes in order to leave space for 'fully rigged Folbots'. *Unison* immediately sailed for Sardinia, to rendezvous with Cayley's *(P 311)* charioteers.

Simpson was very anxious about these big submarines making the transit through the Sicilian minefields and across the enemy's Palermo-Tunis convoy route. The huge containers they carried rendered them slower at diving, more difficult to trim and naturally made their silhouette dramatically more conspicuous. In addition to which, extracting the chariots from the containers took fifteen minutes. Simpson therefore ordered *P 311* to report when she was through the minefield and well clear of the enemy's A/S sweep; he was holding the other two *T*-class boats back until he had confirmation that *P 311* had made it.

Cayley signalled at 0130 on 31 December, giving his position as thirty miles west-north-west of Marittimo. Simpson then released *Trooper* (Lieutenant Wraith) and *Thunderbolt* (Lieutenant-Commander Crouch) to follow *P 311*'s track through the Sicilian Channel, but they were then to make for different landfalls*.

P 311's destination was La Maddalena, an important naval base at the northern tip of Sardinia. RAF reconnaissance had discovered that two 8-inch cruisers were in port at the time. They were the target of *P 311*'s two valiant charioteers. After the attack the chariots were to be sunk while their crews made their way on foot to a prearranged spot on the island's eastern coast. Here, at a given time on a given day, *Unison*'s Folbot team would pick them up.

Anthony Daniell, captain of *Unison*, had arranged to meet *P 311*'s charioteers on the night of 8 January, or, failing that, at the same time on the 9th. Daniell writes:

> I decided that Derek Palmer, our fourth hand, would paddle ashore with one of our crew and two Folbot canoes to contact the expected charioteers. He was to whistle or hum some bars of 'Rule Britannia' at intervals to demonstrate his *bona fide*. Alas, no charioteers came.

Daniell and *Unison* returned to Malta without the brave charioteers on 16 January. It is almost certain that they never reached their destination and that *P 311* was mined in the dense minefields around La Maddalena.

The loss was deeply felt by all at Lazaretto. 'Harmonica Dick' had been a popular figure and a particular friend of Simpson's. His officers and crew, and the four charioteers on board, had

---

* *Thunderbolt's* original destination was Cagliari. *P.37*, after landing agents on the Tunisia coast, moved up to Sardinia as rescue submarine.

worked like Trojans to prepare for this operation. It was difficult to realize they had gone.

The other two submarines, *Thunderbolt* (Lieutenant-Commander Crouch) and *Trooper* (Lieutenant Wraith), launched their chariots for a joint attack on Palermo on the night of 2/3 January, 1943★. Despite squally winds, the chariots were all launched successfully, but ran into trouble thereafter.

One chariot broke down and the crew had to wait for recovery by *P 46/Unruffled*. Another sank and drowned one of her crew. The captain of the third, negotiating a net, tore his suit and was drowned. His crewman drove the chariot ashore, blew it up and was taken prisoner. But the two other chariots had better luck. One, driven by Lieutenant R. T. G. Greenland, RNVR, and crewed by Leading Signalman A. Ferrier, reached Palermo's innermost wharf. The two men detached their 400lb explosive bow and attached it to a brand-new, still uncommissioned *Regolo*-class cruiser, *Ulpio Traiano*; they then went on to fix limpet mines to three destroyers. The other chariot took Sub-Lieutenant R. G. Dove, RNVR, and Leading Seaman J. Freel right under the 8,500-ton *Viminale*, a troop transport.

Palermo was woken at dawn by such a violent explosion that the citizens and port authorities were thrown into confusion. It was *Viminale* that had exploded. At 0800 the new cruiser went up. Realizing at last what had happened, the authorities then managed to clear the limpet mines before the destroyers were lost too.

Meanwhile *P 46/Unruffled* had picked up the crew from the broken-down chariot: 'my namesake, Sub-Lieutenant H. L. Stevens, RNVR, and Leading Seaman Carter', as Stevens recalls. Ninety minutes after *Unruffled* should have retired, she was finally able to leave the scene of the crime.

The success at Palermo was a slight consolation for the loss of *P 311*. For their gallantry the Palermo charioteers were later honoured: Lieutenant Greenland and Sub-Lieutenant Dove were each awarded the DSO, Leading Signalman Ferrier and Leading Seaman Freel the CGM.

★ For a full account of this operation see *Above Us The Waves*, C. Warren and J. Benson (Harrap, 1953).

The tide was turning in the Mediterranean. Albeit at a high cost to themselves, the British submarines were slowly strangling the supply line to Tunisia. The Germans could scarcely persuade their Italian allies to put to sea. At the end of December, 1942, the Admiralty signalled a rare expression of their 'admiration for the Mediterranean submarines' tenacity and ingenuity in maintaining their offensive'.

It was hardly a time for great celebration, the New Year of 1943, but it looked a good deal more cheerful than the year that had passed.

25

JANUARY, 1943

'What a place to spend New Year's Day,' wrote our spare crew telegraphist in his log, 'passing through a minefield!' He was still in *P 43*, now *Unison*, and her orders were to rendezvous with the 'Jeep riders', as he calls the charioteers, from *P 311*. Sadly, as we know, the mission was never fulfilled, as *P 311* had been lost with all hands. On 16 January *Unison* returned to base:

> Arrived Lazaretto 1500. All public places, including bars, out of bounds. An epidemic of Infantile Paralysis has broken out on the island.

On the following day the second attack in the 'Principal' series began when *Thunderbolt* sailed for Tripoli with two more chariot crews embarked. Intelligence had suggested that the Germans were planning to sink two vessels as blockships in Tripoli harbour, to immobilize the port and thus deny it to the British who, even now, were knocking at the gates. The task of the charioteers was to sink these two potential blockships where they were, safely to one side.

Simpson was against the plan. The waters were shallow, badly charted and thick with mines, as his *U*s knew to their cost. The full moon period was approaching, which would be a particular hazard for the *T*-class boat with her huge double burden fore and aft of the conning tower. But as the C-in-C, Admiral Harwood, pointed out, the Mediterranean Fleet's duty was to supply the British when they took Tripoli and thus it was very much in our interests to keep the harbour clear.

The night of 18 January was breathlessly calm — no cloud and the moon almost full. *Thunderbolt* arrived off Tripoli and Lt-Cdr Crouch gave the order to launch the chariots. They were in mid-operation when an E-boat was sighted leaving harbour. She approached steadily, then stopped 3,000 yards away. *Thunderbolt* waited, completely vulnerable with her hatches open, the chariots still in the containers. Nothing happened; the enemy had not seen her. Silently the charioteers completed their job, slipped over the side, mounted their torpedoes and crept away into the dark sea, while *Thunderbolt* slid gratefully beneath the surface and retired.

The mission had mixed results. One chariot developed mechanical troubles and had to be abandoned; her crew were captured but escaped a few days later when the Eighth Army entered Tripoli. The other chariot, XIII, manned by Sub-Lieutenant H. L. H. Stevens, whom Stevens had collected from Palermo in *P 46/Unruffled*, and Chief ERA S. Buxton, was approaching her target when it blew up in front of them. The Germans had chosen that very moment to sink the blockship. The charioteers were only 150 yards away, and lucky to escape with their lives; but, undeterred, they made for the other potential blockship, attached limpet mines and fled. The limpets did their job and the second target vessel sank safely away from the harbour entrance. But XIII's crew found a suitable landing place, then dispatched their chariot seawards to scuttle herself; then they too were captured, transported to Italy and interned in a POW camp near Rome. They escaped to the sanctuary of the Vatican, and finally recovered their freedom when the Allies arrived nine months later. Courageous men, indeed.

Admiral Harwood signalled his 'high appreciation' of *Thunderbolt*'s and the charioteers' achievements; despite the sunken blockship there was still a chance that our shipping could enter and leave Tripoli harbour. But Simpson remained sceptical; in addition to the three *T*s, the *U*s had been tied up on Operation 'Principal' for about two weeks, at a crucial stage in the North African campaign. In his opinion, the results were simply not worth the effort.

Meanwhile the young John Roxburgh and *P 44* (or *United* as she now became) were back on patrol. On the night of 6/7 January, zigzagging northwards towards Marittimo for the Palermo-Bizerta convoy route, Roxburgh was on the bridge with the author as Officer of the Watch. It was a glassy calm night, but visibility was low, mists obscuring the horizon. 'Already we had made one emergency alteration of course for the torpedo-like phosphorescent surface trails of marine eels. Roxburgh had a strong presentiment that E-boats were listening on their hydrophones; he ordered our generators to be stopped and we proceeded silently and slowly on main electric motors.

Two torpedoes were shooting through the sea towards us. The first passed some way ahead, the second under the fore-hatch. We dived. Minutes later we heard the HE of approaching E-boats, and we were forced to remain deep for much of the following day as the enemy energetically pursued us.

Three days later, at 0400 on the morning of the 10th, we were caught in the glare of a searchlight beam off Cape San Vito – which also lit up a nearby E-boat. Again we dived, and managed to throw off the hunters. Still moving north-westwards we next joined *Una* to form a patrol line west of the volcano island, Stromboli, where a convoy was expected. But the combination of atrocious weather conditions and efficient escorts kept us from our target. *Una* was no luckier than *United*. Both submarines now turned back.

On 17 January, we were again off Marittimo. The HSD, Able Seaman Duckers, had heard fast diesel and turbine HE approaching and, coming up to periscope depth at 1715, Roxburgh sighted a modern 7,000-ton motor vessel, *Roselli*, escorted by two *Artigliere*-class destroyers. Twelve minutes later Roxburgh fired four torpedoes at a range of 3,000 yards. Two minutes later the noise of a torpedo hit was heard and Duckers reported that the diesel HE had ceased.* At 1733 the destroyers launched their counter-attack – thirty charges dropped in the first half hour. None were particularly close but we had now been dived since 0601 that morning and were looking forward to a change of air.

At 2224 Roxburgh felt it was safe to surface but an E-boat was sighted nearby and we immediately had to dive again. The hatch had been open a bare minute. Evidently suspicious, the E-boat

---

* In fact it was the destroyer *Bombardiere* that our torpedo hit; she sank. *Roselli* survived.

was now operating her asdic; we could hear the familiar 'pings'. Two more destroyers and a second E-boat joined the hunt. Roxburgh's patrol report notes at 2309:

> At one time, the whole team were right overhead, pinging for all they were worth on the same frequency. This was as well for *P 44* as they appeared to interfere with each other and so *P 44* was never detected.

At 0400 the next morning, 18 January, we were getting desperate for air, but now there were four E-boats up top, and at 0515 they were joined by another destroyer. Roxburgh's report says at 0650:

> *P 44* had now been persistently hunted and depth-charged for thirteen hours. Throughout this time, the HSD, Able Seaman Donald Duckers, had been closed up at his set without relief. Without his very skilful and unruffled demeanour, *P 44* may well have found herself in difficulties. He proved invaluable to the Commanding Officer and is deserving of the highest praise.

It was now daylight. We had at least another twelve hours to face, before being able to surface.

At 0715 a convoy was allowed to pass; the torpedoes had not been reloaded during the hunt for fear of noise-making and loss of trim. It was also essential now to husband the remaining air in the boat and to conserve the battery. The submarine therefore went deep as the convoy thundered overhead.

As many men as possible were lying horizontal, immobile, silent, in order to hoard the rapidly diminishing oxygen. Cooking and eating were out of the question. There was just sufficient lighting for safety. After twenty-two hours, the Chief ERA, Leon Tout, released a burst of life-giving canned oxygen into each compartment, guessing how much to provide because the gauges had not yet reached Malta.

The *U*s were supplied with a granulated carbon dioxide absorbent, called Protosorb, but this was contained in long unwieldy metal trays which continually got in everyone's way; we had deliberately left them behind.

After thirty hours the carbon dioxide poisoning became acute, the oxygen less and less effective. Breathing was a severe effort; heads were pounding. Everyone was mentally counting the minutes till 1806, when it was calculated that darkness would have fallen and we could surface. We came up from deep and cautiously Roxburgh raised the periscope for his first look in thirty-six hours. He immediately ordered: 'Seventy feet.' It still was not dark enough to surface. Roxburgh writes: 'I can still remember the groans and expostulations from all and sundry, when I announced the unpalatable fact.'

Finally at 1826 on the 18th *United* surfaced, her company all gasping for air.

If it had not been for that one minute when the hatch was open, late on the 17th, releasing the atmospheric pressure in the submarine, we would not have survived. Roxburgh's patrol report goes on:

> By the time *P 44* surfaced, practically the whole crew and officers were showing signs of considerable distress through carbon dioxide poisoning. On surfacing, the Commanding Officer, whose mental powers were much reduced, was feeling far from aggressive, and he spent the first five minutes on the bridge being extremely ill, as did the Officer of the Watch up there with him, and a large number of the crew below.

Cyril Balls, the gunlayer, puts it more bluntly. 'Most of the crew were violently sick,' he writes. 'It was ages before there was sufficient oxygen to light the first all-important cigarette.'

On 20 January we arrived safely back at Lazaretto.

P 51/Unseen was watching small craft moving along the south Tunisian coast, on 17 January, when a merchant vessel (*Zenobia Martini*, 1,455 tons) was sighted off the island of Djerba with a single escorting destroyer. *Unseen* made a three-torpedo attack and obtained two hits, as her Telegraphist Jim Richards remembers. Richards goes on:

> In between picking up survivors from her sunken charge, the escort hunted *P 51* for over two hours, dropping depth charges;

six were close and shook the crew alarmingly, but inflicted no serious operational damage on the boat. The enemy escort eventually departed and, shortly after noon, *P 51* sighted the wreckage of her victim: a lifeboat numbered '2'; a raft; empty oil drums; petrol containers; and a corpse. It was satisfying to know that Rommel's army would not be using this material against our advancing Eighth Army.

That night the submarine sighted several more supply ships but they were judged 'too small to warrant a difficult torpedo attack'. These were shallow waters and *P 51* had already touched bottom once; besides, she was almost certainly being tracked by the enemy's radar installations on the shore.

The following morning, heading eastwards, the submarine was off Zuara when she sighted 'an Italian *Calypso*-class destroyer, a merchant vessel [later identified as *Sportivo*, 1,600 tons] . . . and a 400-ton petrol carrier,' writes Jim Richards. Three torpedoes were fired and one hit obtained on the merchant vessel. With the destroyer in hot pursuit, the submarine fled for safety; the water here was sixty feet deep and the thirty-five depth charges dropped were unpleasantly close. Although *Unseen* sighted the same destroyer and petrol carrier that afternoon, she was unable to attack; like *United* the previous day, she was running out of air, although the situation was not so dangerous as to prevent her crew reloading the torpedoes. Jim Richards again:

> Undressed to the waist, all hands not on watch helped the fore-ends men to haul on the blocks and tackles to hasten the operation, until the torpedo chief, Percy Porter, and the torpedo officer, Subbie Ron Linden, could report to 'Jimmy-the-One': 'Reloading completed.'

Fortunately, the hard-working crew were rewarded with fresh air that night when the submarine was able to surface.

It was a nervous night, for there was considerable A/S activity. With ships and aircraft joining in, *Unseen* decided that the better part of valour was discretion and, having received orders to clear the area, returned to Malta safely on the morning of 21 January. Richards concludes his account of this patrol with a note on 'the faithful mine-sweeper *Hebe'* who met the submarine in the app-roaches to Marsamxett Harbour and escorted her 'back to the relative safety and calm waters of Manoel Island'.

Unseen had been ordered to leave the area because the surface ships of Malta's Force K were about to commence a preliminary assault off Tripoli, before Montgomery launched his great land offensive. As Richards explains: 'The submarine did not always have the opportunity to fire recognition signals.' During her next patrol off Crotone, Calabria, *Unseen* torpedoed and sank *Le Tre Marie* (1,085 tons).

Rorqual, the mine-laying submarine who had been such a staunch friend to Malta during the siege, when she ran stores from either end of the Mediterranean, was at last reverting to her proper role.

According to Lieutenant Ian Stoop, first *Rorqual*'s third hand, later her Number One, this submarine had led a charmed life. One dramatic incident that he cites occurred when she was leav-ing Malta one night and was challenged by an enemy submarine. *Rorqual* dived immediately, when an enormous explosion was heard astern. The Italian U-boat had fired an acoustic torpedo, and evidently reported that she had sunk *Rorqual*. Ian Stoop explains:

> When the Italians finally capitulated, *Rorqual* was in Malta and we were able to visit an Italian submarine: on her wardroom bulkhead was a plaque presented by Mussolini 'for the sinking of HMS *Rorqual*'! We had the pleasure of showing her captain the real *Rorqual* safely alongside in Lazaretto Creek.

On another occasion, described in Captain Simpson's book, *Ror-qual* had been laying mines off the Cani Rocks, six miles from the Bizerta roads (mines that later claimed *Graz* (1,870 tons) as a vic-tim) when another U-boat attacked. Simpson received a signal from Lieutenant L. W. Napier, *Rorqual*'s CO:

> Four torpedoes have just passed under me, between forehatch and stern. Am proceeding.

After the war it was learned that the U-boat CO had glimpsed the huge bulk of *Rorqual* through his binoculars in the darkness and hastily ordered a deeper setting on the torpedoes. He was convinced that his target was an aircraft carrier.

Now, on 17 January, Simpson had again been obliged to send *Rorqual* to the Cani Rocks; a hazardous operation at the best of times, this would be during the full moon period. In his book Simpson recounts what happened:

> Acting on the double-bluff theory, Lennox Napier took *Rorqual* straight through on the surface. His guess that the enemy would never think a submarine could be so foolish proved correct. *Rorqual*'s lay of fifty mines, fifteen miles north-east of Bizerta, in sight of the Cani Rocks for an accurate fix, claimed a victim the next afternoon.

That victim was *Ankara*, a tank carrier for the Afrika Korps, who had won the tag 'unsinkable' for the numerous occasions when she escaped the attacks of our submarines.

What Simpson's account does not mention, according to Ian Stoop, is that

> on arriving in the laying area, we could not open the mine doors, because they were jammed. As a result, we withdrew and spent the night close in to Pantelleria, in bright moonlight, charging batteries whilst Rudd Cairns [first lieutenant] and the Chief, Charles Saunders, fixed the mine doors . . . Whilst this operation was going on, the captain and I watched a large convoy, heavily escorted, pass quietly by towards Tripoli.

'There was nothing we could do at the time,' Stoop adds, but the sinking of the *Ankara* the following day was suitable compensation for this disappointment.

In future *Rorqual* would be working mainly from Algiers with the Eighth Flotilla, although she remained a familiar sight in Malta's harbours, when she occasionally passed through on passage to Beirut.

United returned to Malta, as we have seen, on 20 January, a day later than expected, and naturally everyone had been thinking the worst. Her captain still remembers going to the wardroom bar to celebrate his return and asking the bar steward for his bottle of beer – 'one a month, I think, was the allowance at the time' – and being told: 'Ow, signor, Lieutenant Stevens drink it to drown his sorrows and to drink your health in eternity!' John Roxburgh had a word or two for Steve after that.

That same day, 20 January, was the day that the Tenth Submarine Flotilla lost its first and formative Captain (S). Although Simpson's relief did not arrive in Malta for another three days, Simpson had done his stint. His Commander-in-Chief sent him the following personal signal that day:

> On completion of your command, I wish to express to you my high appreciation of the fine work you have done. The 10th S/M Flotilla has distinguished itself in a branch of the Service whose reputation has never stood higher than it does today. The great achievements of the S/Ms operating under your control are a reflection of your resolute and inspiring leadership.

Simpson wrote later that he was 'glad to hand over' to his successor, George Phillips, although he 'refrained from telling him how much I loathed the way in which it had developed during the past two months on the Palermo-Tunis route':

> Instead of some respite afforded by the relief of Malta and the success of our armies, there was that gnawing anxiety every hour of every day and night over how my men were standing up to the strain of operating within a narrow channel with barely sea room to manoeuvre. Ceaseless enemy air patrols overhead and convoys to attack which now contained invariably twice the escorts than there were targets. The loss of four submarines in five weeks, and no prospects of change. . . . In retrospect it is obvious that I was getting tired, and it was time I left.

Simpson had shared his doubts with Wingrave 'Gravy' Tench, the civilian administrator whose house and family became a second home to Simpson. 'The cruel joke is this, Gravy,' Tench remembers him confiding; 'just when things might be getting better for Malta, they're becoming much worse for my men.' Tench understood what he meant; he knew all about the enemy concentrating his anti-submarine measures as he was forced to

53. Cloak-and-dagger activities were routine affairs for the Malta submarines. Here Lt N. McHarg RNVR (right) with another officer of the Combined Operations Pilotage Party, Lt Sinclair, take passage in *Unruffled*. COPP parties surveyed the enemy beaches before the invasion of Sicily.

52. Leading Stoker Charlie Fall stands by *Unbroken*'s 3″ gun, the first of the *U*s to be so armed.

54. Outside the Wardroom, Spring, 1943. From left to right:- Lt Waterhouse, Lt-Cdr Giddings, ? , Lt Turner, Cdr Hutchinson (Cdr (S)), Cdr (E) Sandars, Lt Barlow (capless), Rear-Admiral Barry (FO(S)), Lt Prideaux, Lt Marshall, Lt Daniell, Capt Phillips (Capt (S) 10), Lt Crawford, Capt Roper (COS), Lt Patter, Lt Roxburgh, Lt McGeoch, ?, ?, Lt Hammer.

55. The staff office has been hacked out of the rock at Lazaretto. Lt T.E. Barlow, Deputy SOO, and Lt M.L.C. Crawford, CO *Unseen*, read through the signal logs.

56. *Unshaken* and her ship's Company. Her Captain, Lt. Jack Whitton, stands in front of the gun.

57. Right: *Unshaken*'s
boarding party who
captured the Italian
U-boat *Menotti*, and
brought her back to
Malta.

58. Left: *Unseen*
recovering survivors :
note the fore-planes
turned out, ready for
diving. The Adriatic,
September, 1943.

59. Left to right:
Lt J.C.Y. Roxburgh
(CO, *United*); Major
Geoffrey ('Apple')
Appleyard, DSO, 2nd
SAS, No 1 Small Scale
Raiding Force, who
commanded the raids on
Pantellaria; Lt 'Johnny'
Cochrane,
(Second-in-Command);
Lt-Cdr 'Johnny'
MacCarter, South
African Naval Service,
CO *Charioteer*. Standing
at rear: Lt Jackie
Whitton, (CO,
Unshaken).

60. With telegraphs at slow ahead, grouper switch down, *Unseen* glides at walking pace through the depths; the officer of the watch, with spare earphones and stop watch, listens with the asdic (sonar) rating to a passing ship.

61. *Sokol*. The Captain at the attack periscope: Commander George Koziolkowski, Spring, 1943. "Bearing : 'Green seven-O'."

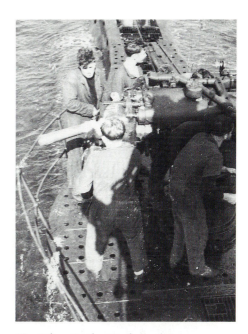

62. *Ultor* (Lt G.E. Hunt) at Malta. Both she and *Unrivalled* were fitted with wooden chocks on the casing, abaft the conning tower, to carry 'chariots' (two–man human torpedoes).

63. *Ultor*. In the *U*-class, there was no gun tower. At 'Gun action' the bridge team, gun's crew, supply numbers and ammunition had all to use the upper conning tower hatch.

64. *Sokol*, showing the fine lines of her class, in a floating dock. The *U*s were handy little submarines, ideal for their Mediterranean patrols, despite their poor turn of speed.

65. *Sokol* at Gibraltar, homeward-bound after her second commission.

66. Right: One of *Sokol*'s torpedomen 'stands by' with hands on the firing levers of two of the four torpedo tubes : "*All tubes ready!*"

67. Commandos getting used to a Folbot; this canoe could be manhandled through the forehatch of a *U*-class submarine.

68. *Rorqual* (Lt-Cdr R.H. Dewhurst; Lt-Cdr L.W. Napier; Lt G.S. Clarabut): external minelayer of the *Porpoise*-class, 2157 tons. Despite her large silhouette and two wartime commissions packed with incident, from August, 1940 to December, 1943, she survived (the only survivor of her class) to serve her final wartime commission in Malayan waters.

69. Although not so well known as *Sokol*, the Polish submarine ORP *Dzik* (ex-*P 52*) was an equally aggressive fighter. She carried out a dozen patrols in the Mediterranean under the command of Lt-Cdr 'Bolek' Romanowski, ex-first Lieutenant of *Sokol*.

70. *Clyde* (Lt-Cdr D.C. Ingram; Lt R.S. Brookes; Lt J.R.H. Bull), 2,723 tons, a fleet submarine (21 knots) of the *River*-class. After one successful Mediterranean patrol, because of her size and speed, she was adapted for carrying supplies (including aviation spirit) to beleagured Malta.

operate in ever more constricted areas. 'I'm asking my submariners almost for the impossible,' Simpson muttered more than once. 'And then,' Tench adds, 'with that phrase he so often used, "Pay no attention," his face would break into its infectious grin.'

It was typical of the man that, tired and dispirited as he must have felt, as he left Lazaretto he paid tribute 'to the wonderful courage and skill of those who have gone to sea and fought the enemy', when he wrote to Captain (S) 1, Phillip Ruck-Keene. Then, listing 'with pride' the results that the Tenth Submarine Flotilla had achieved under his command, he notes that 'approximately 250,000 tons of shipping has been torpedoed and damaged and this includes battleships and four cruisers'.

> The following have been actually sunk: 5 cruisers, 8 destroyers, 8 submarines, 2 armed merchant cruisers, 8 liners, 8 tankers, 65 merchant vessels, 13 schooners and 12 various, including such things as . . . . salvage vessels, tugs, lightships, etc.

If Simpson was proud of his men, they regarded him with something akin to reverence. His hunches, born of experience and careful study of such intelligence as was given him, seemed to them like clairvoyance*. His concern for his COs and crews was obvious to all, yet he 'never shrank from fair and firm administration of justice', in the words of Anthony Daniell. 'He was imbued with a generous humanity and humour that was readily sensed by everyone with whom he came into contact,' writes Daniell. 'That was the main ingredient which made him an apparently effortless leader of men.'

'Shrimp made the flotilla,' Ben Bryant writes, adding that he had 'tremendous stamina':

> He needed it; he was practically 'watch on, stop on' twenty-four hours a day, seven days a week. Nearly every signal you got on patrol from (S) 10 was fairly certain to have been drafted by Shrimp personally.

Just once in a while there were those who saw him with his guard

---

* *Ultra*, we now know, provided Captain Simpson and Captain Phillips with one of their main sources of intelligence.

down, like the Tench family at whose home in St Julian's Bay he sometimes managed to relax. One who remembers him in this family atmosphere was Paul Thirsk, who had worked with him briefly at Lascaris during the autumn of '42, and who was 'fortunate enough to be asked to spend a few days with the Tench family':

> Away from the crushing responsibilities he bore so lightly, and as a relief from the overwhelming grief this sensitive man hid so successfully over the loss of too many of his distinguished officers, Mrs Tench told me that Shrimp would read himself to sleep with one of her children's books.

Thirsk also remembers Simpson joining the wardroom for a sing-song: 'His rendering of "I paid one franc to see the tattooed lady" was superb.'

'He was friendly to all, full of compassion,' writes Cyril Balls:

> If a rating was found in the gutter of the base, sleeping off the previous night's drowning of sorrows, Shrimp would say, 'Get that body out of sight'. He understood. He knew his men. They loved and respected him.

And perhaps Balls was not the only one to glance wonderingly back at that short, thickset figure standing on the harbour steps while the men swarmed on board their boat for another patrol:

> With these terrible decisions on one pair of shoulders he should have been twice as tall and twice as broad. How could one man take all that he did and survive for so long?

But Captain Simpson had one more trial to survive before he could return home.

26

JANUARY/MARCH, 1943

Captain George Phillips was a quiet, slightly reserved man whose presence and reputation commanded immediate respect. He flew out to Malta, landing on 23 January, 1943, which gave him one week to assimilate all that Simpson could pass on before leaving on the 31st.

It was Admiral Sir Max Horton, FOS, who had selected Phillips as Simpson's successor and he could hardly have made a more suitable choice. Phillips knew the *U*-class submarine better than almost anyone else, having participated in the class trials before the war and then commanded *Ursula* in the Norwegian campaign. It was there that he had been honoured with the DSO, where incidentally, he had invented the foul weather 'Ursula suit' which helped to keep us warm and dry on the bridge. And now he was among us, also wearing the ribbon of the George Medal, awarded in recognition of his act of great gallantry in extricating men from a blazing Norwegian submarine, late in 1941.

Despite Simpson's impending departure, there was a faint air of excitement, even optimism, in the air as the elusive prize finally fell into Montgomery's hands. The Eighth Army recaptured Tripoli on 23 January and Montgomery was generous enough to acknowledge the enormous assistance his army had had from the Mediterranean Fleet, in keeping his troops supplied via the recaptured Libyan ports and in destroying the enemy's supplies.

Simpson later wrote to Captain (S) 1, Philip Ruck-Keene, that when he arrived in the Mediterranean 'the Commander-in-Chief said to me: "Your object is to cut the enemy's sea communications between Europe and Tripoli". It was therefore particularly thrilling to me when Tripoli fell to the Eighth Army before I left Malta'.

Taking passage in *Welshman,* the minelayer that had made such daring supply runs to aid Malta in the island's time of greatest need, Simpson sailed for Alexandria on 31 January, 1943. On the evening of the next day *U 617* torpedoed and sank her fifteen miles north of Tobruk. Over half her ship's company of 240 were saved, picked from the water by two destroyers from Benghazi. Among them was George Simpson.

Back in the UK Simpson was appointed Commodore, Western Approaches (Londonderry), where, under his old friend Admiral Sir Max Horton, now Commander-in-Chief Western Approaches, he operated the destroyers and frigates fighting the Battle of the Atlantic. Later he was promoted Rear-Admiral and appointed Flag Officer, Submarines. In 1947-8 he was Chief of Naval Staff to the Royal New Zealand Navy. Eventually he retired to that country, with his wife and family, where he ran a beef farm at Whangerei. He died there on 2 March, 1972.

Meanwhile the Tenth Flotilla's patrols continued, with the *Us* concentrating on the east Tunisian coast during the latter half of this month and most of February. On 19 January, off Tourg-en-ness, *P 42/Unbroken* (Lieutenant Alastair Mars) sank the 6,105-ton *Edda*. Returning to Malta on the 23rd, she reloaded, refuelled and sailed off again two days later, this time on a special operation codenamed 'Felice'. On board were 'a cosmopolitan collection of thugs', in the words of the new Captain (S) 10 — a party of Free French commandos led by Captain J. Eyre of the Royal Engineers. The party comprised Free French fighters because in this French colony they would obviously stand a better chance of escape if things went wrong than British commandos. Their objective was a railway bridge near the shoreline just outside Hammamet.

Unbroken surfaced at 1847 on the 28th. It was a dark night and a flat calm. While the submarine closed the beach, four Folbots were passed out through the fore hatch. By 1930 the Folbot party had been launched and the submarine returned to seaward. A brilliant flash erupted from the shore, followed moments later by the sound of three explosions. It was 2030 and the operation had been successful. But flares lit up the sky, exposing the waiting submarine; she would have to retire. Firing the prearranged signal, two rounds of starshell, to warn the commando party, she was forced to withdraw by the approach of surface craft.

P 45/Unrivalled, commanded by Lieutenant H. B. Turner (known as 'Mossy' because he sported a 'full set' of facial whiskers) was enjoying 'some very nice rough shooting,' as his Commander-in-Chief later commented, during this last fortnight of January, 1943. Off Sousse on the 17th, she gunned a small tug, and then, off nearby Cape Africa on the 20th, she sighted an Italian naval auxiliary and two schooners, one towing the other, escorted by a torpedo boat, the *Lince* (679 tons). The following is taken from Italian records:

> The towed schooner suddenly exploded. Thinking that she had struck a mine, *Lince* then sighted two torpedo tracks, one torpedo of which blew the auxiliary vessel to bits. The towed ship altered course and beached herself.
>
> *Lince* then ran down the torpedo tracks. She hoped to ram, assuming that the submarine could not dive in these shallow waters. *Lince* increased speed, and, a minute later, estimated that she was above the submarine. But *Lince,* who had been based on Tripoli, had disembarked all her depth-charges there after she had been damaged by RAF bombing, her stern having flooded.
>
> One schooner was picking up her consort's survivors; the other, the towed ship, was rescuing the auxiliary's crew from the water, while *Lince* zigzagged for ten minutes until joining up again with the remnants of her charges.

Needless to say, Mossy Turner had managed to dive his submarine and *Unrivalled* retired gracefully. But that was not the end of her patrol. Off Monastir on the 24th, watching four Beaufighters shooting up a ketch, she then surfaced and, boarding the vessel, sank her with a demolition charge. There were only two days during her fourteen-day patrol when she was not at gun action or blowing up ships with torpedoes and charges.

P 46/Unruffled (Lieutenant J. S. Stevens) was playing havoc in the same area. Using her gun wherever possible, she was shooting up small supply ships coast-hugging in the Gulf of Hammamet, resorting to torpedoes only when her gun provoked retaliation from the shore. On one occasion, on 25 January, watched by an audience on the nearby waterfront of Hammamet itself, she used a single torpedo to dispatch the small tanker *Teodolinda* (350 tons). On the 26th she gunned a motor schooner and left her waterlogged. On the 31st, after a long chase, she caught the German supply ship *Lisbon* (1,800 tons). One torpedo found its mark and the vessel exploded in flames before finally sinking.

The single *U*-class submarine not in Tunisian waters at this time was *P 37/Unbending* (Lieutenant E. T. Stanley). She was in the southern approaches to the Strait of Messina when, at dawn on 23 January, she sighted two tugs towing an 8,000-ton ship, escorted by two E-boats and a torpedo boat. She was the *Viminale* (8,500 tons), the charioteers' victim at Palermo, patched up and on her way to the repair yards at Messina. Stanley fired three torpedoes, scoring two hits, but the counter-attack was immediate and accurate. The depth-charges having caused considerable damage in the submarine, including thirteen cracked batteries, she was forced to return to base. *Viminale* survived this second attack and limped round to Messina where repairs took six months to complete. She was on passage to Naples, in July '43, when she was finally sunk by Allied aircraft.

January thus ended, for the Tenth Submarine Flotilla, with a new Captain (S) and a creditable series of hits to add to the tally. But success came in small parcels now. Of the supply ships sunk off the Tunisian coast — many by gun action — the largest was only 2,000 tons. The enemy was increasingly obliged to use these small coast-hugging supply ships as the larger ones provided irresistible targets for the RAF.

If anyone felt despondent at this state of affairs, he was soon cheered by a message from the First Sea Lord, Admiral Sir Dudley Pound:

> The total tonnage sunk in the Med. by H. M. Submarines has just topped the one million mark. My sincere congratulations and thanks to all submarines now serving or who have served in the Med. who have achieved this magnificent result under most difficult conditions.

And good news was continuing to come in from North Africa.

Eighth Army troops were at the Tunisian frontier by the end of the month, and from the west the Anglo-American First Army, now joined by Free French forces, was closing in on the enemy's last foothold in North Africa.

But Rommel, the legendary 'Desert Fox,' was not finished yet. He withdrew the Afrika Korps behind the Mareth Line, a series of fortifications raised by the French against a potential Italian invasion from Libya. It was truly impregnable and Montgomery's only option was to circumvent it by making a 150-mile detour.

Roughly 1,200 miles to the west, in French Morocco, the Casablanca Conference had just ended − a ten-day meeting between the Prime Minister, Mr Churchill, and President Roosevelt to discuss strategy to end the Mediterranean campaign. They were laying the foundations for the Allies' return to Europe. Operation 'Husky' was born.

Una (Lieutenant Joe Martin) opened the February innings off Hammamet on the 1st with a gun attack on two schooners. Both were badly damaged, but when the shore batteries opened up they hit one of the gun's crew, wounding him in the arm. *Una* then dived, returning to Malta on the 3rd in order to land her casualty; she then sailed the same day but with a new destination − eastern Calabria.

On 10 February *Una* sank the 4,260-ton *Cosala* in the Gulf of Squillace and on the 15th, investigating RAF reports that a ship had been beached north of Crotone, she sank it with a torpedo. The RAF reported the next day that only the ship's upper works were above water. With this Parthian shot to her credit − the *Petrarca* (3,360 tons) − *Una* was returning home. In eighteen patrols she had sunk a total of 13,000 tons of enemy shipping, damaged much more, and carried out several special operations. She had had a long stint in the Mediterranean. After a tragic start when she sank the *Lucania* by mistake, she had been welded into a very happy ship by the cheerful and unflappable Pat Norman, and by Joe Martin, Norman's great friend, who carried on the run of successes.

P 43/Unison (Lieutenant Daniell) and *United* (Lieutenant Roxburgh) were both in the Gulf of Hammamet this February, the former in the Sfax area, the latter off Sousse. *Unison* had already used her gun to good effect, sinking three south-bound motor barges, when she came upon a 450-ton coaster 'which proved to be a German', as Anthony Daniell remembers, on 11 February. 'She wasn't worth a torpedo', her CO writes, so the submarine surfaced to use her gun, and despite the range — about 3,000 yards,' Daniell estimated — managed to hit the coaster:

> We hit her the first time and she stopped and lowered a lifeboat. After about ten rounds, we had set her on fire. We retired from the scene and about one and a half hours later, when darkness had fallen, the vessel blew up. A very spectacular Guy Fawkes night display, with lots of noise, plenty of stars going up — quite a satisfactory 'do'.

Noting that *Unison* had 'a very good man, a New Zealander, as gunlayer,' Daniell goes on to explain why a gun attack was such a morale booster for the crew:

> Normally, with an ordinary torpedo attack the ship's company didn't see anything, hear anything or know what was going on: pretty dull stuff. But in a gun action everybody joined in, as well as getting some fresh air through the boat during the day, a very unusual occurrence.

Returning to Malta after this satisfying patrol, *Unison*'s telegraphist recorded in his log:

> *14 February*. Arrived Lazaretto at 1030. Ban lifted ashore, everywhere in bounds again.
> *15 February*. All submarines given names by Admiralty. Ours is *Unison* so now we have to drop our unofficial name of *Ulysses*.

By 26 February *Unison* was back on billet in the Gulf of Hammamet once more.

Unruffled (Lieutenant Stevens) had also been active in the Gulf of Hammamet. On the 18th, off the village of Neboel, she fired a torpedo at each of two anchored schooners. Both torpedoes missed but the startled crews, mesmerized by the sight of torpedoes running up the beach, wasted no time in abandoning ship. The wind later blew the schooners ashore and Steve records, 'Their wreckage was observed high and dry on the sand.' Although the end result was just as good as a hit, Stevens was exasperated that the two torpedoes had missed. 'The incident demonstrates the difficulty of torpedoing small stopped vessels,' he notes. 'Imperceptible rates of tidal stream or current during the torpedo's running time can suffice to cause a miss.'

Unruffled next moved off towards Pantelleria, where RAF reports had warned of a two-ship escorted convoy. She promptly found the convoy and attacked, one torpedo sinking *Baalbek* (2,115 tons), a French merchant vessel commandeered by the Germans. The submarine then returned to Malta on 24 February, her captain's twenty-seventh birthday.

Following the Casablanca Conference, the British Prime Minister paid fleeting visits to Tripoli and to Algiers, where he was satisfied to note that all His Majesty's Submarines now displayed names on their conning towers instead of numbers.

In February there was some reorganization of naval commands in the Mediterranean to take account of the changed requirements. Admiral Cunningham, now promoted to Admiral of the Fleet, resumed the position for which all sailors will remember him: Commander-in-Chief, Mediterranean. His command now included the central and western basins of the Mediterranean, west of a dog-leg line stretching from the toe of Italy to the Tunisian frontier, with Malta in the crook of the dog-leg. East of the line, Admiral Harwood was Commander-in-Chief Levant. But Harwood was not in good health and in less than a month he was relieved. Temporarily the Levant Command was held by Sir Ralph Leatham, Vice-Admiral Malta during the past year, whose own appointment was then taken by Vice-Admiral Sir Stuart Bonham-Carter.

Bonham-Carter had presided over the official opening of the new canteen at Lazaretto, a very popular ceremony, noted Captain (S) 10 in his first monthly report, 'owing to the free issue of a glass of beer to each man present'. The excavated workshops and accommodation had been long since completed, and workers had now started to dig submarine pens in the rock across the creek from Lazaretto. Captain (S) 10 hoped they would be completed 'in time for the next war'.

At the end of February Lazaretto had a surprise visit from the great ABC himself: Admiral Cunningham flew into Malta in a Flying Fortress loaned by the Americans. Tom Lancaster, navigator of *Una,* remembers that day well.

> One quiet afternoon, while talking to a friend near the entrance to the base, both of us in khaki shirts and shorts, the Commander-in-Chief and Flag Lieutenant arrived unannounced, clad in immaculate No. 10s,* to see S 10, Captain Phillips. As it was about tea time, I led the visitors along to the Mess. You can imagine the consternation caused when these two figures appeared in the doorway!
>
> Following on the surprise call by ABC, I do not think he made any adverse comments about our standards of dress, because we continued as before without any bother. I believe he was big enough to appreciate our difficulties.

In one way or another, like Lancaster, many submariners in Malta at that time had lost their uniforms and could not replace them. New uniforms were hardly a priority item on the supply convoys. As a result, many of us dressed in army battle-dress in winter, or in whatever warm clothing we could find. Our appearance was unconventional, to say the least − particularly in summer when home-made sarongs were *de rigueur.*

Already the first cryptic moves were being made for the huge impending Operation 'Husky,' the Allies' return to Europe. Malta, again by virtue of her position, would become a vital launching pad for the invasion of Sicily, as soon as the Axis armies were vanquished in North Africa. The final planning of this great operation depended on very accurate intelligence. Thus the COPPs were born − the reconnaissance of Sicilian landing sites by Combined Operations Pilotage Party patrols.

The Commander-in-Chief ordered that four of the *U*s be diverted from anti-convoy patrols to survey the invasion beaches. In fact, the first one was carried out towards the end of February

---

* Tropical uniform for officers: white tunic and trousers.

by one of the Eighth Flotilla submarines, *Safari,* previously *P 211* (Commander Bryant) and COPP No. 4. Her reconnaissance of the Gulf of Castellammare, north-west Sicily, nearly ended in disaster when one Folbot crew failed to return, but the two men had been provided with a good cover story and escaped with their lives. Though the recce was favourable, the 'Husky' planners decided only to use beaches on the southern and south-eastern coasts of Sicily, so the remaining COPPs were run by the *U*s.

Another secret that February concerned 'QV4,' a new piece of equipment to help submarines escape detection by enemy radar. Only two of the *U*s were equipped with the device. Fitted to each side of the conning tower was a small aerial connected to a receiver below. When the enemy radar pulse was detected, the submarine would swing either side of the signal until the strength of the signals from the two aerials was balanced. The ship's head then indicated the bearing of the attacking aircraft. The submarine was thus alerted to an aircraft or shore station that had gained radar contact. Unfortunately the submarine could not tell whether her attacker was ahead or astern.

Unbending (formerly *P 37)* and *United* (*P 44*) left the dockyard after having QV4 fitted on 26 February. *United*'s first patrol with the apparatus was spent off Cape Spartivento, where a gigantic radar aerial of the 'bedstead' type rotated upon a high cliff. Needless to say, the new device received constant and continuous impulses from the huge aerial, so that the submarine was in a permanent state of flux, swinging to every contact. After a few nights of continually diving for each alarm, the set was switched off and remained off for the rest of the patrol. Men had to sleep.

As Captain Phillips wrote in his first Monthly General Letter, at the end of February, 1943:

> The offensive activities of the Flotilla for some time to come will be much curtailed owing to a special operation of a most secret nature which is now in progress.

He was referring, of course, to the COPPs.

Each of the four *U*s taking part in the COPP missions would carry a special party of men with two or more Folbots. The COPP party would paddle ashore, complete the reconnaissance and paddle back to the submarine. Should they fall into enemy hands, the men were all provided with cover stories.

United sailed on her first COPP mission with Lieutenant Philip ('Bob') Smith, RN, in charge of the two reconnaissance parties making up COPP ME1. Their destination was the beach at Gela on the south coast of Sicily. Bob Smith would take one canoe, with his bowman Lieutenant David Brand, RNVR, and if they did not return the other Folbot crew would paddle ashore, though further along the coast, to avoid compromising the landing site.

Bob Smith later recorded the tension and drama of that first patrol: 'struggling into waterproof clothing' in the confines of the wardroom; 'the strain of waiting' those last fifteen minutes in pitch darkness to allow adaptation to night vision, followed by the 'draught of cool air and a dim circle of sky' as the hatch was opened; then paddling ashore, while the submarine 'with a loud venting of tanks' submerged behind them. Then the mission itself: two hours of paddling, 'noting soundings, bearings and distances, always keeping a careful watch on the beach some 200 feet away'. And finally back to the submarine.

The submarine was not there. Heavy seas and some malfunction in the very elementary homing gear (an infra-red light receiver) combined to make the two men lose their position. To make matters worse, one paddle snapped. By dawn they were ten miles offshore, the sea was getting rougher and they knew their best chance was to paddle back to Malta. Taking it in turns, one would paddle while the other baled. The fragile craft was repeatedly swamped by huge waves. All that day, and all that night, they paddled and baled, paddled and baled; and just after sunrise they glimpsed the faint outline that was Malta. But by noon they were still several miles off the northern tip of the island.

About five miles from Mellieha an MTB appeared, hauled the two exhausted men and their canoe on board and delivered them to safety. They had been paddling for thirty-seven hours. When they examined the Folbot they found it had a three-inch gash in the side, 'presumably caused during her launching from the submarine'. Brand collapsed with exhaustion and had to be taken to hospital, but Smith was not finished yet:

> Feeling slightly recovered, I paddled the canoe back to Lazaretto. The first person I saw on the jetty was Tom Barlow, who looked at me in amazement. He asked accusingly: 'What have you done with *United*?'

United, having failed to rendezvous with Smith and Brand, had moved to the alternative site to launch the second canoe. While waiting to pick this crew up, the author was on the bridge as Officer of the Watch with the captain, John Roxburgh; Goddard, who was our 'Bunts' (signalman), was training the infra-red shaded Aldis lamp inshore, and Cyril Balls was port look-out.

It was Balls who saw the darkened shape approaching and Roxburgh who identified it as a U-boat, which his orders forbade him to attack for fear of compromising the operation ashore. 'Clear the bridge', Roxburgh ordered and pressed the klaxon.

We scrambled down the ladder, but somehow the cable of the Aldis lamp was caught, entangled around the clips of the upper lid. With the captain jumping impatiently on my head, for water was starting to lap the bridge, I fought for interminable seconds to free that flex, knowing that at any moment the control room would have to shut the lower hatch to save the submarine. But at the last moment the cable came free, and we dived just in time. The U-boat, apparently oblivious to our presence, thundered above our for'ard jumping wire.

When *United* surfaced again to pick up the second canoe, this rendezvous failed as well. By this time the weather had deteriorated and the presumption must be that the crew were overwhelmed in the rising sea.

Bob Smith wrote later:

> Looking back on the operation, I am astounded how badly equipped and trained we were. Canoes bought in the sports shops in Cairo and adapted by ourselves. Equipment largely invented by ourselves and put together by the resources of Malta Dockyard under the most adverse conditions. Largely untried infra-red homing gear, which should never have been

> thought suitable for use in a pitching canoe . . . all distinctly
> amateur!

Brave men these. Despite the inevitable doubts they must have felt, they paddled off to spend hours immersed in cold water while making accurate soundings of the contours of the seabed, always with the chance of discovery hanging over them, the beach often being less than two hundred feet away.

Unbending (formerly *P 37*) had sailed with COPP 3, led by Lieutenant-Commander Teacher, on the same day as *United*. Unhappily, all four of her COPP party were lost, and it was a sad boat that returned to Malta on 6 March.

COPP ME2, led by Lieutenant De Kock of the South African Naval Force, was equally ill-fated. Launched from *Unrivalled (P 45)** on 4 and 9 March, both Folbot parties went astray. Again the loss was blamed on adverse weather conditions. Gradually it became clear that the Folbots were not suitable for these operations and, later, the COPPs beach reconnaissances would be carried out mainly by chariots.

These were sad weeks for the Mediterranean submarine flotillas, for one after another the *T*s were being lost. First, *Tigris* (Lieutenant-Commander G. R. Colvin), was thought to have struck a mine north-west of Zembra Island in the Gulf of Tunis on about 27 February.

On 12 March, *Turbulent* (Commander J. W. Linton) attacked but missed the mail steamer, *Principessa Mafalda,* off Punta Arco, Bastia, Corsica. Counter-attacked by the A/S trawler, *Teti II,* Tubby Linton and his crew are believed to have been lost off Bastia, though no traces of her have been found by the French Hydrographer. It is *just* possible that *Turbulent* may have been mined off La Maddalena, on her return passage to Algiers†.

Then *Thunderbolt* (Lieutenant-Commander C. B. Crouch), was depth-charged by the Italian corvette *Cicogna* off Cape San Vito

---

* During her Calabria patrol in February, *Unrivalled* off Cape Stilo sank the *Sparviero* (500 tons) and the *Pasubio* (2,215 tons). Having fired all her torpedos, *Unrivalled* returned to Malta on 19.2.43.

† This last-minute information has kindly been supplied by Mr Paul Kemp, author of *The T-Class submarine,* Arms & Armour Press, 1990.

on 14 March. She sank with all hands in a depth of 1,350 metres.

All three boats were manned by experienced crews and commanded by outstanding COs, and all three were well-known in Malta, though perhaps 'Tubby' Linton was best-known for he had also commanded *Pandora* with distinction. In *Turbulent* he and his splendid company had sunk over 90,000 tons of enemy shipping, including a destroyer, and for his exceptional service Commander Linton was posthumously awarded the Victoria Cross.

27

MARCH/MAY, 1943

Rommel was on his way back to Germany, sick, disillusioned and relieved by his rival, General Sixt von Arnim. Rommel had given his Afrika Korps all that he could, but he could not make up for the petrol, food, ammunition and spares which were being sunk with every convoy. He had given the Americans a bitter first taste of warfare in central Tunisia, and caused General Alexander no little anxiety. Now he had quit, gone, even before Montgomery began his offensive on the Mareth Line.

The Eighth Army assault began on 20 March and by the 29th our troops had broken through. It would be another five or six weeks before the enemy was finally thrown out of Tunisia, but by now it was clear the submarines' attention was mainly required further north.

The submarines now had assistance from their allies. In February the Dutch submarine *Dolfijn* (commissioned as *P 47*), one of the *U*-class, arrived in Algiers to work with the Eighth Flotilla. Her captain was Lieutenant-Commander H. Van Oostrom Soede, Royal Netherlands Navy, with a ship's company of remarkably experienced men. *Dolfijn's* Number One, Lieutenant W. C. M. de Jonge van Ellemeet, had served in submarines since 1936, and even the youngest of her crew had five years' submarine experience. Lieutenant-Commander Soede, known to all as 'Soda', would shortly be joining the Tenth Flotilla.

Eight French submarines had also been welcomed into the Eighth Flotilla at the beginning of March, though they continued to operate from Oran. Because of unreliable torpedoes and lack of spares, the French boats were used mainly for special operations, where the crews' local knowledge often proved invaluable when agents or sabotage parties had to be landed in southern France. Two of their number would later join the Tenth — FF S/M (Free French Submarine) *Curie,* commanded by Lieutenant de Vaisseau P. J. Chailley, and much later, in June '44, FF S/M *Casabianca,* commanded by Capitaine de Corvette de l'Herminier.

Another *U*-class submarine was heading for the Mediterranean at this time. Originally designated *P 52,* she became ORP (Polish Navy Submarine) *Dzik;* many of her crew had previously served in the other Polish submarine *Sokol,* whom we last saw leaving for England in April '42 (see page 171). And *Sokol* herself was about to return to Malta, as we shall see.

In mid-March *Unbending* sailed with a train-wrecking party, three commandos led by Lieutenant Lee, Dorset Regiment, whose target was 'a railway tunnel close to the beach' on the east coast of Calabria. Lieutenant 'Otto' Stanley remembers the infectious enthusiasm these men exuded, a welcome antidote to the gloom the ship's company had been feeling since the loss of their COPP crews earlier in the month.

Stanley writes of 'the usual anxious moments' before surfacing, 'until the bridge had been manned and a search of the horizon had confirmed that no ships were in sight'. But 'reason quickly prevailed over nerves.' The Folbots and their occupants were slipped over the side and *Unbending* withdrew while the raiders paddled off into the dark. Stanley goes on:

> Lee reached the shore in the planned position, but unfortunately tore the skin of his Folbot against a rock on beaching. He and his companion carried out a reconnaissance and completed their plans for entering the tunnel. Exact details of what happened at the other end of the tunnel have never been obtained; it appears that both men landed safely but the moment was too great for one of them, who lost his head and opened fire with his Sten gun, effectively alerting the guards at both ends of the tunnel.
>
> To proceed with the operation became impossible and Lee and his companion had to beat a hasty retreat . . . They set out to search for a boat and were fortunate, around dawn, to find a

small fishing boat which its owner was about to launch. Both were immediately commandeered. The boat put to sea, pulled by the reluctant Italian, and headed for the line 180° from the west end of the tunnel, which had been agreed as the rendezvous line.

On board the submarine everyone was fearing the worst.

We dived at dawn and Lee's hammock was sadly taken down from its position in the gangway, where it had been so roundly cursed by every sailor for the past three days. A diving patrol was established up and down the rendezvous line 'just in case'. Sleep proved elusive.

It was a couple of hours after dawn when the welcome summons was passed forward: 'Captain in the control room.' An excited Officer of the Watch pointed out a smudge of smoke to the eastward, just visible through the high power periscope . . . The convoy steamed steadily on, hugging the coast, and was soon seen to consist of three cargo ships and a small destroyer. An E-boat could also be heard.

A fresh breeze was blowing, which would satisfactorily hide torpedo tracks and any feather the periscope might make through careless handling. Altogether, attack conditions were perfect and by the time the submarine was abeam of the convoy, and within 2,000 yards range, two ships were conveniently overlapping, so that the four torpedoes fired could be spread over both their lengths.

That morning of 14 March *Unbending* sank both *Citta di Bergamo* (2,163 tons) and *Cosenza* (1,471 tons). It was some consolation both to the submarine, and to Lieutenant Lee who had been a witness from a distance. According to Stanley, the two soldiers and their Italian companion, after many vicissitudes, finally landed in Sicily:

There, unfortunately, the Italian fisherman proved a liability and, before they could put to sea again, they were captured. Lee did not remain a prisoner of war for very long, and it was a great day, some four months later, when he sought me out in a shore establishment in England and told me his side of the story.

A further consolation for *Unbending* (and a miraculous escape for one Australian airman) came two days after the successful torpedo attack. Just as the submarine received a signal saying that an American Baltimore had ditched somewhere in the area, the Officer of the Watch sighted a Verey light, and the airman was found and pulled aboard. Sadly, he was the only member of his crew to have survived.

Three old friends had arrived at Lazaretto in March for their six-monthly docking: *Sahib, Splendid* and *Saracen* (formerly *P 212, P 228* and *P 247* respectively). All had been operating from Algiers and all were helping to make the enemy's continued existence in North Africa increasingly untenable. On passage to Malta *Splendid* (Lieutenant Ian McGeoch) had sunk the 3,177-ton tanker, *Devoli,* despite her escort of four torpedo boats and an aircraft. Four days later, on 21 March, he sent another heavily laden tanker to the depths — *Giorgio* (4,887 tons).

Saracen (Lieutenant M. G. R. Lumby), her docking complete, sailed again on the 16th, heading for north-west Sicily and Ustica. *Sahib* (Lieutenant J. H. Bromage) sailed the same day, laden with stores for the Eighth Flotilla (supplies were now reaching Malta regularly from Alexandria) and then headed north for the Tyrrhenian Sea. Bromage took *Sahib* close into Milazzo harbour to make a torpedo attack on the coaster *Sidamo* (2,384 tons).

> The first torpedo just missed the bows but, as it hit the harbour wall under two coasters, it wasn't wasted; the second hit just forward of the bridge. By this time . . . the seaward side of the breakwater was no more than a few yards away — so close that, when I invited the coxswain to have a quick look through the HP periscope, he found himself looking at a donkey and a wildly gesticulating Italian with his barrow-load of *frutas*. It was with some trepidation that I awaited Italian reaction to this rudeness but, to my surprise and gratification, there was absolutely none.

On 20 March, *Unshaken* (Lieutenant Jack Whitton) joined the Tenth Flotilla. Under Whitton's leadership, the submarine was to distinguish herself in the Mediterranean; but she had had a tragic start to her commission under her first captain, Lieutenant C. E. Oxborrow, DSC.

In November, 1942, *Unshaken* was operating from Gibraltar when she ran into some extreme weather conditions, 'the worst that anyone in the boat had ever experienced', writes Leonard Horan, a leading stoker in *Unshaken:*

> The interior of the boat was in a shambles, even the electric stove in the galley had broken away from its fittings; it had ended up in the gangway, with the Chief ERA's bunk, which broke adrift under the incessant pounding of the seas.

Lieutenant Oxborrow (who, Horan notes, had served as first lieutenant to Dick Cayley in *Utmost*) decided to dive the boat 'to obtain respite from the weather and to clear her up'. After an hour the boat resurfaced, Oxborrow telling the crew that 'they were not only fighting the enemy but also the sea: the discomfort had to be endured'.

Conditions had worsened. The submarine was rolling and pitching in the dark seas, and everyone was clinging on as best they could. Suddenly, after one particularly violent roll, the sea came pouring down the conning tower into the control room:

> The coxswain shouted, 'She's slipping back!' Someone managed to get hold of the lanyard of the lower lid and pulled it; the lid shut under the weight of water pouring into the boat and the next order was, 'Check main vents!'
>
> It was discovered that 6 Main Vent was open . . . Someone, thrown by the rolling, probably put his hand out to grab something, but unfortunately grabbed 6 Main Vent lever. It was realized that the captain and the two look-outs must have been lost.

It took the crew two hours to pump out the conning tower, because the sea kept breaking over the bridge, but when Sub-Lieutenant H. P. Westmacott, the acting first lieutenant (standing in for Lieutenant Davis, who was sick ashore in Gibraltar), called for two look-outs on the bridge, 'everyone volunteered'. Micky Shields and another sailor were picked and clambered past the cascading water onto the bridge, where they lashed themselves to the bridge fittings with rope. But there was no sign of the captain or the other two men, Yeoman of Signals S. B. Bennett and Able Seaman C. Thorn.

Westmacott dispatched an immediate signal to Captain (S) 8 and the result was that four days later, on 29 November, *Unshaken* was directed to rendezvous with the corvette, HMS *Samphire*, who had brought Jack Whitton, the Eighth's Spare CO, to take over command of the submarine. The transfer was effected without difficulty and *Unshaken* then went on her way with a new captain.

Unshaken's arrival in Malta coincided with a 'sprite' alert. Intelligence had warned that the Italians were planning a human torpedo attack. The COs of all submarines in harbour were therefore instructed to remind their 'trot sentries' of the drill, which included dropping 2¼lb TNT charges into the water at irregular intervals. Leading Seaman Cyril Balls, *United's* gunlayer, remembers John Roxburgh ordering the whole crew to muster on the fore-casing so that Balls could demonstrate what to do. Balls carefully prepared two charges, lashing two together and linking them with a short mercury fuse. The fuse would be 'set off by stamping on it or pinching it with a pair of pliers', Balls writes, then dropped into the water immediately, because it would explode within seconds. Roxburgh asked Balls to give the prepared charge to a stoker named Sidney, remarking, 'If you can do it, anybody can.' Balls goes on:

> Sidney duly pinched the fuse and threw the *pliers* over the side. Now matelots have always been men of fast reactions, but I've never seen about thirty of them vanishing from sight so rapidly; in fact, I can't even remember where I went. Sidney watched the pliers gently wafting from side to side in the clear waters; suddenly realizing the error of his ways, he just about managed to chuck the charge, where it exploded a couple of feet under.

Fortunately, no one was hurt. Fortunately, too, the anti-'sprite' measures proved unnecessary.

Towards the end of March *Unison* was patrolling the east

Calabrian coast and hoping for 'a little excitement' in the words of our telegraphist, by now stuck barnacle-like to this boat. On the 23rd his hopes were fulfilled:

> At about 1300, sighted 1 tanker, 3 destroyers and 1 A/S vessel. At 1408, fired 4 torpedoes. 1 min. 10 secs. later, one torpedo was heard to hit the target. Unable to see result of attack as we were going deep to avoid the destroyer attack. At 1417 the counter-attack started with a pattern of 5 depth charges across the bows, very close. The impact shook us like a dog shaking a rat. We were at 90 feet but when the charges had exploded we found that we had bounced off the bottom at 380 feet. We were lucky . . . These boats are only supposed to be guaranteed to 300 feet. This one must have been good.

Unison's captain, Anthony Daniell, remembers that the target ship was close inshore and that he had fired at a range of only 500 yards: 'We were considerably shaken by the close explosion of our two torpedoes'. As soon as he had fired, he writes:

> I decided to go even closer inshore, because of the very rocky coast there. The enemy would be confused, trying to differen-tiate his hydrophone or asdic echoes on the submarine from the echoes coming from rocks and cliffs. As it turned out, that decision saved us . . . If we had turned out to sea we would have been lost in about *2,000 fathoms* of water, because the coast is very steep-to there.

If the enemy was confused about *Unison's* position, he was making remarkably good guesses. According to our telegraph-ist's log, at 1700 there had been 133 depth-charge explosions, some of them uncomfortably close: 'Lights and small fittings are breaking.' Finally, however, the submarine surfaced at 2215, 'much the worse for wear and glad to breathe some fresh air after eighteen hours dived'. On the last day of the month, *Unison* returned to Lazaretto and heard, as the log records: 'Our tanker *Zeila,* 1,835 tons, confirmed sunk.'

Unrivalled (P 45) was having similar success. On 29 March, off Palermo, she torpedoed and sank the *Bois Rose* (1,374 tons) and on her way home, in Castellammare Bay, one of Mossy Turner's two torpedoes blew a 231-ton schooner to pieces — the *Triglav*, commandeered from the Yugoslavs. *Unrivalled* returned to base on 4 April, the day after *Unseen (P 51)* returned home.

Unseen had been on patrol off Marittimo and the north coast of Sicily. She was 'returning submerged from patrol when Lieutenant Sallis (Third Hand) put up the periscope for a normal sweep', writes *Unseen's* first lieutenant, Barry Charles:

> To his amazement, it turned in his hand. The reason became apparent when he found himself staring into a rusty mine, the horns of which had turned the periscope as it had been raised.

Both Charles and Tubby Crawford, the CO, took the periscope and stared the mine in the eye. Fortunately it did not become attached to them and was soon bobbing away astern, while the three officers slowly breathed again.

March ended with welcome news from Tunisia. Montgomery had broken through the Mareth Line and even now the Eighth Army was advancing up the coast. Gabes fell to the British troops on 29 March and Sfax would fall by 10 April, then Sousse . . . Meanwhile, the combined squadrons of the Fleet Air Arm and RAF made daily forays against enemy shipping and the notorious corridor of the 'Tunis run' was being saturated with mines laid by *Rorqual* and the surface minelayer *Abdiel*.

The Tenth Flotilla submarines continued to concentrate further north , with one exception. *Unshaken,* being the newcomer, was sailed for her first patrol to the ostensibly quieter area of east Tunisia . . . First, she shelled a schooner hauled up on a beach, but was warned off by spirited action from shore batteries. Then, off Sousse on 8 April, Jack Whitton sank the 1,245-ton *Foggia* with one of his three torpedoes. Lingering off Kelibia in the hope of catching a reported convoy, *Unshaken* continued southwards to beat up an important road bridge until shore batteries again forced her to desist.

But the shore batteries were soon silenced by Montgomery's men, and this proved to be the last of the Fighting Tenth's patrols off the Tunisian coast.

Unbroken (P 42) was encountering different problems off eastern Calabria — five days of bad weather. On 3 April Alastair Mars carried out a long-range attack on a northbound *Regolo*-class cruiser, but without success. Shifting a little further up the coast, towards Cape Stilo, on the 4th, *Unbroken* sighted a large tanker and attacked again. This time one torpedo hit the *Regina* (9,545 tons), badly damaging her and causing her later to be beached. With no torpedoes left, *Unbroken* returned to Malta on 7 April and, this being Mars's eleventh patrol in her, he asked for a rest. He was relieved by the Spare CO, Lieutenant B. J. B. Andrew.

Mars was a skilful and intrepid submarine officer with a reputation as something of a martinet. John Jones tells the 'sorry saga' of two able seamen, himself and Geoff MacTeare, who were late in joining the newly commissioned *Unbroken* (then *P 42)* because they had been enjoying a 'convivial evening' in London. 'Suffice to say we got drunk and enjoyed a night of horizontal refreshment with two ladies of the night.' By the time the two sailors reached Barrow-in-Furness, their late arrival had caused the cancellation of a 'basin dive', inconveniencing not only the rest of the crew but the rest of the shipyard too.

'You two are right in it,' the Coxswain, Joe Sizer, told them, leading them in to see the 'Jimmy', Lieutenant Taylor, RNR. Taylor administered baleful warnings and ordered them to report to the captain the next morning.

> 'MacTeare, Jones,' the Cox'n barked. 'Quick march. Halt. Off caps.'
> We halted in front of the desk and got our first glimpse of the captain, Lieutenant Alastair Campbell Gillespie Mars, RN. He sat grim-faced while the Cox'n read out the charge against us: 'Did wilfully miss the draft. Twenty-four hours adrift . . .'

Mars then administered an almighty rollicking and awarded the two men 'ten days' stoppage of leave'. As this could not yet be implemented because the boat was ashore, he assured the two men that 'he would see to it that we would work our fingers to the bone'. And, remarks Jones, 'he was as good as his word.'

Yet Mars had a soft-hearted side too, as the Tench family found out when he volunteered to escort their five-year-old daughter back to England. He thereby missed the RAF flight that was arranged for him and had to take passage in a destroyer. Not until he had safely delivered the child did he return to his young wife, having lost half his leave.

Unruffled (P 46) spent most of the first half of April off Syracuse in southern Sicily, landing another COPP party by Folbot to survey the intended invasion beaches. Despite bad weather, the Folbot crew completed their task successfully and returned to the submarine without incident. The rest of her patrol was equally quiet.

Unfortunately, three submarines were to have sadly eventful patrols during the latter half of April.

Regent (Lieutenant W. N. R. Knox) had only just returned from America where she had undergone a full-scale refit. She arrived at Malta in late March, en route to join the First Flotilla. On 10 April she set sail for the southern Adriatic, before continuing to Beirut. She never completed the passage.

Italian records show that she attacked a two-ship convoy on 18 April. No counter-attack was carried out, but later that day a large explosion was heard in the same area, five miles north-east of Monopoli. Four corpses wearing British DSEA sets were recovered from the water. The conclusion must be that *Regent* was sunk by a mine.

Splendid (formerly *P 228*) had also arrived in Malta at the end of March, where her captain enjoyed a warm reception from those at Lazaretto who remembered him as the Tenth Flotilla's Spare CO from the previous year — Ian McGeoch. *Splendid* was now operating from Algiers and had come to Malta for her regular docking. She sailed on 18 April for her sixth Mediterranean patrol — off Naples. On the calm, bright morning of 21 April she was off the island of Capri when McGeoch saw through his high-power periscope a puzzling sight — the German destroyer *Hermes,* formerly the Greek *Agios Giorgos,* British-built and very similar to an *H*-class destroyer. Alas, *Hermes* had seen the submarine too.

The Germans dropped a very accurate series of depth-charges. *Splendid* was fatally wounded, sinking to the seabed, but somehow McGeoch managed to get her back to the surface, only to find the destroyer opening fire with equally devastating accuracy. He ordered 'Abandon ship' and some of his crew were caught by the enemy's 12.7cm shells. Within twelve minutes of surfacing, the submarine had sunk again, this time for ever.

In all, thirty survivors were picked up, including McGeoch and his first lieutenant, Robert Balkwill, RNVR, but nineteen men were lost. The survivors now faced the rigours of life in a POW camp, though McGeoch eventually managed to escape, as did his officers and several ratings. Many years later, on the anniversary of *Splendid's* loss, 21 April, 1981, a memorial service was held in an Italian warship over the exact spot where she had been sunk. Among those attending was Vice-Admiral Sir Ian McGeoch, KCB, DSO, DSC.

The third loss that month was *Splendid's* sister ship *Sahib,* formerly *P 212* and commanded by Lieutenant John Bromage. After her Malta docking, she was again on patrol for the Eighth Flotilla, north of Messina. Off Cape Vaticano on 22 April she made a gun attack on the tug *Valente,* towing a lighter, and drove both ashore. Then, moving south-west towards the hot billet off Milazzo, on the 24th she sighted a convoy comprising one Italian merchantman, two corvettes and two torpedo boats. At 0600 *Sahib* struck. One of her torpedoes hit the supply ship *Galiola* (1,428 tons) who sank within five minutes.

The enemy's reaction was swift and violent. Within a period of just seven minutes *Sahib* received a total of fifty-one depth-charges. She suffered some irreparable damage and was forced to the surface. The two corvettes and one torpedo boat (the other being busy picking up survivors from *Galiola)* opened fire on the submarine, but stopped as soon as they saw that she was sinking and that her crew were abandoning ship. At that moment a Ju 88 swooped low overhead, machine-gunning both the submarine and the men swimming in the water. Miraculously only one man was killed, and the rest of *Sahib's* company were saved.

The loss of these three large and highly successful British submarines was a terrible blow to the whole submarine service. In all, seven Mediterranean submarines had been lost since the beginning of the year, but three in a week was almost too much to bear.

The Tenth Flotilla's score for April, 1943, was not yet complete.

In the early hours of the 19th, *Unrivalled (P 45)* received RAF reports of two north-bound ships and moved to intercept them. Mossy Turner watched through his periscope as an RAF aircraft stopped one ship with its bombs and then came under attack from the escort. He then took *Unrivalled* in towards the helpless 850-ton ship, the *KT 7,* and finished her off with torpedoes. During that same afternoon, proceeding round Cape San Vito, *Unrivalled* encountered a tanker with both surface and air escort. From a mile range, her four torpedoes struck home. The tanker *Bivona* (1,642 tons) disappeared in a gigantic explosion. An immense pillar of smoke rose into the sky as though marking her grave.

On 18 April, off Cape Gallo to the west of Palermo, *Unseen (P 51)* had torpedoed and sunk a German A/S ship, *2205* (600 tons), who was escorting a three-ship convoy, but she had to break off the attack when a signal from Captain (S)8 ordered her to move eastwards. It was hoped that the Italian battlefleet might be on the move, but the hopes were in vain.

Unison (P 43) had encountered nothing more interesting than illuminated hospital ships, and Daniell watched enviously as the smoke column to the south indicated the scene of *Unrivalled's* triumph. But on the 21st, moving south-west of Marittimo, despite bad weather and a heavy swell, Daniell, firing his salvo along the swell, sank the modern, 6,406-ton *Marco Foscarini.*

For a final touch that month, *Unshaken* (Lieutenant Whitton) was operating in the Eighth Flotilla area, off Marsala on the 28th, when she attacked a torpedo boat — the 652-ton *Climene.* Hit by one torpedo, *Climene* sank in three minutes.

At the very end of April a new submarine arrived to join the Tenth — *Unruly* (Lieutenant J. P. Fyfe). She was, in a sense, a replacement for *Unbending* (Lieutenant E. T. Stanley) who had gone home on the 12th. Having completed nine patrols and distinguished herself with a score of 15,673 tons of enemy shipping sunk; and a further 10,000 tons damaged, possibly destroyed, as well as chariot and special operations and many gun actions, she was due for a rest.

Tunis was under siege from the RAF and the Royal Navy. Not a single supply ship had managed to get through the Tunis run since 19 April; the rest had been recalled to Sicily. Von Arnim was still receiving aircraft-loads of troops and supplies, but fuel was fast running out. He sent an urgent signal to Berlin requesting that the supply convoys be resumed.

In Berlin the list of supply ships sunk and damaged on the Tunisian run made depressing reading. In February thirty-four ships had sailed the route, a total of 113,000 tons; forty-one per cent had been sunk or damaged. In March forty-four ships had sailed (129,000 tons) and fifty-seven per cent had been lost. In April the figures were twenty-six ships (87,000 tons), seventy-eight per cent lost. Von Arnim would not be receiving any more supplies by sea.

Nor was he going to be allowed to evacuate his troops, as we had evacuated ours at Dunkirk, Norway, Greece and Crete. While the Eighth Army and the Anglo-American First Army made their final joint push for Tunis, Admiral Sir Andrew Cunningham signalled the start of Operation 'Retribution' on 8 May with the words: 'Sink, burn and destroy. Let nothing pass.'

Von Arnim surrendered on 13 May. General Alexander signalled the Prime Minister that same day: 'We are masters of the North African shores'.

28

MAY/JUNE, 1943

The first scent of victory was heady stuff. It wafted across from North Africa like spring itself, bringing new life and hope to Malta. Everyone went about his appointed tasks with renewed determination, confident that at least the beginning of the end was in sight.

The plans for Operation 'Husky', dating from the Casablanca Conference in January, were settled at last. The Allies were planning to invade Sicily, despite the formidable German and Italian forces there, and then progress to mainland Italy in due course. A total of 160,000 troops, 600 tanks, 1,800 guns and impedimenta would have to be landed on the island's southern shores, all transported by an armada of 2,000 warships and merchant vessels for the initial assault, with a further 1,200 ships for the follow-up. Already the ships were converging on the Mediterranean, arriving from all quarters of the globe. The date of the landings was settled on the day before Von Arnim and the Axis forces capitulated: D-Day for Operation 'Husky' would be 10 July, 1943.

With only eight weeks to go, there was much to be done. While the Mediterranean Fleet fought to clear the minefields and keep the enemy guessing where and when exactly the great offensive would be, the Tenth Flotilla was earmarked for two separate tasks — one a continuation of COPP sorties, the other a renewed assault on enemy shipping in the Tyrrhenian Sea.

Several changes were beginning to appear in the submarines themselves: three new members of crew, for example. As cooperation improved between the submarines and the RAF aircraft, an additional W/T watch had to be kept on the Air Reconnaissance Wireless Wave, which meant that another telegraphist was needed, and an extra able seaman was required to look after the QV 4 radar-pulse receiver, for the 'Rooster', as the device was named, had now been fitted in six of the Us. But, even more important, the Admiralty had approved, 'additional to complement', one cook rating. No matter that he would add to congestion, his arrival was awaited with relish.

And several new Us were joining the Tenth. As well as *Unruly* (Lieutenant Fyfe) who arrived on 29 April, *Ultor* (Lieutenant G. E. Hunt) arrived on 3 May. The two were sent off for their first 'blooding' patrols to the eastern coast of Sicily. *Unruly* scored a hit on a 4,000-ton armed merchant cruiser, probably the *Tommaseo*, off Catania on the 16th; but the AMC was later repaired. *Ultor*, moving down to Augusta on the 23rd, managed to sink a 500-ton trawler at anchor in the harbour entrance.

The third new U-class submarine was ORP *Dzik* (Lieutenant-Commander Boleslaw Romanowski). 'Bolek' had been Boris Karnicki's Number One during *Sokol*'s first commission. Soon the Tenth Flotilla had two Polish Us in her midst, for *Dzik* was followed out to Malta by *Sokol* herself, now captained by Lieutenant-Commander Jerzy 'George' Koziolkowski, but still with Lieutenant George Taylor as her British Liaison Officer.

Dzik sailed for her first patrol on 16 May, and off Cape Spartivento on the 24th she scored two torpedo hits on the massive 12,000-ton *Carnaro*. The ship refused to sink and was later towed to Messina for repairs, but it was, nevertheless, an impressive start to *Dzik*'s innings.

Unbroken, too, had a few satisfying moments this May. Now under the command of Lieutenant B. J. B. Andrew, she was in the Gulf of Santa Eufemia on the 19th when she hit *Enrica*, a 269-ton tug. The following day she missed another tug, but hit and sank *Bologna*, formerly the Vichy *Monaco* (5,140 tons).

With growing urgency, four of the Us were now engaged in special operations with COPP parties, preparing to visit the specific beaches where the 'Husky' landings would take place in July. Rather than Folbots, the surveys were usually carried out by modified chariots, carried in chocks on the submarine's after casing. The two-man crews spent half of May rehearsing the drill to disembark and re-embark the chariots from the submarine.

Unrivalled, Unruffled, Unseen and *Unison* all took part in these recce operations during May and June, and on D-Day itself would act as 'beacons', like giant marker buoys indicating where the assault ships should land. It was crucial that everyone knew his job thoroughly, not only with these reconnaissances but with the great offensive itself.

Unison (Lieutenant Daniell) endured a blank patrol during the first half of May, although, as our telegraphist's log shows, it was obvious that someone else was busy:

> 9 *May*. On patrol, ten miles from Palermo. Sunday. Hundreds
> of explosions heard during forenoon and afternoon. Dense
> clouds of smoke seen through periscope. On surfacing, BBC
> announced big daylight raids by over 400 planes on Palermo.

On the 17th *Unison* returned to Lazaretto and embarked the 'Jeeps' or chariots. For several days she made practice runs with the chariots fitted, then on 1 June she sailed for her first reconnaissance patrol but the sea was too rough and the patrol had to be cancelled. On 6 June *Unison* tried again. This time she also carried a Folbot party and, though the Folbot pair carried out their part of the operation, the chariot sank. Happily the two crew were saved.

It would be impossible to overstate either the importance of these COPP surveys or the bravery of the men who carried them out. After the invasion Admiral Cunningham paid them handsome tribute, and they deserved every word. But at the time we did wonder if it was worth so much effort. As Captain (S) 10 wrote, 'the equivalent of thirteen normal-length patrols were spent on reconnaissance . . .when we might have been out hammering the enemy'.

But the Tenth had already been depleted by an even less conventional operation.

With the enemy having capitulated in North Africa, the chief remaining threat to invasion plans in the central Mediterranean was Pantellaria, the heavily fortified Italian island lying north-west of Malta in the Sicilian Channel. The island's airfield was a potential threat to our impending assault on Sicily. The question was whether to batter the island into submission or to invade. General Alexander appointed Major J. G. Appleyard, DSO, MC, from the 2nd SAS Regiment, to find out.

Geoffrey Appleyard ('Apple', as he was known) was twenty-seven years old but already had a formidable reputation. His specific objectives were to survey the best landing beaches for an Allied invasion on Pantellaria and to capture an Italian soldier for interrogation about the enemy's strength on the island.

Operation 'Snapdragon' would require Appleyard, his second-in-command, Lieutenant John Cochrane of the Toronto Scottish, and a band of eight SAS sergeants, with all their impedimenta, to be landed on Pantellaria by submarine. *United* (Lieutenant Roxburgh) sailed from Malta on 10 May. Unfortunately, rough weather prevented the SAS men from landing in their inflatable dinghies on the 12th, as planned, and for the next fortnight the moon was waxing which would add an unnecessary extra hazard to their job. Reluctantly, Roxburgh and Appleyard had to cancel the operation.

Then on the 18th, Appleyard and his 'No. 1 Small-Scale Raiding Force' sailed in *Unshaken* (Lieutenant Whitton) to make a periscope observation of the island's beaches where assault troops could be landed. The recce proving satisfactory, on 20 May *Unshaken* turned for home. Halfway back to Malta she was met by an MTB with an aerial escort which Jack Whitton describes as 'an impressive and lively umbrella of three Spitfires, each clearing the periscope standards by inches'. The MTB had come to collect Appleyard, to save time. He was safely transferred and soon disappeared with his escort. *Unshaken* returned to Lazaretto the following day.

The second attempt at the 'snatch job' began on the 24th, when *Unshaken* again sailed with the SAS party.

The conditions being good, the inflatable dinghies paddled off into the darkness. After scaling the vertical and crumbling cliff, they eventually pounced on a sentry whose terrified yells alerted the defenders. Reinforcements were immediately on the spot, a burst of automatic fire killing Sergeant Herstall, a policeman from Bristol. The raiders escaped down the cliff by sliding down it from top to bottom. Whitton and *Unshaken* were waiting for them and they reached Lazaretto on 30 May.

Five days later they made a third attempt, but again in vain. By now D-Day was only five weeks away, and it was clear that Pantellaria remained a real threat to the success of 'Husky'. The Allied Supreme Commander ordered that the island be captured immediately. While waiting assault forces under Rear-Admiral R. R. McGrigor set forth from Sfax and Sousse, Allied aircraft joined the Navy in bombarding the island. The assault troops met scant resistance and the enemy surrendered on 11 June. On the following day the enemy garrison on Lampedusa, subjected to similar bombardment, followed suit.

Major Appleyard's visit to Malta is particularly remembered by the Tenth's new SOO (Staff Officer, Operations) at this period, Lieutenant-Commander P. J. H. Bartlett. He was the former captain of *Perseus* and hence an experienced submarine officer, as well as an old Malta hand. Peter Bartlett writes that 'we were instructed from on high to give him everything he wanted': the one thing Appleyard needed was an aeroplane. He wanted to be able to fly back and forth to Algiers, to save time, but also he wanted an aircraft for reconnaissance of Pantelleria. But 'the Air Staff at Algiers deemed this impossible'. Presumably they thought it was acceptable to risk a submarine, but not an aircraft.

Bartlett managed to arrange an aerial recce, however, and Wing-Commander Warburton returned with 'eighty wonderful close-range photographs, which I pressed into Major Appleyard's hands the next day'. Bartlett adds:

> The sequel was a signal from the Supreme Commander to Captain (S) 10, asking for further copies; and later we were asked to arrange reconnaissance photographs for the landing beaches in Sicily — an unusual request for a Captain in charge of a submarine flotilla to receive.

Sadly, as Bartlett notes, 'Both Appleyard and Warburton were killed that year.'

All along the coast of North Africa and in every Maltese creek

LCTs (Landing Craft, Tanks) and LCIs (Landing Craft, Infantry) were assembling and men were training for 'Husky'. Malta's harbours now were bustling with activity as surface ships arrived with troops, munitions, supplies of every kind. While the Levant Command, now under Admiral Sir John Cunningham (no relation to 'ABC'), made feint operations in the eastern basin of the Mediterranean, the enemy knew only that an assault was being prepared: not where, nor when.

On 1 June Admiral of the Fleet Sir Andrew Cunningham's command was extended eastwards to Longitude 20°E, so that the whole of the central Mediterranean now came under his control. His three submarine flotillas would all be involved in 'Husky'. The First, still at Beirut, would keep the enemy guessing in the eastern Mediterranean. The Eighth would do the same in the western basin, including the island of Sardinia and the waters north of Sicily. The Tenth would thus be at the centre of the action.

Throughout the month Lazaretto was seething with life, as George Phillips, Captain (S) 10, noted in his Monthly General Letter No. 24 to the Commander-in-Chief, June '43:

> In spite of repairs to damaged cabins, the congestion of officers' accommodation has beaten all previous records, this being mainly accounted for by chariot teams and COPP parties, in addition to Flotilla reinforcements. This establishment is now often referred to as 'The Talbot Arms', 'Lazaretto Hotels, Ltd' and official correspondence has been received addressed to 'Combined Operations Headquarters, Lazaretto'.
>
> All sorts of odd types turn up seeking shelter and refreshment, among the more recent being newspaper editors, photographers, persons awaiting passage, convalescent commandos, barrage balloonists, various cloak-and-daggers and a Tindal of Zulu divers. While my accommodation officer is an expert at getting a quart into a pint pot, metaphorically speaking of course, the majority of these applicants have had to be politely but firmly turned away.

The Press gave Captain Phillips particular problems: 'having descended like locusts on Malta after the fall of Tunisia' the reporters now 'began to infest *Talbot*' (the depot ship and by extension the whole submarine establishment in Malta). As Captain Phillips complained in his June Monthly Letter:

> The reconnaissance carried out by the Flotilla for Operation 'Husky' resulted, inevitably, in a large number of young officers and men knowing very well what part of the enemy's territory would next engage our attention. To avoid an unfortunate breach of security, the Press were politely asked to attend weekly conference in the Base, when all the good stories would be given out and personal interviews granted with officers and men concerned. They were requested not to visit us unofficially. It is unfortunate that this not unreasonable arrangement was taken very badly by the Press, who distinguished the first conference by a remarkable display of bad manners. It is difficult to know how to deal with these people until they show a greater sense of responsibility.

A very much more welcome visitor to Malta this month was King George VI. He flew to Algiers on 12 June, embarked in the cruiser *Aurora*, and sailed into Malta's Grand Harbour on the 20th with an escort of four destroyers and, overhead, streams of RAF fighter aircraft. His one-day visit was greeted with enormous emotion and enthusiasm by the Maltese islanders, and served further to hearten everyone whose efforts were now concentrated on 'Husky'. All the crews of the Tenth Flotilla submarines that were in harbour at the time lined the Sliema route along which the King's car was driven. 'In order to distinguish ourselves from the lower orders,' Captain Phillips recorded in his newsletter, 'Jolly Rogers were brought out and displayed prominently by the submarines owning them.'

The submarines, meanwhile, pursued their various tasks. *Unrivalled* and *Unseen* both continued with chariot recces of the landing beaches around Cape Passero at the south-eastern tip of Sicily, while *Unruffled* took another Folbot party to her sector south of Syracuse.

Unruffled had made a very satisfactory hit early this month, as if to celebrate the DSO recently awarded to her CO, Lieutenant John Stevens, for his crippling of the *Attilio Regolo* five months earlier. On 3 June, in the Tyrrhenian Sea east of the Lipari

Islands, Stevens had added a large tanker to his bag: 'our largest target of the commission', he later wrote, 'the ex-French *Henri Desprez* of 10,000 tons gross':

> Hugging the Calabrian coast, she had one corvette as escort; as the high-power periscope which had the sky-search system was out of use with an optical defect, I do not know whether she had an air escort. Of four torpedoes aimed from close range, three were heard to hit. She blew up and sank. Taking *Unruffled* close inshore near the steep-to cliffs, I confused myself, as well as the hunting corvette. Noises as of more hunting vessels were reported by the asdic operator. These noises were, in fact, generated by surf breaking on the rocks near to us. When this little problem had been solved, we were able to withdraw unscathed.

While *Unruffled* now went about her work south of Syracuse, her billet was taken over by *Unruly* (Lieutenant Fyfe).

To her CO's mortification, *Unruly*'s attack on a 3,000-ton southbound ship at dawn on the 12th, at a range of 2,000 yards, missed. All four torpedoes somehow failed to make contact. Two nights later, she had a chance to redeem herself when the *Velentino Coda* (4,485 tons) was sighted at 10,000 yards with a destroyer escort. Fyfe brought *Unruly* to full buoyancy and ran in on the surface. At a distance of 3,500 yards he fired his last salvo. Two torpedoes found their mark and the target went to the bottom. The panic-stricken escort made a wild and ineffective counter-attack by dropping only six charges.

Ultor (Lieutenant 'Geordie' Hunt) was off the north Sicilian coast on 10 June when she sighted a naval auxiliary and began a torpedo attack, but the attentions of an aerial escort persuaded the submarine to retire. Two days later 'an air-sea search was seen to be in progress', in the words of the Admiralty Weekly Intelligence Review, 'and *Ultor*, baulked of an attack upon the surface ship concerned, was partially consoled by finding the tail-fin of an Italian aircraft'. The Review goes on to quote Geordie Hunt's patrol report:

> Found little of interest, as most of the fuselage had sunk, but bits of the rear-gunner were floating about. Cut the Italian crest out of the tail as a souvenir and proceeded.

Now *Ultor* turned her attention to the Aeolian archipelago and on the 13th she found an ideal target — a wireless station by the shore on Salina Island. This is how the Review tells the story:

> At 2113 *Ultor* surfaced; forty-three rounds were fired at 2,000 yards range. This was her first gun action, and the high spirits natural to the occasion were raised still higher when the third round was seen to fall squarely on the target. Many hits were scored, both on the building and on the mast. The villagers close east of the station were seen to follow the action with pardonable excitement.

The submarine continued her patrol north of the Messina Straits and managed to sink a cable-laying ship (not identified), but was then counter-attacked most efficiently by two destroyers. Despite their attentions *Ultor* made good her escape.

South of the Straits, on the 14th, *United* (Lieutenant Roxburgh) sighted a sizeable target and moved in to attack. By chance, a Spitfire was high overhead at 25,000 feet with a member of the RAF's Photographic Reconnaissance Unit who captured the whole attack with his camera, as Roxburgh remembers, taking a 'graphic series of photos'

> of our torpedoes hitting a 5,000-ton motor vessel; of the ensuing bomb attack on us by an escorting aircraft; of the escorting destroyer turning at speed to come back and depth-charge us; and of the motor vessel finally breaking in two and sinking. By the time we returned to Malta, the experts knew the range from which we fired (900 yards, I believe) from knowledge of the height and time of the photo; from the number of concentric explosion rings out from the target; and from knowledge of the speed of sound in water.

Our target had been the *Ringulv* (5,153 tons), built in Glasgow for a Greek shipping line in 1903. Then called *Keramiai*, she had changed names five times by 1942, when the Germans requisitioned her. The aircraft's bomb attack was wide, but the depth-charges were pretty accurate, smashing thirty lights in the submarine.

Roxburgh added another liner to his score on 20 June. *United* was fifteen miles south of Cape Spartivento when he sighted an unescorted east-bound ship whom he first thought must be a hospital ship. 'On further investigation I realized that she was a very nice modern-looking liner with a raked bow and flying the Italian ensign,' he wrote in his patrol report later. 'It seemed sheer madness for the Italians to send a ship unescorted through this area, but very obliging of them.' She was the armed merchant cruiser *Olbia* (3,514 tons).

United fired a salvo of four torpedoes, three of which hit the AMC. She stopped, listing to starboard and enveloped in smoke. She took over an hour to sink, though Roxburgh commented later:

> The Italians must have been fully prepared to be sunk, for within five minutes of the first explosion I saw a boat in the water, off her quarter, pulling madly away from the ship; there was another very agitated 'abandon ship' party lowering Carley floats and diving into the sea forward from the break in the forecastle.

Roxburgh left the periscope up for all *United*'s crew to take a look at the results of their handiwork.

The log of *Unison*'s telegraphist contains the bare facts of the dramatic action she initiated on 16 June:

> Attack convoy of 1 liner, 1 destroyer and 2 torpedo boats. Sunk liner (3,000 tons) with rebate of 37 depth-charges.

Unison was off the east coast of Sicily, just north of Augusta, when she sighted the Italian liner *Terni* (2,998 tons), formerly the French *Azrou*. Daniell pressed home his attack to 700 yards and fired a full salvo. Two torpedoes hit the target and *Terni* was blown sky-high. The force of the explosions gave the submarine a severe shaking, far worse than the escort's feeble counter-attack, but the damage was slight.

Immediately to the south of *Unison* was *Unshaken* (Lieutenant Jack Whitton), released from her expeditions with Major Appleyard and now patrolling off Syracuse and Augusta. Close inshore, on the afternoon of 22 June, she hit a laden schooner,

Giovanni G (69 tons), with two torpedoes at a range of 2,400 yards. The schooner disintegrated. This was a historic moment. Small though she was, this schooner earned a place in the history of the Fighting Tenth, for she had been sunk by the one thousandth torpedo to have been fired in action by a *U*-class submarine of the Tenth Flotilla.

On the following day *Unshaken* fired her last two torpedoes at the rear ship of a two-ship convoy in ballast, and sank the *Pomo* (1,425 tons), formerly the Yugoslav *Niko Matkovich*, seized by the Italians in 1941. The two escorting destroyers stopped to lower boats and pick up survivors, while the submarine, having heard the noises of her target breaking up, slid quietly away.

With the 'Husky' D-Day approaching, Captain Phillips was summoning his *U*s back to base for last minute preparations and a chance for the crews to rest. June, 1943 had been the Tenth's most successful month since December, 1942, but there was scarcely time to ponder on this satisfying fact. One by one, towards the end of the month, the submarines returned to Lazaretto to accelerated bustle, as the log of *Unison*'s telegraphist makes clear:

> *24 June*. Thursday. Arrived Lazaretto at 1100 . . . During our patrol, Generals Montgomery and Alexander and units of the 1st and 8th Armies — also tanks — have arrived in Malta. Thousands of Combined Operation ratings have arrived, also tons of equipment and stores, including tanks and invasion barges.

Operation 'Husky' was not far off.

29

JULY, 1943

With so much depending on the outcome of the great sea-borne assault on Sicily, and so much frenzied activity continuing around Malta, it was not easy to relax during those last few days before 'Husky', and matters were not made any easier by a sudden attack of sandfly fever at Lazaretto. The majority of the base, including Captain Phillips, went down with the fever, and many of those who escaped were suffering from 'gyppo tummy'.

In all, there would be twenty-six Allied submarines involved in Operation 'Husky', including the two Polish submarines, *Dzik* and *Sokol*, whom we have met, and the Dutch submarine, *Dolfijn*, another *U*-class boat who had been operating out of Algiers.

Dolfijn was not the first Dutch submarine in the Mediterranean. In 1941 three others had been based with the Eighth Flotilla at Gibraltar and had jointly dispatched 18,385 tons of enemy shipping: *O 21* (Lieutenant-Commander J. F. van Dulm, DSO); *O 23* (Lieutenant-Commander G. B. M. van Erkel, DSO); and *O 24* (Lieutenant-Commander O. de Booy, DSO).

Dolfijn and her commanding officer, Lieutenant-Commander Hans van Oostrom Soede, Royal Netherlands Navy, had opened their Mediterranean score card on 9 February 1943, by sinking the Italian U-boat *Malachite*, south of Sardinia. On her next patrol *Dolfijn* had sent *Egle* (1,145 tons) to the depths in the Gulf of Cagliari. On her eighth patrol from Algiers she paid her first, very brief visit to Malta, and not under the happiest of circumstances.

Lieutenant-Commander Soede has written a lively account of

this eighth patrol which took *Dolfijn* to a billet north of Sicily in late May. After a blank few days, on 25 May Soede found 'a beautiful tug, too small for torpedoes but a very nice target for our gun' in a bay on the island of Ustica. While manoeuvring for a good position, *Dofijn* grounded on some rocks and was forced to surface, whereupon an MTB anchored in the bay opened fire. *Dolfijn* returned the fire with machine guns, to devastating effect. Soede goes on:

> It being just after siesta time, the Italians ashore were wide-awake for once, and a well-hidden light machine gun started firing at very short range, presently being joined by two heavy machine guns from the other side of the bay. ... Conditions getting unpleasant, I sent the gun-crew below and while they were entering the hatch, two of them were hit. I jumped down as well and we dived. The MTB did not move, so presumably she also had casualties. How I got away without a scratch, being first on the bridge and last down, I still don't understand; we had some ninety holes in the bridge-screen alone, several quite near my position at the voice-pipe, port side.
>
> Leading Seaman Hennevelt, in charge of the medicine chest, efficiently bandaged our Third Officer, Sub-Lieutenant Brakema, without reporting that he himself was wounded, until we saw that blood was running down his trousers. His wound was serious, so that night I requested and obtained permission to proceed to Malta, which was nearer than Algiers. On arrival I reported for the first time to Captain (S) 10, Captain George C. Phillips.

In Malta Hennevelt had to be kept in hospital, but Brakema fortunately was able to sail with *Dolfijn* when she left later the same day.

Dolfijn's role during Operation 'Husky' was to form a patrol line with four other submarines from the Eighth Flotilla — *Trespasser*, *Saracen* (formerly *P 247*), *Simoon* and *Sibyl* — between northern Italy and the French island of Corsica. Their objective was to shield the invasion armada from Italian warships at present in the northern ports of Genoa, Spezia and Leghorn.

Three other boats from the Eighth Flotilla would act as beacons off the more westerly landing beaches, where the American assault force would be landing – *Safari*, *Shakespeare* and *Seraph*. They would take up their positions late on the 9th and, after the landings began, they would sail for Malta.

The Eighth Flotilla had loaned one of their submarines, *Tactician* (Lieutenant-Commander A. F. Collett who previously commanded *Unique*), to join an 'iron ring' patrol across the Gulf of Taranto. Aerial reconnaissance had reported two Italian battleships to be in Taranto, with supporting cruisers and destroyer screens: they posed a major threat to the Allied invasion fleet and at all costs must be contained. The iron ring boats, like all their sisters, were obliged to observe torpedo restrictions while Operation 'Husky' was in force. No supply ship under 4,000 tons was to be attacked, and one salvo had to be conserved for attacks on cruisers and heavier ships.

The other boats in the iron ring were *Uproar* (at the north-east end), then *Dzik*, *Unbroken* and *Unshaken*. At the last minute, delayed because of the sandfly fever, *United* took *Tactician*'s place in the ring and the latter sailed instead for a position in the Adriatic. *Uproar*, though the name was not familiar, was on her second commission with the Tenth. Formerly *P 31*, she had just returned from her refit, during which she had acquired the latest radar set and a new Commanding Officer, Lieutenant L. E. Herrick.

Three of the Tenth Flotilla's *U*s were positioned north of the Strait of Messina, *Sokol*, *Unruly* and *Ultor*, with orders to detain any hostile shipping north of Messina.

At last, but certainly not least, the four *U*s that best knew these beaches, after all their months of COPP parties and Folbot recces, would take up marker positions off the more easterly of the landing beaches – *Unruffled*, *Unseen*, *Unison* and *Unrivalled*. Each landing force had been assigned its own sector and each sector would each have its own beacon submarine to mark the release position where the convoys would launch their assault craft.

All the beacon submarines had to be in position by the night of 8 July because, such was the need for precision, special asdic transmitter buoys had to be laid offshore. The following night each submarine would launch her COPP crews in their Folbots to paddle ashore and mark the beaches. And then on that night of 9/10 July the beacon submarine was to start operating a radio beacon and an infra-red ray lamp to guide the approaching assault force.

On 1 July Vice-Admiral A. J. Power as VAM (he had taken over after Sir Ralph Leatham became Acting Commander-in-Chief Mediterranean) welcomed to Malta Admiral Sir Bertram Ramsay who was commanding the Eastern Naval Task Force in 'Husky'.

On 4 July, Admiral of the Fleet Sir Andrew Cunningham also arrived in Malta and gave the signal that the invasion fleet was waiting for: 'Carry out Operation "Husky".'

While Eighth Army troops embarked in landing craft from recently captured North African ports and from Malta, the supply convoys that had left the Clyde two or more weeks earlier began to progress eastwards through the Mediterranean: troop transporters, store ships, petrol carriers, oilers, LCTs, LSIs and LCIs all began to converge on Sicily. 'Husky' was under way.

On the day before the landings, 9 July, the weather was appalling. Strong north-westerly winds increased to gale force that afternoon. There was a widespread feeling that the invasion would not be possible and would have to be cancelled. But the huge fleet of merchant ships was committed. To turn them back at this final moment could cause only disastrous confusion.

United, patrolling in the iron ring, had surfaced in the Gulf of Taranto when the author clambered pessimistically up to the bridge at 0100 to take his night watch. If it had been unpleasant deep below the surface in a submarine, how much more miserable would it be for small landing craft, running onto those open beaches through crashing surf and vicious, raging spray. Miraculously, the wind had died.

But the wind had caused problems for some of the craft sailing for Sicily that night, including the motor launches (MLs). The MLs were supposed to lead the convoys in towards the beaches, using infra-red receivers to pick up the beacon submarine's transmissions. But with the adverse weather, the MLs had been unable to keep up with the convoys, as Anthony Daniell, Commanding Officer of *Unison*, remembers. Having 'had to sit on the bottom to make sure that we did not move our position', *Unison* surfaced at 0400 on D-Day, Saturday 10 July, 1943:

> The first thing I saw was a minesweeper very close, who had not, of course, received the signals we were sending out on the infra-red transmitter. It was no good making a formal recognition signal, so I used all the four-letter words at my command. I got a reply in the same sort of vein from the bridge of the minesweeper. It was quite a close thing.

Other victims of the gales that night were the airborne assault forces: paratroops being delivered to the coasts of Sicily in gliders towed by American bombers. *Unison*'s telegraphist noted in his log that at 2300 the night before, 'one of our bombers was seen to crash into the sea . . . These were our airborne troops which were to attack the airfields before the seaborne attack.' A few hours later he added that the first of the landing craft had passed the submarine, making for the beaches:

> There seems to be plenty of AA fire ashore. A few coastal defence guns opened up, but were soon put out of action by our cruisers and destroyers. We left Sicily on the surface at 0830, with the invasion in full swing.

'As dawn broke,' Daniell recalls, 'the sight was very memorable. All round the horizon, there were all the liners one had ever heard of − all the landing craft, all the escort ships, minesweepers . . .'

Unruffled was acting as the most northerly beacon, and her Commanding Officer, Lieutenant Stevens, has recorded his memories of that night in his book *Never Volunteer*:

> By midnight the sky had cleared and there was a dim starlight. Soon a dark shape could be discerned to the south-east; it grew larger and there was a blurred confusion of other dark outlines behind it. In the circumstances, the Challenge and Reply by light for recognition was forbidden. There was no need to worry, we had sighted a destroyer leading in a group of ships detached from the main convoy. They included many famous ocean liners being used as assault troop ships. They loomed nearer, until we were surrounded by silent, stationary, large

vessels, and on this occasion, instead of being spooky, their unchallenged presence was comforting indeed.

The following morning, Steve, too, was impressed by the 'magnificent sight' of 'the vast force of ships which stretched over the southern horizon':

> Small landing craft were scurrying between their parent ships and the beaches as though the occasion was a goodwill visit rather than an opposed amphibious assault. A few bombs were dropped from very high-flying aircraft without effect: otherwise Allied domination of the scene was total.
>
> At 0800 a small minesweeper approached *Unruffled*; she was to escort us to Malta. Obtaining permission to proceed by signal from the Naval Force Commander, we pointed south and followed the sweeper as she threaded her way through the vast floating assembly.

Unseen, who had marked the sector between *Unison* and *Unruffled*, had an equally successful night, but one of *Unrivalled*'s Folbot crews had failed to return from her mission the day before, when lowering the beacon buoys off the beaches. It was presumed that the crews had been overwhelmed by the heavy seas. The rest of the night passed without incident, and *Unrivalled* joined her sisters by retiring from the Sicily beaches.

While the four beacon submarines were in the thick of the action, with a grandstand view of the great Allied onslaught, *Sokol* and her crew were enjoying themselves.

The three *U*s north of the Strait of Messina had had a frustrating patrol before the 'Husky' landings. *Unruly* and *Ultor* sighted three U-boats each, and *Sokol* one, while the torpedo restrictions were in force. At least six German submarines had passed through the straits because of the ban, two of which went on to torpedo our cruisers *Newfoundland* and *Cleopatra* who were covering the landings. But *Ultor* (Lieutenant Hunt) did manage to score three torpedo hits on a southbound ship on the night of the 8th. The *Valfiorita* (6,200 tons) sank the following day.

With nothing else around to keep her interest, *Sokol* was

patrolling the waters off Stromboli. Her liaison officer, George Taylor, remembers the weird glow from the volcanic island reflected on the now-calm surface of the sea. For that night, 9/10 July, *Sokol*'s Polish crew, 'not being completely imbued with the spirit of submarining in accordance with Royal Navy rules, decided that this was a good opportunity to have a bath.'

> Believe it or not, we went over the side, attached to heaving lines, and with saltwater soap we had a very enjoyable bath in the sea. It was a pity that somebody mentioned the incident when we got back to Malta because we got a right royal rocket.

No doubt much refreshed, the Poles proceeded with their patrol, but it did not prove fruitful.

Unruly (Lieutenant Fyfe) found herself another U-boat on the 12th, the day after the torpedo restrictions were lifted; but the salvo, fired at a range of 3,000 yards, missed. The following day Fyfe fired at yet another U-boat. Though he did not realize it at the time, for *Unruly* lived up to her name and lost trim at the moment of firing, one torpedo had sunk the 630-ton Italian submarine, *Acciaio*.

Following their 'Husky' patrols, these three submarines, *Sokol*, *Ultor* and *Unruly*, were to return not to Malta but to Bizerta in northern Tunisia, to obviate the hazard of an attack by our own forces, now streaming back and forth between eastern Tunisia, Malta and southern Sicily. On 24 July, when the convoy and assault lanes had become less crowded, the three Tenth Flotilla *U*s would be escorted back to base.

Their Messina billets were taken over by *Unison* and *Unrivalled*, who, after a few days' rest in Malta, were once again ready for action; but these two boats would find even less to do, and they too returned to Malta via Bizerta, as *Unison*'s telegraphist recorded:

> *30 July*. Friday. Arrived Bizerta with *Unrivalled*. During the short stay in, we had one day's leave in Tunis, travelled down by lorry. Saw all the German equipment and tanks left behind in their flight through Tunisia.

Life was full of such satisfying sights these days. On *Unison*'s return to Malta on D-day afternoon, her telegraphist had marvelled to his log at the 'large units of the fleet, battleships, A/C carriers, monitors, cruisers and destroyers' that were now in harbour:

> A year ago we never thought the fleet would be in Malta again. Malta is now like a huge tanker: the fleet calls in, oils, and away to sea again. ... Landing craft of all descriptions are arriving and leaving more regularly than the local bus service.

Another pleasing sight was the new *U*-class submarine arriving at Lazaretto at the end of the month: *Unsparing* (Lieutenant A. D. Piper, RNR, *Unbeaten*'s one-time first Lieutenant). She had sailed from Algiers on 15 July to relieve *Ultor*, east of the Lipari Islands, where she sighted a 6,000-ton ship but was prevented from attacking by an alert escort. One of her generators burned out on the next day and she was compelled to follow the other two *U*s to Bizerta and thence to Malta.

Two more new *U*s were now operating from Algiers, *Usurper* (Lieutenant D. R. O. Mott) and *Universal* (Lieutenant C. Gordon). Carrying out working-up patrols off Corsica and the south of France respectively, they were warned to keep outside the 100-fathom line to avoid minefields. On 27 July *Usurper* torpedoed and sank *Chateau Yquem* (2,536 tons), a Vichy French ship, the sinking of which sent Vichy radio into paroxysms of fury.

Two of the *U*s had nearly completed their tours of duty in the Mediterranean. On the 28th *Unbroken* sailed for the UK after a very successful commission, first under Mars and more recently under Andrew. As the Admiralty commented:

> The skill with which she was handled throughout this long period [March, 1942 – July, 1943] in most hazardous waters, and her many successes against the enemy, reflect the highest credit on her two Commanding Officers, Lieutenant A. C. G. Mars, DSO, DSC, who commanded her until April 1943, and Lieutenant B. J. B. Andrew, DSC, and her ship's company.

Among her successes she had damaged two cruisers and sunk 15,000 tons of enemy shipping.

And as we shall see, *United* was now on her penultimate patrol before returning to Britain.

Dolfijn had had a most successful patrol, starting on 4 July when she torpedoed the 6,000-ton *Sabbia* off the north-west Italian mainland. Her victim was towed into Civitavecchia but later sank. Later that day the Dutch submarine also sank an A/S trawler, *Adalia* (165 tons), by gun and demolition charge. During the week of the Sicily landings she faithfully patrolled off the island of Giglio; and, not daring to make use of her mine detection unit, she crossed and recrossed thirty-six times in nine days four lines of mines, a fact she discovered from the Italian mine charts when *Dolfijn* returned to base. On the 13th her gunlayer displayed outstanding prowess in sinking an AA schooner presenting a head-on target, *Stefano Galleano* (137 tons). On 20 July *Dolfijn* returned to Algiers.

The five *U*s in the iron ring, by comparison, had a very dull time. On 14 July it was clear that the Italian battlefleet had no intention of sallying forth from its Taranto base, and so two of the five were recalled — *Uproar* and *Unbroken*. That same day, a little further south, their sister *Unshaken* (Lieutenant Whitton) torpedoed and sank an unidentified schooner. She and the Polish submarine *Dzik* were then recalled on the 15th. On the 18th, on passage, *Unshaken* spent some time in conversation with a mysterious submarine who turned out to be the enemy.

She might have been the same U-boat that followed *Unshaken* back to Malta. When *Unshaken* and *Dzik* were approaching the end of the swept channel at dawn on the 19th, the Polish submarine sighted a periscope menacing *Unshaken*. *Dzik* promptly launched a full salvo of torpedoes at the unknown U-boat. Unfortunately she missed, but she had undoubtedly saved *Unshaken*.

The fifth *U* in the iron ring patrol was *United*, now on her penultimate patrol. Her Commanding Officer, Lieutenant Roxburgh, remembers this patrol well:

> On the night of July 10th, whilst on the surface charging our batteries, we heard news of the Allied landings in Sicily. This heartened everyone on board, as it now seemed likely that the

reluctant Italians might at last put to sea and possibly furnish us with a worthwhile target. However, we waited in vain.

On the afternoon of the 15th the long wait was over. The Officer of the Watch, having sighted a U-boat, summoned Roxburgh to the control room. Roxburgh could hardly believe his luck as the U-boat swanned in broad daylight across the surface towards him:

> The range continued steadily to close and still the U-boat foolishly remained on the same course. I could now count seven sunburnt figures on the conning tower. One, whom I assumed to be the commanding officer, since he was smartly dressed in white tropical uniform and cap, was sitting nonchalantly on the bridge rail with his back to me.

The U-boat was only 500 yards away. Roxburgh gave the order to fire. A full salvo of torpedoes sped towards the enemy.

> The seconds ticked by. Surely we could not have missed such a sitting target from so short a range. It seemed an age, but it was in fact only some ten to fifteen seconds after firing when *United* was shaken by a tremendous explosion, shortly followed by another. Up went the periscope, in time for me to see the U-boat throw her stern high, her screws thrashing the air, and then sink without trace.
>
> It was all over in a matter of seconds. Such a rapid end to one's own kind, after such a cold-blooded attack and viewed from so close, gave me no sense of elation, rather one of momentary awe.
>
> This was no time for philosophizing, however – heads could be seen bobbing in the water and men were waving at our periscope. ... As I discussed with my Number One, John Wingate, the pros and cons of surfacing in broad daylight so close to a major enemy naval base, I could not fail to overhear the broad Scots tones of the helmsman, Able Seaman Jock Barry, mumble *sotto voce* from his corner in the control room: 'Pick 'em up, you cruel bugger!'
>
> Barry, nearly forty years of age, was an old man to most of us in our twenties. A huge, tough man, far from being the best-looking member of the crew, he was a great favourite on

board. Before being called up he was a Glasgow policeman, well used to dealing with the razor gangs of the Gorbals. Such tender feelings were therefore somewhat unexpected.

But Roxburgh got his own back; on surfacing he sent Barry out onto the casing to haul the survivors on board, a vulnerable place to be if the boat was suddenly forced to dive. Barry could find only four, and minutes later *United* had dived.

> The survivors turned out to be Italian: the U-boat's command-ing officer, Tenente di Vascello Salvatore Vassallo from Imperia, his navigating officer, and two ratings. They were clearly startled by my appearance when finally I interrogated them, my head being bound with a blood-stained and dirty ban-dage, covering a nasty gash I had sustained two nights earlier from fainting on my own bridge, shortly after leaving Malta, when I was suffering from a touch of sandfly fever.

The prisoners were not at first very forthcoming, and it was only later that we learned their boat had been the *Remo*. Roxburgh continues his account of this memorable patrol:

> That night, whilst on the surface charging the batteries, we received a cryptic signal from Malta ... containing the one word 'Grommet'. This announced the birth of my daughter. Had 'it' been a son, the signal would have read 'Toggle'. It so happened that Lieutenant Vassallo's wife was also expecting a baby and one of his first requests during interrogation was whether or not she could be informed of his survival. Such a culmination to the day called for something special, in addition to the usual Jolly Roger which submarines hoisted on returning from a successful patrol. When, therefore, *United* entered Malta harbour nine days later, she also proudly flew a Stork flag, specially constructed from Number One's 'sarong'*.
>
> *Remo*'s survivors did not have an entirely uneventful nine days on board *United*. Apart from proving an enthusiastic cook and producing excellent spaghetti, the Italian Commanding Officer was treated to a demonstration of an attack on an Italian cruiser, some two days after his rescue. He remained a quiet, though very interested and somewhat anxious spectator in the

* Now in the Royal Navy Submarine Museum at Gosport.

corner of the control room, as I endeavoured to manoeuvre the submarine for a shot at a *Regolo*-class cruiser which flashed past at some 36 knots. With a range of 8,000 yards and from an unfavourable position, we did not complete the attack.

Roxburgh goes on to add:

> Vassallo and I became quite friendly during his time on board, cooped up as we were in our tiny wardroom, a box some eight feet square, which we shared with four other officers. Our only common language was French. I was, however, careful to bid him a friendly farewell and to wish him luck whilst we were below in the submarine, away from prying eyes after we got back to Malta.

There were many who did not understand that friendship could arise even between dedicated opponents.

United returned to Malta on 24 July, eager for news of progress in Sicily. While at sea, the submarine was inevitably very isolated and, although an occasional BBC broadcast was received, everyone longed for the details that could only come from news bulletins posted in Lazaretto, or better still, the first-hand accounts of those who had been on the battlefront.

By this time the assault phase of 'Husky' was complete. The seaborne landings had produced remarkably few casualties and by now the invading Allied troops were busily mopping up resistance across Sicily.

On 25 July Mussolini was forced to resign, was imprisoned and replaced by Marshal Pietro Badoglio. Badoglio declared his intention to continue the struggle within the Axis partnership, but the German leadership rightly judged his declaration to be unreliable. The Italians showed little inclination to resist the Allied invaders and were soon evacuating their troops from Sicily. The Germans, led by Field-Marshal Kesselring, fought on, but within weeks they too would be withdrawing to the mainland and regrouping for the inevitable Allied invasion of Italy.

30

AUGUST, 1943

The plans for Operation 'Avalanche', the return to mainland Europe, were still being formulated. Much debate later centred on the vexed question of why we allowed the Germans to retreat in such good order from Sicily; the submarines from Malta and Algiers, the RAF and American bombers, the heavy ships could all have been used to attack the streams of evacuating troops crossing the Strait of Messina during August '43.

General Montgomery, for one, was outraged at the Allied planners' failure to see beyond the Sicily landings. During Operation 'Husky' it was difficult to coordinate the next moves when all the Allied leaders were so widely dispersed. As Montgomery wrote in his memoirs in 1958:

> Eisenhower, the Supreme Commander, was in Algiers; Alexander, in command of the land forces, was in Sicily; Cunningham, the Naval C-in-C, was in Malta; whereas Tedder, the Air C-in-C, had his headquarters in Tunis. When things went wrong, all they could do was to send telegrams to each other.

And again according to Montgomery, 'Avalanche' was not even considered until late July.

The intention was that, while Montgomery and his Eighth Army crossed the Strait of Messina, the main landings would be made by the Fifth US Army, 150 miles to the north at Salerno, in the first week of September. With RAF bombing of selected Italian cities, the enemy would be kept guessing about the Allies' precise intentions. But events overtook the plans as we shall see.

At the beginning of August *Unseen* (Lieutenant Crawford) was off Cape Rizzuto on the south-eastern coast of Calabria, with a COPP party surveying the beaches for potential landing sites. The survey team had completed their task, despite molestation from our own surface forces, and the submarine was continuing her patrol when she sighted a minelaying cruiser. Crawford made a torpedo attack, which missed; but he then managed to follow the cruiser's moves and thereby plotted the new field. This was of enormous help to submarines and surface ships alike in the weeks that followed.

This was an anxious time for the submarines, with our surface ships pursuing their own ends and the enemy becoming desperate.

At the beginning of July, *Parthian* (Lieutenant C. A. Pardoe, RNR) had arrived in Malta from Beirut, shortly after returning from a major refit in the United States. The original plan had been for her to land a clandestine team in Sicily during 'Husky', but this was cancelled at the last minute. On passage to rejoin the First Flotilla in Beirut, she was to patrol the southern Adriatic, and she sailed from Malta on 22 July. It was her last journey. Due at Beirut on 11 August, by the 14th she was officially posted missing, presumed mined. A tragic end for a fine submarine.

Saracen and her CO, Lieutenant Michael Lumby, were old friends of the Tenth Flotilla, for *Saracen* had often visited Marsamxett Harbour. *Saracen* (formerly *P 247*) was the oldest Cammell Laird *S*-class boat in the Mediterranean and when she sailed from Algiers on 7 August it was expected that this would be her last patrol before returning to England.

'We were sent to patrol off the east coast of Corsica,' Mike Lumby later recorded, 'an area with which we were well acquainted.' On the morning of Friday 13 August, *Saracen* dived outside Bastia where she was planning to investigate reports of unusual shipping activity:

> It was a real Mediterranean summer's day; hazy, no wind, and a glassy calm sea. Sonar conditions were terrible. During the day, we passed several patrols, but there was no HE and no transmissions were to be heard.

But the submarine had been sighted. Two Italian corvettes put to sea, *Euterpe* and *Minerva*, and spent the whole day searching for her. Finally, just after midnight, *Minerva* started to get a good contact and according to the Italian records 'dropped a total of forty depth charges in five patterns of eight.' 'After no great interval of time, one of the escorts revved up to full speed and dropped its carpet of 36 depth charges. This was all extremely noisy, but not too bad,' Mike Lumby continued:

> Until the final charge which was very close and made the boat whip in an alarming manner, such as I had not met before. The helmsman reported that the shaft to the steering wheel had sheared and a voice from the engine room said that water was coming in aft; otherwise all systems appeared to be working. The EO (engineer officer) was sent aft to stuff his socks in the leak, but he returned to say that the after-ends were flooded. They could not open the door.

Saracen was 'fighting a losing battle', in the words of her CO, and the crew mustered in the control room and prepared to abandon ship. Lumby goes on:

> When everyone had gone up the tower, I opened main vents and beat a hasty retreat myself, arriving on the bridge as the water started to lap the bridge deck. The main body of the ship's company had jumped into the sea, but I found three loyal souls waiting on the bridge for me. We four jumped together but, of course, we were by then some distance from the remainder.

The two corvettes had opened fire on the surfacing submarine, but stopped as soon as they saw her crew abandoning ship. All but two men had survived. 'We were very well looked after,' Lumby notes. While his clothes were taken off to be dried he was given brandy and coffee. 'But I was kicking myself for leaving my pipe on the wardroom table. I could have done with it.'

The Tenth Flotilla, too, had suffered a tragedy at the beginning of the month. *Unison* and *Unrivalled*, both in Bizerta at the end of July, had received orders to join a Malta-bound convoy on 2

August. They sailed from Bizerta and formed up at dusk, astern of the escorted merchant ships.

Unison, 'tail-end Charlie' in the port column, was suddenly fired on by the rearmost American merchant ship. This laconic entry in her telegraphist's log tells the bare outline of the story:

> 2 *August*. Monday. Left Bizerta to sail in convoy to Malta. At 2345, fired on by an American merchant ship. One shell entered fore-ends where everyone was sleeping. No casualties. One exploded inside the bridge, on the for'ard periscope. Captain (Lt. Daniell) injured. Torpedo Officer (Lt. King) died of wounds on the way to the US Casualty Clearing Station. Both look-outs injured. Returned to Bizerta with *Unrivalled* and Polish destroyer. Arrived 0230. Removed blood from bridge, control room and crew space.

Daniell was knocked out by the exploding shell and John King very seriously wounded. The coxswain, Petty Officer George 'Happy' Day, was wounded in the legs, as was Acting Leading Signalman James Halliday, who fell through the conning tower to land, bleeding profusely, in the control room.

Lieutenant John Haward, *Unison*'s first lieutenant, took command while the Polish destroyer *Slavak* escorted the stricken submarine back to Bizerta with *Unrivalled*. A motor launch took the wounded on ahead, to be transferred to the 56th United States Army Hospital. John King, a first-class navigating officer and close friend of the author's, died the next day.

Anthony Daniell spent six long months in hospital but was maimed for life. He had to leave the Royal Navy. James Halliday survived his terrible wounds and went to live in Canada. 'Happy' Day, never one to miss a trick, advised his messmates, struggling to lower him over the side in a stretcher, 'Smash a jar of rum. It'll never be missed in this shambles.'

Back in Britain, Lieutenant Daniell, already honoured with the DSC, was awarded the DSO. His ship's company also were honoured for *Unison*'s fourteen patrols.

On 8 September, after repairs and 'ping-running' in Malta, *Unison* sailed for the UK in company with *United*.

United's final patrol before going home began on 15 August, when she sailed from Lazaretto for the Gulf of Taranto. Here she was to try and intercept the Italian minelaying cruisers and destroyers.

Roxburgh was only too well aware that this was *United*'s last patrol: The 'ghouls in the mess' would not let him forget the old superstition. Of course it was nonsense – but, just in case, Roxburgh took particular care to avoid the minefields that *Unseen* had mapped out. Even when he sighted a 'sitting duck', a destroyer that had gone aground, he thought twice about attacking because there were mines somewhere between *United* and the target.

Ten days later, returning from a blank patrol through the Gulf, Roxburgh saw the destroyer was still aground, still with salvage workers trying to refloat her. It was so tempting:

> Mines or no mines, I took *United* inside to the 75-fathom line. The range was still too great for any reasonable chance of success. If I can get in to the 50-fathom line, I said to myself. . . Just then, a still small voice whispered in my ear, '*They always get you on our last patrol.*' I turned south and headed for Malta.

United was shortly thereafter making her way home in company with *Unison*.

While the Eighth Flotilla, and particularly *Shakespeare* (Lieutenant-Commander Ainslie), surveyed the 'Avalanche' beaches around Salerno, the Tenth continued patrols in Taranto Bay and the Adriatic. The Italian fleet had to be contained and kept guessing about where the landings would come.

The first *U* to make herself felt in the Adriatic was *Unruffled*. On 1 August, lurking outside the port of Brindisi, Stevens found himself an unusual target: 'a three-funnelled passenger ship, painted drab grey as befitted her transport role'. Not many ships of her size remained afloat in the Mediterranean. Stevens fired his salvo of torpedoes which missed. A dejected *Unruffled* withdrew to deeper waters. Two days later the same ship appeared in *Unruffled*'s periscope field of view, and this time Stevens scored three hits; the ship sank within minutes. But he was curious as to her identity, hoping, as he said in his book, 'that we had clobbered something sizeable'.

Alas, she proved to be an Italian cross-Adriatic ferry of 3,400 tons. She had started life with two funnels; a third dummy funnel had been added in the war. She was the *Citta di Catania*.

At Bari, just up the coast, *Uproar* (Lieutenant Herrick) made history at 2118 on 6 August when her newly-fitted radar picked up two escorted ships leaving harbour. Herrick, firing three torpedoes at a range of only 500 yards, took *Uproar* astern. The target's speed had been underestimated and the first torpedo was seen to hit abreast the mainmast. One of the escorting destroyers was now only 1,000 yards off, but *Uproar* dived to elude her hunters without difficulty. Her target was the Italian passenger ship *Brindisi* (1,977 tons).

Both *Unruffled* and *Uproar* returned to Malta in mid-August to a spell in the dockyard. Both, coincidentally, had generator problems.

Unshaken (Lieutenant Whitton) was patrolling in the same area a few days later, on 10 August, when a 7,000-ton naval transport, *Asmara*, approached from the south. At a range of 6,000 yards, one torpedo hit the transport which soon began to list and was abandoned. The following day Whitton sighted his victim stranded on a shoal just east of the port and decided to administer the *coup de grâce*. But as *Unshaken* closed in Whitton was astounded to see the ship capsize and sink, bottom up.

On the night of 12/13 August, a calm, moonlit night, *Unshaken* was at full buoyancy on the surface in the Strait of Otranto when a U-boat was sighted. Knowing that at any moment the enemy look-outs could sight *Unshaken*, Whitton wasted no time in firing four torpedoes. But the first torpedo made a great splash, then ran off to starboard. In the bright moonlight the Officer of the Watch in *U.453* sighted this plume of white water, put the helm of his submarine hard-over and succeeded in combing *Unshaken's* other three torpedoes. His vigilance had saved not only his life but the lives of all his shipmates. *Unshaken,* already reloading, pursued the U-boat, but she was too fast and made good her escape.

Also in the Brindisi-Bari billet in August were *Unruly* and the Polish submarine *Dzik*, due to be relieved on the 15th by her sister *Sokol*.

Unruly had been stirring up trouble by hitting and beaching a tanker in ballast. She had barely finished reloading when an eight-ship convoy was sighted approaching from the north. A long-range salvo was fired. Although the results could not be seen, because of a smokescreen laid down by the convoy's destroyer escorts, explosions were heard in the submarine.

Dzik was about to leave her billet when Romanowski sighted this thick blanket of smoke to the northward and decided to investigate. For three hours *Dzik* ran in on the surface. Closing in cautiously lest the bright moonlight betray her position, she fired a full salvo. As she did so, the submarine lost trim. Only one torpedo was seen to hit and the counter-attack began immediately.

Dzik went deep while twenty-two charges were dropped, then returned to the surface when all seemed quiet again. To Romanowski's bemusement the night was now pitch black and he could see nothing.

Sokol had sighted the convoy too. According to George Taylor, her liaison officer, she had manoeuvred into 'an attacking position nicely ahead of the convoy' when the same puzzling phenomenon occurred:

> The night was pitch black: no moonlight. The convoy escaped in the complete blackness. The enemy made A/S contact with *Sokol* and for our pains we received some thirty depth-charges. We felt no little frustration when later we learned that we were receiving *Dzik*'s 'heat'!

What no one in either *Dzik* or *Sokol* had anticipated was that on that night the moon underwent a total eclipse!

For the next five days *Sokol* suffered constant 'heat' until she was relieved by *Unseen*.

Late on 22 August *Unseen* (Lieutenant Crawford) made a torpedo attack on a small escorted vessel outside Bari, but the escorting destroyer began instantaneous retaliation. 'Once again,' writes

Jim Richards, one of *Unseen*'s telegraphists, 'we were thankful for the strength and sound building of our craft by the Barrow-in-Furness workforce.' An hour later, surfacing cautiously, *Unseen* searched for the fruits of her labour:

> As we suspected, the torpedo had proved to be a dud, and barely caused any damage. The ship was safely entering Bari harbour. The torpedo failure was blamed on our use of the First World War Mark IV torpedo warhead, instead of the modern Mark VIII which were in very short supply.

The patrol, although providing 'no worthwhile targets', was far from uninteresting. From the bustle of destroyers, corvettes and aircraft it seemed that something was about to happen. And, writes Richards:

> During the early morning dark hours of August 26th the bridge look-outs were entertained by an Allied air raid on Bari.
> The following midnight *Unseen* moved to a new billet off the Albanian coast. At 0740 on the 27th, the periscope watchkeeper, Sub-Lieutenant Worth, sighted masts at eight miles. The captain promptly went to Diving Stations and started the attack. At 0852 *Unseen* had reached her firing position, with a range of 1,250 yards. One of the torpedoes hit the target after a twenty-five second running time. There was a loud explosion.

The target was *Rastrello* (985 tons), formerly the Greek ship *Messaryas Nomikos,* requisitioned by the Italians in 1942.

Surfacing cautiously at 1045, Crawford found that the target's destroyer escort had fled, leaving survivors floating on a raft. Jim Richards again:

> Though there were three badly wounded seamen among the twelve survivors, it was certain that enemy aircraft would soon appear on the scene. It would have been a long and hazardous operation to take these shocked men below into the submarine . . . so four of the survivors were taken prisoner on board *Unseen*, among whom was a twenty-nine-year-old Yugoslav who was only too keen to be captured.
> The boat remained on the surface for a little over half an hour,

passing down to the raft morphine tablets for the wounded, and a little food. The wardroom wine locker, which in common with the majority of submarine 'Captain's Orders' was never opened at sea, was unlocked for a couple of bottles to be handed down to the raft. We were only twenty to thirty miles from the Italian coast, so we thought that the eight remaining seamen on the raft would soon be rescued by their own people. When an Italian flying boat was sighted advancing towards the wreckage, *Unseen* was obliged to dive.

The four prisoners included a Yugoslav, Giordano Tulach, who was 'a true patriot', according to Richards, and provided useful confirmation of something the Allies had long suspected: 'The Germans were transporting prefabricated U-boats overland to Yugoslavia'.

The following morning *Unseen* surfaced off the Albanian coast, near Valona, to make a gun attack on *Fabiola*, a 103-ton anti-sub-marine vessel. The gun jammed, but some of *Fabiola*'s crew of seventeen were already abandoning ship, so Crawford called for a boarding party. When the submarine closed the vessel, it became clear that the Italian captain and boatswain had remained on board.

A boarding party jumped across, armed with revolvers and demolition charges. Dressed in the normal submarine garb of dirty and oily sport shorts or working overalls; naked above the waist, sockless and with only sandals on their feet, the boarding party looked like pirates of olden days. With a couple of weeks' growth of whiskers, they could terrify the bravest opposition.

The captured vessel's log books and documents were taken on board. The captain and boatswain were taken prisoner and the vessel began to drift away from the submarine. Petty Officer Percy Porter had already set the demolition charges and he and his aides had safely returned to the boat; but some of the board-ing party, in their search for souvenirs, were forced to take an involuntary though refreshing swim back to *Unseen*.

One of the swimmers was Leading Stoker Alfie Simmonds, who had loaded himself with heavy gear; he was compelled to jettison most of it when he sank two fathoms down because of the weight. His leg was unmercifully pulled by the rest of the crew, including the Skipper. One of the captured souvenirs was a machine gun which is now in the Royal Navy Submarine Museum at HMS *Dolphin* in Gosport.

The shore batteries having opened up, *Unseen* dived, just as the demolition charges went off.

Returning to Malta, as she had no torpedoes left, *Unseen* sighted *Ultor* and the two sisters swopped recognition signals at three miles before returning to base on 1 September.

At the end of August, *Ultor* (Lieutenant Hunt) and *Unrivalled* (Lieutenant Turner) were training for a chariot operation to attack the Italian battleships in Taranto harbour. The charioteers had spent most of the month practising. On three occasions their dummy attacks on Grand Harbour had succeeded in penetrating the defence nets.

When the two *U*s sailed from Malta on 24 August everyone was confident of success. But on passage to Taranto the operation was cancelled by the Commander-in-Chief. The reason was not obvious at the time, but Marshall Badoglio had been induced to sign an armistice. Italy was about to surrender and there was no longer any need to sink the Italian battle fleet. The news was not made public until the last minute before 'Avalanche', for fear that the forthcoming surrender might lead to dangerous complacency among the invading troops.

Unrivalled was recalled to Malta, but *Ultor* was diverted to Calabria for an operation designed to deceive the enemy. On board she was carrying two Folbots, a small buoy and other incriminating items to be distributed on the beaches around Point Alice, which, it was hoped, would persuade the Germans that an Allied landing there was imminent. On the way, *Ultor* noticed the grounded vessel that John Roxburgh had considered dispatching, but whereas Roxburgh had the ghouls whispering 'last patrol' in his ear, George Hunt went straight for the target. As Roxburgh himself writes:

> Undeterred by rumours of minefields, George had taken *Ultor* close to the destroyer off Point Alice and put paid to further salvage efforts by hitting her with two torpedoes. But then, it was only George's first patrol!

The target was the torpedo boat *Lince* (679 tons), who had run her stem aground, though her stern was still afloat. An army of toiling Italians had been furiously digging a trench, but in vain. *Ultor's* torpedo hit squarely under her mainmast and the after part broke off and sank — 'so saving the Italians from a hot day's work in the August sun,' George Hunt noted later:

> Ten minutes later what was left of *Lince*, with a great show of spirit, fired one round from her foremost and only remaining gun; luckily this was not pointing in *Ultor's* direction. The torpedo explosion caused heavy casualties which later could be seen laid out on the beach.

This was the same torpedo boat that had been unable to attack Mossy Turner and *Unrivalled* (then *P 45*) off Sousse in January, because she had no depth-charges, her outfit having been landed after RAF bomb damage to the ship off Tripoli.

Ultor then proceeded with her mission by surfacing that night and launching the Folbots and buoy. She then dropped a sailor's cap overboard for good measure; an onshore breeze did the rest.

Unruffled, her generator now repaired, was about to set sail on her eighteenth and penultimate patrol, which would include another clandestine errand. Stevens had spent a few days relaxing in Beirut and had rejoined his boat refreshed, though undoubtedly less thin. When she left Malta on 22 August she had on board two Greek army officers who were to be landed on the island of Cephalonia. As Steve has written 'They were brave men; if captured in German-occupied Greece, they faced penalties horrible to contemplate.'

The two Greeks were landed without incident and paddled off into the unknown. *Unruffled* now returned to Brindisi and on 27 August, despite two seaplanes overhead, managed to torpedo the *Citta di Spezia* (2,475 tons) — Stevens' second *Citta*-class ship in a row.

And on her first patrol during this August of 1943, the new *Unsparing* (Lieutenant A. D. Piper, RNR) attacked the naval water-carrier, *Flegetonte* (1,182 tons), on the 31st off Bari; one of her two torpedoes sank her.

All in all, it had been a successful month for the Fighting Tenth.

31

SEPTEMBER, 1943

The terms of the Italian armistice were finally agreed on 3 September, the same day that Montgomery and the Eighth Army made their landings on mainland Europe. But as we have seen, it was considered necessary to hold back news of the surrender until the evening of 8 September, the day before 'Avalanche', the main landings at Salerno.

One of the conditions to which Badoglio had agreed was 'the immediate transfer of the Italian fleet and aircraft to such points as may be designated by the Allied Commander-in-Chief'. The Germans, suspecting their Axis partner of double-dealing, had seized control of all key ports and naval installations. It thus required some manoeuvring before the Italian naval commanders were able to honour the armistice, but honour it they did.

With most of the Italian fleet at Spezia, in northern Italy, Admiral Cunningham gave the order to sail at 0300 on 9 September, half an hour before the Salerno landings were to begin. The Taranto fleet would leave harbour on the 9th. They would be met by an escort of Allied warships from Malta at daybreak on 10 September at a point twenty miles north of Bone on the Algerian-Tunisian border.

The news of the armistice was greeted in Malta with a joyous clangor of church bells. The long-awaited tidings reached the submarines at sea in the form of the usual encoded signal. According to Jack Whitton, CO of *Unshaken*, the signal arrived at 2230 on the 8th, stating simply that the Italian forces had surrendered, the Italian fleet was making for Allied ports forthwith and that 'ships failing to comply with this order would be treated as hostile'.

At the time *Unshaken* was off Brindisi, having made a splendid torpedo attack on a 7,000-ton tanker outside the port on 5 September. Whitton had attacked through a formidable screen — two sea planes sweeping ahead of the target; two corvettes on each beam and zigzagging with the tanker; and a *Generale*-class destroyer weaving broadly astern. But the tanker had managed to limp into the port so Whitton could not finish the job.

Unshaken was being recalled to base. On the morning of 9 September she was making her way south around the heel of Italy when the hydrophone operator reported: 'High speed revs.' Suspecting an enemy submarine, Whitton ordered Diving Stations. The problem was whether this was a German U-boat or an Italian one. Through the periscope it was hard to tell: the enemy submarine was hull-down, the conning tower glinting in the bright morning sun. Whitton takes up the tale:

> At about 1500 yards range, and with but a few minutes to go before firing torpedoes, I had a long and careful look at the target: the submarine was Italian. She was also flying her ensign and had an unusually large number of chaps on the bridge, whom I could clearly see were gazing to the north-west and, no doubt, at their beloved country a few miles away. With that bunch on the bridge, she was hardly in a position to do a quick dive. . . . We would try to stop her, then board her.

By chance, Whitton's great friend and the flotilla's Spare CO, Lieutenant 'Shaver' Swanston, happened to be along for the ride. Whitton now appointed him commander of the boarding party, with orders to take over the Italian submarine.

Unshaken surfaced and fired a warning shot across the U-boat's bows:

> There were even more chaps on the bridge than before; I suppose they had come up to see what the hell was coming next. By this time *Unshaken* was alongside, stopped, with our bows against the Italian's bow. The boarding party, led by Shaver brandishing a .45, were jumping across. They raced along the forward casing and climbed up the enemy's conning tower. The objective: to secure the conning tower hatch and so to stop him diving, then to subdue any further resistance.

71. Originally the home of the Italian Tenth Submarine Flotilla, this base at La Maddalena to the north of Sardinia became the new home of The Fighting Tenth.

72. *Uproar* (Lt L.E. Herrick) leaves La Maddalena to act as a beacon for the Anzio landings. Standing second from right is *Ultor*'s 'Bunts' (signalman), Gus Britton, ex-champion Navy swimmer and now Head Archivist at The Royal Navy Submarine Museum at Gosport.

73. Lt 'Wiggy' Bennett climbs through the 'upper lid' to *Uproar*'s bridge.

74. *Unsparing* (Lt A.D. Piper, RNR) undergoing trials. *Unsparing* carried out twelve patrols with considerable success in the Mediterranean.

75. Lt G.E. Hunt, CO of the very successful *Ultor*, comes ashore at La Maddalena after patrol.

76. Lt S. Koitschka, CO of *U.616*, who operated in the Mediterranean with success, until sunk in a three-day 'swamp' operation by eight American destroyers.

77. A *UJ* - boat, the very effective type of anti-submarine vessel used by the Germans: their depth-charge attacks were extremely accurate in the later stages of the war.

78. *Champagne*, 9,945 tons, lies derelict near Bastia, after being hit by two torpedoes from *Ultor* on 24 September, 1943. Three days later one torpedo from *Uproar* finished the job.

79. *Ultimatum (P.34)* (Lt W.H. Kett, RNR) prepares to leave La Maddalena for patrol off the French Riviera, while Commander (S), Commander Christopher Hutchinson, and the staff wait to wave, 'God speed!'.

80. Aided by the local populace, *Upstart* lands four spare torpedoes at Khios in the Aegean, for collection by *Untiring* on 6th October, 1943.

81. The crowded bridge of *Ultimatum*. Nearest the camera is Lt W.H. Kett who commanded the submarine during her second commission. The newly-fitted radar aerials are visible.

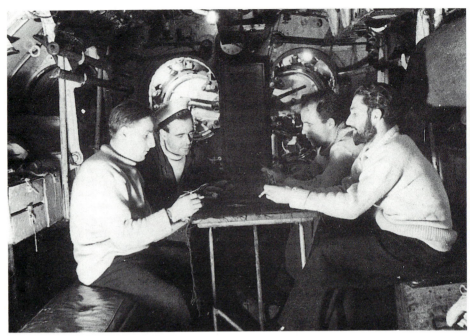

82. Off-watch in *Upstart*'s fore-ends. It is night-time, the boat has surfaced and the diesel generators are running to charge the batteries. "Carry on smoking. . ."

83. *Untiring* (Lt R. Boyd) ammunitions before setting off to the Mediterranean. She missed *U.616* with torpedoes off Toulon in October, 1943.

84. The crowded bridge of the Free French submarine *Curie*, commanded by Lieutenant de Vaisseau P.M. Sonneville. Under this Commanding Officer and, later, under Lieutenant de Vaisseau P.J. Chailley, *Curie* served with distinction in the Tenth Flotilla.

85. The long-awaited mail comes on board : *Unruly* (Lt J.P. Fyfe) at Beirut, 25 January, 1944.

86. *Vox* (Lt J.M. Michell), *Vigorous* (Lt J.C. Ogle) and *Vivid* (Lt J.C. Varley), with many other *V*-class submarines, after operating in the Aegean, continued the struggle in the shallow waters of the Malacca Strait and in the Pacific. The boats are seen here in Melbourne, Australia.

THE WINDOW IN THE CHAPEL OF OUR
LADY AND ST.GEORGE HAS BEEN PRESENTED
BY RELATIVES, SHIPMATES AND FRIENDS IN
MEMORY OF OFFICERS AND MEN OF THE
10TH SUBMARINE FLOTILLA AND OTHER
SUBMARINES OPERATING FROM MALTA WHO
LOST THEIR LIVES IN THE WAR 1939-45

87. Fifty submarines of the Royal and Allied Navies did not return from their Mediterranean war patrols : some 1,900 officers and men. Two plaques in the Anglican Cathedral opposite Manoel Island honour these Companies whose last resting places are the submarines in which they served.

But there was no resistance. The enemy CO wanted to go to Brindisi; Whitton wanted to go back to Malta. 'A somewhat heated exchange followed,' Whitton writes, as the two COs, each on his own bridge, side by side, voiced their intentions:

> 'Brindisi,' he shouted. 'Malta,' I yelled.
> 'Brindisi . . .' 'Malta . . .'

Percy Westmacott, the Number One, passed up Whitton's uniform cap, 'to give the proceedings a little more dignity'.

> I put it on. Also the 3-inch gun, still manned and ready for action, was ordered: 'Load one round HE.'
> The loading number, a seaman with considerable initiative, held up the 3-inch high explosive shell; he displayed it, rather like a music hall conjuror, to a very impressed Italian audience. He then slipped the round home into the gun, slamming the breech shut. The muzzle of the gun was trained on the Italian captain's stomach, at a range of about thirteen feet. Shaver, who was standing close to him, was requested to stand aside. With a shrug of the shoulder and hands in the air, the Italian agreed: Malta. We were now both singing from the same song sheet — and I don't think my cap did the trick.

With Shaver Swanston and the boarding party in control, the Italian boat, *Menotti*, would sail for Malta. Four Italian hostages were kept in *Unshaken* to encourage their shipmates to behave.

Now began the two-day passage for Malta, mainly on the surface so that *Unshaken* could keep an eye on her charge. Each evening the two submarines closed while Whitton made sure all was well. Swanston complained at the dirt and lack of discipline, but he evidently had no problems with the officers who roundly expressed 'their loathing of the Germans in particular and the war in general'. *Menotti's* captain later told Whitton:

> He had no orders to proceed to an Allied port, except a signal which he considered false, the Allies having made use of captured Italian cyphers. He was upset at being defeated; he loathed the Germans but did not mind surrendering to the British.

Unshaken, with her prize, arrived back at Malta on 11 September, as Whitton says, 'to pass through an impressive collection of Italian naval ships anchored off the Grand harbour'.

That afternoon *Unshaken*'s CO was handed what must be one of the most unusual receipt notes in history. Typed on HMSO crown-embossed paper by the Lazaretto typewriter, it was addressed to His Majesty's Submarine *Unshaken* and dated Saturday 11 September, 1943. Signed by George Phillips as Captain (S) 10, it read:

> Received from Lieutenant J. Whitton, RN, one Italian submarine named *Menotti* and sixty-one crew.

Unrivalled was also on patrol when the Italians surrendered, having sailed for Bari on 2 September. On the 8th, only hours before the armistice was announced, she made a torpedo attack on a small Italian vessel outside Bari, but missed. On the 10th Mossy Turner stalked and boarded a trawler; then, while Sub-Lieutenant J. Evans and Able Seaman Lower took their prize into Bari, *Unrivalled* followed with two Italians on board as hostages.

With *Unrivalled* berthed alongside the inner harbour mole, Turner ordered that the Port admiral should repair on board forthwith. And there, seated at the minuscule wardroom table, Turner ordered Admiral Panunzio to sail all the seaworthy ships inside Bari harbour immediately for Malta. The dumbfounded Panunzio agreed but, while they were still discussing details, a report was received that the Germans were about to enter the town.

Putting Panunzio ashore to complete arrangements, *Unrivalled* sailed to patrol outside the harbour. The Germans were indeed approaching Bari, but Panunzio kept his word and sent a motley collection of coasters to sea that evening. Rounding them up like a herd of sheep, *Unrivalled* then set sail for Malta, her gun manned and tubes at the ready. Behind her trailed a convoy of *Rinucci* (1,217 tons); *Acilia* (329 tons); *Lucrino* (5,536 tons); *Apuania* (2,286 tons), *Belugosa* (669 tons) and *Luana* (1,140 tons).

Meanwhile *Unruly* (Lieutenant Fyfe) had arrived on the scene. She bowled into harbour to help persuade some of the more reluctant ships' captains to join the convoy and brought up the rear. On passage to Malta the convoy was attacked by a German aircraft. *Unruly* fired one round of 3-inch at the raider and her shell burst surprisingly near the aircraft. It dropped one bomb, which missed, then flew off.

No-one who saw Mossy Turner shepherding his heterogeneous flock into harbour will ever forget the sight. Admiral Sir John Cunningham, C-in-C Levant, commented later that Lieutenant Turner had shown 'considerable enterprise' in arranging this convoy of merchant ships and getting it to Malta.

'The official record does not convey the fact that there was a dearth of direction as to what action to take,' writes Andrew Prideaux, who three months earlier had been *Unrivalled's* first lieutenant:

> Mossy acted entirely on his own initiative, after the PO Tel reported the BBC news item. At the time, rewards, in the way of honours, were calculated on ships sunk and not on ships *saved*, and the incident was played down.

Sadly neither Prideaux's successor, Charlie Hammer, nor Ken Jones, *Unrivalled's* 'pilot', are alive today to tell us more; and Mossy Turner himself was lost in January, 1944, in the Far East while operating from Trimcomalee as CO of the minelayer *Porpoise* (Shrimp Simpson's second command in 1938).

On the morning of 10 September, patched up in Malta's dockyard after the grim tragedy of 2 August, *Unison* was heading for home with her sister *United*.

Unison, now under the temporary command of Lieutenant Tom Barlow, had during her eleven months under Daniell sorely discomfited the enemy: 16,000 tons of supply ships sunk, 8,000 tons damaged, among other operations to her credit. *United* (Lieutenant Roxburgh) had spent eleven months with the Fighting Tenth, sending 21,000 tons of ships to the bottom, damaging a further 12,000 tons, as well as sinking a destroyer and a U-boat. Both submarines and their gallant crews merited a rest.

The two *U*s were on passage westwards, just off the North African coast, when they sighted the assembled ships of the erstwhile enemy. Roxburgh writes:

It was typical calm, bright Mediterranean weather. To be on the surface in daylight at that time was a novel experience in itself. Then on the morning of 10 September, when about fifteen miles north of Bone, suddenly to see this marvellous sight to the north . . . two battleships, five cruisers, and seven destroyers and torpedo boats who all passed within three miles of us.*

I remember the uncanny silence of it all. Just the chugging of our diesels and the gentle lap of the sea on our hull.

Roxburgh was speechless with the emotion of the moment. He continues:

There were the enemy ships whose silhouettes I knew by heart; ships I had been dreaming about for the past year; ships I had been dreaming of sinking. I watched them steaming off to the east, forming up astern of *Warspite* and *Valiant*.

I somehow felt cheated — there went my targets — but at the same time elated to have been witness of such an historic moment, and moved in a way, in sympathy for the Italians. It was all over fairly quickly but I remember informing the ship's company and allowing some of those off watch to come up on the bridge to see the sight for themselves. They, too, looked on impressed, but said little.

Warspite led the Italian battlefleet into Malta on the 11th, where it was soon joined by the remnants of the Italian fleet from Taranto. On 13 September, 1943, Admiral Sir Andrew Cunningham, C-in-C of the Mediterranean Fleet, made a general signal to all ships:

I have this day informed the Board of Admiralty that the Italian fleet now lies at anchor under the guns of the fortress of Malta.

His historic signal undoubtedly marks the end of a chapter.

---

* When the force had sailed to surrender from Spezia early in the morning of 9 September, it had consisted of 3 battleships, 6 cruisers and 8 destroyers. That afternoon, planes were seen approaching. The Italians, thinking they were Allied aircraft, offered no resistance, only to be attacked by eleven German Dornier 217s, equipped with the new wireless-controlled bombs. The flagship, *Roma*, was hit, caught fire and blew up with heavy casualties, including Admiral Bergamini, the C-in-C. One cruiser and one destroyer remained behind to pick up survivors.

32

SEPTEMBER/OCTOBER, 1943

The surrender of the Italian fleet immediately reduced the Tenth Flotilla's operational areas to the 'distant and somewhat neglected waters of the north Adriatic', as Captain Phillips put it. The Commander-in-Chief had ordered him not to sail any of his flotilla until further orders, and by 14 September all except *Sokol* were in harbour. The following day all seaworthy submarines would be sailed to reinforce the Eighth Flotilla in the Gulf of Genoa.

Sokol had been off Brindisi when the armistice was announced and as her liaison officer, George Taylor, remembers, 'Our next few days were involved in a complex mission.' *Sokol's* CO, Lieutenant-Commander 'George' Koziolkowski, had been ordered to send a party ashore to persuade the Italians there to surrender. The party comprised Taylor himself 'with an armed escort of two ratings, one being the tough gunlayer, Leading Seaman Jerzy Daskkiewicz'. As elsewhere, the Italians proved cooperative, though Taylor notes that they 'expressed astonishment at the presence of a Polish submarine operating in the Adriatic'.

Sokol returned to Lazaretto on the 16th and almost immediately was sent off to the Gulf of Genoa with the rest of the *U*s.

At Salerno the Allies had run into trouble. Even though the Italian forces had surrendered, the Germans were still in occupation and they laid on a very effective counter-attack. Fortunately Montgomery was even now charging to the rescue with his Eighth Army, which had made good progress since landing further south on the 3rd. On 16 September the two Allied invasion forces linked up and Eisenhower made a £5 bet with Montgomery that the campaign would be over by Christmas. But there was a long, hard winter ahead for the troops; and the submarines still had some work to do too.

Ultor, Unseen, Uproar and *Dzik* sailed from Malta on 15 September to take up their new billets off Genoa. The Tenth would now join forces temporarily with the Eighth Flotilla, and on 18 September Captain Phillips flew to Algiers to confer with Captain Fawkes, Captain (S)8. All *S*-class and *T*-class submarines were now being sent to join the fight in the Pacific, and the remainder of the Mediterranean war would involve mainly the *U*s. *Maidstone*, the Eighth's depot ship, would herself sail for the Far East in November. From 8 November onwards operational control of submarines in the western basin of the Mediterranean would be handed back to Captain (S)10.

The three principal areas in which the German naval forces remained active, and in which the Allied submarines would now seek to take control, were in the Aegean, in the southern Adriatic and along the French coastline as far east as northern Italy. Captains Phillips and Fawkes decided that a new submarine base should be opened for the *U*s, with their lesser endurance, in Sardinia. Very conveniently the Germans abandoned that island on 19 September.

The suggestion was that the new British submarine base should be located on the isle of La Maddalena, on the north-eastern tip of Sardinia. This had been a major Italian naval base, including, by coincidence, the home of their Tenth Submarine Flotilla. But as Allied bombers had been active in the area, there was a strong possibility that the base was no longer habitable. Captain Phillips judged it wise to send a team to reconnoitre the place.

Commander Christopher Hutchinson, the Tenth's Commander (S) with Commander Tom Sanders, the flotilla's engineer officer, and Lieutenant C. J. Bennett, the torpedo officer, departed in MTBs to survey Maddalena and report back to Phillips at Algiers. Meantime the work of the flotilla must continue.

Dzik (Lieutenant-Commander B. S. Romanowski) had been delayed with repairs to her muffler valve when she set sail from Malta for her last patrol with the Tenth. As Antoni Banach, an ERA in *Dzik*, remembers, this was one of her most successful patrols. On 21 September she sighted the 6,397-ton German supply ship *Nicolauo Ourania* (formerly Greek) in Bastia harbour, Corsica, and sank her at the harbour entrance 'which prevented other ships in the harbour from escaping'. *Dzik's* torpedo attack on the big German ship also caused the demise of several barges and an accompanying tug, and when the news of her success reached Alexandria, writes Banach, 'RAF bombers were sent to destroy the remaining ships bottled up in the harbour'.

On the following day *Dzik* sank three Siebel ferries (fast, well-armed landing craft) with another salvo of torpedoes, set for surface running. Ironically, it was this success that brought most satisfaction to everyone in *Dzik*, this being the first time that they were certain their target was German. Banach adds:

> Within seven days of the start of the patrol, *Dzik* had fired all eight torpedoes . . . so we returned early to base. We surfaced a few miles off the coast of Algiers, with our flag hoisted with the Jolly Roger. Some American planes returning from a raid must have mistaken us for a German U-boat, and, without warning, machine-gunned our submarine, hitting the conning tower. We crash-dived and reached a safe depth underwater without any casualties. We were thankful that the Americans had no bombs left, because they could not have failed to hit us.

Eventually *Dzik* made it safely into Algiers, but had to wait for her reload torpedoes. When they came, she was sent to join the First Flotilla. 'From then until April, 1944, *Dzik* operated from Beirut,' Banach adds, 'hunting in the Greek islands.'

Several other *U*s were having success in these less familiar waters. *Unseen* was off Spezia on 21 September when her CO, 'Tubby' Crawford, attacked a two-ship convoy escorted by E-boats. By firing a full salvo when the two target ships were overlapping, Crawford achieved the remarkable result of putting a torpedo into each. Both *Brandenburg*, the 3,894-ton auxiliary minelayer, and *Kreta* (2,600 tons) went to the bottom. Another remarkable feat was achieved the following day, off the island of Elba, when Lieutenant Herrick of *Uproar* hit the *Andre Sgarallino*, a 731-ton naval auxiliary, with three torpedoes out of three fired.

Ultor (Lieutenant Hunt), off north-east Corsica, was loitering in the hope of catching some of the evacuating Germans. She struck lucky on the 24th. As the Admiralty Weekly Intelligence Report notes, *Ultor* had seen 'a large tanker loading lorries in Bastia harbour' and at 1945 the tanker emerged from harbour: she was 'none other than *Champagne*' (9,945 tons):

> Every precaution against attack had been made; two corvettes and four E-boats were disposed, one astern and two on either side. Such devices serve only to whet a submariner's appetite, and at 1954 *Ultor* made an advancing attack and passed inside the port bow escort. At 1958 four torpedoes were fired at 1,800 yards range; the enemy, proceeding at twelve knots, was hit twice. The counter-attack was feeble and unworthy of the impressive force which had been laid on to protect *Champagne*. At 0800 next morning the tanker with her cargo of lorries was seen to be beached about half a mile south of the harbour. After having sunk one of the enemy Siebel ferries with which the area was infested, *Ultor* tried to dispose finally of the beached tanker. The torpedo, her last, did not hit.

Nevertheless, *Ultor* had severely inconvenienced the enemy at a time when he was desperately regrouping his forces for a counter-offensive on the Allied armies. And, just to put the bubbles in the champagne, *Uproar* passed by on the 26th, saw the beached tanker and fired one torpedo into her stern.

So ended this climactic month for the Fighting Tenth. The Italians had surrendered. The evidence lay moored in Malta's harbours. On the last day of September the first six Italian submarines arrived in Marsamxett harbour. Berthed with the Italian seaplane tender *Miraglio*, in Lazaretto Creek as accommodation ship', as Captain Phillips remarked in his monthly report, they were but 'a poor substitute' for his *Us*.

In the same report Phillips notes the 'embarrassing amount of intelligence' which was now being provided by the Italians, but comments dryly on the information supplied concerning minefields:

> These are so numerous and widespread that it is difficult to see

how our submarines could have operated had the position of these fields been known previously. The Sicilian Channel, on paper, was certainly impassable on the routes we used regularly for twenty-four months.

While the Italian ships now lay idle until useful work could be found for them in territories recently liberated from Fascist rule – Libya, for example – the Royal Navy's Mediterranean Fleet still had its work cut out, particularly in the Aegean where German resistance was fiercest.

On 1 October Naples fell to the Allies and, with the enemy now slowly retreating in Italy, the focus would turn increasingly to the eastern Mediterranean. On the 21st a total of nine *U*s would be loaned to Captain (S)1 at Beirut to reinforce the First Flotilla in the Aegean. The islands in the Dodecanese that had been quietly taken by the Allies during 'Husky' and 'Avalanche' were now snatched back by the Germans. This, it seemed, was where the enemy would make his last stand.

The Fighting Tenth had left Lazaretto for the last time. Although the *U*s' new home at Maddalena was not yet prepared, most would return from their Aegean patrols not to the familiar, battered, friendly face of Malta, but to the unknown quantity of a former enemy base. The final phase was about to begin.

Phase V

Finale

OCTOBER, 1943 – SEPTEMBER, 1944

33

'With the armistice with Italy, the main work of the submarines in the Mediterranean was completed.' So ends
the Admiralty's summing up of this period. But, as we have seen,
the Germans had recovered their grip on the Greek islands, and
the Fighting Tenth would be sorely needed in months to come
as support for the First Flotilla.

The nature of this last phase was very different. Targets were
restricted to only German or German-controlled shipping in the
diminishing operational areas. Torpedo targets were increasingly
scarce. As one of the Tenth's COs remarked recently, 'One has
to remember that by the end of '42, most of the really big stuff
had been sunk.' The German ship-builders were not able to make
up for such losses. Consequently, our submarines in future
would make much more frequent use of the gun and the demolition charge.

What was unchanged was the threat that our submarines faced.
Usurper, who had arrived in the Mediterranean only three months
before, was lost in the Gulf of Genoa early in October. Lieutenant
David Mott had taken her for her third patrol, working out of
Algiers. Young, married, having already won the DSC, he had
been expected to go far. But his fate is unknown. Possibly he was
mined; possibly he was sunk by a German anti-submarine vessel
operating in that area on 3 October.

Even less is known of the fate of *Trooper*, whose commanding
officer was an old Tenth man, Lieutenant Johnny Wraith, DSO,
DSC, formerly captain of *Upright*. On 26 September *Trooper* had
left Beirut for a patrol in the Dodecanese. She never returned.

Sokol's last patrol for the Tenth was in the northern Adriatic,
where she was investigating German activities at the Slovenian
port of Pula. On 4 October, remembers George Taylor, her liai-

son officer, she made a brilliant attack on a large merchant ship, *Dea Mazella* (3,080 tons). Despite a strong current and even stronger wind, at a range of only 700 yards, *Sokol* fired two torpedoes. George Taylor writes:

> Thirty-five seconds after firing, the second torpedo exploded, which was followed by a second tremendous explosion that shook *Sokol* considerably, breaking a lot of glass and light bulbs and damaging a number of gauges. The target must have been loaded with ammunition.

Some hours later the target sank. Meanwhile *Sokol* had sighted another ship and fired another two torpedoes. This time, remembers Taylor, neither hit the target, but one of them 'very nearly scored an "own goal" ':

> This torpedo had a gyro failure. It passed directly above our conning tower, and then we saw it leaping about like a demented porpoise, with the target ship firing its stern gun at it . . . Even those enthusiastic fighting men, the Poles, were a little subdued at the thought of how very nearly we had torpedoed ourselves.

Three days later, still patrolling off Pula, *Sokol* found another large target, the 7,095-ton *Eridania*, originally Italian but commandeered by the Germans. At 0701 on the morning of 7 October *Sokol* fired another two torpedoes. One struck *Eridania* in the area of the boiler room and she exploded and sank twenty minutes later.

Despite the intense A/S activity she had provoked in the area, *Sokol* continued her patrol and was delighted to come upon the same ship that she had missed three days earlier. 'But now she was returning from Dalmatia and was crowded with troops on the upper deck,' Taylor recalls. *Sokol* fired her last torpedo:

> Speed was correctly estimated at 11 knots and the torpedo aimed at the funnel was running perfectly true. The asdics heard the torpedo 25° off course; then it veered 40° in the opposite direction. It was leaping out of the water again like a wild porpoise. It was so disappointing that this, which should have been

a successful attack, was frustrated for the second time by a faulty torpedo.

George Koziolkowski brought *Sokol* to the surface and attempted to sink the vessel with her gun. A few devastating hits were made, but *Sokol*'s efforts were interrupted by shore batteries and patrolling aircraft, and she was forced to dive.

This was the end of *Sokol*'s second commission with the Tenth Submarine Flotilla. She would now sail for Beirut, to join the First Flotilla. But on the way she had to call in at Malta and happened to see a mislaid barrage balloon floating on the edge of the swept channel. Being a public-spirited sort of man, Koziolkowski stopped to pick up the barrage balloon and carted it in to Malta, secured to the bows of his boat — 'producing quite an unusual sight', admits *Sokol*'s patrol report. As the same report adds, the surface ship sent to escort *Sokol* into harbour 'must have been pretty puzzled by our appearance as, after exchanging recognition signals, she flashed: "Are you a submarine?" '

Unsparing (Lieutenant A. D. Piper, RNR), the newcomer who had hit the *Flegetonte* on 31 August, had sailed for Beirut on 23 September. On 29 October, prowling around the Dodecanese, she made a night surface attack on the 1,160-ton troop transport *Ingeborg*, sinking her, and the following morning she also sank a rescue vessel crammed with troops picked out of the sea. Her patrol report notes that the pale skin of the bodies in the water indicated that these were German reinforcements, new to the Mediterranean.

On the 31st *Unsparing* surfaced to attack a caique with her gun, but the enemy's return fire, at a range of 3,000 yards, was deadly accurate, killing *Unsparing*'s gun trainer, Able Seaman Harry Wilson, and injuring two of the gun crew and gunnery officer. Sadly, *Unsparing* returned to Beirut, unable even to warn Captain (S) 1 of her impending arrival because one of the aerial lead-ins had been damaged. On passage she was met by the new *Surf* (Lieutenant D. Lambert) who passed a signal to Beirut on her behalf.

Unsparing's CO, Aston Piper, had been Teddy Woodward's Number One in *Unbeaten*. Piper would spend his entire submarine service, except for one patrol in *H 32*, in his beloved *U*s.

By the end of the war he would have carried out a record forty-one war patrols. David 'Shaver' Swanston was a close runner-up, completing thirty-five patrols before his 'perisher' and then continuing as CO of *Shakespeare* (formerly *P 221*) in the Pacific.

At Maddalena Commander Christopher Hutchinson was doing his utmost to goad the Italians into tidying up their bombed-out base so that it would be a home fit for the Fighting Tenth. But progress was slow. His patience was severely tested by their lackadaisical attitude and he personally faced a double challenge in that he was not only Commander (S) but also Chief of Staff to Captain P. Q. Roberts,* who was the Naval Officer in Command. 'Hutch' remembers life at Maddalena:

> I took over responsibility for administering the dockyard area, which included the ex-Italian barracks which we occupied. An Italian vice-Admiral continued to have his office in the dockyard, though how he spent his time I cannot imagine, as our Commander (E) ran the workshops we needed and I allocated the berths for our submarines, the American PT boats, Polish and Free French trawlers . . . AA defence was provided by the American army.
>
> Somehow or other this motley collection of mostly unarmed British, heavily armed Americans with every man a holster, lazy Italians with carabiniere rifles and knives, excitable Frogs and perky Poles managed to avoid civil war. None had enough work to do and boredom set in with the removal of active local hostilities . . . One night things did flare up and looked ugly for a time. The local Carabiniere tried to get control by firing *feux-de-joie* in the air, but this made the Yanks and Poles reach for their holsters and the French and Italians for their knives. Fearing bloodshed if things were not brought quickly under control, I led a patrol of twelve *unarmed* sailors, with webbing equipment, at a slow march. Away went the rifles, pistols and knives . . .
>
> The submarine barracks were previously occupied, coincidentally, by the Tenth Submarine Flotilla of the Regia Marina as their detention barracks. Ratings' accommodation was bad, but everything possible was being done to rectify the poor standard.

* Captain Roberts' initials were used to designate the Russian convoys, which he planned. Hence, for example, P.Q. 17.

Accommodation for officers was better, but there was no ward-room. A team of submarine officers found a wooden hut; they erected it and, after painting it out, transformed it into a very reasonable anteroom and wardroom.

At the moment there were no submarines at the base. Most of the Tenth's *U*s were patrolling in the Aegean during late October and early November, or still operating from Algiers under Captain (S) 8. Those in need of repairs returned to Malta.

On 8 November, Captain (S) 8 turned over operational command of the western Mediterranean to Captain (S) 10 at the new HMS *Talbot*, Maddalena. For the rest of the month the base staff at Lazaretto packed up all the stores, spares and impedimenta for transporting to Maddalena. On 1 December Captain George Phillips sailed from Malta to open the new base. The first *U* to arrive at La Maddalena was *Uproar* (Lieutenant L. E. Herrick) on 13 December.

Uproar had spent some time undergoing repairs at Malta before leaving for her patrol with the Eighth Flotilla on 28 November. Her billet was off Cannes and Monaco, where she experienced the weather conditions typical of this area in winter — high winds, short unpleasant seas and low visibility. It was on such a day, 6 December, that Herrick sighted a large modern liner, escorted by one destroyer. The liner was the 11,718-ton German *Vergilio* (previously Italian, and before that the Yugoslavian *Dubrovnik*). From 7,800 yards' range Herrick fired a salvo of which one torpedo hit, but the liner disappeared over the horizon before *Uproar* could reload her tubes. She claimed just to have damaged her target, but enemy records confirmed later that *Vergilio* did eventually sink. She was the last big ship, over 10,000 tons, to be sunk by an Allied submarine in the Mediterranean.

Uproar thus arrived at Maddalena for the first time, on 13 December, with her Jolly Roger flying from the periscope.

Untiring (Lieutenant R. Boyd) was a new arrival in the Mediterranean and one of her first patrols for the Tenth was off the Cote d'Azur. She had spent a few days at Malta and left Marsamxett Harbour in company with *Ultor* on 7 December, sailing for the south of France. Like *Uproar* the week before, she met atrocious weather, but on the 14th she caught a German minelayer in the act and pursued her into Monaco harbour. Robert Boyd then launched a memorable torpedo attack.

Lieutenant Donald Wilson, RANVR, who had been 'Shirty' Kershaw's second 'Jimmy' during *Uproar/P 31*'s first commission, was now *Untiring*'s Number One. 'We fired at an oblique angle,' he writes, 'I seem to remember that we only had two degrees to get through the [harbour] gate.' Lieutenant Johnnie Coote, Third Hand and torpedo officer, agrees:

> To get the depth of water necessary for the fish not to explode on diving straight from the tube . . . we had to stand off. This narrowed the angle for the shot down to about one degree either side. The first one went up on the breakwater, by which time we were too close for a second shot. So we circled to seaward, waiting for the reaction which surprisingly never came. So we lined up for a second shot. This was a bull's eye. The remaining mines went off, breaking every window in Monte Carlo.

'The explosion also caused a great deal of damage to the International Geographic Building on the waterfront,' adds Don Wilson, while Captain (S) 10 noted: 'Lieutenant Boyd hoped that the wheel in the Casino, 400 yards away, did not "come off the board" in Nazi favour.'

On 7 December *Untiring* moved billet, having been fired at by a destroyer probably using radar, and on the following day torpedoed and sank two 500-ton ammunition-carrying coasters. The two escorts, A/S drifters, according to Don Wilson, 'zigged around in a complete panic, firing every available weapon into the sea around them.' *Untiring* then made her way south-east to the new Tenth Flotilla base at Maddalena.

Bonifacio Straits had been heavily mined, remembers Johnnie Coote, 'so we had to rendezvous with *MGB 660* and be led in on the surface':

> It proved to be the start of a party which lasted with brief interruptions for patrols for a year. Maddalena was the Scapa Flow of the Italian Navy. Officers got sent there if they had made off with their CO's wife. We were billeted in the ratings' detention quarters. You can imagine the squalor. There was an Officers'

Club, with nothing to eat and only very rough Corsican wine
to drink.

Sad news had come from the Aegean. One of the First Flotilla
submarines had been lost. *Simoom* (Lieutenant G. D. N. Milner)
had arrived in Beirut only in October, and on her first patrol she
vanished. German records suggest that a submarine was sunk off
the island of Khios on 19 November, but if this was *Simoom* she
was a long way out of position. It seems as probable that she was
mined.

The enemy was fighting a bitter and seemingly pointless
struggle in the Aegean, and the combined Allied services continued to take heavy casualties from the Luftwaffe stationed in the
islands. The submarines could do very little in the way of retaliation — a coaster shot up here, a caique boarded there. But *Dzik's*
ERA, Antoni Banach, remembers the satisfaction, during one
patrol in the Greek islands, of boarding a Greek vessel that had
been commandeered by two German soldiers. The Greek captain
now became *Dzik's* guest for the remaining week of the patrol,
while the two Germans were set to work, 'usually cleaning jobs'.
Apparently they had been going on leave; now they were heading
for a POW camp. One was stupid enough to make the Nazi salute as he was leaving the boat and shouted 'Heil Hitler!' at the submarine crew, but, as Banach writes, 'The duty sentry at the end
of the gangplank pointed his bayonet at the sergeant's groin and
we all cheered him.'

By the end of November the Germans realized this battle was
pointless and withdrew from the Aegean. But in mainland Italy
there was no withdrawing. On 26 December General Eisenhower
paid the £5 he owed to Montgomery. Both men were now leaving this theatre of war to plan next summer's Operation 'Overlord', the Normandy landings. Behind them they left Allied
troops bogged down in the mud of an Italian winter, deadlocked
until another push was launched at Anzio in January, 1944.

Two of the Tenth Flotilla's *U*s were once again required as beacon submarines, marking the release positions off Anzio for the
British and American assault beaches — *Ultor* (Lieutenant G. E.
Hunt) and *Uproar* (Lieutenant L. E. Herrick), both now working
out of Maddalena. Their beach-marking was a complete success

and the naval phase of the assault plan went with a swing. On 22 January the British and Americans landed nearly 40,000 men and met practically no opposition, a situation which unfortunately did not last. Within days these troops were encircled by the enemy and bogged down.

The C-in-C, Mediterranean, Admiral Sir John Cunningham, was critical of the army's failure to exploit its initial success. He stated his views to Admiral of the Fleet Sir Andrew Cunningham who, on 5 October, had taken over as First Sea Lord from Sir Dudley Pound. The devoted Pound, who had carried the burden of the sea war for the four most critical years, died on Trafalgar Day, 1943, worn out by service to his country.

By the end of '43, with the exception of certain well-defined areas, the Allies were firmly in control of the Mediterranean. The main threat to supply ships now came from torpedo bombers and U-boats.

Ultimatum (Lieutenant W. H. Kett, RNR) was on her second commission in the Mediterranean. We last met her under the name of *P 34*. This commission started on 19 October, 1943, when Hedley Kett sailed her from Algiers to patrol the southern coast of France. At 0716 on 30 October *Ultimatum* encountered a German U-boat returning to Toulon. The enemy submarine was on the surface, her officers on the bridge, her crew lined up on the fore-casing; evidently she was preparing to enter harbour. Kett fired a three-torpedo salvo. The U-boat exploded and sank.*

Unfortunately there were more where she came from, and there was another U-boat base at Marseilles. The Germans had started building submarine pens as soon as they entered Marseilles in late 1942, and it was only through repeated Allied bombing raids that the U-boat menace could be contained.

By the end of December, 1943 *Ultimatum* had joined her sisters at Maddalena and the Tenth was now reinforced by another new

---

* At the time the enemy submarine was thought to be *U.431*, but her identity remains uncertain as a Ministry of Defence re-assessment in 1988 claimed that *U.431* fell victim to an RAF attack in the Gulf of Lyons on 21 October, an assessment difficult to sustain because a survivor has been found who was picked up by a fishing boat off Toulon.

U: Universal (Lieutenant C. Gordon) who arrived on the 27th and was followed in mid-January, '44 by *Upstart* (Lieutenant P. C. Chapman). In this same month, the Tenth Flotilla lost its Captain (S). Captain George Phillips was returning to England. After a much-needed break he was appointed Chief Staff Officer (Administration), to organize the submarine run-down when victory came. He was then appointed Captain (S) 5 at *Dolphin*, Gosport, to put his ideas into action.

Commander Hutchinson took over the Tenth until the end of January, when Captain P. Q. Roberts, Flag Officer at Maddalena, was formally appointed the flotilla's third Captain (S) 10.

'P.Q.', as the new Captain (S) 10 was known, was a forceful personality, as several of the Tenth's COs testify. Johnnie Coote, third hand in *Untiring,* has vivid memories of Roberts commandeering an Italian general's white charger and riding around Maddalena 'putting the fear of God into the 20,000 Italian troops, now supposedly our allies, but given to taking pot-shots at late-night revellers'. It was also on horseback that Roberts mustered everyone on the base to greet *Untiring* after one successful patrol: 'He personally led the "three cheers" on horseback, which was oddly moving.'

Maddalena was not a popular base. Being on a small island it was cut off from the rest of Sardinia, and seemed to the submariners to be isolated, forgotten, out on a limb. At this stage 'there was no patrol leave and absolutely nowhere to go,' writes Johnny Coote, remembering how food and thoughts of food consequently took on untoward significance. One particular memory concerns the paymaster at Maddalena – 'an exceedingly wet RNVR', snorts Coote – who was finally goaded into action. Taking a suitcase full of money, he crossed to Sardinia in a landing craft to buy some fresh fruit and vegetables. The word went round Maddalena. Men who had lived for days, even weeks, on tins of 'Meat & Veg', according to Coote, gathered at the dock to greet the paymaster on his return.

> He stepped ashore empty-handed. 'Too expensive,' he explained. 'So I didn't buy anything.'

Coote adds tersely: 'He was nearly lynched.'

At the beginning of February, 1944, there was a further reorganization of submarine forces in the Mediterranean, with the First Flotilla now moving to Malta, a flotilla which now included the four Greek submarines and their depot ship *Corinthia*. The Tenth was still at Maddalena, but Algiers — now home to the Free French submarines such as *Curie* and *Casabianca,* who were operated by Captain (S) 10 — became a regular port of call for the British submarines during their rest periods. French hospitality was all the more appreciated after the dullness of Sardinia.

In March, 1944, *Untiring* went back to Malta for her periodical docking and happened to be there when the two Polish submarines, *Dzik* and *Sokol,* were taking their leave of the Mediterranean. Johnnie Coote writes:

> There was a terrific party in the wardroom, drinking out of sawn-off beer bottles. Just before they (the Poles) were due to slip at 2200, we had the BBC news relayed into the wardroom, a matter of daily routine. The general carousing fell silent, as we heard the announcement that we had agreed with Roosevelt and Stalin to carve Poland up . . . The likes of Romanowski, Koziolkowski and Teddy Bernas were in tears. Their reward for five years of fighting with unflinching bravery on the side of the ally who went to war to preserve their country was suddenly for nothing. They mostly now had no home to return to after the war. The shame and poignancy of that moment remains with me. They went down to the trot in tears — and it wasn't all gin.

'It is with much regret that we part with Lieutenant-Commanders Romanowski and "George" Koziolkowski,' Captain (S) 1 commented in March, 1944, 'and their most efficient submarines.' The Admiralty also registered approval of the Poles' 'offensive spirit'. Meanwhile, in *Dzik*'s last patrol report, Romanowski wrote:

> Our officers and men are very proud to have been part of the famous Tenth and First Submarine Flotillas and that we could add our paltry quota to their magnificent score.

Their gallantry was equalled only by their modesty.

The continuing impasse on land was at least serving to tie down German troops, which allowed the Allies a useful breathing space before 'Overlord'. Naval forces, too, were gradually leaving the Mediterranean, although in May the first of the new *V*-class submarines arrived to join (S) 1 at Malta — *Vampire* (Lieutenant C. W. Taylor, RNR).

Upstart, who had arrived the month before, began her work for the Tenth with a satisfying hit on an auxiliary minelayer. She had been patrolling as close as possible inshore, off Toulon, harassed both by terrible weather and by anti-submarine patrols. Then on 15 February, off Cape Cepet, the *Nieder Sachsen* was sighted — the 1,796-ton vessel that had originally been the French *Guyane,* then was sequestered by the Italians in 1942 and renamed *Acqui.* She had been scuttled in Pezia on 9 September, 1943, but was salvaged and recommissioned in December with the German crew of *Brandenburg,* sunk by *Unseen* in September, 1943.

Nieder Sachsen/Acqui/Guyane was almost certainly involved in laying a field to entrap the submarines of the Tenth flotilla, for this billet was a regular haunt of theirs now. At a range of 1,000 yards Chapman fired three torpedoes. One was enough. She sank before his eyes.

Another memorable hit off Toulon came on 21 June when *Universal* (Lieutenant C. Gordon) finally penetrated the very determined anti-submarine measures to sink a 250-ton yacht on hydrophone patrol. This was followed by a greater success on the 22nd. Repeating her stalking tactics on three chasseurs patrolling off Cassis, she sighted two liners close inshore. From a range of 3,500 yards Gordon fired two torpedoes at each liner and achieved four hits. The bigger ship, *President dal Piaz* (4,930 tons), exploded in flames and subsided, half-submerged on the bottom. The smaller vessel, *Sampiere Corso* (3,823 tons), sank with a broken back, her stern on the seabed, her bows cocked skywards. The hunting chasseurs scurried to and fro, but without any idea of *Universal*'s whereabouts Gordon was able to give some of his ship's company the rare opportunity of admiring their own handiwork through the periscope.

By the time *Universal* returned to Maddalena there was bad news from Malta: one of the First Flotilla's S-class submarines was missing — *Sickle.* Her CO, Lieutenant J. R. Drummond, had been first lieutenant to Lieutenant-Commander David Wanklyn in *Upholder*. As captain of his own boat, he had taken *Sickle* on several patrols already in the Aegean, and she had several sinkings to her credit. But after a signal reporting enemy shipping movements on 12 June, nothing more was heard from *Sickle*. She is presumed to have been mined, possibly in a minefield off Lemnos.

Sickle was the forty-fifth and last British submarine to be sunk in the Mediterranean.

Undoubtedly the true successor to *Upholder*, in these last months of the war in the Mediterranean, was *Ultor,* constantly on the prowl, constantly adding to her list of hits. George ('Geordie') Hunt's brilliant results, like those of Wanklyn in *Upholder,* reflect the dedication and competence of her whole crew.

In mid-May *Ultor* continued the Fighting Tenth's harassment of enemy A/S shipping off the south coast of France. On 11 May she managed to sink a KT ship, a transport vessel of 850 tons, under the noses of two escorting E-boats. On the 15th she spotted 'a welcome novelty', in the words of the Admiralty Weekly Intelligence Report: 'an 80-ton deeply laden coaster'. *Ultor* surfaced and opened up with her gun, forcing the coaster's crew to beach her and abandon ship.

On *Ultor*'s next patrol, her fourteenth, she headed for Cape Camarat and was soon rewarded with a multiple target; a 1,000-ton armed salvage ship was towing a motley collection of very bedraggled-looking lighters, evidently on their way to lay A/S nets or booms. At a range of 800 yards, with one torpedo *Ultor* managed to dispose of two enemy vessels at once. The tremendous explosion gave the submarine herself a considerable shaking.

On the following day, 31 May, she followed two enemy minesweepers from Cassis and at sunset, while they were silhouetted against the horizon and she was well covered by darkness, *Ultor* surfaced for an attack with her Vickers gun. Soon the target was ablaze, but the other minesweeper was now hunting the submarine, and the shore batteries had all opened up. *Ultor* made a timely withdrawal, though not before she saw her target explode and sink. Two days later she caught an armed merchant vessel emerging from Port Vendres, *Alice Robert* (2,610 tons), with a destroyer for escort. By 0910 on that morning of 2 June the merchantman had been sunk by another of *Ultor*'s accurate torpedoes.

After a very well-earned break *Ultor* was back on patrol on 16 June, again making for the south coast of France. As the Admiralty Weekly Intelligence Report remarked, 'This, her fifteenth Mediterranean war patrol, was to prove the most eventful, arduous and successful of all.' After several days dodging A/S patrols, and on one occasion having her periscope fired at by E-boats, she fired two torpedoes at a lighter and obtained at least one hit. The target sank.

On 27 June, before dawn, *Ultor* sighted a large merchant vessel who proved to be the German-requisitioned former French ship *Cap Blanc* (3,315 tons). Undeterred by her escort of three destroyers and a corvette, Hunt fired a salvo of four torpedoes and scored two hits. The target vanished in a huge explosion. He now took *Ultor* deep while the hunters sought in vain. A couple of hours later, with his reload torpedoes in the tubes, he brought the boat to the surface and sighted an even larger target — *Pallas,* a 5,260-ton steamer. Not only did *Pallas* have four destroyers, one corvette and a UJ-boat (submarine hunter) as defence, she also had an aerial escort of five circling aircraft. But *Ultor* skilfully eluded them all, weaving through the screen to fire her remaining torpedoes. Less than an hour later she had safely escaped the hectic but inaccurate A/S measures and Hunt surfaced to let some of his crew look through the periscope at the mortally damaged target. Shortly afterwards *Pallas* sank.

With no torpedoes left, *Ultor* returned to Maddalena on 29 June. Her successes of two days earlier were described by Captain Roberts, Captain (S) 10, as 'the most superlative exhibition' and the Commander-in-Chief, Mediterranean reported to the Admiralty, 'for the information of their Lordships':

Great credit is due to the Commanding Officer of H.M. Submarine "ULTOR", Lieutenant G. E. HUNT, DSC, RN, for this most satisfactory Patrol during which one "F" Lighter, one 3,000-ton Motor Vessel and one Tanker were sunk. H.M.

Submarine "ULTOR" 's actions on the morning of 27th June rank with some of the most outstanding of the War.

Sgd. J. H. D. CUNNINGHAM, Admiral

On 18 July *Ultor* sailed for her sixteenth and final patrol, which was 'hindered, and eventually cut short, by technical defects' in the words of the Admiralty WIR. Nevertheless, *Ultor* made a successful torpedo attack on a 500-ton coaster and returned to base with valuable information about minefields off the Riviera.

Ultor had achieved the highest number of ships sunk by any British submarine during the Second World War.* During her sixteen patrols she had sunk or destroyed over 43,000 tons of Axis shipping, her largest victim being *Champagne* (9,945 tons) in September, 1943. The sinkings included seven supply ships or tankers totalling 33,185 tons; a 1,200-ton cable ship; a 1,000-ton salvage ship; the torpedo boat *Lince*; an armed trawler; and seventeen other small ships and craft. Her scorecard reads: 20 ships sunk, 2 damaged by torpedo; 8 small vessels sunk, 2 damaged by gunfire. 1 bombardment, 1 beach-marking, 1 special operation.

As *Ultor* sailed for her hard-earned rest, the Commander-in-Chief, Mediterranean noted:

> Considering the paucity of targets off the south coast of France this year, the successes achieved by *Ultor* have been most outstanding and are due to the consistently conspicuous daring of her Commanding Officer.

'Geordie' Hunt, as third hand in *Unity,* had escaped during that tragedy on the Tyne in 1940. Thereafter he went from strength to strength. He was twice Mentioned in Dispatches, won the DSC and Bar, and was honoured with two DSOs in his command of *Ultor*. He was further awarded a year's seniority 'for good services' and was directed by their Lordships to have his official portrait painted. The painting by Anthony Devas is now in the Imperial War Museum, London.

---

* David Wanklyn in *Upholder* sank the most tonnage of any British C.O.

Lieutenant Hunt himself said, '*Ultor*'s successes were entirely due to a marvellous team on board and the fantastic support from the Depot Ship's staff.'

34

On 21 September, 1944, HMS *Talbot* at Maddalena hauled down her White Ensign for the last time. The Tenth Submarine Flotilla had been disbanded. By this time the focus of the war in Europe was on the River Rhine though it was not until 4 May, 1945, that the Allies took the German surrender. But still there were mopping-up operations in the Mediterranean, and several of the *U*s remained at Malta or Algiers, like *Curie* (Lieutenant de Vaisseau Pierre-Jean Chailley), the Free French submarine.

Jean-Pierre Brunet was first lieutenant in *Curie*. He had witnessed the commissioning of his submarine in May, 1943, the ceremony at Barrow-in Furness being honoured by General de Gaulle in person. *Curie* had made herself useful with the Eighth Flotilla at Algiers, patrolling in the western Mediterranean, and soon after the liberation of France she had paid a call on St Tropez. Her crew was therefore in high spirits. Eager for action in the Aegean, they first found themselves living 'like upper-class tourists', swanning around the Dodecanese by moonlight, while Brunet absorbed 'the most glamorous and historic coast anywhere in the world: that is, at the foot of the Pelion and Ossa mountains, which, mythology aiding, have been sung by countless poets in many languages'.

Reality came home to the French submariners when they reached Khios just after the island had been liberated. They found the islanders 'literally dying of hunger', remembers Brunet. 'We shared our provisions with them, but that was, of course, just a drop in the bucket.'

On 2 October *Curie* was hoping to catch a convoy of vessels reported to be heading her way, carrying retreating German troops, and that evening *Curie*'s Third Hand, François A'Weng, sighted the convoy's smoke. 'That night we were not going to try a periscope attack,' recalls Brunet; 'we were too afraid of losing sight of the convoy once submerged.' Unbelievably, in bright moonlight, *Curie* managed to cross the convoy's path unseen, manoeuvring inshore and doing a U-turn so that she could fire her torpedoes at the leading ship.

'The explosions were what we expected,' Brunet says, 'shudderingly thunderous.' *Curie* had sunk the German-requisitioned Bulgarian steamer, *Tsar Ferdinand* (1,950 tons), who sank in thirteen minutes. The French tourists now dived and eluded the convoy's escorts, but, to their delight, they found another convoy in exactly the same place on the following night. This time they fired at 'a curious contraption' which turned out to be a Siebel ferry. Their patrol became fairly peaceful and they amused themselves with practical jokes — surfacing suddenly beside a caique, not so much to check the boat as to surprise the fishermen.

When *Curie* came off patrol she returned to Malta flying her Jolly Roger and was given 'a formidable welcome', remembers Brunet. *Curie*'s was not the last strike in the Mediterranean. That honour went to another *U*.

Unswerving, commanded by Lieutenant M. D. Tattersall, RNVR (He was the first RNVR commanding officer★ and all his officers were RNVR too) had been operating some distance north of *Curie* and had caught another ship in the same convoy attacked by the Frenchmen. Her target was the 1,900 ton tanker, *Bertha,* sunk off Cape Kassandra on 3 October, 1944. *Unswerving* had won a place in history by scoring the last sinking in the Mediterranean theatre of war.

We cannot leave the Mediterranean without a final word about Malta, home of the Tenth Submarine Flotilla for most of its life. The people of Malta had shared their island with us, shared the terrors and the joys. The suffering they had undergone, in their determination to hold out against the barbaric German and Italian aggression, earned not only the unique award of the George Cross, but also an enduring place in the hearts of the British.

After the war it was calculated that Malta had suffered a total

★ Lieutenant-Commander E.P.Young, RNVR, was the first RNVR officer to command an operational submarine HM S/M *Storm*.

of 3,343 air raids, in which 16,000 tons of bombs and parachute mines were dropped, 35,000 homes and buildings were flattened; 1,597 civilians were killed, thousands mutilated for life. Although the siege was lifted in 1943, the years of austerity continued well past the end of the war. Like Britain herself, Malta faced a long wait before prosperity returned.

In 1947 the island acquired limited self-government, finally winning Independence in 1964. To many younger Britons the name of Malta is now familiar more as a holiday destination than as a valiant comrade-in-arms and companion in suffering. Until, that is, they see those proud letters after her name: *Malta GC*.

Gradually the *U*s made their way back to Britain, first for a much-needed break, then to continue patrols in colder northern waters until the end of the war. These small submarines had their drawbacks,* it is true, but they had nevertheless achieved wonders in the Mediterranean. It was our marvellous good luck that the *U* was already in production two years before the war, and especially that the submarine was so well suited to Mediterranean conditions, with the low silhouette and swift diving ability.

Both Phillips and Simpson liked the *U*s, not only because of their suitability for the job in hand but because of their simplicity; they were easy to maintain, even when spares were unavailable: 'sealing wax and string' kept the boats operational, thanks to the ingenuity and determination of MacGregor and his team.

By comparison with German U-boats, our submarines were sadly ill-equipped. Due to the parsimony of inter-war governments, our submarine commanders went into action during the Second World War with torpedoes their fathers had known in 1914-18. The Germans, on the other hand, provided their submariners with attack computers and torpedoes that would run not only silently and without tracks but on a course selected by the CO; and the Americans in the Pacific used radar-linked computers to target their torpedoes.

And yet, despite living conditions which modern submarine

* Two of their principal weaknesses were the slow surface speed and the shallow tested diving depth.

crews would regard as intolerable, the Us came to be regarded with affection by their officers and men. It is, after all, the qualities of leadership and teamwork that make a submarine successful, and these we were fortunate to have in abundance.

All of the Tenth's early records sank with *Medway* on the last day of June, 1942: the least of our worries at the time, but a blow to historians and statisticians. The tonnages cited in this book have been gleaned from Admiralty records, and checked with Italian and German sources.

In summarizing the achievements of the Tenth Flotilla, the score card begins with the first attack on 25 February, 1941, by a submarine of the U-class, *Upright* on *Armando Diaz*; and ends with the last (unsuccessful) attack on 8 August, 1944, by *Universal* on a French chasseur.

Successes by submarines working from Malta and on loan to the Tenth Flotilla have been included, as have those caused by minelays carried out by submarines on loan to the Tenth Flotilla.

The results of attacks by U-class submarines operating from other flotillas have not been counted; excluded also are targets of less than 500 tons that have been sunk or damaged.

During these three and a half years, the Tenth Submarine Flotilla sank a total of 648,629 tons, and damaged 400,480 tons of enemy shipping: a grand total of over one million tons denied to the enemy.

The fighting spirit of the Royal Navy is not something accidental. It has been bred over the centuries, schooled and handed down through the heat of battle, the core of its ideal being the defence of our Christian values against oppression. This was what gave men like Wanklyn, Tomkinson, Cayley, Wraith, Woodward, Hunt *et al*, the valour to fight on against all odds. And their example is our source of inspiration. It is to them and their companies that our Tenth Submarine Flotilla owes its *nom-de-guerre: The Fighting Tenth*.

APPENDIX – The *U*-class Submarine

NB: There were two versions of the U-class submarine: where there were significant differences, the figure in brackets refers to the second group.

Dimensions	length overall: 191 ft (196 ft 9in) beam: 16 ft draught: 14 ft 5 in (14ft 6in)
Displacement	630/720 tons (648/735 tons) positive buoyancy on surface: 90 tons
Armament	4 x 21-in bow torpedo tubes (*Ursula*, 6 x 21in) 4 x 21-in reload torpedoes 1 x 12-pdr HA/LA gun (3-inch gun) 2 x Lewis M/G (Vickers 0.303 M/G)
Propulsion: *diesel-electric*	2 x 400 h.p. Paxman diesel engines, each coupled to one electric generator. 2 electric motors coupled directly to each propeller shaft
Speed	10 knots surfaced; 8/7 knots submerged
Fuel	38 tons diesel
Endurance	surfaced: 3800 n.m. at 10 knots submerged: 'grouped down' (batteries in series) 60 hours at 2½ knots; 'grouped up' (batteries in parallel) 2½ hours at 7 knots

Complement	4 officers, 27 (29) ratings
Safe diving depth	250 feet
Main ballast tanks	6 (two end tanks free flood; four internal centre tanks fitted with Kingston valves); high pressure air blows
Quick diving tank	fitted with Kingston valve. Quick Diving time: 16 secs. High Pressure air blows
Periscopes	2 Barr & Stroud periscopes. *For'd:* search, bifocal (large diameter) high and low magnification lens. *Aft:* (thin upper tube) attack, monocular
Periscope depth	27 ft. Highest part of bridge only 12 ft below surface
Radio (wireless transmission)	W/T masts hinged at after edge of bridge and stowed at the after-casing; could be raised hydraulically. (Removed later)

GLOSSARY

Asdic (sonar)	The device by which submarines are detected. Submarines are also fitted with asdics which are used mainly as hydrophones. When operated in the transmission mode, submarines could communicate with each other by Morse code (SST, Subsonic Transmission) or 'underwater telephone'.
Blowers	Machines with which to blow out the water in the tanks by using low pressure air.
'Bunts'	The signalman.
Casing (fore- after-)	The 'deck' welded on to the pressure hull of the submarine. The casing is 'free-flood', i.e. allows water to pass through. At sea, the berthing wires are stowed beneath the casing.
CCR	Contact Control Rod; (Non-contact), torpedo warhead pistol.
CERA	Chief Engine Room Artificer.
Chariot	Two-man human torpedo.
Conning tower	(or bridge). The raised part in the centre of the submarine. The only tenable part of her when on the surface.
Control room	The nerve-centre of the submarine.
DA	Director Angle: the amount of 'aim-off' required to allow for the course and speed of the target.
D/F	Direction Finding.
Dghaisa	Maltese all-purpose, colourful boat propelled by one man. He stands upright and pushes against his two oars.
DR	Dead Reckoning position.
DSEA	Davis Submerged Escape Apparatus.

E-boat	(or 'MAS' for Italian). Term for German or Italian 35-knot Motor Torpedo or gun Boats, or submarine chasers: length about 75 feet.
EO	Engineer Officer.
ERA	Engine Room Artificer.
ETA	Expected Time of Arrival.
Faithful Freddie	The magnetic compass used in emergency.
F-lighter	German 'flak', shallow draught craft, armed often with an 88mm gun.
Fish	Torpedo (slang).
Folbot	Two-manned collapsible canvas canoe.
FOSM	Flag Officer, Submarines.
FO (S) or FOS	Flag officer (Submarines): WW II abbreviation.
Fruit Machine	The calculating machine into which all relevant attack data is fed, and from which the necessary information is extracted to carry out a torpedo attack.
GAF	German Air Force.
Gash	Rubbish: Collected in buckets for 'ditching' on surface at night.
Gens	Surface ship service in the Royal Navy (slang).
Group down	Batteries in series: for low speed and using little electric power.
Group up	Batteries in parallel: for relatively faster speed, but using up batteries rapidly.
HE	Hydrophone Effect; i.e. propeller or engine noise.
HE	High Explosive.
Heads	Lavatory and washplace.
Heat	Slang for being at the receiving end of a depth-charge attack.
HP	High Pressure.
HSD	Higher Submarine Detector: the non-substantive rate of a skilled asdic operator.
Iron Ring	A patrol line of several submarines established outside a port to catch the enemy.
Jimmy	Jimmy-the-One, Jim or Number One: First Lieutenant and Second-in-Command.
'Kipper'	(or 'Fish'). Torpedo, (slang).
LP	Low Pressure.
Main Ballast Kingstons	Valves fitted to the bottom of the internal main ballast tanks.

Main Ballast tanks	The tanks which give the submarine its buoyancy. All are fitted with main vents; in the Us 'One' MB was for'd; 'Six' MB was aft.
Main Vents	The large mushroom valves on top of the Main Ballast tanks; operated by telemotor pressure or by hand. When the vents are opened, the air in the tanks escapes, allowing sea water to enter through the flooding holes and Kingstons.
Night Vision (or Sight)	The ability of a man to see ships in the dark. It was found that it took 20 minutes for the eyes to adjust from normal lighting to darkness, thereby attaining true night sight: the essential requirement for look-outs.
Number One	First Lieutenant and Second-in-Command.
Outside ERA	The Engine Room Artificer whose duty is at the blowing panel in the control room. Being responsible for all auxiliary machinery 'outside' the Engine Room, he is also known as the 'Outside Wrecker'. He works the periscope hoist.
Panel	The conglomeration of valves and blows centralized in one position on the starboard side of the control room.
Perisher	Slang for Commanding Officers 'Qualifying' Course (COQC).
Pilot	Slang for 'Navigator' (Sometimes 'Vasco').
Planes	Slang for hydroplanes, the horizontal 'fins' which control the depth-keeping and trim of the submarine. Fitted fore and aft on each side of the pressure hull, they are operated by hydraulic oil pressure.
Q Tank	The emergency quick-diving tank. When flooded, the tank makes the submarine ten tons heavier than her normal dived trim. In wartime, Q is always kept flooded when the submarine is on the surface.
RANVR	Royal Australian Naval Volunteer Reserve,
RNR	Royal Naval Reserve.
RNVR	Royal Naval Volunteer Reserve.
SANF (V)	South African Naval Forces (Volunteer).
S 1, S 8, S 10	Captain (S), 1st Submarine Flotilla 8th Submarine Flotilla 10th Submarine Flotilla

Sailing Orders	Instructions issued to a warship before going to sea; details of where to go, how to get there and what to do under all circumstances are given.
SO	Senior Officer.
Stick	Slang for periscope.
SST	Subsonic Transmission (see 'asdic').
Swept Channel	The channel kept clear of enemy mines by mine sweepers, to give safe passage to shipping.
Telemotor system	Hydraulic oil pressure lines for actuating mechanical systems.
TI	Torpedo Instructor: Senior rating in charge of torpedoes and department.
Trim	The state of buoyancy when the submarine is submerged, i.e., light or heavy; bow up or bow down.
Uckers	
UJ-boat	Naval version of the game of Ludo.
	(U. B. Jäger) German Anti-Submarine Escort Craft.
Ursula suit	Waterproof jacket and trousers, designed by the captain of HM Submarine, Ursula.
Watertight doors	The submarine is divided in the Us into watertight compartments by five bulkheads. Watertight doors are fitted into each bulkhead to provide crew movement along the passage way.
W/T	Wireless Telegraphy.
WT	Watertight
Zigzagging	Steering on either side of the mean course in order to confuse the aim of an enemy submarine.

ACKNOWLEDGEMENTS

I am greatly indebted to Captain George Phillips, DSO, GM, and his wife Pamela, for their encouragement, advice and friendship; Mr Wingrave Tench, OBE, for his invaluable contributions; Rear-Admiral C. H. Hutchinson, CB, DSO, OBE, and his wife, Nancy, for their kindness in placing their home at our disposal, while I finished the manuscript; Commander Peter Bartlett, OBE, for his help and long-standing friendship; Commander Richard Compton-Hall, MBE, Director of the Royal Navy Submarine Museum, for his unstinted support; and Mr Gus Britton RN (Ret'd) Archivist to the Museum (who was *Uproar*'s 'Bunts' during her second commission in the Mediterranean) for his constant and patient help; Mr Francis Dickinson, grandson of the late Lieutenant-Commander E. P. Tomkinson, DSO★★, for access to family papers and photographs; Captain A. G. M. A. Provest, Director of Public Relations (Navy), Ministry of Defence, and Lieutenant-Commander Michael Wilson (Ret'd) of the Naval Historical Section; Mr Howard Davies and his Staff in the Search Department of the Public Record Office; the Director of the Imperial War Museum and his Staff and, particularly Mr Paul Kemp of the Department of Photography whose assistance has been invaluable; Captain Pietro de Michelis di Slonghello, IN, Naval Attaché to the Italian Embassy, Paris, who kindly spent many hours translating Italian war records on to tape; Mr Victor Coppini of Valletta, Malta, GC, whose help has been immense; and to Captain M. L. C. Crawford, DSC★, RN, for permission to quote fully from the history he wrote in 1971 of HM Submarine *Upholder* whose first lieutenant he was; and to Captain John Stevens, DSO★, DSC, RN, for the similar privilege with his book, *Never Volunteer*.

And, finally, we are greatly indebted to Miss Tania Simpson, the late Rear-Admiral Simpson's daughter, who has allowed me unreservedly to quote from her father's autobiography, *Periscope View*, published in 1972 by Macmillan, London. The publishers have also granted me permission to quote from this, Admiral Simpson's 'professional autobiography', and I am very grateful for Lord Hardinge's help and advice, for he was Shrimp's editor: as a Sub-Lieutenant, he was Secretary to Captain (S)10 at Lazaretto.

May those whose names follow accept our thanks for their essential contributions and help:

Lt-Commander E. Bagnasaco, IN; Mr Cyril Balls, RN; ERA A. Banach, KW; Lt-Commander R. Bannar-Martin, DSC, RN; J. H. Beattie, Esq.; Commander J. H. Bromage, DSO, DSC*, RN; Lieutenant de Vaisseau Jean Pierre Brunet, FNFL; Rear-Admiral Ben Bryant, CB, DSO**, DSC; Petty Officer F. F. Buckingham, RN; Commander P. C. Chapman, DSO, OBE, DSC*, RN; Lt-Commander James Craven, DSC; A. R. Daniell, Esq, DSO, DSC; Commander J. H. Eaden, DSC**, RN; Mr Kenneth England, RN; Commander W. T. J. Fox, RN; Mr G. G. Gregory, RN; Commander P. R. H. Harrison, DSO, DSC*, RN; Vice-Admiral Sir Arthur Hezlet, KBE, CB, DSO, DSC; Commander L. F. L. Hill, RD*, RNR; Mr W. A. Horton, RN; Brian Hudson, Esq; Captain G. E. Hunt, DSO*, DSC*, RN; Lt-Commander R. L. Jay, DSC, RN; Mr Geoffrey Jones; Mr John Jones, RN; Captain W. H. Kett, DSC*, RD*, RNR; Lt-Commander T. W. Lancaster, DSC, RN; Captain M. G. R. Lumby, DSO, DSC, RN; Lieutenant Donald McEwen, DSC, RN; Lieutenant F. E. Macvie, DSC, RN; Captain K. H. Martin, DSC, RN; Mr Fred Matthews, RN; Mr Alec McCandlish, RN; Vice-Admiral Sir Ian McGeoch, KCB, DSO, DSC; Lt-Commander J. F. Michell, RN; Captain R. G. Mills, DSO, DSC, RN; Mr J. Murdoch, RN; Captain C. P. Norman, CBE, DSO, DSC, RN; Captain E. D. Norman, DSO, DSC, RN; Commander J. P. H. Oakley, DSC*, RN; Monsieur Joseph Pierre, FNFL; Captain A. D. Piper, DSO, DSC*, RD**, RNR; Rear-Admiral B. C. G. Place, VC, CB, DSC; Lt-Commander A. G. Prideaux, DSC, RN; Commander R. P. Raikes, DSO, RN; Mr Jim Richards, RN; Vice-Admiral Sir John Roxburgh, KCB, CBE, DSO, DSC*; CPO Gordon Selby, DSM*, BEM, RN; Commander P. G. R. Smith, DSC, RN; Captain H. van Oostrom Soede, DSO, R.Neth.N; Commander E. T. Stanley, DSO, DSC, RN; Mr Ray Steggles, RN; Lt-Commander I. M. Stoop, DSC, RN; Lt-Commander Sir Godfrey Style, CBE, DSC, RN; Mr J. H. Sutcliffe, RN; Lieutenant G. G. Taylor, KW (Polish), RNVR; Lt-Commander Paul Thirsk, DSC, RNR; Mr Harry Thomas, RN; Captain R. M. Venables, RN; Mr. B. R. Williams, RN; J. F. Williams Esq; Lt-Commander Donald Wilson, DSC, RANVR; Lt-Commander Jack Whitton, DSC, RN; Commander E. A. Woodward, DSO**, F.I.Nuc.E., KSJ, RN.

BIBLIOGRAPHY

Bagnasco, Erminio, *Marina Italiana* (Arms and Armour Press, 1976)

Bryant, Ben, *One Man Band* (William Kimber, 1958)

Crawford, M. L. C., *HM Submarine Upholder* (Warship Profile, 1971)

Cunningham of Hyndehope, Viscount, *A Sailor's Odyssey* (Hutchinson, 1951)

Gerard, Francis, *Malta Magnificent* (Cassell, 1943)

Hart, Sydney, *Submarine 'Upholder'* (Oldbourne, 1960)

Lenton, H. T., *British Submarines* (Macdonald, 1972)

Mars, Alastair, *Unbroken: The Story of a Submarine* (Frederick Muller, 1953)

Martiensen, Anthony, *Hitler and His Admirals* (Secker & Warburg, 1948)

Roskill, S. W., *The War At Sea 1939-1945* (4 vols: HMSO, 1956-61)

Simpson, George, *Periscope View* (Macmillan, 1972)

Stevens, John, *Never Volunteer* (Woodleigh, Emsworth, 1971)

Vella, Philip, *Malta: Blitzed but not Beaten* (Progress Press, 1985, for National War Museum Association, Malta GC)

Warner, Oliver, *Cunningham of Hyndhope* (John Murray, 1967)

Warren, C. E. T., and James Benson, *Above us the Waves* (Harrap, 1953)

Young, Edward, *One of our Submarines* (Rupert Hart-Davis, 1952)

La Lotta Antisommergibile: Ufficio Storico della Marina Militare (Stato Maggiore della Marina, 1978)

INDEX